THE RECEPTION OF RAUSCHENBUSCH

MERCER UNIVERSITY

MERCER UNIVERSITY PRESS

Endowed by

TOM WATSON BROWN

and

THE WATSON-BROWN FOUNDATION, INC.

THE RECEPTION OF RAUSCHENBUSCH

The Responses of His Early Readers

WILLIAM L. PITTS, JR.

MERCER UNIVERSITY PRESS | MACON, GEORGIA

2018

The James N. Griffith Series in Baptist Studies

This series on Baptist life and thought explores and investigates Baptist history, offers analyses of Baptist theologies, provides studies in hymnody, and examines the role of Baptists in societies and cultures around the world. The series also includes classics of Baptist literature, letters, diaries, and other writings. For a complete list of titles in the series, visit www.mupress.org and visit the series page.

—C. Douglas Weaver, Series Editor

MUP/ H961

Published by Mercer University Press
1501 Mercer University Drive
Macon, Georgia 31207

9 8 7 6 5 4 3 2 1

Books published by Mercer University Press are printed on acid-free paper that meets the requirements of the American National Standard for Information Sciences—Permanence of Paper for Printed Library Materials.

Printed and bound in the United States.

This book is set in Adobe Caslon.

ISBN 978-0-88146-681-2
Cataloging-in-Publication Data is available from the Library of Congress

CONTENTS

To Ruth

PREFACE

My discovery of Walter Rauschenbusch occurred at university. The professor of an American history course had developed an extensive reading list for his course. He did me a great favor in selecting Rauschenbusch's *Christianity and the Social Crisis* as my assignment. Reared in a family that regularly attended church three times each week, I was immersed in traditional emphases on Bible study, missions education, and evangelistic worship. Reading Rauschenbusch opened my perception to the breadth of Christianity in refreshing and liberating new ways. This is one of the books that changed my outlook on religion and on life. It made Christianity richer, fuller, more inclusive, and more relevant. Only later did I learn that Rauschenbusch had long been judged one of the more creative and influential American interpreters of Christianity, and only later still did I read scores of letters to Rauschenbusch, declaring readers' indebtedness to him for articulating a much larger understanding of Christianity and for giving many of them renewed resolve to serve their churches. They saw in Rauschenbusch's vision of Christianity new ways of affirming the relevance of Christianity to daily life. These earlier readers had been affected as I had been. The goal of this book is to tell the story of Rauschenbusch's books and their reception by his earliest readers.

Rauschenbusch studies have flourished in recent years. Scholars have provided an excellent biography, a history of liberalism that places Rauschenbusch in a long line of creative thinkers, and numerous studies of his social ethics. Rauschenbusch dissertations have appeared roughly every two years since 2000, and the centennial of Rauschenbusch's death has drawn even more attention to him. By focusing on reception, this study seeks to add historical context to understanding Rauschenbusch's professional life and his writings. Among other roles, people interacted with him as pastor, Baptist, professor, and Protestant leader. Based on personal contact and observation, how did they judge the man and his contributions? Furthermore, thousands who never met him responded to Rauschenbusch primarily as readers. What were the arguments in his major books, and how did the reading audience respond to his message?

Rauschenbusch was creative, productive, and well organized. He kept and dated lecture and sermon notes, typed drafts of his articles and books, dated his extensive correspondence, and retained diaries of travels and family trips. He directed that his papers be destroyed, but they were preserved along with those of his family. Based on these as well as his major publications, there are ample resources for ongoing studies of Rauschenbusch.

I have consulted two major collections of Rauschenbusch materials. The Rauschenbusch Family Papers, held in the American Baptist Historical Society

(ABHS) archival collection at Mercer University in Atlanta, Georgia, fill several scrapbooks and 180 boxes. The North American Baptist Heritage Commission (NABHC) archives housed at Sioux Falls Seminary in Sioux Falls, South Dakota, also contain a significant Rauschenbusch collection. Other collections such as the Ambrose Swazey Library of Colgate Rochester Crozer Divinity School house additional materials.

Rauschenbusch was a person of his own era and followed its conventions. Whereas more gender inclusive language is preferred today, Rauschenbusch, like most leading writers down to the 1960s, used "man" for humanity. He also used capitalization more freely than is common today; where I am quoting him, I have usually left his writing completely intact. The academic conventions of the day did not require extensive source documentation. Rauschenbusch used footnotes infrequently in some volumes and not at all in others. He does not include bibliographies for his books, and some of his books were published without an index.
I am indebted to many people and institutions for assistance in researching this book. Executive Director Dr. Deborah Van Broekhoven, assistant director Jan Ballard, former communications assistant Betsy Dunbar, current Executive Director Priscilla Eppinger, office manager Janet Winfield, and the entire staff of the American Baptist Historical Society in Atlanta, Georgia, have been extraordinarily helpful. Director Dr. Jackie Howell of the North American Baptist Heritage Commission generously assisted in making significant Rauschenbusch materials available to me. I am grateful to the staff of the Baylor Moody Library, who have rendered much assistance, especially by securing materials through interlibrary loan. I am also indebted to Baylor University's College of Arts and Sciences and its Department of Religion for funding part of the research for this project. Thanks to my graduate assistants, who have contributed to this project in numerous ways, especially Scott Prather, Brandon Morgan, and Malcolm Foley. I deeply appreciate the encouragement and support given by Pam Durso, Executive Director of Baptist Women in Ministry and Bruce Gourley, former Executive Directive of Baptist History and Heritage. I am particularly grateful to Christopher Evans, Professor of the History of Christianity at Boston University School of Theology, for his careful reading of the manuscript and his constructive suggestions. Marc Jolley, Director of Mercer University Press, and his staff have offered superb support in the process of publication. My thanks most of all go to my wife, Ruth, who has been a great collaborator in this project. She has assisted at every stage with research, typing, and editing. Even more important is the unfailing encouragement and support she has given for this project. It gives me immense pleasure to dedicate this book to her.

—Bill Pitts
January 2018

Walter Rauschenbusch: student at Gütersloh, Germany, 1882

Courtesy of the American Baptist Historical Society

Walter Rauschenbusch:
seminary student at Rochester Theological Seminary, 1884

Courtesy of the American Baptist Historical Society

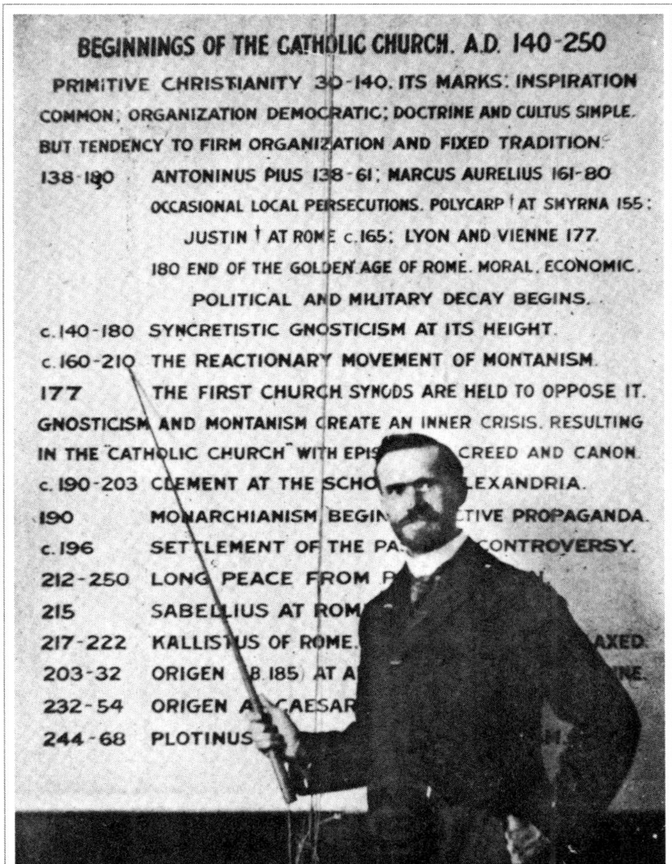

Walter Rauschenbusch in the classroom

Courtesy of the American Baptist Historical Society

Walter Rauschenbusch: Professor and Social Gospel Writer

Courtesy of the American Baptist Historical Society

Walter Rauschenbusch with Leighton Williams

Courtesy of the American Baptist Historical Society

Walter Rauschenbusch: American Protestant Leader

Courtesy of the American Baptist Historical Society

THE RECEPTION OF RAUSCHENBUSCH

INTRODUCTION

The heart of Rauschenbusch's message was that Jesus proclaimed the Kingdom of God, and this concept included both individual salvation and the transformation of the entire society. This proposal put the task of the church in an entirely new perspective. If he was correct, the church bore part of the responsibility for the welfare of the nation. Readers gave his proposal a divided response: some rejected it outright; others accepted it as a mandate for the church. Those who accepted Rauschenbusch's thoughts experienced a new sense of responsibility not only for the church but also for its interaction with society. The new challenge was exhilarating for many readers.

My focus in this study is the immediate reception by Rauschenbusch's contemporary audiences. Why did Rauschenbusch become famous in 1907, and what evidence can be found to document his influence? The vision for this book was inspired by reading letters written to him following the publication of his major works; hence my choice of the term "reception." Reception is a flexible term. I survey his long-term reception in the final chapter, but in this study, I am particularly interested in documenting the earliest responses to Rauschenbusch as a person and as a writer. Especially revealing are letters written to him immediately following publication of each of his books. These letters allow modern readers to hear the voices of the readers of Rauschenbusch's era. They illumine factors in the process by which Rauschenbusch became influential during his lifetime and beyond.

In Part 1, I devote the first chapter to Rauschenbusch's religious and intellectual development and the second chapter to the American society where he observed troubling dimensions of suffering and injustice. Chapter three traces key developments in Rauschenbusch's discovery and articulation of the social gospel through 1907: the story of Rauschenbusch's national recognition derives from his publication of *Christianity and the Social Crisis* in that year. In this book he articulated an understanding of the social gospel with more clarity, insight, and persuasion than most people had ever seen. The book sold thousands of volumes and made him famous. In this chapter, I trace major stages in his development of the ideas of the social gospel and discuss the major lines of his argument. The fourth chapter is devoted fully to the reception of Rauschenbusch's message in *Christianity and the Social Crisis*, documented in the particularly rich collection of letters preserved in the Rauschenbusch Family Papers. Numerous readers wrote letters of appreciation to him. I have also explored aspects of the publication culture of Macmillan Press and networking patterns of American ministers that contributed to the surprisingly rapid success of the book. Part 1 thus presents Rauschenbusch's core ideas and the reception of his first major book.

In Part 2, I explore a different dimension of the notion of reception. Apart from his major books, contemporaries often spoke about Rauschenbusch's vocational achievements and his personal character. The details of his life are properly left to biographies, but there is also a story of the reception of Rauschenbusch in the performance of his professional roles. I have selected four strands of his influence, each with its own chapter: first, I examine his work as a pastor-scholar, illustrating how seriously he pursued scholarship while serving as pastor. Second, I show how he also made significant contributions to Baptist life throughout his career. He clearly articulated Baptist identity, and he offered guidance for his denomination during his lifetime. Third, I turn to Rauschenbusch as a professor of church history and discuss aspects of his approach to the history of Christianity as well as his legacy as a teacher. His personal contact and influence were as important to the generation of students he taught as were his writings to the wider public. Finally, the fame brought by *Christianity and the Social Crisis* catapulted Rauschenbusch into a position as public Protestant leader. In this fourth role, Rauschenbusch demonstrated leadership, positioning himself on major Protestant trends of the day—missions, unity, theology—as well as promoting the social gospel. These four chapters combine assessments of Rauschenbusch's direct personal influence on people he met and groups he served. Substantial evidence exists for examining his roles as minister, Baptist, seminary professor, and Protestant leader. These varied interests demonstrate Rauschenbusch's versatility, and they form an important dimension of his legacy.

In Part 3, I examine the broad range of Rauschenbusch's Christianity. He is too often presented as a one-dimensional thinker whose only idea was the social gospel, but he is a far more complicated figure than that. He provides a superb example of a person who experienced and articulated great diversity of Christian experience. Whereas some Christians favor expressing their faith in contemplation, prayer, and worship, others live out their Christianity through activism and service. Still others identify as Christian principally through their beliefs. Rauschenbusch devoted serious attention to all of these dimensions of the faith by writing separate books from all three perspectives. In *For God and the People*, his prayers for the social awakening, Rauschenbusch made a splendid contribution to the concerns of modern Christian spirituality. His prayers are little gems, prepared for laity of all walks of life. His *Christianizing the Social Order* provided an extended discussion of American society—its achievements and its failures. Urgently pressed by ministers for ways to proceed in establishing the kingdom of God, he offered practical guidelines, directions and principles for taking action to redeem the nation. In *A Theology for the Social Gospel* Rauschenbusch devoted himself to theological reflection. Here he pitted the kingdom of evil against the kingdom of God and developed these theological ideas in depth. The year before his *Theology* was published, Rauschenbusch published *The Social Principles of Jesus*, a course of study guidelines for college students. This book provided students with guidance for Christian ethical action. Based on selected readings from the Gospels, Rauschenbusch explained in this book that Jesus and his teachings provided a new force in history. Rauschenbusch's Christianity was multifaceted.

Abundant letters and book reviews survive and comment on all of Rauschenbusch's later works as well as his first major book, and I explore the theme of reception for each of them. Each book was declared to be his best; opinion clearly varied according to readers' preferences. Where evidence exists in letters and copies of contracts with publishers, I describe circumstances surrounding the writing of his major books. Before describing reception, I provide an extended account of the contents and argument of each book. Like many prolific writers, Rauschenbusch was both innovative and repetitive. He restated key ideas, arguments, and areas needing reform, but his language was vigorous, and he kept devising new ways to deliver his message.

Whereas most of the sources cited in this study were written during the year following the publication of each book, I devote the final chapter to a survey of the reception of Rauschenbusch over the past century. This book is published on the occasion of the centennial anniversary of Rauschenbusch's death. His legacy is important, and every book written about him is in some way a tribute to his ongoing relevance. Few American religious leaders have accomplished as much in a lifetime of fifty-six years. Through his personal influence, and especially through the extended reach of his writings, Rauschenbusch's influence has been sustained throughout the century following his death.

I have chosen the term "reception" as the major motif of this study. The idea of reception history is open to a variety of understandings. I distinguish reception from both legacy and response. "Legacy" is a broad term with legal roots suggesting all that is left by a person to those following. Rauschenbusch elicited immediate response, but to respond or answer usually includes negative as well as positive reactions. Sections of the church rejected Rauschenbusch's notion of a social gospel, and that reaction is of course part of the broader history of social Christianity. By using the term "reception," I focus primarily on the positive responses to Rauschenbusch's proposals. Positive responders often did not accept all that Rauschenbusch said and many thought that his work needed modification, but they believed his work was constructive and on the right path. They viewed Rauschenbusch's proposals with appreciation and appropriated them for their own use. This is the connotation of the term "reception" used in this study. The multiple responses to Rauschenbusch's writings came from otherwise unknown ministers as well as from highly visible religious leaders. The letters thus reveal something of popular religion in America as well as reflections by the elite. Historians searching for the elusive common voice of the laity will find that voice in these letters. Rauschenbusch's influence was strongest among readers who favored moderate reform. His proposals were accepted most readily by the Protestants who came to be known as mainline liberal Protestantism. They were typically associated with the Federal Council of Churches (later called National Council of Churches of Christ), and they exercised powerful cultural influence during the twentieth century. Acting on the vision of social redemption was for them an important task of the church. The reception continues.

PART 1

A LARGER UNDERSTANDING OF CHRISTIANITY: CHURCH AND SOCIETY

Walter Rauschenbusch (1861–1918) is best known as an advocate for the social gospel. This is the most referenced, most studied, and certainly most influential new idea that he proposed for Christian thought and for the church's understanding of its task. What is involved in the concept of the social gospel? Why did it flourish during his generation? How did Rauschenbusch arrive at this position? What did he add to the movement? What was the importance of this concept? Part 1 approaches these questions in four chapters, each with a specific theme and each related to the broader idea of the social gospel.

Rauschenbusch's personal development is the subject of chapter 1. This chapter focuses especially on the educational and religious influences that shaped the young Rauschenbusch. Academically he was brilliant and motivated to achieve excellence in the task of learning. Religiously he was deeply committed to his faith—to understanding it and conveying its message through his work as a minister. Before he engaged the problems of the parish ministry in New York City, he wrestled as a student with intellectual trends of his day. Significant advances in scientific and historical methods in this era raised important questions of biblical and historical interpretation. How might the Christian deal with the idea of evolution? How should Scripture be interpreted? As a student, Rauschenbusch studied these current topics and adopted progressive interpretations. Positioning himself in this fashion on current intellectual trends created a mental outlook that allowed him to be open to exploring additional new ideas.

Chapter 2 turns from the early formation of Rauschenbusch to the rapidly changing conditions in American urban life in 1886–1918, the era of Rauschenbusch's adult working life. The difficulties faced by working people struck Rauschenbusch with particular force. The social conditions he encountered in New York City were unlike anything he had experienced at home or in school. He was minister to German immigrants, and he wanted to help them. He wondered if the gospel had something to say to their current social condition as well as offering the traditional promise of heaven. He was aware that many workers were turning away from the church in Europe. He wanted his ministry among his parishioners to be constructive and relevant. He needed to articulate the

Christian faith in the new context created by the industrial economy. He did not try to address this vast problem alone. He made friends with two other young ministers to talk about the nature of their ministry. What exactly should they do? He wanted to understand the society in which he was attempting to minister, and therefore he spent many hours reading analyses of the social and economic structures of American society as well as discussing the relationship of the church to society with these close friends. Chapter 2 explores salient features of his society and his understanding of it.

Chapter 3 analyzes the development of Rauschenbusch's response to the problem—his discovery of the social dimension of the gospel and its application to contemporary society. Historians have labored over dating the development of Rauschenbusch's social thought, especially by looking for social gospel themes in his early sermons and published articles. Critical to the fuller articulation of his key ideas was a sabbatical leave Rauschenbusch took to Germany in 1891. There he wrote an extensive manuscript in which he argued for the revolutionary character of the Christian faith. The essential themes of the social gospel appeared in this long text, but the manuscript remained unpublished, and he shared it with only a few friends. He continued to think and write about his central idea that the Bible taught both individual and social Christianity. He eventually published his understanding of Christianity in *Christianity and the Social Crisis* (1907). Here he forcefully argued for the biblical basis for the social gospel and for the need for the contemporary church to adopt this broader understanding of Christian practices. This book brought him immediate fame. Chapter 3 traces the argument of the social gospel as Rauschenbusch developed it in his *Christianity Revolutionary* manuscript, his "New Evangelism" article, and his stunningly successful *Christianity and the Social Crisis.*

Part 1 closes with an extended assessment of the reception of Rauschenbusch's publication. The book had a profound impact on its first readers. Its message was fresh, grounded in Scripture, and morally challenging. Rauschenbusch presented his argument in vigorous prose. In terms of sales and circulation, it was an overwhelming success. Study groups formed in churches and ministerial associations to discuss the ideas in the book. Many levels of networking by churches and individuals went into making this the most popular book published in the field of religion during the next three years. Rauschenbusch received an avalanche of letters of gratitude. The letters show readers' personal feelings. They indicate that his message revealed for many ministers a new understanding of the gospel message, gave them energy for a fresh start in their ministries, and provided a new sense of purpose in their lives. In order to judge the immediate impact of *Christianity and the Social Crisis,* chapter 4 is devoted to examining evidence of the immediate reception of this classic book in American religious history.

CHAPTER 1

FORMATION OF A PROGRESSIVE YOUNG MINISTER

Walter Rauschenbusch lived during an era of extraordinary intellectual and social ferment in American history. The changes of the era influenced him to view the world from new perspectives. Several factors shaped Rauschenbusch's life: his early home life, his educational and religious experiences, the new ideas he encountered at university and seminary, especially those affecting religion, and the responses he developed to the new trends in Western thought. Religious experiences grounded him in lifelong commitment to a life of faith, and challenges posed by new ideas moved him to reshape his understanding of Christianity. The chronological, detailed narrative of Rauschenbusch's life has been carefully researched and narrated.[1] While including some essential biography, the approach taken here is thematic. The task of the present chapter is to explore the formative influences in Rauschenbusch's early life and their impact on his intellectual and religious outlook.

Home and Family

The Rauschenbusch family joined the great tide of nineteenth-century European immigrants to America. Rauschenbusch's father, August, was a Lutheran pastor who trained in Berlin where he was greatly influenced by the Pietism of

[1]Rauschenbusch has had three major biographers. Dores R. Sharpe, Rauschenbusch's Canadian student, published the first biography, *Walter Rauschenbusch* (New York: Macmillan, 1942). This was followed by Paul Minus, *Walter Rauschenbusch: American Reformer* (New York: Macmillan, 1988), and most recently by the thorough work of Christopher Evans, *The Kingdom Is Always but Coming: A Life of Walter Rauschenbusch* (Grand Rapids: Eerdmans, 2004). Sharpe collected much primary material, and Minus and Evans had access to the extensive collection of Rauschenbusch Family Papers, which are now housed in the American Baptist Historical Society (ABHS) in Atlanta, Georgia (hereafter cited as Rauschenbusch Family Papers). While most of the materials are held in one of the 180 boxes (and are noted with a box number and the terms "Rauschenbusch Family Papers"), there are other major sources not contained in the boxes. Rauschenbusch collected articles and other materials and pasted them in scrapbooks which are too large to fit in boxes. Also, many free-standing volumes are shelved outside the boxes, notably the *Brotherhood of the Kingdom* leaflets which are bound as a single volume.

his church history professor, Johann Neander.[2] Neander's theology stressed the centrality of the influence of the divine on individual human lives. His church history writing emphasized biographies of individual Christians and focused on living out the Christian life rather than retracing the traditional accounts of monasticism, papacy, and preeminent theologians. This attention to the practice of Christianity deeply influenced the approach to church history taken by August Rauschenbusch and his son, Walter. August came to America in 1846 to work with the American Tract Society as a missionary among immigrants; some 1,200,000 fellow Germans had arrived in the United States by 1850.[3] Although August was the sixth in a line of Lutheran pastors, after he arrived in the United States, he engaged in extended dialogue with Baptists and converted to the Baptist denomination in 1850.[4] Thus Walter was brought up in a German Baptist household. He deeply admired his father for taking this bold step despite the sacrifices it entailed.

August married Caroline Rump, and according to his daughter the marriage occurred on the rebound from a failed romance.[5] The couple was often estranged, and August left the home for extended periods. The unhappy relationship of his parents was a source of enduring pain to Walter. Although August was often absent and demanding with his children when present, Walter adored his father and adopted his Pietism, his love of learning, and his commitment to a life of service.[6] As a tribute to his father, Walter finished August's autobiography posthumously.[7] Rauschenbusch was also protective of his mother and expressed his deep admiration and love for her as well. He recalled with fondness the religious training his mother had provided. He later sought to establish relationships within his own family that would avoid the failed relationship of his parents.

Walter Rauschenbusch grew up in Rochester, where his father taught in the Baptist Theological Seminary. Rochester, located in western New York, was connected with the interior of the state and with the populous East Coast by the Erie Canal, completed in 1825. Longtime Rochesterian Augustus Hopkins Strong remarked in 1916 that in its day the canal "was as great an achievement as is the

---

[2] For a recent comprehensive study of Pietism, see Shantz, *An Introduction to German Pietism.*

[3] Sharpe, *Walter Rauschenbusch*, 3; Evans, *The Kingdom Is Always but Coming*, 5–6.

[4] See August Rauschenbusch's account of his shift to the Baptists in *Life and Ministry of August Rauschenbusch*, 88–91.

[5] Winifred [Rauschenbusch] Rorty to Dores Sharpe, December 17, 1938, box 50, Rauschenbusch Family Papers.

[6] For an analysis of August Rauschenbusch's own religious commitment and his contribution to German Baptists in the United States and Canada, see Pitts, "Shaping a German Immigrant Church," 194–214.

[7] A. Rauschenbusch, *Leben und Wirken von August Rauschenbusch.*

Panama Canal in our day, the longest canal in the world."[8] The Erie Canal revolutionized transportation and communication and spurred the rapid growth of the city.

Following the era of canal building, Rochester was at the geographical center of vibrant religious activity. Whitney Cross demonstrated that the region was home to numerous significant American religious innovations before the Civil War.[9] Moreover, Rochester experienced repeated waves of revival that swept the region. Charles Grandison Finney was the great revivalist of the first half of the century in America. He was particularly effective in cities, his earliest success coming during his Rochester meeting in 1830. Finney's influence remained significant in the region. Strong, president and professor of theology at Rochester Theological Seminary for forty years (1872–1912), was converted by Finney in 1856.[10] Dwight L. Moody continued the revival tradition during Rauschenbusch's era and deeply influenced Protestantism of his era. Carl E. Schneider perceptively observed that in August Rauschenbusch's thinking, German Pietism was gradually recast as American evangelicalism.[11] The expectation of personal conversion was central in Rauschenbusch's religious formation.

Baptists grew rapidly in the region. The New York Baptist Union established the new seminary at Rochester in 1850, designed to train the young men who sought to serve the denomination. The seminary flourished following the Civil War. By 1867 the regular English course of instruction included biblical literature (which included biblical languages, biblical criticism, and exegesis), ecclesiastical history, theology, homiletics, and pastoral duties.[12] By 1869 the seminary had added "Evidences of Christianity" to the curriculum.[13] The seminary continued to develop and rapidly achieved a reputation for excellence.

As Baptists successfully established churches among German immigrants, some of their church members committed themselves to ministry. Rochester

[8] Strong, *Reminiscences of Early Rochester*, 10.

[9] See W. R. Cross, *The Burned-over District*; this book became a classic study of pre-Civil War religion in the region. A later important study focused on the role of the economy and its influential place in supporting Rochester's temperance movement. See Johnson, *A Shopkeeper's Millennium*.

[10] Hudson, ed., *Walter Rauschenbusch: Selected Writings*, 8–9.

[11] Schneider, "Americanization of August Rauschenbusch, 1816–1899," 3–14.

[12] Rochester Theological Seminary, *Seventeenth Annual Catalogue of the Officers and Students of the Rochester Theological Seminary, 1867–68*, 13–15.

[13] Rochester Theological Seminary, *Nineteenth Annual Catalogue of the Officers and Students of the Rochester Theological Seminary*, 13.

Theological Seminary welcomed them, but the training center for German Baptist pastors initially struggled, attracting only a small response.[14] The major drawback was that the instruction they were receiving was in English, but they needed to be taught in German. The seminary addressed the problem by creating the German department in 1858. Early in its existence the seminary had acquired a treasured resource, the 4600-volume library of German church historian Johann Neander.[15] The curriculum of the German department was flexible by design. Some younger seminarians took a full curriculum of instruction. Some older church members also experienced a call to preach, but they did not pursue a full degree and took only the essentials of ministerial training before assuming leadership of their churches. Because of his strong educational background and his missionary and pastoral work among German immigrants, the seminary called August Rauschenbusch in 1858 to be head of the new department, where he served until 1888. He was effective in this position, and his reputation as the major architect of German Baptist theological education spread in the United States.[16]

Walter was born in Rochester on October 4, 1861, the year the Civil War began. In an early childhood memory prompted by Lincoln's assassination in 1865, Rauschenbusch recalled that black wreaths honoring the fallen president had been placed on the front porches of homes on his street.[17] This was one of his earliest memories of Rochester. Except for his eleven-year ministry in New York City and extended periods of study abroad, Rochester was home for Walter Rauschenbusch throughout his life.

Education and Religion

Education and religion combined to shape the young Rauschenbusch. These pervasive influences intermingled in his experience. Despite Rochester being his home, Rauschenbusch spent an extraordinarily long time in German schools. The first of these ventures began in 1865 when Walter was three years old and Augustus moved the family to Germany for four years.[18] Thus Rauschenbusch's earliest formal education began in Germany. Because Augustus insisted that the children speak only German at home, Walter was fluent in both German and

---

[14]See the account of the department's early years in Gabelmann, "The German Department of Rochester Theological Seminary," 308–12.

[15] Rochester Theological Seminary, *Catalogue of the Rochester Theological Seminary, Founded November 4, 1850, by the New-York Baptist Union for Ministerial Education, 1854–5*, 16. Also see Hayes, "The History of the University of Rochester Libraries—120 Years," 63.

[16] Gabelmann, "The German Department of Rochester Theological Seminary," 310.

[17] WR, "Reminiscences of My Life," typescript (1900), box 139, Rauschenbusch Family Papers.

[18] Ibid.

English.[19] His bilingual skills would be an important asset for his work, giving him ready access to intellectual currents shaping modern theological, biblical, and historical studies in Germany, some of which he appropriated for his own theology. The dual language skill was also critical for providing effective leadership to the German Baptist constituency in the United States. Like his father, Rauschenbusch maintained a passionate devotion to German culture. Walter would return to Germany for additional education during high school, for a critical sabbatical year of writing in 1891, and for additional periods of study and academic conferences.

The family returned to Rochester in 1869, and August bought a home on Arnold Park Avenue, where the family lived until 1888.[20] Walter and his older sisters, Frieda and Emma, went to school in Rochester during the 1870s.[21] The family attended Rochester German Baptist Church. In a YMCA address later in his life, Rauschenbusch recalled the religious influence of his home: "I was brought up in a very religious family, and I thank God for it. We had household religious services every day, and from childhood I was taught to pray, read the Bible, go to Sunday school, to be in church often, and all those things I have no doubt trickled down into my mind and did their work there."[22] As he grew up he also experienced feelings of guilt for engaging in what his sister called "the meaner kind of boyish mischief."[23] Rauschenbusch confessed, "I ran with a gang; for a time I tried very hard to become their leader in swearing, but I never could. I think, however, that other people who observed me thought I was on the road to the devil."[24] Rauschenbusch also recalled a dawning consciousness of God:

> When I was leaving boyhood behind me and the seriousness of life began to come over me, I felt the call of God, and after a long struggle extending through several years, I submitted my will to his law. Henceforth God was consciously present in my life, and this gave it a sense of solemnity and worth. This gave a decisive reinforcement to my will, and turned my life in the direction of service and when necessary self-sacrifice; so salvation came to me.[25]

Walter experienced a period of skepticism and questioning of religious faith

---

[19] A. Rauschenbusch, *August Rauschenbusch, Life and Ministry*, 17.

[20] Ibid., 174.

[21] Ibid., 170. Rauschenbusch's oldest son, Winfrid, died in 1858..

[22] WR, "The Kingdom of God," *Cleveland's Young Men* 27 (January 9, 1913), cited in Handy, *The Social Gospel in America*, 264.

[23] Winifred [Rauschenbusch] Rorty to Dores Sharpe, December 17, 1938, box 50, Rauschenbusch Family Papers.

[24] WR, "The Kingdom of God," *Cleveland's Young Men* 27 (January 9, 1913), cited in Handy, *The Social Gospel in America*, 264.

[25] Barnes, "Walter Rauschenbusch—His Personal Testimony," *The Watchman Examiner*, August 1, 1918, 985. The original letter is found box 39, Rauschenbusch Family Papers.

before conversion during his senior year in high school at age seventeen. He reported that the conversion process involved a long struggle but was deeply meaningful. He later said that conversion meant "a break with debasing habits." Moreover, from a constructive perspective "it [conversion] means more self-control, more responsiveness to duty, more capacity to take a long outlook, and consequently better work. We can observe this in ourselves and others."[26] This reflection is presumably in part autobiographical. Near the end of his life Rauschenbusch recalled, "It [his conversion] was a tender mysterious experience. It influenced my soul down to its depths."[27] Rauschenbusch interpreted his religious conversion in terms of his own resolve to serve, and he used the familiar image of the prodigal son to interpret his experience:

> I began to feel the stirring of human ambition within me; and what I said to myself was: 'I want to become a man; I want to be respected; and if I go on like this, I cannot have the respect of men.' This was my way of saying: 'I am out in the far country, and I want to go home to my country, and I don't want to tend the hogs any longer.' And so I came to my Father, and I began to pray for help and got it. And I got my own religious experience.[28]

Rauschenbusch was baptized at the First German Baptist Church in Rochester on March 16, 1879.[29] Rauschenbusch recalled that at the time of his conversion he thought every Christian should work to redeem humanity. He said that he "wanted to do hard work for God."[30] This comment suggests a deep level of commitment by the young Rauschenbusch. The conversion experience and the example of his father combined to provide the foundation for his call to the ministry.[31] These influences profoundly shaped the course of his adult life. Immersed in religious practice from childhood, Rauschenbusch briefly pushed against his training, but as a youth he grew serious about life. He viewed his conversion negatively as a time of decision for abandoning mischief, but also constructively for giving him direction and purpose in life. In his last reflection on his life, Rauschenbusch linked his own conversion with his "public work" of opposing the "social iniquity" of "injustices."[32]

---

[26] WR, *The Social Principles of Jesus*, 1927 ed., 72–73.

[27] Barnes, "Walter Rauschenbusch—His Personal Testimony." *The Watchman Examiner,* August 1, 1918, 985.

[28] WR, "The Kingdom of God." *Cleveland's Young Men* 27 (January 9, 1913), cited in Handy, *The Social Gospel in America*, 264.

[29] Minus, *Walter Rauschenbusch*, 17.

[30] WR, "The Kingdom of God." *Cleveland's Young Men* 27 (January 9, 1913), cited in Handy, *The Social Gospel in America*, 264.

[31] Evans, *The Kingdom Is Always but Coming*, 19–20; Minus, *Walter Rauschenbusch*, 17.

[32] Barnes, "Walter Rauschenbusch—His Personal Testimony," 985.

> In my efforts to secure more freedom and justice for men I acted under religious impulses. I realized that God hates injustices and that I would be quenching the life of God within me if I kept silent with all this social iniquity around me.... My life would seem an empty shell if my personal religion were left out of it. It has been my deepest satisfaction to get evidence now and then that I have been able to help men to a new spiritual birth. I have always regarded my public work as a form of evangelism, which called for a deeper repentance and a new experience of God's salvation.[33]

Walter excelled in academic work. He recalled the delight he felt when he first experienced an intellectual awakening: an acquaintance "lent me a fascinating illustrated book of history. It told about invasions of the barbarians, looting and burning of cities by the Huns. That is the first book, the content of which thrilled me and made me remember it."[34] His sister recalled that he and his friend Ed Hanna competed to see who could translate Latin texts more quickly.[35] Although intellectually astute, Rauschenbusch was socially shy.[36] Convinced of the superiority of the German educational system, August arranged for Walter to return to Germany to study at the Gymnasium in Gütersloh during the years 1879–1883. Rauschenbusch recalled that at school he was required to memorize passages from Scripture, the *Small Catechism*, and the *Augsburg Confession*. He worked hard on his Greek and Latin, spending less time on French, history, religion, and other subjects. He was very conscientious about his responsibilities. In a tiny pocket diary, he meticulously recorded expenses he incurred and the number of minutes he devoted to the study of each of his subjects.[37] He combined natural intellectual gifts with disciplined study and finished at the top of his class at the Gymnasium.[38]

While in Germany, Rauschenbusch pursued his quest for knowledge outside of formal education. He traveled to several German cities where he attended lectures by notable scholars such as the historians Theodore Mommsen and Ernst

---

[33] Ibid.

[34] WR, "Reminiscences of my Life," typescript (1900), box 139, Rauschenbusch Family Papers. He does not indicate his age when he read this book.

[35] Winifred [Rauschenbusch] Rorty to Dores Sharpe, December 17, 1938, box 50, Rauschenbusch Family Papers.

[36] Ibid. He attempted to overcome some of this shyness by the time he was in seminary. (See WR to Munson Ford, December 21, 1884, in Hudson, ed., *Walter Rauschenbusch: Selected Writings*, 54.) But his later assessment of himself was "I was born shy" (see WR to Rev. G. Herbert Elkins, January 20, 1916, box 46, Rauschenbusch Family Papers).

[37] WR, pocket diary, box 38, Rauschenbusch Family Papers.

[38] His students later reported his linguistic prowess. According to Sharpe, he wrote a Christmas letter to his family in Greek, and for his Hebrew exams, rather than translating Psalm 90 into German he rendered it into Latin hexameter (Sharpe, *Walter Rauschenbusch*, 45).

Robert Curtius, and he visited major art galleries.[39] Minus writes that the youthful Rauschenbusch was also exposed to terrible human suffering when he visited a house of epileptics.[40] Rauschenbusch's success at school was shaping him for an academic perspective on life—first as a scholar-minister and later a professor.

Religious influences during his years in Germany affected Rauschenbusch deeply. He observed the long-standing tensions between Lutheran and Catholic cultures. He would also later use this method of comparing denominational characteristics in his teaching and writing. He learned new hymns, including those of the seventeenth-century Lutheran Pietist Paul Gerhardt, whose poetry expressed the believer's complete trust in God. Toward the end of his life Rauschenbusch wrote that the German Lutheran hymns had remained favorites throughout his life.[41]

In Germany Rauschenbusch also encountered current conflicting interpretations of Protestant Christianity. The leading German Protestant theologian of the era was Albrecht Ritschl. His recasting of theology sought to communicate traditional Christian ideas in modern terms. New Testament studies supported the view that the idea of the kingdom of God was Jesus' central message, and Ritschl gave particular attention to Jesus' preaching of the kingdom of God in his theology. Ritschl understood the task of the theologian was to apply Jesus' message of the kingdom to modern culture. On the other hand, Rauschenbusch's host was Heinrich Bertelsmann, a traditionalist who opposed the new liberal theology of Ritschl and his growing influence in German Protestant thought. Bertelsmann established a school and a press that he dedicated to promoting traditional ideas. Thus Rauschenbusch experienced first-hand the Protestant tensions that arose between the traditional conservatism embraced by a host family and the new theology centered on Ritschl's recovery of Jesus' teaching of the kingdom of God. As his personal theology developed, the idea of the kingdom of God would later take the central position in Rauschenbusch's theological reconstruction.

Rauschenbusch's Understanding of Ministerial Training

Toward the end of his stay in Germany, and on the eve of returning to Rochester for seminary training, Rauschenbusch reflected on preparation for ministry, including both academic curricula and spiritual formation. His written summary of his thoughts reveals a mature understanding of seminary curriculum and the logical order of his thinking.[42] In his address book, Rauschenbusch wrote

---

[39] Sharpe, *Walter Rauschenbusch*, 49.

[40] Minus, *Walter Rauschenbusch*, 26.

[41] WR, "Instructions in case of my death," box 106, Rauschenbusch Family Papers.

[42] What follows is a summary of theological education which Rauschenbusch outlined for himself. See the small diary/address book, box 38, Rauschenbusch Family Papers. The

in outline form: "In every plan [there should be] (1) an understanding of end [and] (2) of means for attaining it. [The] *End* [is] ministerial service, i.e., [to] save men and honor God. [The] *Means* [is] such preparation as shall give a proper knowledge by proper habits. (1) Acquisition of proper knowledge [and] (2) acquisition of proper habits are end of theological course."[43] In this brief note Rauschenbusch analyzed the purpose of ministerial education and the importance of disciplined habits to achieve the goals of seminary training.

Next Rauschenbusch analyzed the means to the end. Here he shifted from disciplined habits to a review of the seminary curriculum:

> [The] knowledge to be acquired [is] (1) Biblical, (2) Historical, (3) Systematic, & (4) Practical. *Biblical* Theology gives facts of revelation, therefore know O.T. and N.T. Knowledge of original languages is desirable. *Historical* Theology takes biblical facts and shows how the church has apprehended them (History of Doctrine) and what effects this approach has brought in the church. *Systematic* Theology. *Practical* Theology [is] the unfolding and impressing of these facts (1) in public address Homiletics [and] (2) in private pastoral work.[44]

Having summarized the components of the three-year curriculum, Rauschenbusch described systematic theology, which he had earlier omitted to discuss: "*Systematic Theology*: [Its] *Aim* is not to impose a ready-made system, but (1) to cultivate habit of theological thought by comparison of Scripture and the writers (2) settle down upon a few important principles (3) show their connection so that it will be an organic system."[45] Already he indicated suspicion of a theological system. Instead he advocated focusing on a few principles and showing their organic interrelationship. Finally he turned to "Methods" where he created a list of common pedagogical practices: "*Methods* of obtaining the aim [are] (1) printed lectures (2) accompanying explanations and illustrations (interleaved) (3) side reading (references in the book) (4) questions and discussions arising by study (5) essays, original investigation [during the] middle and senior year (6) examinations end of term."[46]

These brief notes reveal knowledge of seminary requirements and an analytical mind working systematically to make sense of an entire curriculum. They also show that Rauschenbusch had reflected on the variety of pedagogical methods

---

notebook appears to be from Gymnasium days; the date 1883 appears twice in the book. These comments were apparently written in Gütersloh as Rauschenbusch anticipated returning to Rochester for his seminary education, yet they show close familiarity with seminary life. Rauschenbusch wrote these notes in outline form. I have kept the structure of his remarks but slightly edited them to improve readability.

[43] Ibid.

[44] Ibid.

[45] Ibid.

[46] Ibid.

used during his era. He adds to this reflection on education notes to himself on intellectual habits he should adopt: "*Habits to be formed*: Intellectual (1) regularity necessary (2) exclusive devotion to work of Seminary (3) mental discipline, vigorous study (4) loftiness of mind—not being rude and boyish, using slang, talking of trifles."[47] Rauschenbusch's list reveals a serious approach to learning, and his practice of these habits doubtless helped him attain the highest levels of academic achievement.

In a third set of comments for seminary training, Rauschenbusch also addressed the issue of appropriate "religious habits." He reviewed intellectual preparation, and here he added his reflections on habitual practices desirable for the future minister: "I. Seminary is a religious institution where work is done with the help of Christ, including attendance at prayers...and willingness to speak for Christ.... II. Relations with each other are very valuable and a powerful influence. III. Relation to our churches. Membership in town is desirable. We should work there. IV. These duties can be fulfilled only if private reading and prayer is kept up. We are dependent on the Word as on daily bread."[48]

These unpublished notes provide evidence of a remarkable grasp of ministerial education of his day. Rauschenbusch probably heard much of this at home from his seminary professor father before experiencing seminary life himself as student and professor. The comments show that he was attentive to essential dimensions of spirituality and religious practice—prayer and Bible reading, relationships with others, and active participation and service in the local church—as well as classic disciplines of seminary training. These short notes summarizing his reflections show that Rauschenbusch had developed a serious approach to religious and intellectual practice. He had prepared well. But the university and the seminary experience ahead of him would bring new visions and challenges to his intellectual and religious world.

Rauschenbusch returned to Rochester in 1883 ready to train for the ministry, but he also wanted to secure a university degree as had his Rauschenbusch forebears in ministry. He therefore enrolled simultaneously at University of Rochester to complete his university degree and at Rochester Theological Seminary to begin his first year of seminary training. Rochester granted extensive credit for his Gütersloh Gymnasium work, and he achieved both of his goals, earning his A.B. in 1884 and his seminary degree in 1886.[49] The time Rauschenbusch devoted to academic exploration in Germany and at Rochester was critical

---

[47] Ibid.

[48] Ibid.

[49] *Rochester Theological Seminary General Catalogue 1850–1920*, 36 ("Rauschenbusch" [brief biographical information under "Faculty"]) and 160 ("Rauschenbusch" [brief biographical information under "graduates"]). The University of Rochester also awarded Rauschenbusch the D.D. in 1902, and Oberlin University granted him another honorary doctorate in 1916.

for his intellectual formation. In the midst of his New York ministry, Rauschenbusch returned to Germany for a third time, where he once again experienced a decisive intellectual awakening. Rauschenbusch was in his element in academic life. He readily met its challenges. He was a young intellectual with a strong religious commitment.

Intellectual Trends and the New Theology

Rauschenbusch was deeply influenced by the intellectual ferment of his era. Western culture experienced a profound intellectual upheaval during the late nineteenth and early twentieth centuries. This revolution changed the outlook of Americans and Europeans in virtually every area of study. New ideas challenged the older views in the natural sciences (notably in geology and biology), in understanding of people in groups and as individuals (with the emergence of the new disciplines of sociology and psychology), and in the perception of history and religion. Perhaps the dominant new idea of the era was the notion of development.

The idea of development provided a framework and a perspective that were appropriated by many disciplines. It was at the core of Darwin's view of evolution. Historians had traditionally written narratives, but now they became increasingly interested in identifying causes of change, growth, and development in human experience.[50] This historical view of things seemed to offer a key to understanding many aspects of nature and culture. Everything seemed to have developed and to have a history. The dynamic paradigm of development both in nature and in human society challenged an older static view of things as fixed and unchanging. The European and American presses circulated the new ideas widely, and the challenge of new ideas created an intellectual chasm in Western society. Whereas many people continued to hold to older views of science, time, and history, others began to accept the compelling logic of new evidence that seemed to leave them no choice but to adopt newer views.

The new outlook fueled furious debates and was particularly stressful in religious circles since traditional religious ideas were often based on the assumption that religious truth was fixed, settled, and unchanging for all time. The idea of development of doctrine undermined the older presuppositions. Confronted with powerful arguments for new interpretations of nature and human history, thoughtful readers chose a position to defend; others were doubtless left with a sense of uncertainty that left questions unresolved. Reared in tradition, Rauschenbusch struggled to accept the new outlook and the new organic/developmental view of society and history.

The new ideas of thinkers such as Marx, Comte, and Freud gained widespread acceptance. As founders of communism, positivism, and psychiatry, they

[50] Persons, *American Minds*, 338.

were among the most influential innovators of the era. None of them had a place in their thinking for traditional views of God. This was a crucial period for intellectual history, and these new nineteenth-century ideas presented enormous challenges to religious belief.[51] Comte, for example, divided history into three stages: mythical, religious, and positivist. The implication was clear: the modern positivist world had outgrown the need for religious belief. This was a part of the intellectual framework Rauschenbusch encountered.

In addition to the perspective of development in society, the achievements of science led increasingly to the view that science and the scientific method as the most reliable path to truth. Scientific discoveries challenged long-held views, and few disciplines remained unaffected. The scientific method relied on observation and experimentation, and people began to accept the method of discovery employed by the sciences. Scientists seemed to be consistently making new discoveries and establishing fact after fact. The results of the scientific method seemed to offer certainty and were therefore compelling to many. During this era the prestige of science permeated the culture as never before. New scientific discoveries in geology and biology illustrate how science challenged the Western intellectual tradition and Christian assumptions. In both instances scientific method combined with models of development to explain first the world and then life itself.

Developments in the discipline of geology during the nineteenth century dramatically illustrate the growing tensions between traditional ways of viewing the world and emerging new perspectives. New geological knowledge opened the way to a re-evaluation of time. In the mid-seventeenth century, Archbishop James Ussher (1581–1656) calculated the age of the earth, which he published in *Chronicle of the Old and New Testament* (1650–1654). He relied on the chronologies that appeared in the Bible to calculate the age of the earth by working back through the lists of kings of Israel and Judah with their periods of rule, the Judges, Moses, Abraham, and the antediluvians. His effort yielded the date of 4004 BCE. This date began to move from limited antiquarian interests to an influential popular cultural idea a half century later: By about 1700 CE printers began to publish Ussher's dates along with the text of the Bible. When nineteenth-century geologists began to look seriously at the age of the earth, the popular notion that the earth was about 6000 years old had been widely circulated for well over a century.

---

[51]Darwin's influence was massive in science, but these three men also challenged thinking about the past. Karl Marx saw a dialectical struggle between classes to explain the economic dynamic at work shaping much of history. A leading founder of positivism, Auguste Comte, thought humanity now relied on reason, not religion. Sigmund Freud explored the workings of the individual mind. For discussions of modern European intellectual life during this era see the interpretations of Baumer, *Modern European Thought*, and Tarnas, *The Passion of the Western Mind*.

Geologists sought to understand the formation of the structure of the earth's surface. They studied the evidence presented by layer upon layer of rocks, which, moreover, were often filled with the remains of sea creatures. Charles Lyell's uniformitarian geology held that the dramatic shape of the earth—mountains, gorges, sediments—appeared by natural causes such as the relentless movement of wind and water, seismic shifts, and volcanic activity. The evidence presented by geology meant that the processes of change were gradual; the geologists believed that the surface of the earth took millions of years to reach its present status. Geologists seemed to have discovered dimensions of time undreamed of before.

The new perspective on time had enormous implications for both science and religion. The question of the age of the earth was impossible to ignore. Some interpreters rejected the new science; others rejected the traditional biblical account of six days of creation. But many ministers and congregations searched for new interpretations of accommodation, finding ways for people to affirm their belief in essential claims of both science and religion. The days of Genesis 1, for example, were interpreted as epochs or ages rather than twenty-four-hour periods. The evidence of the geologists extended time immeasurably, and the notion of a very old earth began to be assimilated into general Western scientific and intellectual culture.[52]

Biology challenged traditional views of the origins of humanity, and its claims initially received much more dramatic responses than the new geology. In 1831 Charles Darwin was appointed naturalist on the voyage of *The Beagle*. His task was to gather information on the flora and fauna of the South American coastline for future use by the British navy. As he collected evidence, patterns of relationships eventually emerged in Darwin's mind. He observed finches and other birds on the Galapagos Islands whose beaks varied from island to island. Darwin noted that they had different food sources. Turtles varied according to their island of origin; a resident official in the Galapagos told Darwin that he could identify the home island of each turtle because of variations in their physiology. In later reflections on his observations Darwin argued that the animals adapted to whatever conditions nature provided; thus a key concept in his thinking was "natural selection" in creating variations of species. He suggested that the variations in species were countless; some survived and others did not. The key to survival was the ability to adapt. In an arresting illustration of his views, Darwin pointed out that the modern farmer practiced cross-breeding to secure desired traits in his animals.[53] This was a simple and familiar example of Darwin's view

[52] The major change in understanding the age of the earth is insightfully told in Gillespie's *Genesis and Geology*.

[53] Darwin, *The Origin of Species*. See chapter 1, "Variation and Domestication," 71–100, esp. 89–94.

of the mechanics of life. Darwin examined hundreds of species, looking for connections between them, and he developed the model of a tree of life in which all living things were related. He knew that this theory would be controversial, so he delayed publication of his views. However, when he learned that Alfred Russell Wallace was about to publish his theory of evolution, Darwin proceeded to publish *On the Origin of the Species* in 1859. His book offered an explanation of life based on natural laws. This scientific theory of evolution revolutionized the understanding of life in the modern world.[54]

Evolution had immense repercussions on religious thought. Traditional views of creation of the species, including humanity, were drawn from Genesis 1 and 2. Darwin sought a scientific answer based on natural evidence. The new view did not see nature as good and gentle, but rather as violent, an arena of struggles for survival. Moreover, the theory suggested that many species had come and gone. There was no fixed order in nature. It was instead a giant process of conflict in constant flux and motion. The religious perspective looked to divine creation; the scientific view sought to understand natural causes for the workings of nature. The tension between science and religion demanded attention.

Immediately a famous debate took place in 1860 at Oxford over the claims of the new theory, and the outcome was divided. As with geology, so now with biology: whereas traditionalists sought to preserve a literal reading of Genesis and therefore conceded little to new scientific views, some scientists felt compelled to reject traditional religious views. However, once again many religious defenders of the new science sought ways to accommodate the truths of Christianity to the truths of science, arguing that one could accept the truths found in religion along with those discovered by science. Revolutionary understandings of the world prompted rethinking of Christian belief and was called simply New Theology. This theology would adapt interpretations to accommodate religious belief: it scientific discovery. Scholars adopting this approach included theologians such as Theodore T. Munger, Washington Gladden, William Newton Clarke, and Newman Smith.[55] During his university studies Rauschenbusch wrestled with these ideas presented by the new science, and he began to adopt perspectives of the New Theology under the influence of his professors.

The notion of development had a profound impact on understanding history and religion as well as science. Using the method of historical criticism, scholars of the discipline of historical theology insisted that Christian doctrine itself had a history of change and development. They noted that doctrines enshrined in

---

[54] This issue continues to attract significant attention. For example, studies from each of the past three decades include Roberts, *Darwinism and the Divine in America*; Numbers, *Darwinism Comes to America*; and Bowler, *Monkey Trials and Gorilla Sermons.*

[55] Wacker, *Augustus H. Strong and the Dilemma of Historical Consciousness*, 147–59.

creeds were not fixed from the beginning of Christianity; rather, beliefs were debated and shaped over a long period of time. Some views were adopted by Christian interpretations as orthodox, while others were eventually declared heretical. The study of the documents of historical theology repeatedly demonstrated precisely this point. The history of the development of doctrine was a central pursuit in the writings of great scholars of Rauschenbusch's era such as the prodigious work of Reinhold Seeberg and especially Adolpf von Harnack, whom Rauschenbusch viewed as the greatest of all church historians. The scholarship of this era reshaped the way readers understood how Christian doctrine had been formed. Their historical approach challenged the notion that Christian doctrine was fixed, static, and eternal, and this perspective was a deeply unsettling notion for many. Rauschenbusch's era was perhaps the golden age of the influence of the discipline of the history of Christianity. People in growing numbers began to understand that much could be gained by recovering the history of their own disciplines such as music, art, philosophy, and science, as well as the history of Christianity. Moreover, many disciplines sought to imitate the scientific method and to show that they too based their conclusions on observation and evidence in their approach to knowledge. Historians based the claim that they were "scientific" on the fact that they had adopted the method of historical criticism.

Biblical scholars preceded historians in adopting new methods of studying the past. They concluded that Scripture also had developed, and they worked to trace sources of biblical texts, to reconstruct how biblical texts might have originated, been edited, and transmitted. Scholars noted the variety of historical settings and audiences of each book in the Bible and pointed out differences in theological perspectives within the Bible itself—for example different presentations of Jesus among the writers of the four Gospels. The new method of analysis was given the name "higher criticism." William Arnold Stevens, Rauschenbusch's New Testament professor, who adopted and taught the new method wrote, "It is plain that the Bible is for the most part history, primarily it is not so much itself a revelation as the record of a revelation. In other words, it is a revelation in process of transmission."[56] Higher criticism clearly assumed historical perspectives of development. Whereas traditional pre-critical approaches harmonized the various voices of the scriptural texts, the new method readily accepted the variety within the text of Scripture. A favored perspective adopted during this era was to contrast the religion of Jesus with the theology of Paul, giving priority to the former. The new theological views favored the authority of experience over dogma, and the new method held that the diversity in Scripture was a product of the human role in its origins. Since there were many authors of the Bible, there were therefore multiple viewpoints. This perspective engendered controversy. Publication in

[56] Stevens, "Inspiration of the Apostles," 80.

England of *Essays and Reviews* (1860) ignited debate over the nature of the Bible and its authority; American Protestants also began an endless debate over this issue. Several professors endured heresy charges and trials over this heated issue. The most notable American episode was the trial of the Presbyterian minister Charles A. Briggs, who was brought to trial in 1891 for adopting higher criticism and questioning Mosaic authorship of the Pentateuch. Briggs switched denominations, and his school supported him; other professors were not so fortunate. Rauschenbusch was introduced to the new method of biblical interpretation during his seminary training and soon adopted it.

The scientific method looked for evidence to arrive at conclusions. It stated a finding, and often claimed the finding as "fact." But the scientific method also remained open-ended. It did not seek to claim to have discovered a fixed truth once and for all time, but rather it was willing to change conclusions based on discovery of newer evidence. Historical criticism adopted a similar position: new evidence or better interpretations might change the way the past was understood. Historians believed they must remain open to a more valid interpretation in the future. Dogmatic theologians tended to see the belief of the church in terms of fixed, unchanging teachings that must be believed. The historians, on the other hand, had described how these doctrines came to be shaped and adopted, and they revealed the role of fallible bishops and theologians of the past in the formation of dogma. The anchor of an absolute truth appeared to be something of an illusion. The New Theology therefore preferred to simplify the Christian message by looking to the teaching of Jesus—which many theologians commonly summarized as the requirement of love for God and others.[57] The combination of the ideas of development and truth as open-ended created a very different understanding of the world, including its religious expressions.

Similar intellectual battles occurred in Catholicism. Ernst Renan's *Life of Jesus* (1863) was one of the most influential religious books of the nineteenth century. Its underlying working assumption was that Jesus should be studied like any other historical person. Prominent Catholic scholars such as Alfred Loisy and George Tyrrell adopted this outlook. The Roman Catholic Church called the new development "Modernism," and Pius X formally condemned its assumptions and method in 1907. Renan, Loisy, and Tyrrell all lost their teaching positions. For a generation, Catholic biblical scholars were denied use of the modern methods of biblical study. This reaction eventually gave way to modern views, and in 1943 the Roman Catholic Church permitted the new critical method of biblical interpretation.

Both the new science of the late nineteenth century and the understanding

[57] Harnack reduced the message of Christianity to this and other simple formulations (see Harnack, *What Is Christianity?*).

of history rested on the assumption that the earth, human societies, institutions and ideas, and all living things had experienced change. Apparently, nothing was fixed forever. Added to this, the new scientific method demanded evidence based on observation and experimentation as well as an open-ended view of truth. How was the church to respond? How was Rauschenbusch, the young seminarian, to respond? On these critical issues the seminary curriculum and professors gave him guidance.

The response of theologians to the new trends in Western thought developed broadly in one of two directions: they tended either to resist or to embrace new ideas. This division was part of the foundation for the conservative/liberal dichotomy that developed more sharply in the twentieth century and profoundly shapes American Protestantism today. Theologians needed to grapple with the implications of Darwin and evolution, geology and time, historical criticism of texts, and critical reconstructions of the historical past. Whereas traditionalists defended older patterns of thought in their efforts to present the Christian faith, advocates of the New Theology adopted modern methods of interpreting Scripture, church history, and key theological themes. Making a change of this magnitude was not easy. Rauschenbusch's personal experience is instructive. His own professors were divided on the best way to respond to modern thought. The Rochester seminary president, Augustus H. Strong, was a prolific and influential theologian who constructed his theology around traditional Calvinist views. Minus declares that in 1885 "among Baptists, Rochester was admired for its allegiance to the old faith and its resistance to new winds of doctrine."[58] Although Strong's original outlook was conservative, he also encouraged his faculty to welcome new ideas. Minus attributes this attitude to Strong's commitment to Baptist traditions of free intellectual inquiry.[59] But Grant Wacker's study of Strong reveals how profoundly the current cultural shifts were affecting him and Rochester seminary.[60] Only a few professors had adopted the New Theology when Rauschenbusch arrived as a student, but a generation later a majority of the faculty at Rochester and at many other Protestant seminaries had adopted the outlook of the New Theology.[61] By 1900 "nearly all of the chairs of theology at American elite seminaries and divinity schools were held by liberals."[62] The revolutionary new ideas of the modern world stimulated construction and widespread adoption of the New Theology. As one student of this era wrote, this was "one of the most crucial periods in the intellectual history of Christendom."[63] People were having

[58] Minus, *Walter Rauschenbusch*, 38.

[59] Ibid., 42.

[60] Wacker, *Augustus H. Strong and the Dilemma of Historical Consciousness.*

[61] See Moore, Jr., "Academic Freedom," 66-68.

[62] Dorrien, *Soul in Society*, 23.

[63] Foster, "Albrecht Ritschl," 49.

to cope with many challenging new ideas.

Transformative Education: Rauschenbusch's Reception of the New Theology

Academic work provided Rauschenbusch with much satisfaction. On several occasions he commented on how his Rochester education had reshaped his entire intellectual outlook.[64] He pointed to landmarks of new insights during the course of his biblical studies. He remembered that he linked the thought of Jesus with that of the Old Testament prophets in his first seminary paper.[65] This idea would shape a key chapter in his first major book almost a quarter of a century later. In the history of Christianity he found a congenial model of Christianity in the writings of Johann Neander, his father's favorite professor. Rauschenbusch's church history professor at Rochester, Benjamin True, explained to him Neander's view that in Jesus Christ a divine power had entered human history.[66] Philip Schaff aptly described Neander's view of church history:

> It is distinguished for thorough and conscientious use of the sources, critical research, ingenious combination, tender love of truth and justice, evangelical catholicity, hearty piety, and by masterly analysis of the doctrinal systems and the subjective Christian life of men of God in past ages. The edifying character is not introduced from without, but naturally grows out of his conception of church history, viewed as a continuous revelation of Christ's presence and power in humanity, and as an illustration of the parable of the leaven which gradually pervades and transforms the whole lump.[67]

Neander's writing of church history emphasized the story of lives changed by the power of the spirit of Jesus, rather than the history of doctrines. In Strong's class Rauschenbusch discovered that speculative theology did not resonate with him personally. But the idea that the coming of Jesus represented a new power introduced into the course of human history was persuasive for Rauschenbusch, and he advocated this view throughout the remainder of his life. During his seminary studies Rauschenbusch was increasingly attracted to historical rather than theological modes of understanding Christianity.

During his B.A. studies at Rochester Rauschenbusch also encountered the

---

[64] In 1912, a Rochester graduate wrote a tribute to the five professors who formed the Rochester Theological Seminary family, 1881–1902, some serving longer: Strong, Stevens, Osgood, Pattison, and True. See Carman, "A Great Theological Quintet," 533–34.

[65] Minus, *Walter Rauschenbusch*, 40.

[66] Ibid., 41.

[67] Schaff, *History of the Christian Church*, 1:41.

new views of science. His physiology professor, Harrison Webster, was particularly influential in helping Rauschenbusch come to terms with the new science. Webster, who became a personal mentor for Rauschenbusch and others, gave his students "assurance in turning their backs on obsolete traditions."[68] Webster emphasized in class that it was important to abandon traditional views if they were erroneous. He specifically modeled a way forward in dealing with the question of evolution by affirming the teachings of both evolution and Christianity. He called himself a Christian evolutionist, and he found evolution to be no threat to his faith. In his youth Rauschenbusch had already spent significant time in observing nature and had little problem with adopting the evolutionary understanding of nature. That the relationship of religion and science has often been characterized as conflict is evident in the titles of two of the most influential American books of the era, J. William Draper's *History of the Conflict Between Science and Religion* (1874) and Andrew Dixon White's *History of the Warfare Between Science and Theology in Christendom* (1896). However, modern research suggests that rather than emphasizing conflict, many people sought ways to accommodate the new science.[69] Rauschenbusch's solution to the religion and science issue is evident in a speech he prepared for delivery to students at YMCA in Philadelphia and Milwaukee in 1892.[70] He told the students that this was a delicate subject but also an important one and must be addressed. His resolution of the issue was to develop a two spheres approach: whereas science had its method of explaining the natural world, religion dealt with realms beyond the reach of science as it sought to understand the relationship between the human and the divine. If each of these was recognized as a legitimate sphere of inquiry dealing with different kinds of questions, there would be no need to view them in conflict with each other. The way forward for the Christian was to accept both. Some interpreters used Darwin's picture of nature in terms of struggle for survival as justification for competition in society. This form of social Darwinism was favored by many in the establishment. Rauschenbusch rejected application of Darwin's thought to society. The counter argument held that the model of animals fighting for survival does not apply to humans who value other humans and intervene to help them. Rauschenbusch wrote that Jesus did not talk about eliminating the unfit but rather saving weaker members of society.[71] The New Theology sought accommodation of science to faith. Surely, both were striving for truth. This was the option chosen by many liberal and moderate Protestants during Rauschenbusch's era and during the century following. It helped him resolve one great intellectual problem of the

[68] Minus, *Walter Rauschenbusch*, 37.
[69] Brooke, *Science and Religion*. Brooke reviews numerous examples of accommodation.
[70] WR, "Bible and Science," vol. 19:341–47, box 150, Rauschenbusch Family Papers.
[71] WR, *Social Principles*, 1927, 13.

day. More unsettling was the new understanding of the Bible.

Rauschenbusch encountered conflicting interpretations of the Bible and doctrine at both university and seminary. Howard Osgood, his conservative Old Testament professor, read higher criticism—but only to refute it. In an *Introduction to the Pentateuch,* prepared for use by the classes at Rochester Theological Seminary, Osgood explained the twofold Elohist and Yahwist authorship identified by German scholarship, but rejected these in favor of Mosaic authorship.[72] On the other hand, Rauschenbusch was drawn to the historical method of his New Testament professor Stevens. In the same year that Rauschenbusch graduated from the seminary, Stevens wrote that the Bible has the same limitations always associated with human languages. He observed, "The defect is not merely in the writers; it lies in the very nature of language itself. Words are but fine figures; they speak figuratively; they are merely rude signs of our facts and notions, not their exact organic equivalents."[73] His position was that the Bible should therefore not be viewed "as composed of infallible or erroneous documents, or as being expressive of absolute truth."[74] Stevens, along with Ernest DeWitt Burton, published *A Harmony of the Gospels for Historical Study* in 1893. These two authors wrote that their purpose was not to harmonize the Gospels in the sense of bringing them into agreement, but rather to arrange their corresponding parts. They were convinced of the value of historical critical studies, and they affirmed that "the four writers differ and how they differ is precisely what the intelligent reader wishes to know; eventually he comes to value their writings even more for their differences than for their exact agreement."[75] Rauschenbusch said that Stevens taught students that above everything else they should seek truth.[76] This was the students' main task, and this lesson remained fixed in his mind. Rauschenbusch reported that during the course of his biblical studies he experienced "the travail of religious unsettlement."[77] He said that he had come to the seminary with no outlook "except the common evangelicalism."[78] By carefully comparing the four Gospels he found that some passages claimed one thing about Jesus while others claimed something different. In the notes he took in 1884 in his course on the Gospels, Rauschenbusch included a section on discrepancies between the synoptic Gospels and the Gospel of John relating to the date of Passover. He followed this discussion with a section on attempts to harmonize the problem.[79] He said

[72] Osgood, *A Short Synopsis of Introduction to The Pentateuch.*

[73] Stevens, "Inspiration of the Apostles," 81.

[74] Ibid.

[75] Stevens and Burton, *A Harmony of the Gospels for Historical Study*, iii–iv.

[76] See Stevens, "Biblical Criticism," 14–15.

[77] WR to C. E. Smith, 21 March 1912, cited in Minus, *Walter Rauschenbusch*, 40.

[78] WR to John S. Phillips, May 24, 1909, box 39, Rauschenbusch Family Papers.

[79] See Rauschenbusch's class notes on "Harmony of the Gospels," part 1 (February 1884),

that his traditional ideas about the theory of inerrancy of Scripture simply became untenable.[80] No longer able to hold inherited views, Rauschenbusch embraced the new methods of biblical interpretation, but he confessed that this path "cost me a hard struggle."[81]

Under close study of the biblical text while he was at the seminary, Rauschenbusch's view of Scripture began to change. In addition to changing the direction of biblical studies, the New Theology recast traditional theological categories. Augustus Strong taught all three years of theology courses to the seminary students. Rauschenbusch wrote a paper for Strong on the view of the Trinity offered by the theologian Sabellius. Rauschenbusch ultimately concluded that it is futile to speculate on the nature of God since it is a mystery beyond our knowing.[82] He showed in this early essay that he really had little interest in speculative theology. In his senior year Rauschenbusch wrote another paper for Strong, this one on "The Bushnellian Theory of the Atonement."[83] Bushnell, an American Congregationalist minister (1802–1876), taught that Jesus had come to reveal God's love and to draw people to new life. Bushnell said that in the suffering of Jesus, humanity can see the love of God, and this experience moves people to desire to return to God. Rauschenbusch criticized the traditional substitutionary view of atonement articulated by Anselm, and widely adopted by Protestants, asserting that Jesus never taught it; moreover, he said that Anselm's theory relies on a "business transaction in which human souls are the merchandise and merit earned or pain suffered is the price."[84] He thought that the idea of a father demanding the death of his son is not something in which Christians in general find much satisfaction. What kind of God would demand the death of his son? By contrast, however, the young seminarian argued that Bushnell's view of atonement comes right out of the Gospels; it is intelligible and it is comforting.[85]

Changing theological views he had held all of his life was a difficult course to follow. Yet Rauschenbusch did so, encouraged by his teachers to free his mind to pursue the truth. This basic rule for education was also emphasized by Rauschenbusch's early reading of the influential Anglican, Frederick Robertson, minister of Trinity Chapel, Brighton, England (1816–1853). Robertson had adopted a

---

F-4, held in the North American Baptist Heritage Commission archives, Sioux Falls Seminary, Sioux Falls, South Dakota (hereafter cited as NABHC archives).

[80] WR to C. E. Smith, March 21, 1912, cited in Minus, *Walter Rauschenbusch*, 40.

[81] Ibid., 41.

[82] WR, "Sabellius and Sabellianism," for Dr. A. H. Strong's class in dogmatics, in the middle year, 1884–1885, box 14, Rauschenbusch Family Papers.

[83] WR, "The Bushnellian Theory of the Atonement," November 17, 1885, box 14, Rauschenbusch Family Papers.

[84] Ibid.

[85] Ibid.

broad or liberal view of theology, preached to the neglected working class, and counseled his readers to be a servant only to the truth.[86] Robertson's guidance in Rauschenbusch's life was enormous. Rauschenbusch later wrote, "I owe more to Frederick W. Robertson than to any other writer."[87] Even more direct was the personal counsel offered by his undergraduate physiology professor, Harrison E. Webster, and his New Testament seminary professor, William Arnold Stevens, to pursue truth no matter what. Thus Rauschenbusch was beginning to embrace positions of the New Theology. To abandon some of the conservative interpretations of his father, whom he admired and wanted to please, required extraordinary courage. Heeding the influence of mentors, he believed he was called to seek the truth, and in them he found models of men with courage to change their fundamental views. Rauschenbusch modified a number of his religious views, but the most important idea he embraced was the counsel of Stevens, Robertson, and Webster to pursue truth. He had learned reasons for adopting the New Theology. His years spent in education had not stifled him to simply repeat and defend older theological traditions; rather, education liberated him to discern and develop new perspectives on the Bible and doctrine and eventually on the relationship of Christianity to the larger American culture. The New Theology thus engaged major trends of the day including the findings of science, the method of historical criticism and a new understanding of theological language and reflection. Rauschenbusch accepted these elements of the New Theology. Terminally ill in 1918, Rauschenbusch wrote from his hospital bed describing his religious and intellectual development through its critical stages. He described the importance of his personal conversion, but declared it was only the beginning of his personal religion: "When I came to intellectual maturity, I had a second great struggle for salvation, perhaps of equal importance. During my theological education I confronted the choice between the imposing authority of human traditions and the self-evidencing power of God's living word.... This was the personal religious problem of faith applied to intellectual duty.... I am inexpressibly grateful that I made the choice right."[88]

Rauschenbusch had adopted the pursuit of truth as the purpose of education. This conviction gave him courage to grow intellectually and change his views. Rauschenbusch's intellectual pilgrimage was central to his religious experience. He had chosen the path of the New Theology and found it to be liberating. The

---

[86] Minus, *Walter Rauschenbusch*, 44.

[87] WR to Maria Döring, July 13, 1886, in NABHC archives. Robertson died at age thirty-seven; his sermons and lectures were published posthumously. See Brooke, ed., *Life and Letters of the Rev. F. W. Robertson*.

[88] Barnes, "Walter Rauschenbusch—His Personal Testimony."

sense of liberation freed him to explore other new problems he confronted, including the social dimensions of Christianity. His intellectual independence and openness to new interpretations were essential to his life's achievement. Without exercising intellectual freedom, it is doubtful that he would ever have developed a new perspective on the gospel.

Called to Ministry

Rauschenbusch was deeply impressed by his practical experience of serving a German Baptist congregation in Louisville, Kentucky, during two summers of his seminary training. This experience introduced him to the struggles and the rewards of the life of a pastor. He had to deal with factions in the church; he had visitations to make; he had to encourage suffering people. But the church appreciated his work during these short periods of service, and he felt he had accomplished good work among them. When he finished seminary, Rauschenbusch considered his vocational options. Because of his lifelong academic success and the work of his father at Rochester Seminary, Rauschenbusch considered an academic career, but he decided during his seminary training that the more valuable work was ministry.[89] Halfway through seminary he confided to his good friend Munson Ford, "It is now no longer my fond hope to be a learned theologian and write big books.... My studies are progressing quietly. I don't mean to fall in my standing, yet I no longer regard them as an end in themselves, if I ever did. I look more for the great thoughts that shake mankind than for certainty in regard to a disputed date in Acts or an obscure root of a Hebrew verb."[90]

Rauschenbusch also seriously considered missionary work. In a 1913 address to a Cleveland YMCA audience, he said, "I wanted to go out as a foreign missionary."[91] He developed a lifelong commitment to foreign missions and frequently promoted the movement in sermons, speeches, and writings. In the end, however, Rauschenbusch took a different course. He became a pastor. At the end of his seminary training he wrote to Ford, "I want to be a pastor, powerful with men, preaching to them Christ as the man in whom their affections and energies can find the satisfaction for which mankind is groaning."[92] The Second German Baptist Church in New York City called Rauschenbusch to serve as minister. In describing his initial understanding of his work, he used the traditional language of Protestant revivalism. To Ford, he wrote, "I can help people most by bringing

[89] Handy, *The Social Gospel in America*, 254.

[90] WR to Munson Ford, December 21, 1884, in Hudson, ed., *Walter Rauschenbusch: Selected Writings*, 53–54.

[91] WR, "The Kingdom of God," cited in Handy, *The Social Gospel in America*, 265.

[92] WR to Munson Ford, December 21, 1884, in Hudson, ed., *Walter Rauschenbusch. Selected Writings*, 53–54.

them into loving and personal relation with our Lord Jesus Christ."[93]

Rauschenbusch was as well prepared and as highly motivated as any young seminarian of his day. He had studied the Christian heritage and was fully aware of the pervasive intellectual difficulties posed by evolution, biblical authority, and religious skepticism. He began his pastoral work in a traditional mode to a traditional German Baptist congregation. This was the form of Christianity he had experienced as a child in Rochester and as a seminarian serving German Baptists in Louisville. But the conditions he faced as a pastor in New York City revealed to him massive changes occurring in American life. He would soon sense the need to address these realities, and he rapidly came to believe that addressing the social adversity produced by poverty was part of the responsibility of the Christian church and of all Christians. He brought with him from Rochester a strong religious commitment to minister combined with an intellectual curiosity and capacity to learn and adapt. He rapidly broadened his understanding of society and of the capacity of the gospel to address its needs. What exactly was the nature of the problem? What was American society in New York City like during Rauschenbusch's young adult life?

[93] WR to Munson Ford, June 30, 1886, box 23, Rauschenbusch Family Papers.

CHAPTER 2

RAUSCHENBUSCH'S AMERICAN SOCIETY AND CHURCH

Immediately after seminary graduation in 1886 Rauschenbusch left to become the pastor of the Second German Baptist Church, located near Hell's Kitchen in New York City. He served as minister to this German-speaking congregation for the next eleven years. Rochester was a relatively busy center of activity, but in New York City Rauschenbusch met the full force of the rapid change occurring in American society. Rauschenbusch's social setting powerfully shaped his life and thought. His training had introduced him to the language and literature of the Bible and to the academic study of Christianity and ministry. He had excelled in his studies. He had some practical experience of leading a church after two summers of service in Louisville, and he had embraced a new theology that helped him cope with intellectual challenges presented by modern thought. However, confronting conditions in New York City made it clear that he still had much to learn. He soon realized he needed to understand the living conditions of the people where he ministered. Seminary work had equipped him with critical skills of reading and analysis, but it had poorly prepared him for understanding American society.

The New Economic Order

The era of Rauschenbusch's adult working life, 1886–1918, was one of enormous change in American life. Not only was the end of the nineteenth century a period of fermenting intellectual activity; it was a period of immense social, economic, and political transformation as well. Social and intellectual revolutions combined to influence Rauschenbusch profoundly. At the international level, the United States was catapulted into a position of world leadership by its success in the Spanish-American War in 1898. Near the end of Rauschenbusch's life, the country was drawn into World War I in order, President Wilson had said, to make the world safe for democracy. This mantra rang hollow for Rauschenbusch. The war with his beloved homeland brought him agony and despair. The era also saw astounding social developments as American women worked for fuller participation in society. They made their greatest stride forward by securing the vote in 1920. In 1920 Rochester Theological Seminary voted to admit women.[1] However, it would be another generation before women enjoyed significantly greater opportunities in the nation. Emancipation had ended slavery, but the plight of African Americans remained grim, with widespread segregation, discrimination, and injustice. Rauschenbusch did not substantially address issues of justice for either women or African Americans. Instead, his attention was drawn to the plight of American workers and through them to the economic structures that determined their lives.

The Industrial Revolution began in England in the mid-eighteenth century. By harnessing the power of coal, steam, and later electricity, machines could produce vast quantities of goods. This economic revolution spread to other European nations and to the United States during the nineteenth century. By the time Rauschenbusch reached New York City, industry was producing at accelerated rates, creating unprecedented economic wealth in the nation. Following a brief era of canal-building (over 3000 miles between 1825 and 1840) that connected the West to major eastern population centers, Americans built railroads that revolutionized transportation. Two hundred thousand miles of track eventually connected the major areas of the nation, symbolized by the completion of the transcontinental railroad at Promontory Point, near Ogden, Utah, in 1869. Inventors facilitated additional revolutionary changes. Communication breakthroughs included the telegraph (1861), the Atlantic cable (1866), and the telephone (1876), all invented during or soon after the Civil War. Edison revolutionized the possibilities for extending productive work as well as evening social life with his invention of the light bulb in 1878. In addition to human ingenuity, the nation was fortunate to have plentiful natural resources—whether the need was for land, minerals, water, timber, or other basic materials. Americans found efficient ways to harness their immense natural resources and to put them to use to support the burgeoning economy. Temperate climate and arable land made food production readily available to support a growing population.

The country produced business leaders who displayed vision and drive. Entrepreneurs abounded in the early nineteenth century. After the Civil War businesses continued to proliferate, but now the scale of companies reached enormous size. For industry to thrive, steel was essential (Carnegie), as was oil (Rockefeller), and banking on a large scale (J. P. Morgan); McCormick produced farm implements; Armour, meat; Kraft, cheese. Vanderbilt was only one of many tycoons who provided essential transport in railroads and shipping for American commerce; Edison lighted cities. The list of business giants of this era is stunning.

Evaluation of these entrepreneurs has been debated and is evident in the

[1] "Rochester Takes a Step Forward," 728.

choice of language employed by journalists and others who wrote about the business tycoons. Advocates called them "captains of industry." They had the vision and business acumen to identify major needs and to organize companies to respond. The result was that they built factories that could provide clothes, food, transportation, and all sorts of commodities to masses of people who had never enjoyed such resources before. The range of goods they provided was remarkable. These same people were also called robber barons. Many observers thought their business practices were unfair. They undercut prices set by competitors with the goal of driving them out of business, then controlling and raising prices. Or, more simply, they could agree with other major players in a given industry on prices of goods and services. These trusts combined several businesses in a single sector to achieve monopolies. Again, their goal was to defeat competition in order to be free to set prices for their products. These practices created immense wealth for the few at the expense of the ordinary wage earner and earned entrepreneurs the hostility of reformers, including the muckrakers, journalists who exposed these practices. Moreover, the "robber barons" took advantage of workers, paying them as little as possible and working them for extended hours. So much wealth was accumulated in the hands of a few that polarized classes were clearly demarcated in the cities. The masses of workers struggled for wages, lived in cramped and unhealthy tenements, and often turned to alcohol for escape while the "robber barons" grew wealthier than European monarchs. The new rich displayed their wealth with lavish homes and parties—a practice Thorstein Veblen labeled "conspicuous consumption."[2]

The "robber barons" seemed to ignore widespread suffering in the nation, and, in fact were the cause of much of it. The economic system relied on the concept of "wages for labor" without any guarantee of a job or insurance for the disabled or aged. Owners paid the lowest wages possible. The result was that the huge number of workers who made up the lower class in the United States were poor. There was almost always a fresh arrival of immigrant workers at hand, and many of them were willing to work for less than the previous arrivals. The social consequences of aggressive capitalism were readily evident. The economic imbalance seared the consciences of reformers; journalists reported injustices and dangers of the system; novelists excoriated the wealthy in their stories. This dynamic interaction of wealth and poverty was most visible in the country's large cities; it attracted Rauschenbusch's attention and concerned him deeply once he arrived in New York City.

[2] Veblen, *The Theory of the Leisure Class.*

Immigration: Workers and the New Social Order

The massive immigration—some forty million new arrivals—to the United States in the nineteenth century was one of the great migrations of people in modern history. Historians of emigration/immigration commonly identify push-pull features associated with the dynamics of leaving home to create life in another country. During this era most of the immigrants came from Europe where a variety of economic and political problems provided powerful incentives for people to leave "the old country" and come to America. Financial distress was a major factor in the decision to emigrate. Disaster struck Ireland in the potato famine of the 1840s, triggering a massive migration of the Irish to the U.S. Political revolutions convulsed European nations as well—particularly in 1848—and were usually put down by more conservative forces. This prompted migration for those passionate for political liberty. Economic opportunity provided the leading "pull factors" for immigration to the U.S. The frontier provided plentiful land for farmers even after its official closure in 1890. Much of the territory of the Midwest was rich farmland. Moreover, U.S. government policy offered attractive economic incentives: people could secure possession of farmland through "improving" it by farming and building homes. In addition to political and economic opportunity, the U.S. offered public education for many of its citizens. Propagandists touted the attraction of new opportunity in America, and relatives invited family members to join them. Ethnic groups organized networks for incoming immigrants, especially important for those who spoke little English. August Rauschenbusch had emigrated in order to serve churches of immigrant Germans.

Walter Rauschenbusch's era coincided with the heyday of immigration. During the decade of 1900–1909, more than eight million immigrants arrived in the United States.[3] Historian Oscar Handlin, son of Russian immigrants, recounted in vivid language the experience of the immigrants.[4] People of the same language tended to live close to one another. They established ethnic stores, restaurants, and newspapers. They worshiped together in Catholic or Protestant or Jewish congregations. The Baptists of New York City recognized immigrant patterns and established German-language Baptist churches. Many of the first-generation immigrants learned English; others learned little English and preferred to use their native language whenever possible, including during worship services. The second generation usually spoke English, a skill critical to assimilation into their new culture.

The German scholar Klaus Juergen Jaehn observed that Walter Rauschenbusch demonstrated a strong solidarity with the German community in which he

---

[3] See Kraut, *The Huddled Masses*, 20. This book contains an excellent collection of photographs drawn largely from the Library of Congress and the U.S. National Archives.

[4] Handlin, *The Uprooted*.

grew up.[5] Walter had lived and studied in Germany for several years, served a German Baptist church in New York City, and early in his career published his views in German as well as in English. When he returned to Rochester, he remained a member of the German Baptist congregation in the city.[6] Like his father before him, both as minister and professor, Walter sought to serve the spiritual needs of German Americans. The immigrant experience was one of the major factors shaping his outlook on life.

In the half century between the Civil War and World War I, American cities grew rapidly. These cities were the home of countless factories and businesses. They provided the major alternative to the farm for American labor.[7] Cities served as magnets to rural American young people and to immigrants seeking work. Many immigrants settled on the East Coast, assuring the rapid growth of Philadelphia, Boston, and New York, three of America's most populous cities. When Rauschenbusch moved to New York City to minister to German immigrants, he found their situation grim. They needed jobs to support their families. Many were unskilled and took factory jobs requiring minimal skill or training.

The lower-class workers in New York City and elsewhere lived in tenements. These five-story buildings virtually filled block after block of the city. The reform-minded Danish journalist and photographer Jacob Riis memorably recorded the plight of the tenement dwellers in his classic photo-book *How the Other Half Lives.*[8] The pictures Riis recorded reveal desperate people and attest to the grinding poverty in the United States. Like many reformers of this era, Riis appealed to justice as the standard for economic practice in American society. He wrote that "there is nothing below that line [Fourteenth Street] that can outdo in wickedness Hell's Kitchen."[9] Rauschenbusch's Second German Baptist Church was located at the edge of this notorious district. He visited people in the tenements and was well aware of the condition of the people living in them. The tenements provided cheap housing to the poorer population, yet Riis reported that "the rent is never less than one week's wages out of four, quite often half of the family's earnings."[10] Riis enumerated problems that flourished in this environment, including ignorance, poverty, bad hygiene, starvation, and intemperance. Saloons proliferated in tenement districts. Riis calculated that "there are

---

[5] Jaehn, *Rauschenbusch*, 81.

[6] Ibid.

[7] Cross, *The Church and the City*, xi.

[8] Riis cites some 1900 statistics in the 1901 edition used here. The other enduring classic of the era is Thorstein Veblen's *The Theory of the Leisure Class: An Economic Study of Institutions*, also an indictment of the American economic system, but seen from the perspective of the wealthy classes.

[9] Riis, *How the Other Half Lives*, 121.

[10] Ibid., 124.

easily ten saloons to every church. Below Fourteenth Street [the ratio] is 111 Protestant churches to 4,065 saloons."[11] He reflected with grim humor on the contrast between the grip of the saloon on lives and the loss of influence of the church: "I am afraid, too, that the congregations [in the saloons] are larger by a good deal; certainly the attendance is steadier, and the contributions more liberal the week round, Sunday included."[12] He was also confident that the saloon bred poverty and corrupted politics.[13] Votes could be bought for drinks. Rauschenbusch was fully aware of all the problems Riis recorded. Recognizing the damage alcoholism inflicted on families and political life, Rauschenbusch was a lifelong opponent of the saloons and a supporter of temperance.

Riis was a reformer but also a fair-minded observer. He distinguished between bad and good tenements and bad and good landlords. He praised the health officials and the business men who worked for improvement in mass housing. He noted that the biggest problem of the tenements was the tenants themselves: "the poorest are shiftless and destructive. It is what the tenements have made them."[14] It was a double-edged sword. The social problems were compounded by rapid population growth,[15] and Riis concluded that the tenements were here to stay. They simply must be made better—as they certainly were when New York City introduced running water. Veblen and Riis produced memorable phrases—"conspicuous consumption" and "how the other half lives"—which summarized the disparity between rich and poor in the social order of their era.

Social Costs of the Economic Order

The social and personal costs of the American economic system were staggering. Unemployment was a problem never resolved, and it was the major cause of widespread poverty. Men, women and children all sought work in order to support their families. Thousands of workers lived in crowded tenement apartments with inadequate light, air, and heat. Riis and Rauschenbusch collaborated as advocates for public spaces such as parks and "sand piles" (sandboxes).[16] Disease, especially tuberculosis, flourished under these conditions. Early in his ministry in New York City Rauschenbusch left his sick-bed too soon to minister to a parishioner in need, resulting in the onset of deafness in 1888 which plagued him for the remaining thirty years of his life. He became almost completely deaf.[17]

---

[11] Ibid., 165.

[12] Ibid.

[13] Ibid., 169.

[14] Ibid., 214.

[15] Riis cited census statistics. In 1869, 14,872 New York City tenements housed 468,492 persons; in 1888, 32,390 housed 1,093,701; in 1901, 37,316 housed 1,250,000 (ibid., 216).

[16] Dahlberg, "Walter Rauschenbusch: Prophet of Social Christianity," 5.

[17] Handy, *The Social Gospel in America*, 254.

Although poverty was common in rural areas and in Europe as well, it was so concentrated in the cities that it drew the attention of reformers. Life in the tenements took a physical toll, but also emotional costs at levels of human dignity and moral responsibility. Jacob Riis reported visiting two elderly women, one of whom had recently had a stroke and was unable to work; determined to live with some dignity, her sister continued to work despite declining health and uncertain wages. The sisters told Riis that they were doing everything in their power to avoid ending their lives in the poor-house.[18] Poverty tempted people to turn to crime, which was so endemic that social workers classified criminals as a recognized social subgroup. Riis's description of the foundlings is heart-rending. He reported that in a city of two million the Foundling Asylum had taken in 25,000 abandoned children in twenty years. Observing that "only the poor abandon their children," he concluded that even the instinct of motherhood was smothered by poverty and want.[19] Riis praised the work of the Sisters of Charity, who cared for thousands of these abandoned children. The mortality rate among children was high, and it pierced Rauschenbusch's soul. In one of his most memorable outpourings of compassion he wrote, "Oh, the children's funerals! They gripped my heart—that was one of the things I always went away thinking about—why did the children have to die?"[20]

In the early stages of economic growth after the Civil War, the federal government adopted a hands-off policy. The assumption of the prevailing laissez faire economic theory supported the status quo; its proponents argued that the market would take care of itself through the natural laws of economics, especially the dynamic of supply and demand. But if demand were slow, workers were laid off from work or they simply lost their jobs. Without protection workers were exploited. They had no job security and no insurance. They had to accept the wages offered them. The government argued that its task was to keep order, not intervene in the economic process. This non-intervention policy led labor leaders to form unions that sought to protect workers' jobs and wages through common action, especially the threat of strikes. In response, owners hired strike breakers; this led to violence, and authorities intervened to try to assure order and peace. Workers demanded protection by law while owners fought this reform of the system. Eventually the state would address the problem with legislation that offered some protection to ordinary workers, but this took time to achieve.

The Churches and the City

What should the response of the church be to the conditions created by the

---

[18] Riis, *How the Other Half Lives*, 189.

[19] Ibid., 145.

[20] WR, "The Kingdom of God," cited in Handy, *The Social Gospel in America*, 265–66.

American industrial revolution? Specifically, do Christians and churches have a responsibility for the plight of the worker? Rauschenbusch had experienced and grappled with the intellectual revolution in the course of pursuing his education. Now he found himself in the midst of vast social and economic changes. He determined as a young pastor to engage this revolution as well. In this pursuit he was creative, a visionary who would offer guidance to the church. The European experience could be instructive, and he determined to learn from it.

In Europe, Socialism provided a popular response to economic inequity brought on by industrialization. Socialism is a political and economic theory that society should be based on the subordination of the individual to the interests of the community and collective ownership of production and distribution. Rauschenbusch's intimate knowledge of Germany made him keenly aware of the growth of socialist trends in Germany. In an 1891 essay Rauschenbusch declared that Germany had been "the scene of the most important events in the social movement. He reported that one sixth of voters had moved to the social vote as Social Democrats."[21] Rauschenbusch judged this to be a positive sign because it represented a shift to government of, by, and for the people. He also reported that German industrial organization had made significant strides toward cooperation.

Because of the impact of the Industrial Revolution, some leaders in the English Church directly addressed the social problems presented by the new economy. Beginning in 1848 theologian F. D. Maurice and novelist Charles Kingsley led a movement of Christian Socialists to pursue serious reflection on economic issues and address problems it presented. Maurice cast the problem in a memorable contrast, pitting capitalism based on competition against Christianity based on cooperation. Humanity's true nature is not designed for competition, he argued; instead, the Christian view is that people are meant for community based on cooperation. People must live in groups, not alone; there is no other option. The question is how well citizens will do this. Maurice purposely adopted the title "Christian Socialism" in order to prompt a response, and his strategy succeeded. Rauschenbusch adopted a similar view: he often wrote of "a cooperative commonwealth"—his vision for the United States in contrast to its prevailing practice of fiercely competitive capitalism.[22]

The nineteenth century was an impressive era of humanitarianism in England. Charles Dickens, the most popular novelist of the century, repeatedly called attention to the plight of the poor in his novels about English life. William and Catherine Booth took a practical approach to poverty, establishing the Salvation Army (1865) for Christian ministry among the poor in East London and beyond. Booth was a former Methodist evangelist who loved the poor and believed he

---

[21] WR, "In Germany," 2–3.

[22] For an introduction to Maurice, see Morris, ed., *To Build Christ's Kingdom*.

should help people with their physical needs of food, shelter and clothing as well as their spiritual needs. Similarly, George Williams established the YMCA (1844) to offer lodging and address social and spiritual needs of the young who moved to English cities searching for work. These developments provide evidence that society recognized the problem of poverty. Para-church movements arose alongside the established churches, but the churches themselves still had to work out their policies regarding the new economic and social conditions.

In the late nineteenth century, the Anglican church created two major organizations to address social problems—the Guild of St. Matthew (1887), which called for Parliament to legislate a limitation of work hours, and the Christian Social Union (1889), which insisted that Christianity must aim at redeeming the whole person. These late Victorian Christian social movements accustomed the Anglican Christians to the idea that the church must act on its social conscience and respond to basic physical as well as spiritual needs. The Anglican Church did in fact accept care for the poor as a moral mandate. In 1897 the Lambeth Conference, the meeting of Anglican bishops worldwide, voted to accept responsibility for the social and economic order. At the following Lambeth Conference in 1908, church leaders sought to implement their goals by appealing to industries to provide a living wage to workers. The American churches borrowed from their British cousins, but they also addressed the problem in their own ways. The importance of the churches' response to the city became increasingly evident. Numerous books published between 1894 and 1911 in the United States called attention to the new obligations of churches in the cities, including *The Challenge of the City*, *The Redemption of the City*, *If Christ Came to Chicago*, and *Christianity's Storm Center: A Study of the Modern City.*[23]

The Catholic/Protestant tensions dating from the Reformation continued to create the sharpest division of churches in the United States. The Catholic Church was the largest single denomination by 1850, but the combined Protestant churches outnumbered the Catholics, and Protestants enjoyed cultural leadership in American society. The organizational model for the Protestants was the denomination—led by Methodists, Baptists, Presbyterians, and others. Each denomination held distinct interpretations, but Protestants also shared many beliefs and practices. A common model of becoming a Christian among many Protestants was the conversion experience, a long tradition that had been adopted by large segments of Protestantism and made even more popular by the prevalence of revivals organized often during the eighteenth and nineteenth centuries. Protestants also adopted a moral code that involved both biblical and cultural

[23] See Strong, *The Challenge of the City*; Sears, *The Redemption of the City*; Stead, *If Christ Came to Chicago*; and Stelzle, *Christianity's Storm Centre.*

guidelines. By contrast, the Catholic model for becoming Christian stressed instruction and observance of the sacraments, beginning with baptism and continuing with regular attendance at Mass as well as observance of the church's moral teachings.

Neither branch of the Christian tradition was prepared for the new social problems it encountered in the modern industrial world. Pope Leo XIII (1878–1903) acknowledged the new problem and issued *Rerum Novarum* (*Of New Things*) in 1891, a critically important statement in support of the workers.[24] For this initiative he was labeled "the working man's pope." Catholic priest John A. Ryan emerged as the most articulate spokesman for social action in the American Roman Catholic Church.[25] Immigration vastly increased Roman Catholic presence in the United States, but adjusting to meaningful ministry in the cities was difficult for the churches. Catholic churchmen often contrasted the city with rural society. The articulate Catholic bishop John L. Spalding drew an idyllic picture of rural life throughout the Christian centuries and compared it with life in the cities of the present. He cited statistical reports demonstrating the superior strength, health, morality, temperance, and lower death rate of the rural populations of Europe and the United States.[26] When Bishop Spalding described the problems of the cities, he found that the foremost problems were the difficulties posed by the economic situation. Trades had given way to machinery, and "the workman now is only part of the machine." Wages were so low that "the operative receives barely enough to keep him from starvation.... [If] he ceases to work, he is at once a pauper...."[27] His family life is broken down, and he is no more than a slave.[28]

The Protestant churches adopted various strategies to succeed in American culture from the beginning. In the nineteenth century, Protestants followed the frontier and planted churches in rural and small-town America. However, like the Roman Catholics, Protestant churches were also ill-prepared to meet the urban industrial challenges. The churches responded to life in the city in a variety of ways. Some sought to continue the rural or immigrant church practices in the big city. Others organized downtown churches that appealed to the successful new merchant classes. Dwight L. Moody, the leading evangelist of the day, along with his singer, Ira Sankey, sustained the revival tradition as an option in the cities. Moody was joined by many fellow evangelists, such as Reuben Torrey, John

---

[24] Leo XIII, *Rerum Novarum*, May 15, 1891, *Christian Social Teachings*, ed. George W. Forell (Garden City, NY: Doubleday & Company, 1966) 339–44.

[25] See Ryan, *A Living Wage*.

[26] Spalding, "The Country and City," 64–100; this chapter from Spalding's book is cited in Cross, *The Church and the City*, 3–28. The statistical reports are discussed in pages 11–15.

[27] Spalding, "The Country and City," 17.

[28] Ibid., 18, 20.

Wilbur Chapman, and Sam Jones, who were striving to reach the urban masses by revivalism.

Nontraditional forms of Christianity also appeared and flourished during this era. Mary Baker Eddy (1821–1910), founder of Christian Science, stressed physical healing through divine means. Charles Taze Russell, founder of Jehovah's Witnesses, gave people much to ponder by focusing religious attention on the end of the world. New holiness denominations appeared during this era, stressing the importance of living a holy Christian life, and the Pentecostal movement emerged with the new century, proclaiming two special gifts of the Holy Spirit—speaking in tongues and divine healing. These new forms of Christianity attracted significant followings, but neither they nor traditional denominations addressed specific approaches to problems created by the industrialization of America. This new set of problems in American society presented itself not so much as an intellectual or theological issue as a social challenge.

As the U.S. rapidly industrialized following the Civil War, American churches searched for ways to meet social needs. British Christian institutions already designed for social service—the Salvation Army, the YMCA, and the YWCA—soon established a presence in the U.S. In Chicago, Jane Addams established Hull House, a much-needed Christian social center to care for needy. Because housing the poor was a pervasive problem, many cities imitated her idea. Some large inner-city churches opened their doors for daily service and ministry, offering child care, education, job placement, counseling, and other social services throughout the week as well as regular Sunday worship. This "institutional church" movement was adopted by churches in many cities of the U.S. These churches grappled with social issues by using their buildings and resources as a place to offer various forms of social assistance to those in need.

Discovering Socialism

At age twenty-five Rauschenbusch began his work as pastor in New York City (1886–1897). Here he experienced first-hand the economic and social conditions produced by the modern factory system, and his social awakening began with his personal observation of suffering people. He wrote, "There among the working people my social education began."[29] Church historian Robert Handy wrote that as a pastor Rauschenbusch was "confronted directly by the pressing social problems of the times—the terrible human effects of insecurity, unemployment, poverty, wretched housing, malnutrition, disease, ignorance and crime."[30]

---

[29] WR, "Report of Talk to Sunday School", *Rochester Democrat and Chronicle*, January 25, 1913, cited in Hudson, ed., *Walter Rauschenbusch: Selected Writings*, 10, fn. 13.

[30] Handy, *The Social Gospel in America*, 254.

Rauschenbusch later confessed, "I had no idea of the social question."[31] In addition to taking care of traditional pastoral responsibilities, Rauschenbusch's chief strategies for informing himself about physical suffering included reading analyses of American society, meeting with like-minded fellow pastors, and publishing his own ideas. He was a man of books and ideas, but university and seminary had left him with little practical understanding of the structures of society in which he was to minister. Nevertheless, books also were a key to the solutions he sought.

Rauschenbusch's lifelong commitment to reading, reflection, and writing is astounding. Had he not kept up his passion for knowledge and learning as a pastor, it is doubtful that he would be known today. Like most ministers, he had responsibility for the pastoral care of his people and for worship. He prepared his sermons and met his other pastoral obligations, but he also sustained a high intellectual work ethic. He began to read leading sociologists and economists.[32] He was keenly interested in the ideas of social Christians who had already explored the mutual insights of Christianity and sociology. He took a two-month sabbatical during his first summer in New York and read more of the pioneering English advocates of a social gospel, F. D. Maurice and F. W. Robertson. Thus, as Jaehn points out, he knew the social teachings of these ministers from the beginning of his career.[33]

The first and most influential social analyst to catch Rauschenbusch's attention was Henry George, who published *Progress and Poverty* in 1879. In 1886, the year Rauschenbusch began his ministry in the city, George ran for mayor of New York, and Rauschenbusch heard him speak during the campaign. George lost the race, but he left an indelible imprint on Rauschenbusch's thinking. George knew the deprivation of wage earners and described their condition as "industrial slavery."[34] He was struck by the fact that while the American economy progressed to create fabulous wealth, it also was attended by widespread poverty. How could this be? This is the question he addressed, and his analysis deeply influenced Rauschenbusch. George believed that God created the land for all people to use but that the modern economic system allowed some people to amass large tracts of land and "charge exorbitantly for them...thereby bringing unearned wealth to themselves and poverty to others."[35] Instead of allowing unused land to increase

---

[31] Minus, *Walter Rauschenbusch*, 61.

[32] Asked about his awakening to the social gospel, Rauschenbusch responded, "Of course my reading very rapidly widened out.... I began to absorb scientific economic literature and gave attention to the study of the statistics of morality in its various phases" (WR to H. G. Roller, March 12, 1915, box 14, Rauschenbusch Family Papers).

[33] Jaehn, *Rauschenbusch*, 10.

[34] Ibid., 62.

[35] Ibid.

in value, George's answer to the problem was to create a "single tax" on all land according to its rental value and use the profits to create new housing, lower rents, and care for the poor. Since rent typically took as much as one-fourth to one-half of the worker's wages, reformers regularly identified it as the worker's biggest financial burden. Moreover, if wages increased, so did rent. George held that labor produced legitimate wealth, but land produced illegitimate wealth. The latter should be taxed.[36] George's influence was crucial for Rauschenbusch's early social theory. Rauschenbusch later wrote, "I owe my own first awakening to the world of social problems to the agitation of Henry George in 1886 and wish here to record my lifelong debt to this single-minded apostle of great truth."[37]

Richard Ely also produced a deep and lasting influence on Rauschenbusch. Ely was an economist who rejected the common theory that some people were meant to enjoy wealth while others were meant to suffer misery. He believed government should intervene to assure the well-being of all. In *Social Aspects of Christianity* (1889) he argued that Christians who taught only individual conversion had overlooked the biblical passion for social righteousness. This insight was another powerful influence in Rauschenbusch's religious conviction. A two-level understanding of Christianity became the fundamental assertion in Rauschenbusch's own re-visioning the nature of Christianity. It was the cornerstone of his thought.

Numerous other authors with a social passion also influenced Rauschenbusch, including the radical novelist Edward Bellamy who wrote *Looking Backward* (1889), a utopian depiction of a more perfect world, and also Leo Tolstoy, who in *My Religion* (1885) stressed that modern Christians should follow the demands of the Sermon on the Mount, especially in matters relating to money.[38] The essays of the Italian political leader Giuseppe Mazzini (1805–1872) combined religious faith with the goal of personal liberty.[39] He devoted himself to service of the state, stressing "community and association, organic relationships and human solidarity."[40] In *Our Country: Its Possible Future and Its Present Crisis* (1885), perhaps the most influential analysis of America during this era, Josiah Strong also called the churches to their social responsibility.[41] The authors Rauschenbusch read provided insight into the structures of society that produced

[36] George, *Progress and Poverty*, xiii–xv.

[37] WR, *Christianizing the Social Order*, 1912 ed., 394.

[38] For Rauschenbusch's debt to Tolstoy and Mazzini, see WR to G. H. Roller, March 12, 1915, box 14, Rauschenbusch Family Papers.

[39] A collection of seven of Mazzini's essays, including "The Duties of Man," may be found in *The Duties of Man and Other Essays*.

[40] Hudson, ed., *Walter Rauschenbusch: Selected Writings*, 17.

[41] See Gaustad, "Our Country: One Century Later," 85–101, for a perceptive analysis of the book.

inequality. As they analyzed and explained the American economy, the causes of suffering became clear to Rauschenbusch. Most of these writers were driven by a sense of justice. They advocated a transformation of society that would establish more equality and more democracy in the ordinary structures of national life.

In their reflections, the Christian Socialists focused on what the church might contribute to the creation of a better society, a better nation. The American social gospel minister Washington Gladden (1836–1918) had often addressed economic conflict with the admonition to both labor and capital to practice the golden rule. At the beginning of *Christianizing the Social Order,* Rauschenbusch wrote, "I want to pay tribute of honor to three men who were pioneers of Christian social thought in America twenty-five years ago: Washington Gladden, Josiah Strong, and Richard Ely. These men had matured their thought when the rest of us were young men, and they had a spirit in them which kindled and compelled us."[42] Rauschenbusch was deeply influenced by reading many studies of contemporary society—by both secular and religious authors.

Theological statements often repeat well-worn formulas of the Christian tradition. In more creative moments, with resources found in Scripture, tradition, reason, and culture, theological perception may respond to changes in society by reformulating the Christian message with new and meaningful approaches to faith. This process is evident in the history of the church at critical junctures—in the work of Augustine, Luther, Schleiermacher, and contemporary liberation theology, to cite well-known examples. They all offered the church new perspectives to meet new challenges. In a similar fashion the social transformations of industrialization created new problems for the church of Rauschenbusch's day. He used the tool of the new discipline of sociology combined with Christian teaching to help him analyze the changing relationship of society and church and offer the church an expanded understanding that Christian identity includes social responsibility. In Hudson's succinct summary, socialism was Rauschenbusch's "most momentous discovery."[43] Rauschenbusch was aware that many people feared the word "socialist."[44] He took the position that he would not join the Socialist Party because it would cause some readers to dismiss him due to the party's association with revolutionary action and reputation for atheism and violence. But he would identify with the goals of Socialists in so far as they stood for working for the betterment of the entire society rather than for advancement of the individual. Perceiving both positive and negative features in socialist theory, Rauschenbusch took a middle path between radicalism and capitalism as prac-

---

[42] WR, *Christianizing the Social Order*, 9.

[43] Hudson, ed., *Walter Rauschenbusch: Selected Writings*, 35.

[44] WR, "In Germany," 2.

ticed in the United States. He affirmed a moderate socialism and adopted socialism's broad themes and goals because he believed both socialism and Christianity stood for caring for other people. He repeatedly said that he advocated gradual and nonviolent change; he often declared that he supported *evolutionary* but not *revolutionary* socialism. Rauschenbusch used the language of the "cooperative commonwealth" and "solidarity" of all people in society. He wanted to apply the Christian gospel to the larger society. He advocated a social gospel, not a gospel limited to individuals. Critics attacked Rauschenbusch, charging him with substituting the social gospel for the New Testament Gospels, for attempting to replace spiritual Christianity with reform of society. These opponents argued that society would be reformed only when each individual was converted one by one. Rauschenbusch rapidly came to an alternative conclusion: original Christianity was both social and individual, a position already articulated by Richard Ely. The church needed to embrace a Christian socialism.

Rauschenbusch's Appreciation of Christian Socialism

Rauschenbusch wanted to contribute to redeeming his nation. The work of socialists helped him understand the problems of American society. What could the church do to help? In his analysis two things were of particular concern—"the unequal distribution of Property...and the spiritual needs of the people around me."[45] In the thoughtful assessment of his life just prior to his death, Rauschenbusch described his life in terms of three conversions: first, his personal conversion experience; second, working out the proper relationship of mind and faith; and third and finally, his embracing of social Christianity. Regarding social justice he wrote, "In my efforts to secure more freedom and justice for men I acted under religious impulses. I realized that God hates injustices and that I would be quenching the life of God within me if I kept silent with all this social iniquity around me."[46] For Rauschenbusch, socialism alone was insufficient; Christianity focused on the salvation of the individual alone was insufficient. His Christian conviction was that the church must now fight injustice and work for the redemption of society as well as transforming individuals.

One of the key questions in Rauschenbusch research is the process by which he arrived at his conception of social Christianity. Seldom mentioned is his acknowledged debt to Harrison Webster, "who took an interest in economic questions and often discussed them with me while I was a student in Rochester

---

[45] WR correspondence, March 12, 1897, #64, in NABHC archives; also cited in Jaehn, *Rauschenbusch*, 16.

[46] WR to Lemuel Call Barnes, *Rochester Theological Seminary Bulletin* (November 1918): 38–40; also cited in Hudson, ed., *Walter Rauschenbusch: Selected Writings*, 45. The original copy of the letter is found box 39, Rauschenbusch Family Papers.

Theological Seminary."[47] Rauschenbusch provided some personal reflections on this topic, and his prodigious output of writing has allowed scholars to trace the development of his thinking, including key influences on him and the dating of his progress toward embracing a social dimension of Christianity. It was a relatively rapid journey. The evidence for Rauschenbusch's traditional Christianity is significant though often now ignored. His description of his personal conversion, his declaration of his goal as a minister, and his early sermons all reflect traditional American Protestantism focused on individual conversions. He never abandoned this commitment. However, Rauschenbusch also developed an added interest in social Christianity because of the daily experiences of his parishioners. Klaus Jaehn was particularly interested in tracing the development of Rauschenbusch's social Christianity. He notes that Rauschenbusch was becoming familiar with some Christian Socialist literature at the beginning of his ministry.[48] He reports that Rauschenbusch was personally "giving thought to becoming involved in the social question already by December 1887 or 1888."[49] As early concrete evidence of Rauschenbusch's social interest, Jaehn points to Rauschenbusch's 1887 manuscript on Henry George, and to his description of it as "my first paper on the social question."[50] Jaehn further notes that in 1888 Rauschenbusch wrote separate essays on the two social classes, "Beneath the Glitter" and "The Saving Efficacy of Money," contrasting the conditions of poor and rich Americans.[51] By 1889 the evidence for Rauschenbusch's social commitment is overwhelming. In that year he wrote a defense of Edward Bellamy.[52] Moreover, Rauschenbusch took his concern into the pulpit. Max Stackhouse studied Rauschenbusch's sermons to determine the date of the young minister's shift to addressing social questions publicly. Although there are scattered references to social questions in the earlier sermons, Stackhouse identifies spring 1889 as the date of Rauschenbusch's first sermon devoted completely to social issues.[53] Rauschenbusch reached a wider and more influential audience at the 1889 meeting of the Baptist Congress. Before this group of Baptist leaders Rauschenbusch set forth his radical position. He wrote that true Christianity is meant to change individual lives, but that is only half the task. The other half is to bring in the kingdom of God by exercising direct influence on society.[54] Rauschenbusch was now completely devoted to what he called

---

[47] WR to G. H. Roller, March 12, 1915, box 14, Rauschenbusch Family Papers.
[48] Jaehn, *Rauschenbusch*, 10.
[49] Ibid., 22.
[50] Ibid., 16.
[51] Ibid., 17. Both of these articles appeared in *For the Right*.
[52] Ibid., 24.
[53] Max Stackhouse, "Formation," 158, cited in Jaehn, *Rauschenbusch*, 24.
[54] WR, "Natural and Artificial Monopolies," 58.

the "social movement." By the time Rauschenbusch was twenty-seven he had experienced the third of his three life-forming conversions.

Friends urged Rauschenbusch to give up social work and devote himself to "Christian work." But he said that he knew that this work was the work of Christ, and he looked to the Bible for guidance and revised his interpretation of Christianity. The next stage of his move to social Christianity came about by writing down his ideas; this process brought clarity to his thought. What did he and colleagues have to say "for the Right" and against what was wrong in America?

Collaboration with Fellow Ministers

Soon after arriving in New York, Rauschenbusch began to attend a weekly meeting of the Baptist pastors in the city. Here he met two fellow ministers with whom he formed a close association—Leighton Williams, pastor of the Amity Baptist Church on West 54th Street, and Nathaniel Schmidt, pastor of the First Swedish Baptist Church on East 20th Street. In 1887 the three Baptist pastors began to meet together regularly on Sunday afternoon for reflection and communion and to discuss the nature of their ministry in the big city.[55] Williams recalled that their friendship was "cemented by a close similarity of ideas and regular meetings." They called themselves the "Society of Jesus," and gave their attention to both "personal regeneration" and "special reform."[56] Williams noted, "Our theological views were much the same and we were still more united in our social opinions."[57] The three Baptist ministers read Christian classics together. Among them was the influential 1856 *Tongue of Fire* by the Irish Methodist William Arthur. In this book Arthur explored the role of Pentecost in the origins of Christianity, concluding that the effects of Pentecost were not confined to the church, but also included society.[58] Arthur affirmed need for redemption of both individuals and society. He said that "the only way to effect regeneration of society is the regeneration of individuals...."[59] He continued, "On the other hand, have not those who see and feel the importance of first seeking the regeneration of individuals too often insufficiently studied the application of Christianity to social

---

[55] WR, diary, 1888–1891, box 97, Rauschenbusch Family Papers Box; Hudson, ed., *Walter Rauschenbusch: Selected Writings*, 10–22.

[56] Hudson, ed., *Walter Rauschenbusch: Selected Writings*, 19.

[57] Leighton Williams, "The Brotherhood of the Kingdom and Its Work," Brotherhood Leaflet 10, 1–2; originally given as an address at the Congress of Religions at Omaha, NE, October 1897, and collected in a volume in *The Brotherhood of the Kingdom: Pamphlets*, ABHS archives.

[58] Arthur, *The Tongue of Fire*, 74, 79 (page citations are for the revised edition).

[59] Ibid., 91.

evils?"[60] Arthur's idea and even his phrasing of the issue anticipates Rauschenbusch's own articulation of two-dimensional Christianity. Later, in 1893, a larger group formed another small association they called the Brotherhood of the Kingdom and met annually for worship and discussion at the home of Leighton Williams' father.[61] Rauschenbusch wrote several key brochures positioning the purpose and goals of the group. Meeting with like-minded pastors and friends was thus a strategy that brought Rauschenbusch intensity of devotion, deep friendships, and professional support during his career. In addition to the three members of the little Society of Jesus and the twenty or so of the Brotherhood of the Kingdom, Rauschenbusch participated in meetings of the Baptist Congress from 1892 until 1897, when he left New York City for Rochester.[62] Once again he found a forum for articulating his ideas among supportive colleagues. These three groups provided important discussion partners who stimulated the development of Rauschenbusch's ideas. His extensive correspondence attests to the importance of these circles of confidants. Thus throughout his ministry Rauschenbusch sought out relationships with other progressive ministers and created opportunities to exchange ideas, especially through conversations, conferences, publications, and correspondence.

Growing Deafness

Responding to his pastoral duties early in his ministry, Rauschenbusch visited the sick during an epidemic variously described as Russian grippe or influenza. He exhausted himself performing this duty and succumbed to the illness himself. He returned to his work too soon, and the illness had the effect of rapidly causing the loss of his hearing. This was a devastating blow to the young minister. Years later he told his seminary class that "when his deafness began, his faith in God was seriously shaken." He felt that he had been doing the Lord's work, yet this affliction had come upon him so that he lived in a world of complete silence. The illness resulted not only in his deafness, but also in a rather high-pitched weak voice.[63] Rauschenbusch eventually made the best of his condition. He told the students that two values came from this loss. First, he could think more effectively because he could organize his thoughts without distraction, and second, his weak voice made it clear that he would not be an effective orator. He would "have to substitute his brains for his vocal chords."[64] Later testimony about his addresses confirmed the effectiveness of his speaking ability. Dahlberg recalled

[60] Ibid.

[61] Minus, *Walter Rauschenbusch*, 85–87.

[62] Hudson, ed., *Walter Rauschenbusch: Selected Writings*, 21–22.

[63] Dahlberg, "Edwin Dahlberg in Conversation," 210.

[64] Ibid.

that he "was a popular speaker because he spoke with a real human feeling."[65] But at the time of this crisis Rauschenbusch was distraught. He left for Germany in 1891 not only for a sabbatical but also for finding help for his hearing. He eventually found that technology had not been able to solve the problem, and therefore he worked at lip-reading. As professor he secured the assistance of student secretaries to communicate in writing what was being said in public writings. The condition had psychological consequences; Rauschenbusch declared that he had been lonely as a result of losing his hearing.[66]

The Pastor Defends the Workers

Rauschenbusch was a gifted writer. His daughter, Winifred, recalled, "During those early New York years...he was learning his craft as a writer."[67] In 1887, only eighteen months after he arrived in New York, Rauschenbusch took up his pen to advocate for the poor by appealing for social justice. In 1889 he publicly endorsed a Christian socialism, and in that same year began a paper with Leighton Williams, Elizabeth Post, and J. F. Raymond, which they called *For the Right*.[68] This small monthly journal addressed concerns of workers, including such goals as better wages and living conditions, the eight-hour workday, the single tax on land, municipal ownership of utilities, and cheap public transportation. Rauschenbusch described the perspective of the paper, indicating that *For the Right* was distinguished from other papers akin to it in that "it stands for personal regeneration and social reform."[69] In the journal articles he began articulating his central perspective on Christianity in 1890, before he had opportunity to work out his views in book form. In an early *For the Right* essay, Rauschenbusch published "A Story of Three Miners." He described three Nevada miners who took turns preparing meals for each other. Their cooking fire smoked endlessly. The first miner took the attitude of "grin and bear it." The second was always just mad at the smoke. The third looked for the cause—a bird's nest in the chimney—and removed it. The moral of the parable was that to solve the problem the cause must be removed. He went on to declare that these were "hard times." Coal prices were high, and rents were getting worse. He concluded his essay with counsel to the workers to remove the "crow's nest."[70] The story was simplistic, but he was attempting to address economic problems by counseling readers to identify and

---

[65] Ibid.

[66] Hudson, ed. *Walter Rauschenbusch: Selected Writings*, 45, n. 5.

[67] Winifred [Rauschenbusch] Rorty to Dores Sharpe, December 17, 1938, box 50, Rauschenbusch Family Papers.

[68] WR, diary, 1888–1891.

[69] WR, "Good Men and Good Governance," 2.

[70] WR, "A Story of Three Miners," 2–3.

remove the causes of injustice.[71]

In the new little journal Rauschenbusch included many issues of interest to workers, such as the problem posed by machines replacing people, resulting in lay-offs.[72] He declared that *For the Right* was against intemperance, but noted that if this were society's only problem, temperate people should be well off. "But are they?" he asked rhetorically, and answered his own question: "There are many things that press hard on a man and that have nothing to do with drink."[73] Rauschenbusch noted that the cause of the problem of injustice—the crow's nest in the chimney, identified in his little story—is "the spirit of selfishness which knows no compassion and sometimes kills the sense of right."[74] He cited examples of economic practices he believed undermined the workers—such as tariffs on trade, limiting coal production for higher profit, and holding vacant land for speculation.[75] He discussed the labor theory of value with the familiar example of the price of a coat: "does it [the value of the coat] not in justice belong to those who have created the value?"[76] Rauschenbusch noted that in the industrial sector it was important to work together instead of against one another, and he gave examples of the advantages that would come to all of society by making the railroad, telegraph lines, and coal mines public property.[77] In "Eight Hours" he celebrated the legislation establishing the eight-hour workday and the power that strikes had demonstrated toward achieving this important goal.[78] Rauschenbusch was keenly aware of the division of classes in American society, and he was also realistic about the process of change. He counseled workers that the goals they sought would not be handed to them: "Do not expect salvation from the rich and the educated...most often they are thinking only of themselves just as you probably would if you were rich. The help must come through yourself."[79] Reform moved slowly. He was fully aware of corrupt politics as well as economic inequities, and he spoke out against both. The measure of the seriousness with which he tried to integrate socialism and Christianity is clear in his counsel to readers to "read *Looking Backward* and the Gospel of Luke. See what our Master had to say about the

---

[71] Rauschenbusch was tapping into the power of story-telling in this article. Years later fellow New York City minister C. A. Daniel recalled this story in detail and also the point Rauschenbusch made: systemic change comes only by addressing causes. See Daniel, "Reminiscences of My Friend," 6–10.

[72] WR, "Drop a Nickel in the Slot," 3–4.

[73] WR, "The Crow's Nest," 4.

[74] WR, "Getting at the Crow's Nest," 2.

[75] Ibid.

[76] WR, "$8,500," 5–6.

[77] WR, "In Germany," 2–3.

[78] WR, "Eight Hours," 3.

[79] WR, "Drop a Nickel in the Slot," 4.

same things."[80]

In *For the Right* Rauschenbusch took positions on a variety of topics that came to his attention, including gambling in Louisiana (it is wrong), public transport (it should be cheap to accommodate everyone), and rent (it is the real problem of the poor—whether in Ireland or in New York City). As a regular contributor to *For the Right,* Rauschenbusch took up the task of writing brief articles in which he analyzed many aspects of the economy and the plight of the workers, but the journal lasted only from November 1889 to March 1891. It did not reach its intended working-class audience: it lacked financial support, and its young authors were sometimes patronizing.[81] But Rauschenbusch had made his positions public: he stood for justice for American workers. His contributions to *For the Right* provided the opportunity for him to develop his ideas.[82] He received negative criticism from fellow Baptists and others, but favorable notice from the major New York newspapers.[83] Meeting deadlines for the paper had been demanding. His deafness was getting worse. He decided to return to Germany to seek medical help for his deafness and for a study sabbatical.

The year 1891 was to be a year like no other in his life. During his nine-month sabbatical, before he was thirty years of age, Rauschenbusch worked out a comprehensive vision of what he called a "Christianity Revolutionary."[84] It was midway along his journey as a minister. He had encountered a complicated social and economic world during his five years of ministry in New York City, and he had used insights of sociology and economics to analyze American society. He decided that the old evangelical conception of Christianity was too small. He said that Jesus was not merely a guide to a disembodied mystical religion. He came to create a new society on earth.[85] But social reform alone would not achieve the goals he envisioned; he believed that in this new society the church and social reform would need each other.[86] Both sought a better society, so they needed to collaborate. He began to articulate what this new and Christianity Revolutionary would look like. The key analytical tool he had acquired since his seminary curriculum was the analysis provided by sociology. This new discipline studied human beings in groups, and Rauschenbusch had come to believe that the earliest

---

[80] WR, "In Germany," 2.

[81] WR, diary, 1888–1891; Hudson, ed., *Walter Rauschenbusch: Selected Writings,* 20.

[82] "The Genesis of *Christianity and the Social Crisis,*" *Rochester Theological Seminary Bulletin: The Record,* LXIX (November 1918), 51-53.

[83] Daniel, "Reminiscences of My Friend," 6.

[84] WR, diary, 1888–1891.

[85] WR, "The Righteousness of the Kingdom," 63. In the following years Rauschenbusch often spoke of the individual conception of Christianity as too small. See WR to Will and Mrs. Will [Munger], July 11, 1896, box 50, Rauschenbusch Family Papers.

[86] He later addressed this issue directly in *Christianity and the Social Crisis,* xxii.

Christian message was created for and directed to both individuals and groups. What would happen if the modern church also adopted this view of things? This would be a worthwhile topic to ponder during a sabbatical.

CHAPTER 3

CHRISTIANITY REVOLUTIONARY: INDIVIDUAL AND SOCIAL REDEMPTION

Rauschenbusch is best known for his advocacy of a social gospel. This achievement eclipses his other work and remains central to his legacy. He never intended for individual Christianity to be obscured or lost by recovering the idea of the social message of the church. He believed in both. The task of this chapter is to examine stages in the development of Rauschenbusch's understanding of Christianity as both individual and social. He had already adopted new views on social Christianity during the early years of his pastorate (1886–1891). In 1891 he had the opportunity to spell out his belief that original Christianity was revolutionary and what that might mean for the present. Especially significant for Rauschenbusch was his insight into the meaning of the kingdom of God in the teachings of Jesus. In 1892 Rauschenbusch and other ministers organized the "Brotherhood of the Kingdom." The purpose of the group was to promote the central biblical idea of the kingdom of God in the present day. A year after he took the major church history position at Rochester Theological Seminary, Rauschenbusch wrote "The New Evangelism" (1904), in which he argued that the old evangelism was failing and that the church must re-conceive its central task. Soon thereafter he began working on an extended argument, which he published in 1907 as *Christianity and the Social Crisis.* This critically significant publication was his manifesto for recovering social dimensions of the Christian faith. What he had proposed in his 1891 manuscript, but never published, was refined, argued with force, and presented to the American public in 1907. It made such an impact that it shaped the remaining eleven years of his life. In his public speaking, articles, and books he continued to promote his ideas about the gospel and its application to all of society. Why should the church be revolutionary in the present age? Rauschenbusch thought about the causes of suffering among America's poor. He made numerous proposals to create a better nation. For workers he wanted reforms such as minimum wage, a forty-hour work week, better housing, insurance, and health and food safety. Workers needed leverage to change labor practices. He supported the right to form labor unions and for them to bargain for these goods. On another level, he advocated city ownership and management of essentials for daily life, such as public transport, electricity, water, and coal. Whereas private ownership for profit meant that prices would continue to rise, public ownership could aim at keeping costs as low as possible. Finally, Rauschenbusch advocated legislation to bring about changes. Eventually these changes would be put into place in American society, but he was writing during the beginning of the twentieth century movement towards a welfare state.

The Righteousness of the Kingdom (1891)

Rauschenbusch left for his sabbatical in Europe in March 1891. On his way to Germany, Rauschenbusch visited England to learn first-hand about social experiments in that nation. He was deeply disappointed with what he observed in Liverpool but delighted with the social progress he saw in Birmingham. The visit further confirmed his view that in the modern world charity is not enough to address poverty. Cities must continue to work as communities devoted to social betterment.

During the months of his sabbatical in Germany Rauschenbusch wrote his first full-length book, *Christianity Revolutionary*. Though it was not published until 1968, it was crucial for Rauschenbusch's development of his ideas. This manuscript contains an extended summary of his early views on social Christianity.[1] The key point Rauschenbusch wanted to make was that original Christianity was revolutionary. His opening sentence is "Christianity in its nature is revolutionary."[2] He argued that the Christian movement had been revolutionary in its origins and also that the modern church needed to be prepared to promote radical change in the present. He affirmed that "the great task of our epoch is the recasting of social institutions."[3] He believed that the church was called to be involved in this task.

Writing his lengthy manuscript was a huge undertaking. Although as a pastor he had no academic requirement to meet, Rauschenbusch went on sabbatical

[1] WR, *Christianity Revolutionary*, box 101, Rauschenbusch Family Papers. The papers include a typescript plus notes in Rauschenbusch's handwriting and some of his reading notes for the manuscript. Max Stackhouse discovered the manuscript, edited it, and published it as *The Righteousness of the Kingdom*. The title of the book evidently went through several iterations: *Revolutionary Christianity*, *Christianity Revolutionary*, and *The Righteousness of the Kingdom*. In light of Rauschenbusch's process for selecting titles for later publications, these variations are not surprising. For several of his books, Rauschenbusch made lists of potential titles before selecting one. In both the handwritten 440-page manuscript and its typed version, Rauschenbusch used the title *Christianity Revolutionary*. The first two titles he considered emphasized the revolutionary character of Christianity; the third, the central theological idea of the kingdom of God.

[2] WR, *The Righteousness of the Kingdom*, 70.

[3] Ibid., 64.

with the purpose of learning about developments in social reconstruction efforts and current theology in Europe. The background for writing this book is illumined by Rauschenbusch's correspondence with Nathaniel Schmidt. Rauschenbusch, Schmidt, and Leighton Williams had formed the little "Society of Jesus" in 1887 and had begun to forge a vision of a socially aware church. Rauschenbusch was a gifted writer who already had much experience in organizing and articulating his ideas in his sermons, in published articles, in Sunday school lessons, and in *For the Right.* As his work on the manuscript progressed, Rauschenbusch wrote to Schmidt: "I have sent you nearly the whole of what I have thus far written of the book. I feel it is a great deal when I request you to read it and critique it. But you know that it was written to be our joint utterance. That was what sustained me in the often exhausting labor of writing it. Now may I tell you some of my wishes about your criticism?"

He lists specific concerns on which he sought Schmidt's comments:

> (1) General conception of the book, (2) Is the spirit in which it is written righteous? (3) Is the style appropriate? (4) Mark superfluous or too long sections (5) Table of contents included. I feel inclined to condense chapter on Law very much and keep it in my book on "The Ethics of Jesus." [Leighton] Williams wants the chapter on the New Law to go on now; he thinks the real meat of the book is in the chapter on the Force (The Revolutionary Power) and on the Law.... Affectionately, WR.[4]

Evidently the three young ministers had agreed that Rauschenbusch should write a book supporting their understanding of Christianity, that they would assist in editing the book, and that in this sense, as Rauschenbusch wrote, "it was written to be our joint utterance." Rauschenbusch had already been in touch with Williams and now solicited input from Schmidt.

During his sabbatical Rauschenbusch spent some research time at Greifswald University. Historian Jaehn searched for evidence of Rauschenbusch's activity in the library and identified some seventy book slips bearing Rauschenbusch's name. He found that most of these books dealt with the messianic idea in Scripture, the notion of the kingdom of God, the life of Jesus, and Christian ethics. Rauschenbusch also read books by the English Christian Socialist F. D. Maurice and by Hermann Cremer, a local German theologian who held conservative theological views but liberal views on social questions.[5] Two themes thus commanded Rauschenbusch's research agenda: the message of Jesus and writings on social Christianity by modern theologians. When he moved to Berlin, Rausch-

[4] WR to Nathaniel Schmidt, January 22, 1892, box 101, Rauschenbusch Family Papers.

[5] Jaehn, *Rauschenbusch*, 42.

enbusch secured a reading card to continue his research at the university and began to write his manuscript on *Christianity Revolutionary*.[6]

Rauschenbusch asserts in his introduction to the manuscript that Jesus was interested in conduct, not in ceremony and not in doctrine. Christianity, he affirms, is ethical.[7] The church has fought over doctrine and ceremony instead of resisting wrong.[8] He concludes that the preoccupations of the church have been misplaced. He attempts to call the church back to its ethical dimension, which he believes was its original purpose. Moreover, he affirms that Jesus was not merely a teacher of individual moral practice; he also came to establish a new society on earth.[9] Rauschenbusch argues that a true sense of justice is essential to the task of social reconstruction. He contrasts the phenomenon of people who are outraged at the dramatic news of children dying in fires but who fail to be outraged by the conditions in the tenements where many have lived and died in obscurity.[10] He affirms that original Christianity was revolutionary and that Jesus' message was also revolutionary. He writes that Jesus associated himself with the prophets who expected their work to involve struggle.[11] Rauschenbusch observes that Jesus himself announced a messianic age and said that it would present a radically new state of affairs. Those with two coats would share with those who had none. Repentance would open up a new spirit, a reversal of values.[12] So, in Rauschenbusch's view, Jesus was a revolutionary, and as the book of Acts put it, his followers "turned the world upside down" (Acts 17:7).[13]

Rauschenbusch was well aware of the conservative nature of the church throughout much of its history. He challenged the appropriateness of this position, seeking to overturn traditional conservatism when he argued that original Christianity was revolutionary. The tension between the church traditional and the church revolutionary was clear to him, and it was abundantly evident in the religious world of Rauschenbusch's day. Rauschenbusch constantly encountered cultural conformist religion that resisted change, but he saw true religion as challenging the establishment. He therefore opened his proposals for reform of the church with the argument that Jesus himself was a revolutionary, who repeatedly opposed Pharisees and other leaders of traditional religious beliefs and practices.

---

[6] WR, diary, 1888–1891, box 97, Rauschenbusch Family Papers.

[7] WR, *Christianity Revolutionary*, manuscript, 63, box 101, Rauschenbusch Family Papers.

[8] Ibid., 64.

[9] Ibid., 63.

[10] Ibid., 68. Rauschenbusch's social activism is apparent early in this book.

[11] Ibid., 71. Rauschenbusch would later use the connection between Jesus and the prophets in the opening chapters of *Christianity and the Social Crisis*.

[12] WR, *Christianity Revolutionary*, 74–75.

[13] Ibid., 77–78.

Rauschenbusch noted that Jesus critiqued the religion of his day and suffered serious opposition as a result: "Christ's work is not educational but revolutionary."[14] It was vital to his argument that Rauschenbusch convince readers that revolution in religious practice was not only acceptable, but desirable and required if recovery of the religion of Jesus was to be authentic. He was clearly aware that people looked to their understanding of the past, especially to their interpretation of Jesus and the earliest church, as the authoritative model for the present church. He wanted to show that Jesus' outlook was reform-minded and that the church today should adopt a similar outlook.

In his second chapter Rauschenbusch turned to an analysis of Jesus' central idea: the announcement of the coming of the kingdom of God. In the concept of the kingdom of God Rauschenbusch found the biblical basis he was looking for to articulate a social gospel. Rauschenbusch believed that all that is recorded of Jesus—his life, his teachings, his miracles, his death and resurrection—comes together in the notion that Jesus had come to establish God's rule in the hearts of people and in society. The influential theologian Albrecht Ritschl especially had drawn attention to solidarity in the idea of the kingdom of God.[15] In one parable the kingdom of God was compared to the growth of the mustard seed; this story suggested for many readers, including Rauschenbusch, the growth and development in the kingdom. Interpreters such as Johannes Weiss and Albert Schweitzer believed instead that Jesus taught the mystery and suddenness of the appearance of the kingdom announced by Jesus. Despite major differences of interpretation, New Testament scholars agreed on the centrality of the kingdom of God in Jesus' thought. To convince his readers, Rauschenbusch needed to establish powerful biblical justification. The idea of the kingdom of God would provide his major biblical/theological support for interpreting Christianity as social as well as individual. The kingdom of God was, after all, now clearly understood to be the central idea in Jesus' own teaching.

Rauschenbusch opens his discussion of the kingdom of God with four observations. First, he emphasizes that Jesus was not stressing nationality, but spiritual fitness.[16] But he adds that the kingdom not only is spiritual and within but also has outward dimensions. Moreover, the messianic rule of God cannot be brought about by the use of force; Jesus refused to use force.[17] Finally, Rauschenbusch declares that individual personality—its value and responsibility—must be

---

[14] Ibid., 76.

[15] WR, *A Theology for the Social Gospel*, 1997 ed., 93–94, 125.

[16] Rauschenbusch later identified his debt to Ritschl. See WR, *The Righteousness of the Kingdom*, 85.

[17] Ibid., 88, 91.

honored.[18] People must be persuaded, not coerced, by the truth of the promises delivered by Jesus in the beatitudes that open his famous sermon (Matt 5:1-12).

Rauschenbusch goes on to develop one of his central ideas: the great mass of evangelical Christians of the present day think that all that God desires is the salvation of many individual souls for heaven.[19] He asserts that this is a limited understanding and is therefore unscriptural. Then he explains, "it is right in preaching the redemption of the individual; it is wrong in not preaching the collective life of humanity."[20] This two-part sentence succinctly summarizes Rauschenbusch's proposal for the church. Again he writes, "The individual and the collective life on humanity act and react of each other.... Each, therefore is a citadel to be captured in the name of God."[21] By fastening on the central biblical concept of the kingdom of God, Rauschenbusch had identified the biblical/theological concept that he employed to construct his program of reform. He often spoke of the "power" that entered history with the coming of Jesus.[22] The nature of his personality is indicated by Jesus' self-sacrifice and his love. Rauschenbusch believed that this revolutionary force has the power to change both individuals and nations.[23]

A key dimension of Rauschenbusch's strategy was to argue that "the religion of Jesus is above all things a practical religion."[24] Rauschenbusch introduced social concerns into his discussion by noting problems in American society: drunkenness, speculative land prices, pauperism, crime, theft, divorce, suicide, and prostitution, among others. He declared that justice is the foundation on which to build a better society.[25] In his view the injustice of the wage system was apparent. Warning against amassing fortunes, Rauschenbusch cited the biblical passage that counsels hearers to lay up treasures in heaven, not on earth, and references the parable of Lazarus and Dives and the rich young ruler.[26] Then he cited current examples of monopoly ownership and contrasted it with the value of public ownership of life's essentials. He declared that the process of acquiring wealth usually ignores the Christian virtues and thus damages the soul.[27] Rauschenbusch asserted that the quest for wealth has in many instances consumed churches as well

---

[18] Ibid., 95–97. This emphasis on person/personalism was common in theological reflection of this era.

[19] Ibid., 98.

[20] Ibid., 99.

[21] Ibid., 104–105.

[22] Ibid., 122, 126.

[23] Ibid., 126.

[24] Ibid., 179.

[25] Ibid., 191.

[26] Ibid., 208–10.

[27] Ibid., 212–18.

as businesses. Clergy often succumbed to the influence of the wealthy in shaping their values, and few stood up for the masses.[28] He had a discerning eye and spared no institution, including the church and its leaders.

In his discussion of "The New Morality," Rauschenbusch used the traditional Christian sermonic trope of duty to self, others, and God. Here he warned against ascetical or ceremonial religion, which he saw as false. Instead, true religion is based on love, justice, and faith. Rauschenbusch concluded with warning and hope. He confessed that the doctrine of human progress appealed to him, but that the actual direction of unguided human nature is downward, not upward. "None of us," he asserted, "drifts into purity, justice, or unselfishness."[29] Here he showed awareness of the power of evil. The kingdom of God will not evolve by natural processes: "It is uphill work."[30] Rauschenbusch then asked, "From where do we get the force to move up?" and answered, "From God."[31] He concluded by affirming that the hope based on the idea of the kingdom of God alone has the power to triumph.[32]

Rauschenbusch never published this manuscript. His later editor, Max Stackhouse, suggests that he was preoccupied with other tasks when he returned to New York City.[33] He was indeed a busy minister, devoted to parish work, writing Sunday school lessons for the churches of his denomination, and courting and marrying Pauline Rother in 1893. Also Nathaniel Schmidt offered extended critique and suggested revisions, as Rauschenbusch had requested. Questions of how to reshape the argument may have further delayed the project. Moreover, Rauschenbusch suggested that he had dealt with "dangerous" ideas. Perhaps he was using caution to protect his position as a minister. He was, after all, articulating a revolutionary statement of Christianity to an audience that understood religion in much more traditional, conservative terms.

The Righteousness of the Kingdom provides an important advance in Rauschenbusch's ideas in 1891. In *For the Right* he had already identified many social problems that needed to be addressed, and his sermons had already exposed problems and proposed the idea of a social gospel. Nevertheless, the study abroad marked a decisive step forward. Rauschenbusch was immersed in German culture, fluent in both English and German, and stimulated by his studies to present a comprehensive statement of his views.[34]

---

[28] Ibid., 231.
[29] Ibid., 282–83.
[30] Ibid., 283.
[31] Ibid.
[32] Ibid., 284–85.
[33] Stackhouse, "Editor's Introduction," 17.
[34] The 1891 sabbatical was the third of six visits to Germany. In all, he spent about ten years of his life there. See Winifred Rauschenbusch, "Notes of Addresses: Apparently on the

Stackhouse identified three ways Rauschenbusch changed as a result of his sabbatical. First, he recognized more fully the role of religion and ethics in history. Second, he adopted the centrality of the kingdom of God in the teachings of Jesus. Third, his overall interests shifted in a decided move to historical issues.[35] Rauschenbusch later recalled how the notion of the kingdom of God gripped his imagination and changed him:

> In 1891 I spent a year of study in Germany.... In the Alps I have seen the summit of some great mountains come out of the clouds in the early morn and stand revealed in blazing purity. Its foot was still swathed in drifting mist, but I knew the mountain was there, and my soul rejoiced in it. So Christ's conception of the Kingdom of God came to me as a new revelation. Here was the idea and purpose that had dominated the mind of the Master himself. All his teachings center about it. His life was given to it. His death was suffered for it. When a man has once seen that in the Gospels, he can never unsee it again.
>
> When the Kingdom of God dominated our landscape, the perspective of life shifted into a new alignment. I felt a new security in my social impulses. The spiritual authority of Jesus Christ would have been sufficient to offset the weight of all the doctors, and I now knew that I had history on my side. But in addition I found that the new conception of the purpose of Christianity was simply satisfying. It responded to all the old and all the new elements of my religious life. The saving of the lost, the teaching of the young, the pastoral care of the poor and frail, the quickening of lowed intellects, the study of the Bible, church union, political reforms, the reorganization of the industrial system, international peace—it was all covered by the one aim of the Reign of God on earth. That idea is necessarily as big as humanity, for it means the divine transformation of all of human life. It alone can say without limitation, "Nil humani a me alienum" ("Nothing that is human is alien to me").[36]

Rauschenbusch had preached on the kingdom of God, but in 1891 the concept provided the unifying theme for all of his religious concerns and the theological center for all of his efforts.[37]

In his view, the kingdom of God was inclusive of all dimensions of Christianity—individual, ecclesiastical and societal. Later Rauschenbusch wrote that his study in Europe in 1891 was the "most striking epoch in my life."[38] This assessment is telling indeed. Much of his vision of the gospel and its relationship to the

---

Subject of His Travels," n.d., box 39, Rauschenbusch Family Papers.

[35] Stackhouse, "Editor's Introduction," 28; Minus, *Walter Rauschenbusch*, 81.

[36] WR, *Christianizing the Social Order*, 1912 ed., 93–94. This is Rauschenbusch's translation.

[37] See Handy's discussion in *The Social Gospel in America*, 255–56.

[38] WR to G. H. Roller, March 12, 1915, box 115, Rauschenbusch Family Papers.

contemporary church and society was shaped during Rauschenbusch's later twenties, and he articulated many of these ideas in *The Righteousness of the Kingdom.* Throughout his life Rauschenbusch would devote himself to developing implications of the concept of social dimensions of the gospel. Rauschenbusch's unpublished manuscript was a landmark in the trajectory of development that made him famous in his own day and influential thereafter. He repeated and refined his ideas in future sermons and publications: Rauschenbusch's articulation and defense of the social gospel perhaps reached its apogee in 1907 when he published *Christianity and the Social Crisis.* He was still concerned with many of the issues he had developed in his 1891 manuscript sixteen years earlier, and he made many significant steps along the way toward 1907.

The Brotherhood of the Kingdom

Following his sabbatical Rauschenbusch continued to seek support from fellow ministers. He became an officer in the Baptist Congress in 1892. Leighton Williams and others formed yet another organization, The Brotherhood of the Kingdom (1892). This was a small group committed to recovering the message of the kingdom of God. The Brotherhood met annually for devotion, study, and discussion of papers at Marlborough, a property on the Hudson River owned by Leighton Williams' family. The group included Williams, Rauschenbusch, and Schmidt, as well as Philadelphia pastor George Dana Boardman, theology professor William Newton Clarke, and pastor and Baptist social service leader Samuel Zane Batten.[39] The Brotherhood published a number of leaflets promoting their ideas of the kingdom of God.[40] Rauschenbusch was eager to promote the centrality of the Kingdom. He wrote:

> We desire to see the Kingdom of God once more the great object of Christian preaching; the inspiration of Christian hymnology; the foundation of systematic theology; the enduring motive of evangelistic and missionary work; the religious inspiration of social work and the social outcome of religious inspiration; the common object in which all religious bodies find their unity; the great synthesis in which the regeneration of the spirit, the enlightenment of the intellect, the development of the body, the reform of the political life, the sanctification of industrial life, and all that concerns the redemption of humanity shall be embraced.
>
> To this task, God helping us, we desire to dedicate our lives.[41]

---

[39] Hudson, ed., *Walter Rauschenbusch: Selected Writings*, 25.

[40] The table of contents of a bound volume of these leaflets lists twenty-eight titles. Rauschenbusch wrote ten of these. This collection of booklets is housed in the ABHS archives.

[41] WR, "The Brotherhood of the Kingdom," Brotherhood Leaflet No. 2, ABHS archives; Hudson, ed., *Walter Rauschenbusch: Selected Writings*, 75–76.

For members of the Brotherhood, the concept of the kingdom of God best expressed the great aim of Christianity because it provided an all-encompassing synthesis of the divine forces in humanity.[42] Rauschenbusch found in this group an important sounding-board for his thinking. Twenty years later, he wrote regretfully about the failure of the Brotherhood to become a larger movement but affirmed that it "had a tremendous influence on the early group."[43]

In an 1892 article published in *The Examiner*, Rauschenbusch explored the notion of the kingdom of God, calling it "A Conquering Idea."[44] He wrote that Albrecht Ritschl, "who has himself done more, perhaps, than any other man to rehabilitate that idea in the theological thought of Germany," noted, "Since the second century nothing has less guided the church in its efforts for moral renewal than the idea of the kingdom of God in the sense in which Christ used the words."[45] In the second Brotherhood leaflet Rauschenbusch readily agreed with Ritschl that establishing the kingdom of God was the great aim of Jesus and the key idea of his teaching. And he also argued that this idea had been abandoned or misconstrued by most Christians.[46] Rauschenbusch identified three great distortions of the idea. First, some people equated the kingdom of God with life after death. Second, although the kingdom is a collective ideal, many interpreters had replaced it with individual salvation. A third error was made by others who substituted the idea of the church for the kingdom. Rauschenbusch conceded these common interpretations were partially true, but each led to distortion. Individualism fostered selfishness; focus on heaven alone meant there was no attempt to bring the kingdom on earth; and focusing only on the church left the remainder of society unredeemed.[47] Rauschenbusch concluded that the kingdom of God is a conquering idea, but only to the extent that its true meaning is adopted by pastors and churches.[48] This was indeed "Christianity Revolutionary."

In another leaflet, "The Kingdom of God" Rauschenbusch elaborated on two additional interpretations of the kingdom. The mystics found it in the inner

---

[42] WR, "Our Attitude toward Millenarianism," ABHS archives; Hudson, ed., *Walter Rauschenbusch: Selected Writings*, 79.

[43] WR to The Brotherhood of the Kingdom, August 20, 1912, box 27, Rauschenbusch Family Papers.

[44] WR, "A Conquering Idea," in Hudson, ed., *Walter Rauschenbusch: Selected Writings*, 71–74.

[45] Hudson, ed., *Walter Rauschenbusch: Selected Writings*, 71–72.

[46] WR, "The Brotherhood of the Kingdom," Brotherhood Leaflet No. 2, ABHS archives; *Brotherhood of the Kingdom* (a bound volume); Hudson, ed., *Walter Rauschenbusch: Selected Writings*, 75.

[47] WR, "A Conquering Idea," in Hudson, ed., *Walter Rauschenbusch: Selected Writings*, 73.

[48] Ibid., 74.

life of the Spirit ("The Kingdom is within you," Luke 17:21) and others emphasized laboring "for a righteous social order."[49] Rauschenbusch was irenic. He did not want to deny the value of these interpretations, but he did judge that all five interpretations he identified in his writings "err by defect. The Kingdom of God is larger than anything contained in any one of these ideas. It stands for the sum of all divine and righteous forces on earth. It embraces all pure aspirations Godward and all true hopes for the perfection of life."[50] Rauschenbusch spoke of the kingdom as an idea that is not fulfilled in this life. Nevertheless, he said that we must work for the kingdom here and now through the laws and institutions of our society. He said that we should aspire to the kingdom, even though it is never completely realized. In language he favored elsewhere, he liked to say, "The Kingdom is always but coming."[51] The church and the kingdom are not identical. Instead, he wrote, "We are the church as we worship together; we are the Kingdom as we live justly and lovingly with one another."[52] In these publications from 1893 and 1894 Rauschenbusch found in the notion of the kingdom of God the best summation of Christianity. Hence his desire to promote the "Brotherhood of the Kingdom."[53] The kingdom idea is biblical, and it includes many traditional ideas, but it also includes social redemption. For Rauschenbusch, it was the perfect vehicle to carry his message.

The New Evangelism

Following his 1891 sabbatical Rauschenbusch had five more years as a pastor in New York City and ten years as a professor in Rochester before he wrote *Christianity and the Social Crisis.* Between 1891 and 1907 he continued to develop social Christianity themes in his sermons and especially in his publications.

In 1904 Rauschenbusch published "The New Evangelism" in *The Independent*, a national religious journal.[54] In this article he made the case for churches adopting new approaches in their work, arguing that a new evangelism was essential for the modern church. He pointed out that church leaders themselves

---

[49] WR, "The Kingdom of God," Brotherhood leaflet No. 4, ABHS archives. *Brotherhood of the Kingdom* (a bound volume); Hudson, ed., *Walter Rauschenbusch: Selected Writings*, 77–78.

[50] Ibid., 78.

[51] WR, *Christianity and the Social Crisis*, 1907 ed., 421.

[52] WR, "The Kingdom of God," Hudson, ed., *Walter Rauschenbusch: Selected Writings*, 78.

[53] Rauschenbusch remained committed to the Brotherhood. He sent the following message to them on August 20, 1912: "Whatever happens, the Brotherhood has not lived in vain. It is justified by its children. It has had a tremendous influence on the early group, and it has been of inestimable value to the entire national movement to have a number of mature minds at its command early" (Minus, *Walter Rauschenbusch*, 131; for date of letter see 219, n. 18).

[54] WR, "The New Evangelism," 1054–59.

were dissatisfied with older approaches to evangelism, recognizing that the older methods were not as effective as they had been in the past. Rauschenbusch contended in his essay that everything in society develops and religion must develop along with society. Society was experiencing rapid and profound change; the church was stuck in the past. He said that the church was "in the position of a mother talking to her son of seventeen as if he were still twelve. What she says is good and loving, but it is not what the boy with his new passions and problems needs."[55] Thus "the old scheme of salvation seems mechanical and remote."[56] The old morality focused on personal or family matters. He said that currently the community accepted many respectable amusements, and much of the morality supported by the church tended to fall into categories of "respectability and good breeding."[57] But Rauschenbusch noted that when moving from questions of moral behavior to the structure of American society, the church was mute. He reminded readers that the church had been viewed as the moral guide for civilization in the past, but it was silent on the most urgent issues of the present day. It is especially in the fields of commerce and industry that the nation faces unsolved problems, and the church "has no clear message, and often claims to be under no obligation to have one."[58]

Rauschenbusch believed that the church was losing the working class, and he thought workers were alienated because they believed the church's ethical life was being guided by the business class.[59] Rauschenbusch was firm in his insistence that the new evangelism would have to address social issues. The church must stand up for justice in society, and it should provide guidance on such issues as fair taxes and wages and the prevention of hunger in society. He wrote that the new evangelism would have to be ready to discuss "how a Christian man should live under modern conditions, and then summon men to live so."[60] This brief article pointedly faulted the churches for failing to keep up and to address the current moral conditions of the nation. In Rauschenbusch's view, the church confronted a serious problem of relevance. By the next year he was at work on his first published book, which was designed to articulate the nature of America's social crisis and the responsibility of the church.

Early in 1907 Rauschenbusch published "What Is a Christian Nation?" in which he laid out in six points his vision of a Christian nation.[61] At the outset he

---

[55] WR, "The New Evangelism," in Hudson, ed., *Walter Rauschenbusch: Selected Writings*, 138.

[56] Ibid., 140.

[57] Ibid., 141.

[58] Ibid., 143.

[59] Ibid., 142.

[60] Ibid., 143.

[61] We may assume that these points are indications of his view of social redemption: A

says, "We shall all agree, I think, that merciful helpfulness toward those who suffer would be a mark of Christian spirit in a nation as in an individual."[62] He cites examples of relief rendered to victims of the Galveston flood (1900), the San Francisco earthquake (1906), the plague in India (1903) and the famine in China (1876-79). He describes this public generosity as impulsive. By contrast, however, with much publicized catastrophes people "pass by without thought where men are suffering and dying in silence. The extinction of child-labor and of tuberculosis would be a higher test of our national Christianity than trainloads of supplies in case of sudden disaster."[63] In describing these contrasting responses to suffering, Rauschenbusch was calling for the nation to address causes of suffering through structural changes. This was the direction the new evangelism should take.

Christianity and the Social Crisis (1907)

Rauschenbusch wrote his final draft of *Christianity and the Social Crisis* in 1905–1906, then left for another sabbatical in Europe. He returned to national acclaim; 50,000 copies of the book sold during the next three years.[64] Clearly this book carried a message that intrigued many readers. In Robert Handy's words, *Christianity and the Social Crisis* became "the most famous social gospel book of them all."[65] What was Rauschenbusch's argument in this landmark book of American religious history? Other authors had written on various social problems. Congregationalist minister Washington Gladden, in *Applied Christianity: Moral Aspects of Social Questions* (1886), admonished application of the Golden Rule by both employers and workers.[66] Charles Sheldon's novel *In His Steps* (1896) placed his characters in various situations demanding moral choice and action and had them ask, "What would Jesus do?"[67] Rauschenbusch took a more comprehensive approach. He recognized the power of self-interest in modern economic struc-

---

Christian nation would (1) render help to the suffering, (2) punish with purpose to save, (3) support development of every personality, (4) value spiritual over material wealth, (5) create a community of love modeled on the family and (6) be conscious of God in national affairs. See WR, "What is a Christian Nation?" in *The Materials of Religious Education: Being the Principal Papers Presented At, and The Proceedings of the Fourth General Convention of the Religious Education Association, Rochester, New York, February 5–7, 1907,* (Chicago: Executive Office of the Association, 1907) 25–30. Also in *The Standard,* 54 (January 23, 1907): 757-58.

[62] Ibid., 26.

[63] Ibid.

[64] Cross, Introduction *Christianity and the Social Crisis* by WR, 1964 ed., viii.

[65] Handy, *The Social Gospel in America*, 331.

[66] Gladden, *Applied Christianity.*

[67] Sheldon, *In His Steps.*

tures that resulted in injustices for ordinary workers. How should Christians respond? Rauschenbusch's proposals challenged current economic, political, and social practice, as well as the passivity of the church. He called his *Christianity and the Social Crisis* a "dangerous book."[68] He thought the American economic system was structured unfairly, resulting in suffering for the working class. He believed that the church should always align itself against injustice. His challenge was to persuade Christian readers to act to change their society and to create a more Christian nation. How could he do this? What was his argument? How did this church history professor proceed?

Writing *Christianity and the Social Crisis*

Rauschenbusch kept many records of his progress in writing, including a summary of his work on *Christianity and the Social Crisis.* He understood his *Christianity Revolutionary* manuscript as the first stage in the development of *Christianity and the Social Crisis.* He indicated that he wrote his second draft in 1902 and the third and final draft in 1905–1906.[69] He also recorded several dates documenting his progress on the manuscript. He finished a draft of chapter 1 on May 27, 1905, noting that he completely rewrote the chapter during the week of May 15–21, 1906. Working quickly, he completed the first draft of the chapters on "The Social Aims of Jesus" in two days in May 1905 and finished rewriting the final draft on June 16, 1906. The report shows that he worked on the book in May and during summer 1905 and again in 1906.[70] When he had completed the first five of seven chapters, he listed forty-six German and nineteen English books he had consulted as sources for his writing.[71]

Rauschenbusch submitted his book proposal to Macmillan on September 17, 1906, explaining to the editors, "It deals with the relation of Christianity to the social movement...." He wrote that there were no books in English on the subject, and he was confident that the book covered a great deal of ground not previously discussed. Moreover, he wrote that "the subject is bound to remain under discussion for years to come...just now a large number of ministers and others are opening their minds to social questions...and are seeking an adjustment between their old views and the new."[72] Having demonstrated need and

[68] WR, "The Genesis of *Christianity and the Social Crisis,*" 51-53; also cited in Dorrien, "Thy Kingdom Come," 82 and in Minus, *Walter Rauschenbusch*, 158.

[69] WR, "Notes on Addresses," typescript, box 39, Rauschenbusch Family Papers.

[70] WR, *Christianity and the Social Crisis*, bibliography, box 46, Rauschenbusch Family Papers.

[71] Rauschenbusch occasionally introduced a footnote or attributed an idea to another author. But this book is not generally footnoted, nor does it have a printed bibliography. See WR typescript of Books Used, box 46, Rauschenbusch family papers.

[72] WR to the Macmillan Company, September 17, 1906, box 46, Rauschenbusch Family

high probability of demand for the book, Rauschenbusch described the content of each of the chapters and submitted chapter 4 for evaluation. He was prepared to send the first six chapters for editorial review and hoped to finish the seventh within a few weeks. He gave the name of well-known academics who could speak for him, including A. H. Strong, Rochester Seminary president, and William H. P. Faunce, president of Brown University. He also enclosed his recent article "The New Evangelism," which had been "widely quoted...and would help you to form your judgment of my literary work."[73] George Brett replied for the Macmillan Company in less than two weeks, encouraging Rauschenbusch to finish the book and submit the completed manuscript.[74]

Rauschenbusch complied; Macmillan accepted the book and sent Rauschenbusch a contract in November. But Rauschenbusch expressed several reservations in his response to Brett. He wanted control of translations of the book since, he declared, "I write German nearly as well as English"; he wanted complimentary copies for friends; he asked for publication rights in England and Canada; and finally, he wanted the right to make thorough revisions in the book. In short, he was asking for considerable control of the book. He had a growing confidence of the book's "ability to make its mark."[75] This was not a misplaced analysis.

The Argument of *Christianity and the Social Crisis*

To begin his argument in *Christianity and the Social Crisis* Rauschenbusch stated the human condition in its most basic terms: "humanity is always...hungry for bread, sweaty with labor, struggling to wrest from nature and hostile men enough to feed its children. The welfare of the mass [of people] is always at odds with the selfish force of the strong."[76] Rauschenbusch first offered biblical support for his argument. He asserted that the key idea of the Hebrew prophets was God's demand for righteousness; they taught that the true worship of God is right moral conduct.[77] In their thinking religion and ethics were inseparable. Rauschenbusch affirmed that whereas Americans based their outlook, including religion, on individualism, the prophets' interest was the national condition.[78] The sympathy of the prophets was with the poor, and they warned against oppression by those who

---

Papers.

[73] Ibid.

[74] George P. Brett to WR, box 46, Rauschenbusch Family Papers.

[75] WR to George Brett, December 5, 1906, box 46, Rauschenbusch Family Papers. Rauschenbusch indicated in this December letter that he was still making revisions.

[76] WR, *Christianity and the Social Crisis*, 1. 1964 ed.

[77] WR, *Christianity and the Social Crisis*, 5; 11.

[78] Ibid., 10.

held power, affirming that Jehovah would vindicate the voiceless and the helpless.[79]

Rauschenbusch points out many strands of prophetic literature to support his contention. The greed for land by the rich is illustrated by Ahab's violent grab of Naboth's vineyard.[80] The laws of the Old Testament protected slaves, immigrants, beasts, and strangers. The law opposed taking of interest and made provision for breaking the cycle of poverty through observing the Jubilee, the practice of periodic restoration of property to debtors.[81] Rauschenbusch strongly contends that the religion of the prophets was not the "quiet devoutness of private religion."[82] The prophets challenged the status quo: "they were the men of the opposition and of the radical minority."[83] But they had the satisfaction of knowing that they were on the side of justice, "and justice is on the way to God."[84] In a resounding crescendo to his opening chapter, Rauschenbusch writes, "If anyone holds that religion is purely personal, or that God is on the side of the rich or that social interest is likely to lead preachers astray—he must prove his case with the prophets, and the burden of proof is with him."[85] Rauschenbusch disclaimed expertise in Old Testament studies, but believed that he had rightly understood the fundamentals of prophetic religion.[86] He identified the age-old problems of the selfish strong oppressing the weak and affirmed that the task of the prophets was to challenge this situation in ancient Israel. They did so by shifting their understanding of the foundation of religion from ritual to ethics, affirming that God cared nothing for ceremony, everything for justice.

Rauschenbusch moved next to make a similar affirmation about the message of Jesus, titling his second chapter "The Social Aims of Jesus."[87] He asked his readers to interpret Scripture a new way. He opened the chapter on Jesus with the astute caution that "we see in the Bible what we have been taught to see there. We drop great sets of facts from our field of vision...."[88] He saw this as a perennial problem for religious reformers: how do you persuade readers to interpret the gospel in a new and very different way? Rauschenbusch declared America to be in the midst of a revolution: he said that the current social movement was as significant as the Renaissance and the Reformation were in their day, and that it

[79] Ibid., 11–12.
[80] Ibid., 17.
[81] Ibid., 21–22.
[82] Ibid., 22.
[83] Ibid., 40.
[84] Ibid., 41.
[85] Ibid., 43.
[86] Ibid. He drew much material from Smith, *The Book of the Twelve Prophets.*
[87] WR, *Christianity and the Social Crisis*, 44.
[88] Ibid., 45.

would take a generation or two for people to shift from an individualistic to a social comprehension of religion.[89] He wrote that Jesus taught love and solidarity rather than selfishness, hate, ambition, and covetousness.

Rauschenbusch linked John the Baptist and the spirit of the prophets; he noted that when the people asked what they should do, John replied, "He that hath two coats, let him share with him that hath none; and he that hath food, let him do likewise."[90] Rauschenbusch then moved to Jesus' teachings. He found spiritual guidance on economics in Jesus' message of the kingdom of God, which for him meant the rule of God in the lives of people. He quoted the saying of Jesus "Ye cannot serve God and mammon" and cited the story of the rich young man's conversation with Jesus.[91] His conclusion was that Scripture does indeed teach that when life is built on the idea that "a man's life consisteth in the abundance of things that he possesseth…he is lost to the Kingdom of God."[92] He emphasized that the sympathies of Jesus were with the "poor and oppressed."[93]

Reflecting on the revisions of his understanding of Christianity, Rauschenbusch wrote at the end of his life, "I had to set myself against all that I had previously been taught…. I had to revise my whole study of the Bible…. My scientific studying of the Bible was undertaken to find a base for the Christian teaching of the social gospel."[94]

In the following chapter on "Primitive Christianity," Rauschenbusch wrote that the evidence for early Christianity is meager. He noted that the book of Acts records communal practice at Jerusalem, which suggests these early Christians shared their property.[95] He noted that this passage had been awkward for interpreters and many dismissed it on the basis that it was recorded only once. Rauschenbusch's retort was that many ecclesiastical bodies would be happy to have this much evidence for a favored church practice. The social ministry of early Christians, declared Rauschenbusch, was not required or forced on the church; it was voluntary and based on generosity.[96] He also reminded readers of the practice of the shared common meal, the selection of deacons to assist the poor, and appeals to churches to aid the poor of another church. His conclusion was that there was

[89] Ibid., 46.

[90] Ibid., 50.

[91] Ibid., 74–75.

[92] Ibid., 74.

[93] Ibid., 82.

[94] WR, "The Genesis of *Christianity and the Social Crisis*," 51–52.

[95] Ibid., 112. Here his cultural context strongly influenced Rauschenbusch's interpretation of Scripture. His view was that Christianity would gradually permeate society and create a better social order.

[96] WR, *Christianity and the Social Crisis*, 120–22.

"abundant and throbbing social life in primitive Christianity."[97]

Rauschenbusch devoted chapter 4 to exploring the question, "Why has Christianity not undertaken the work of social reconstruction?" He affirmed that early Christianity was launched as a great revolutionary movement, but in the early church social concerns were put on hold by factors such as apocalyptic expectations, fear of state persecution, or pursuit of ascetic ideals.[98] Moreover, after three centuries the cultural context changed again, and the church became a dominant power in society where it offered stability, acquired its own property and power, and provided leadership in education and intellectual culture. Though the church was a vast force in society, it still failed to transform society. Occasionally it sought to reform a "single intolerable evil," but in general the church "has accepted as inevitable the general social system."[99] As examples of failings of the church, despite initially elevating the position of women, the church has "exerted a conservative and retarding influence on the rise of women to equality with man."[100] Likewise, before the practice was abolished by law, millions of Christians supported slavery.[101] The church had failed to Christianize society, and injustices abounded.

Not only had the church failed to fight injustices, Rauschenbusch cited a fundamental shift in the nature of the church itself during the second century. The church changed its core message: whereas the original kingdom of God idea was collective, the message of the church shifted to promise of eternal life for individuals. The message of the kingdom of God sought to transform humanity but the hope of eternal life focused on individual escape from this world. In short, the notion of the kingdom of God receded in the teachings of the church. The central teaching of Jesus was thereby obscured.

Rauschenbusch was especially critical of the medieval Catholic Church, which adopted ceremonialism, sacramentalism, and dogmatism. By distorting and obscuring Jesus' idea of the kingdom of God, the medieval Catholic Church had substituted itself for the kingdom of God. Developing the idea of this chapter was critical for Rauschenbusch's explanation for what occurred in the church's history. If Jesus' original message of the kingdom was indeed social as much as it was individual, why was that message not kept alive in the church? Rauschenbusch's central argument was indeed a bold interpretative move. Donovan

---

[97] Ibid., 140.

[98] Ibid., 143. This "revolutionary" language permeated his discussion in his 1891 manuscript (hence the original title proposals *Revolutionary Christianity* or *Christianity Revolutionary*).

[99] Ibid., 149.

[100] Ibid., 150.

[101] Ibid., 158.

Smucker locates the key to Rauschenbusch's view in his appropriation of Harnack's argument that the development of Christian doctrine was a process of Hellenization—that is, of philosophical categories employed to explain the meaning of Jesus and his message.[102] Harnack's task was to recover the message of Jesus. He articulated his findings in a series of lectures, published as *What Is Christianity?*, an enormously influential volume. Smucker observed that "Harnack's perspective obviously opened the gates for a radical attack on previous theological formulations."[103] The findings of history thus undermined dogma, proving that it has been culturally conditioned.[104] In a similar manner Rauschenbusch posited the notion that Jesus' central message of the Kingdom of God had been lost until it was recovered by Ritschl and Harnack. Rauschenbusch boldly concluded, "Harnack's *History of Dogma* [is] a Baptist book."[105]

Rauschenbusch opened his next chapter, "The Present Crisis," with an imaginary conference in which the spirits of the centuries report to each other.[106] The Spirit of the Nineteenth Century reported to the spirits of other centuries the great accomplishments of his era: discoveries, wealth, freedom of thought. The Spirit of the First Century responded:

> You have made men rich.... [Is there no] fear of hunger?...Do children grow...and none die before their time?... You have made men wise. Are they wise or cunning? ... Have they learned to deal with their fellows in justice and love? You have set them free. Are there none, then, who toil for others against their will? You have made men one. Are there no barriers of class...? Do men no longer spill the blood of men for their ambitions and the sweat of men for their greed?[107]

The Spirit of the Nineteenth Century bowed his head and replied, "Your shame is already upon me. My great cities are as yours were. My millions live from hand to mouth. Those who toil longest have least. My thousands sink exhausted before their days are half spent. My human wreckage multiplies. Class faces class in sullen distrust."[108] Here Rauschenbusch's creative imagination takes

[102] Harnack, *History of Dogma*. II, 169-380. Harnack contrasts "the old Christianity and the New Church," II, 94-168, setting up the model of original genuine Christianity obscured in the second century.

[103] Smucker, *The Origin of Walter Rauschenbusch's Social Ethics*, 99.

[104] Ibid.

[105] WR, "A Baptist Re-Interpretation of Church History," 7, typescript of lecture delivered at the Baptist Seminary Faculties Union, University of Chicago, April 1913, box 21, Rauschenbusch Family Papers.

[106] "The Present Crisis" is the title of a poem by James Russell Lowell. Rauschenbusch referred to it on several occasions in his writings.

[107] WR, *Christianity and the Social Crisis*, 211–12.

[108] Ibid., 212.

the reader to a lofty Council of Spirits who listen to evaluations of the social condition of America in 1900. The achievements of the nineteenth century are astounding, but for many the social conditions remain horrifying. It would be hard to miss Rauschenbusch's personal compassion in this compelling passage.

Rauschenbusch linked the present crisis to the American economic system, which had created two classes of people—the employer and the wage earner. His judgment is harsh: "It is hardly likely that any social revolution, by which hereafter capitalism may be overthrown, will cause more injustice, more physical suffering, and more heartache than the industrial revolution by which capitalism rose to power."[109] His assessment is that humanity's moral forces "failed to keep pace with its intellectual and economic development. Men learned to make wealth much faster than they learned to distribute it justly. Their eye for profit was keener than their ear for the voice of God and humanity. That is the great sin of modern humanity...."[110] Rauschenbusch's passion is strong.

Rauschenbusch's historical narrative had arrived at the present, and he was now addressing the dire situation of the American worker—the chief burden of his conscience and the crisis he sought to relieve. For him the crisis was a moral question, thus the responsibility and the opportunity of the church. He commented on the many blessings of the land of America but cautioned that the important issue now was how wealth was distributed. The new immigrants had no land, but only their bodies to offer. According to the labor theory of value, workers created value by what they made, but the industrial wage system gave them only a fraction of the value they created. Rauschenbusch declared that "there is a deep-seated injustice here."[111] Over and over justice was the criteria of appeal in Rauschenbusch's writings. He felt deeply the injustice of the economic system, noting that "the average workingman's family is only a few weeks removed from destitution."[112] They must pay for high rent, expensive coal, and adequate food with wages so meager they are left with little more.[113] The system was costly to human life. Rauschenbusch noted diminished vitality in exhausted workers, breakdown of health, debilitating diseases, and the common turn to alcohol for relief.[114]

Rauschenbusch drew the familiar contrasts in his analysis of American society, noting the rich were getting richer: "The extremes of wealth and poverty are much farther apart than formerly.... There is a rich class and a poor class...."[115]

---

[109] Ibid., 218.
[110] Ibid.
[111] Ibid., 228.
[112] Ibid., 235.
[113] Ibid., 240.
[114] Ibid., 241–42.
[115] Ibid., 249.

The owners and managers of industry are rich or highly paid.... On the other side is the mass who take orders, who are employed or dismissed at a word...."[116] Labor and capital classes were deeply divided and estranged. This condition constitutes what he called the "present crisis." The strongest are taxed least and the weakest most.[117] Rauschenbusch quoted Charles Spahr's calculations that "One per cent of the families in our country held more than half of the aggregate wealth of the country...in 1890." Would they be content "with one per cent of the political power?" he asked rhetorically.[118] Thus economic, social, and political forces converged, and fundamental to everything was the economic system.

Rauschenbusch had articulated a social message in original Christianity, and he analyzed the current crisis of the American worker. His next task was to address the status of the church in the social movement. The church, according to Rauschenbusch, should be the conscience of society. It should speak out against wrong, but the church itself was caught up in the system it should be changing. It held property, needed income, employed people, and sought its own self-perpetuation. Rauschenbusch's analysis was not complex. He believed that the source of the social crisis was the economic structure because its principles were antagonistic to the ethics of Christianity.[119] In the American economy competition prevailed over cooperation. The church, Rauschenbusch said, has a prophetic role to play and cannot afford to remain neutral. It must always address the world as it is and as it should be.[120] Rauschenbusch had taken up a prophetic role in reminding readers of the responsibility of the church in the face of a great challenge. His great underlying theme throughout the book remains his appeal to justice.

If the church has responsibility for creating a better American society, what is it to do? Rauschenbusch offers several general guidelines in his final chapter, but his proposals are wide-ranging, and the guidelines are general. He addressed some of the most common criticisms of social Christianity. He said that we have always been told that "if only all individuals were regenerated and lived right, all social questions would be solved."[121] Some people criticized social preachers for forgetting the soul, and Rauschenbusch replied that forgetting the individual would be a serious defect. However, he pushed on with a constructive response that was broad, sweeping, and bold. Rauschenbusch declared:

> There are two great entities in human life—the human soul and the human race—and religion is to save both. The soul is to seek righteousness and eternal

[116] Ibid., 250.
[117] Ibid., 254, 257.
[118] Ibid., 263.
[119] Ibid, 316.
[120] Ibid., 341–42.
[121] Ibid., 359.

> life; the race is to seek righteousness and the Kingdom of God. The social preacher is apt to overlook the one. The evangelical preacher has long overlooked the other. It is due to that protracted neglect that we are now deluged by the social problems in the present acute form.[122]

Rauschenbusch observed that some ministers "have the gift of dealing with individuals and the loving insight into personal needs; others have the passionate interest in the larger life and its laws. The Church needs evangelists and pastors, but it needs prophets too."[123] This passage succinctly summarized Rauschenbusch's challenge to the church—its ministers and its laity. The society was in trouble, and the church is called to assist in its reconstruction. It must no longer be content only with offering individuals the promise of heaven after death.

Rauschenbusch closed the book by reiterating themes he had often developed in earlier writings. The church should stand for human dignity: people should not be treated as things.[124] Although contemporary public life puts profit first, Rauschenbusch reminds readers of Jesus' observation, "Life is more than food and raiment."[125] He stated his criteria for a Christian nation: it will be Christianized only when it puts people before wealth. He called for fraternity, not selfishness; cooperation, not competition. The Christian spirit, he said, promotes cooperation, brotherhood, and solidarity.[126] These were favorite terms Rauschenbusch used repeatedly in his writing.

In *Christianity and the Social Crisis* Rauschenbusch presented a manifesto for the social gospel. He envisioned a transformed church working to transform the nation. Rauschenbusch's proposals, however, were not pragmatic or workable. How does one go about actually persuading people to give up self-interest in order to change the structures of society? He was unable to provide specific methods to accomplish these goals but he did offer a visionary proposal that inspired readers of *Christianity and the Social Crisis.*

Social Christianity was Rauschenbusch's passion. He would write four additional books that included the word "social" in the title. All of them would contribute to his basic agenda of articulating and seeking to apply the social gospel beyond the individual and the church to the nation. The social gospel found its most powerful expression in this classic of the Christian faith, *Christianity and the Social Crisis.*

Defending Two Christianities: The Personal and The Social

---

[122] Ibid., 367.
[123] Ibid.
[124] Ibid., 369.
[125] Ibid., 370, quoting Matt 6:25.
[126] Ibid., 400.

In *Christianity and the Social Crisis* Rauschenbusch proposed that Christians adopt a revolutionary outlook, that they recognize the two levels of religion found in both testaments, and that they embrace the task of renovating society, especially the nation's economic structure. This twofold nature of the Christian faith became Rauschenbusch's lifelong message to the church. His strategy was not to deny the importance of individual salvation, but to affirm it and build on it—to bring to consciousness the mandate to transform society. It was a noble ideal, but it was not so readily followed. The reception of his major theme was decidedly split in the generations following.

Twentieth-century U.S. Protestantism has been characterized by sharp divisions between conservatives and liberals over theology, Scripture, and culture.[127] The social gospel became yet another source of division in twentieth-century Protestant battles. The Evangelical/Fundamentalist wing of Protestantism has touted the individual conversion experience as the bedrock of the faith. So far as the problems of society are concerned, its most common position has been that only when individuals are changed through personal conversion will society change for the better; therefore, the church need not seriously engage in creating a better society. The church's focus should be on the spiritual world, not on this present earthly existence.

The evangelical focus is an otherworldly salvation based on the "born again" language that the Gospel of John employs in recounting Jesus' conversation with Nicodemus (John 3: 1-18). In this text Jesus asserts that one cannot enter the kingdom of God unless born again of the Spirit. The key passage is John 3:16: those who believe in God's son will not perish. Verse 18 is seen as the reverse; those who do not believe are condemned already. The evangelical model focuses on the individual's personal belief and the obligation to extend this message to others. The church exists for this purpose, and the goal is eternal salvation of individuals. According to Rauschenbusch's social gospel, eternal salvation of individuals is only part of the story.

Equally arresting and powerful in the Gospels is Matthew's earlier recorded version of Jesus' teaching that at the final judgment, people's destiny will be determined not by their profession of belief, but by their treatment of the marginalized. In one passage Jesus declares that it is not those who say, "Lord, Lord, [that] shall enter into the kingdom of heaven; but he that doeth the will of my Father which is in heaven."[128] In this passage, favored by the liberal/progressive side of the debate, God's final word is commendation for action on behalf of the

---

[127] For discussion of the two wings of this polarity, see Hutchison, *The Modernist Impulse in American Protestantism* and Marsden, *Fundamentalism and American Culture*. Szasz, *The Divided Mind of American Protestantism*, summarizes key issues in the division.

[128] Matt 7:21.

dispossessed—the hungry, thirsty, naked, sick, prisoner, and foreigner. God's judgment to everlasting punishment is for those who neglected to help others in need (Matt 25:37-46). In this text the measure of being a Christian is working to achieve relief of the suffering of others. It is a Christianity understood not so much as belief, but as action focused on the needs of others and characterized by service. This model of Christianity is impossible to conceive apart from responsible relationships with others; it is a social view of salvation.

Protestants have not resolved tension between the "two Christianities." Some Christians combine both aspects of Christian teaching in their lives. Today some evangelicals are committed deeply to lives of service for others.[129] Likewise many people of progressive theological or social persuasions affirm the reality and absolute necessity of life-changing personal conversion to provide commitment to the life of faith.[130] Yet Protestants as a whole have not successfully negotiated a rapprochement of these two versions of Christianity despite a century to work out differences. They have tended to opt for one or the other as their primary identity and tend to think in terms of these two Christianities being incompatible rather than complementary. Rauschenbusch affirmed that both the personal experience of God and the social imperative of the gospel must be heeded if one is to be true to the original message of Jesus' understanding the Kingdom of God.

For some interpreters, Rauschenbusch's views provided balance and a step forward. Rauschenbusch followers emphasize that his position on social issues provides an interpretation of Christianity that recovers the relevance of Christianity to life in the world. For his critics, however, Rauschenbusch's advocacy of social Christianity makes him one of the sources of the division in modern American Protestant Christianity rather than a model for "balanced" Christianity. The balance Rauschenbusch advocated in his own writings has not been translated to the wider Protestant community.

Rauschenbusch always affirmed the importance of personal conversion. He grew up with the notion that the heart of Christianity was the personal conversion experience. This was central to his father's Pietism and to the American revivalist experience, promoted by his own Baptist denomination as much as by any group. Rauschenbusch indicated that he became serious about his religious experience during his teenage years, only after he had rebelled in reaction to the demands of

---

[129] As early as 1947, Carl F. H. Henry appealed to fellow evangelicals to accept their social responsibility in a now famous little book *The Uneasy Conscience of Modern Fundamentalism*. For a more recent discussion of evangelicals' struggle with the social demands of the faith, see Tseng and Furness, "The Reawakening of the Evangelical Social Conscience," 114–25.

[130]The deep, personal faith of leaders of the early stages of Life and Work Conferences is transparent. See the discussion of J. H. Oldham in David Miller, *God at Work: The History and Promise of the Faith and Work Movement*(Oxford: Oxford University Press, 2007) 31, 42-46.

his overly strict minister father.[131] He knew that his reading audience had, for the most part, similarly made their commitment to Christianity through a personal conversion experience, and he was careful to affirm the validity of this foundational religious event in his life. He referred to his own conversion experience as "a very true one...it was of everlasting value to me...it influenced my soul down to the depths."[132] This was his early experience.Rauschenbusch recalled that when he first arrived in New York City, "My idea then was to save souls."[133] His early sermons reflected this language for the next three years.[134] Rauschenbusch admired Dwight L. Moody's revival preaching, and Rauschenbusch collected the sermons of Moody and other successful ministers of his day.[135] He collaborated with Ira Sankey on the German translation of a hymnal.[136] He was firmly grounded where most Baptists began their religious pilgrimage, in the confidence that the critical religious issue in life was the personal conversion experience of the individual Christian. As Stephen Brachlow noted, "He never belittled the importance of a personal experience of conversion in the old revivalistic sense."[137]

The two-tiered view of Christianity is not original with Rauschenbusch. He does not footnote sources, but the idea appears in Holiness preacher William Arthur's *Tongue of Fire* (1856) and in sociologist Richard Ely's *Social Aspects of Christianity* (1889), and he was familiar with these books. Rauschenbusch adopted this position as his own view. Once he came to the view that original Christianity had both personal and social centers, the idea became a permanent fixture in his thought. Henceforth he believed that "the old individualistic style of evangelism...offered only a half-gospel."[138] This was his great new discovery. He sustained this idea during his thirty-year career as a public writer. Throughout his life as a minister and as a professor the idea of the personal and social dimensions of Christianity appear repeatedly.

---

[131] Stackhouse, introduction to *The Righteousness of the Kingdom* by WR, 16.

[132] WR, "The Kingdom of God," 2; cited in Handy, *The Social Gospel in America*, 264–65.

[133] WR, "The Genesis of *Christianity and the Social Crisis*," 51.

[134] See section five of Rauschenbusch's 1886–1890 scrapbook, Rauschenbusch Family Papers. Also see his sermons for this period, box 150, Rauschenbusch Family Papers.

[135] See section five of Rauschenbusch's 1886–1890 scrapbook, Rauschenbusch Family Papers.

[136] In 1889 Rauschenbusch edited and published *Neue Lieder*, a translation into German of Ira Sankey's *Gospel Hymns, No. 5*. In 1890 he published a translation of *Gospel Hymns/1*, and in 1894 *Gospel Hymns/2*. Translations by others were used, but about one-third of the hymns were translated by Rauschenbusch himself (see Hudson, ed., *Walter Rauschenbusch: Selected Writings*, 9, fn. 11).

[137] Brachlow, "Walter Rauschenbusch," 366, 368–71. A typescript of the article is in the NABHC archives item #82. The quote is found on p. 16.

[138] Brachlow, "Walter Rauschenbusch," 18.

Rauschenbusch's earliest biographer, Dores Sharpe, noted that he sought to combine the old religious convictions with the task of making the world just.[139] Rauschenbusch did not like the term "social gospel." For him, there is no other kind. The message of Jesus and the Kingdom always included the social as well as the individual. According to the leading church historian of the recent past, Owen Chadwick the "reverence for individual conscience" was nurtured by Christianity, and conscience "is the most important part of a man, that which forms the root of his character and personality."[140] Rauschenbusch would heartily agree.

Whether Rauschenbusch's position can become a model for Protestants today is an open question. While it is fair to say that Rauschenbusch's own understanding of Christianity included both personal and social dimensions, it is also true that he gave most of his attention to social Christianity. In fact, Rauschenbusch probably wrote ninety-five pages arguing for social Christianity for every five he wrote reaffirming the conversion experience. He was, after all, making an argument, and he believed the first point—individual conversion—had already been secured in Protestant thinking. He wrote as if he needed to over-correct. Also he could be harsh on the traditional position, criticizing it as a selfish interest in nothing but one's own benefit. It is readily apparent why he would be misunderstood since his emphasis was so overwhelmingly weighted toward social Christianity; it was simple for his opponents to discredit him by claiming that he had replaced conversion with social reform. That claim is a distortion, but it was widely successful because, while Rauschenbusch won a following, he also suffered criticism and rejection. As Gary Dorrien observed, "The social gospel belonged to the theological liberals...just as the Fundamentalists claimed."[141] So there are two popular narratives operative in Protestant thinking today that tend to diverge into either rejection or acceptance of the social gospel.[142] By contrast, the Christianity Rauschenbusch envisioned included working for the redemption of individuals *and* also the redemption of the common society shared by individuals. He firmly believed that both together comprised Jesus' thoughts expressed in the idea of the kingdom of God.

Rauschenbusch scholars, a half century after his death, understood his two dimensions of Christianity to be the key foundational notion in Rauschenbusch's thought. In his brilliant introduction to *Christianity and the Social Crisis*, Robert D. Cross wrote that in Rauschenbusch's thinking "the two Christian theses—

---

[139] Sharpe, *Walter Rauschenbusch*, 220–21.

[140] Chadwick, *The Secularization of the European Mind*, 23.

[141] Dorrien, "Thy Kingdom Come," 124.

[142] For an authoritative discussion of the continuation of the Protestant division after World War II, see Wuthnow, "The Great Divide," 133–72.

saving the lost and active religious life—were not antagonistic but complementary."[143] Although theologian Max Stackhouse found many deficiencies in Rauschenbusch's theology, he argued that Rauschenbusch attempted to provide a new social structural framework for thinking about the faith; this insight, said Stackhouse, is what is significant, not whether Rauschenbusch fulfilled his own method.[144] Robert Handy, who edited *The Social Gospel in America,* a substantial selection of writings by Gladden, Ely, and Rauschenbusch, declared that "by the 1940s the social gospel movement had largely disappeared. Yet its major contention has not been forgotten."[145] Handy deftly summarized, "Rauschenbusch's challenge has not yet been fully met. He called for the blending of evangelical concern with social passion."[146] In his account of Rauschenbusch's journey to social Christianity, German scholar Klaus Jaehn similarly noted that Rauschenbusch always insisted on the "double duty of individual and social salvation" but that he never made the mistake of simply replacing personal salvation with the call for social salvation, a mistake made by certain of his successors."[147]

This idea of Rauschenbusch continues to inspire many Christians' vision of the faith. Rauschenbusch's second biographer, Paul Minus, observed in 1988 that Rauschenbusch "more than any other person" [moved] "the churches to a new sense of social mission...that the person concerned with saving souls must also be concerned with changing the economic and social conditions that blight souls."[148] And in 1993 Richard W. Fox observed that "social and individual transformation for Rauschenbusch and Rauschenbusch's Jesus were mutually reinforcing."[149] Rauschenbusch has continued to influence readers in the present generation. Christopher Evans, author of the most recent biography of Rauschenbusch, declared, "My introduction to the social gospel, as a historical topic and as a vital theological legacy, came through seminary courses [where I learned] the social gospel emphasis that united a compelling vision of personal faith with social transformation...."[150] Likewise Thomas Halbrooks described his own experience of reading Rauschenbusch as "a transforming event":

> I had understood [the Bible] to teach of individual sin and salvation.... Rauschenbusch did not deny any of my prior understanding.... He argued that the gospel of salvation was only half a gospel.... I also learned that Rauschenbusch held together both piety and social action. He refused to give up one for the other.

---

[143] Cross, introduction to *Christianity and the Social Gospel*, 1964 ed., xiii.
[144] Stackhouse, introduction to *The Righteousness of the Kingdom*, 43.
[145] Handy, *The Social Gospel in America*, 15.
[146] *Handy, foreword to The Righteousness of the Kingdom, n.p.*
[147] Jaehn, *Rauschenbusch*, 45.
[148] Minus, *Walter Rauschenbusch*, x.
[149] Fox, "The Culture of Liberal Protestant Progressives 1875–1925," 655.
[150] Evans, introduction to *The Social Gospel Today*, ix.

> He viewed them both as necessary for the life of the church.... That encounter with Rauschenbusch changed my perspective forever.[151]

As Rauschenbusch would say, he was striving for an enlarged vision of Christianity.

Rauschenbusch was pained over the war of words regarding his idea. Caricatures abound on both sides of the Protestant divide. Perhaps the best approach to understanding the problem of the individual and the social dimensions of Christianity in Rauschenbusch's thought is to recall his personal experience. He says that he grew by decisive stages as a Christian—first his conversion, second his intellectual liberation, and finally his discovery of the social question. He viewed his Christian experience as development by stages rather than as the product of a single moment or event. In this way he accommodated two key dimensions of religious experience as complementary rather than setting them at odds and settling for one by rejecting the other. His was an inclusive model based on his life experience: in his view, the kingdom of God that Jesus preached envisions both redemption of the individual and redemption of society.

---

[151] Halbrooks, preface to *The Social Gospel Today*, xii–xiv.

CHAPTER 4

THE POPULAR RECEPTION OF RAUSCHENBUSCH'S *CHRISTIANITY AND THE SOCIAL CRISIS*, 1907–1909

Immediately following the submission of his *Christianity and the Social Crisis* manuscript to Macmillan, Rauschenbusch left for a year-long sabbatical in Europe. When he returned to the United States, he was famous. He spoke to several hundred people at the Hotel Astor on the subject "The Church and Social Awakening."[1] He spent the remainder of his career articulating the social gospel rather than writing church history.

Christianity and the Social Crisis was the religious best seller in the United States for three years, 1907–1909, selling more than 50,000 copies.[2] In 1910 when journalist Ray Stannard Baker polled clergy on what recent book or what man had influenced them most, he reported that the responses were a resounding affirmation of Rauschenbusch's message: "By all odds the book most frequently mentioned was *Christianity and the Social Crisis* by Walter Rauschenbusch. No recent religious book perhaps has had a more favorable reception among both church and secular journals, or a wider reading among religious leaders than this."[3] "Rarely," wrote biographer Paul Minus, "had an American seminary professor been so widely known."[4] Rauschenbusch's book had an immediate and profound impact on American church leaders.

Many interpreters have claimed that Baptists have produced effective preachers but no theologians of note who are read beyond their own denomination. If this generalization is true, then Walter Rauschenbusch is a notable exception. He influenced a wide range of Christians beyond Baptist circles, and his

---

[1] "Why Socialism Grows."

[2] Cross, introduction to *Christianity and the Social Crisis* by WR, viii. The *New York Times* reported that there were "9,620 books brought out in America during the year." See "Best Books of 1907."

[3] Baker, *The Spiritual Unrest*, 263.

[4] Minus, *Walter Rauschenbusch*, 75.

ideas have entered the larger Christian heritage.[5] The narrative of American religion now almost always includes Rauschenbusch and the social gospel.[6]

Many indications point to Rauschenbusch's sustained impact on American religious life. In the years following Rauschenbusch's death the reach of his influence extended to such prominent American religious leaders as Reinhold Niebuhr and Martin Luther King, Jr., both of whom sought ways to apply the Christian faith to modern social problems. A centennial edition of the book appeared in 2007, edited by Rauschenbusch's great-grandson, Paul Raushenbush.[7] But what of first impressions and the immediate influence of Rauschenbusch's book during those first three years when sales of his book soared? What did people say about the book? How did his writing affect them? How did *Christianity and the Social Crisis* become an instant best-seller? By what channels did the book gain influence? What levels of society were persuaded by Rauschenbusch, and on the other side, who opposed him and why? In short, what were the dynamics of Rauschenbusch's immediate fame? Reading Rauschenbusch is instructive, and his thought continues to draw the attention of ethicists, historians, theologians, and other academics.[8] But why and how ordinary readers of his day embraced his thought is also important. In Charles Strain's judgment the book "astounded the massive reading public."[9] This chapter explores and analyzes initial popular reactions to the book from a cross section of classes and professions: it is a study of the earliest reception history of this key work in the history of American Christianity.

Fortunately, the Rauschenbusch papers include a splendid collection of letters addressed to Rauschenbusch from 1907–1909[10] and present a collection of the earliest reactions to *Christianity and the Social Crisis*. These letters from individuals (mostly clergy but also some laity) mirror the mood of the earliest readers; as such they are a unique source. They offer the opportunity of evaluating the reception of Rauschenbusch "from below," that is, from average readers as well as from academics. The method followed in this chapter will be to analyze the tes-

---

[5] Dillenberger and Welch, *Protestant Christianity*, has been a widely used introduction to American Protestantism. The authors give the Social Gospel a full chapter and cite Rauschenbusch as the key thinker of the movement.

[6] See Ahlstrom, *A Religious History of the American People*, 800–804; Gaustad and Schmidt, *The Religious History of America*, 242–44; Marty, *Pilgrims in Their Own Land*, 347–55; Richard E. Wentz, *American Religious Traditions*, 342–43; and Lippy, *Introducing American Religion*, 148–49, 202–203.

[7] WR, *Christianity and the Social Crisis in the 21st Century*.

[8] Rauschenbusch's long-term legacy is further developed in the final chapter of this book.

[9] Strain, "Toward a Generic Analysis of a Classic of The Social Gospel," 527.

[10] The extensive collection of letters from the years 1907–1910 is found chiefly in folders box 25, Rauschenbusch Family Papers.

timony of the letters written and the methods used to disseminate his views during the months Rauschenbusch achieved notoriety.[11] The collection contains letters conveying largely favorable comments on *Christianity and the Social Crisis,* but it includes some negative responses as well. Contemporary journals also carried editorial comments and book reviews with evaluations of his work.

Rauschenbusch's Message

As a pastor, Rauschenbusch not only felt the desperate economic distress of workers; he also sought solutions to social problems in the United States. He had met with other reform-minded young ministers to share ideas, publish their views, and influence churches. These ministers read sociology as well as theology, and with their new knowledge they sought to assist the working class by altering public opinion through their sermons and their publications.

The majority of Rauschenbusch's reading audience would be very much like him in their religious background. They would have been brought up on Christianity centered around a personal conversion experience, and their churches would have been content to function in essential isolation from other institutions in American society. Therefore, his claim that the church must respond to ordinary human need was new and arresting for many people. It was this message that drew the attention of readers.[12] Judging from the responses in the letters sent to him about the book, Rauschenbusch was more successful than he dreamed in arousing the conscience of readers to affirm the social responsibility of the churches.

Publishing *Christianity and the Social Crisis* was worrisome for Rauschenbusch because of his use of the word "social." Socialism as practiced in Europe carried connotations of anarchism, atheism, and revolution. In the U.S. many people feared the radical politics and rejection of religion associated with Socialist parties. Rauschenbusch agreed with the broad goal of socialism that society should adopt policies benefitting all of its members, but he rejected atheism and anarchism. Several correspondents later confirmed that many members of their churches were afraid of the word "socialism."[13] Rauschenbusch himself worried about trying to join what he saw as the common goals of socialism and Christianity and therefore labeled his own book "dangerous."[14] One of Rauschenbusch's

[11] Most of the citations, in fact, are derived from an avalanche of letters from 1907, written during the earliest months following publication of *Christianity and the Social Crisis*; readers sent additional reflections periodically during the following three years.

[12] Pitts, "The Personal and the Social Christianity in Rauschenbusch's Thought," 138–60.

[13] See F. C. A. Jones to WR, May 13, 1907, and Frederick I. Bamford to WR, November 1, 1907, box 25, Rauschenbusch Family Papers.

[14] WR, "The Genesis of *Christianity and the Social Crisis,*" 51–53; also cited in Dorrien,

great achievements, therefore, was to open the way for people to begin to think in terms of a moderate Christian Socialism. His basic idea was to place the welfare of the community in the foreground of the church's agenda. Was the church not understood from its earliest history to be a community of love and compassion? Could that sentiment not reach beyond its own membership?

Some authors seemed pleased and relieved that Rauschenbusch used the term "social." Christian Socialist Rufus Weeks offered his opinion that "there is nothing more lamentable in the whole world today than the unnatural hostility between socialism and religion on the continent of Europe."[15] A. J. Huizinga, missionary to India, wrote to Rauschenbusch, "Did you read what Mrs. Peabody says in her book...regarding the impression, the deep impression [your book] made on her husband? He had never conceived a Christian Socialism—had always connected it with demagogues and anarchists."[16] And A. O. Alexander lamented, "Now I am engaged in teaching in the public schools here [in Idaho] preparatory to homesteading land if I find a suitable location. I know that I cannot remain in the pastorate with my socialist views."[17] Alexander was grateful for the book but saddened that he could not serve as a pastor while publicly espousing socialist views. Missionary administrator William E. Hutchison expressed his gratitude to Rauschenbusch and added, "The disappointment to me about the Socialist movement is that most of the influential leaders appear to have been estranged from Christianity, and I fear largely through the fault of the Church. Books like yours will serve to bring together what by nature belong together, sane Socialism and true Christianity."[18]

Rauschenbusch was an irenic person, not disposed to attack others, yet he had an argument to make. He closed his introduction with a clear statement that religion is not intended as our bank account; rather, it is meant for righteousness now.[19] He wanted to apply the Christian faith in concrete ways to everyday experience and "to help the plain people...and to ease the pressure that bears them down."[20] This program would involve the church in social construction of the nation. His message resonated with many readers.

"Thy Kingdom Come: Walter Rauschenbusch, Vida Scudder and the Social(ist) Gospel," *The Making of American Liberal Theology: Idealism, Realism, and Modernity*, 82 and in Minus, *Walter Rauschenbusch*, 158.

[15] Rufus Weeks to WR, September 26, 1907, box 25, Rauschenbusch Family Papers.

[16] A. J. Huizinga to WR, November 28, 1909, box 25, Rauschenbusch Family Papers.

[17] A. O. Alexander to WR, September 9, 1909, box 25, Rauschenbusch Family Papers.

[18] William E. Hutchison to WR, June 28, 1909, box 25, Rauschenbusch Family Papers.

[19] WR, introduction to *Christianity and the Social Crisis*, xxv.

[20] Ibid.

Success of *Christianity and the Social Crisis*: Argument and Style

A major question is why and how the book became so successful so quickly. The letters sent to Rauschenbusch offer important clues regarding his achievement of immediate and notable success and almost invariably indicate that the writer has just read *Christianity and the Social Crisis.* Many writers routinely thank Rauschenbusch for writing the book and praise it as the best book on the subject they have read. Some letter writers are content with expression of these basic sentiments, and many book notices published in journals carry a similar tone and content. Providence, Rhode Island, resident Samuel Bottomley's sentiments are typical: "I want to express my hearty appreciation of *Christianity and the Social Crisis.* I consider it the most valuable contribution toward solving the many social and industrial problems of the world.... It should be placed in the hands of every minister.... The church can never repay the debt it now owes you."[21] Other writers often reflected on how the book's message intersected with their own life experiences. The expression of gratitude is simple, but it seems genuine. Edmund Fontaine, a struggling worker, was receptive to Rauschenbusch's argument because he found Rauschenbusch sympathetic to his own personal condition. He wrote:

> I admire your book *Christianity and the Social Crisis* so very much that I must write to you. It is a piece of real constructive work for social betterment.... Your picture of social conditions is not any too severe for I have been up against it to make a living during my 38 years of hard work. I do expert orchard work, but am a machinist by trade (my deafness kept me from college). I enclose two poems that I think you would like. Yours fraternally, Edmund Fontaine. P.S. I will put a notice of the book in the "Richmond Times-Dispatch."[22]

Fontaine was clearly drawn to Rauschenbusch's argument. Beyond that, he confessed his own struggle as evidence of the economic difficulties for the average worker in American society. How ironic that he mentioned his deafness and limited opportunities because he could not attend college. Rauschenbusch must have been deeply moved; he was proposing a better society for thousands of workers like Edmund Fontaine. Other writers noted with favor the way Rauschenbusch embraced socialism, suggesting this bold move as a reason for the book's success. Rufus Weeks, journalist and socialist, suggested that the book had "created for the Christian Socialism Movement a solid intellectual basis."[23]

But other sympathetic readers despaired of church leaders ever responding to such radical suggestions. Addressing Rauschenbusch as "Comrade," Oakland

---

[21] Samuel Bottomley to WR, December 6, 1907, box 25, Rauschenbusch Family Papers.
[22] Edmund Fontaine to WR, July 16, 1907, box 25, Rauschenbusch Family Papers.
[23] Rufus Weeks to WR, June 4, 1907, box 25, Rauschenbusch Family Papers.

California librarian Frederick Bumford declared that Rauschenbusch had touched his heart and his head deeply. Moreover, Bumford noted that he had been a socialist for twenty years, and for the past ten years he had been trying to win ministers to the socialist cause, but "the battle has been futile."[24] James Mullenbach, superintendent in the Chicago Police Department and a former minister, was also distressed at the failings of the church, which "does not realize it is in the midst of a revolution unparalleled in scope and power."[25] He wrote that the church is hampered by lack of vision among its leaders, class conscious interests in the cities, and conservatism in the country churches. "One fears," Mullenbach concluded, "that the churches will line up for the Established Order rather than against it."[26] As a practical man, dealing with problems of law and order in the streets every day, he hoped that the book might inspire the churches "for right action in the present day struggle for industrial justice and liberty."[27] F. C. A. Jones, a Rochester friend, was dismayed to see "the imperviousness of the religious mind which withstood Jesus in his work" in the first century and similarly resists social Christianity in the present. He declared that the position taken against employing a social analysis and remedy was already well established in some of the churches, and some church leaders refused to even consider the idea of social Christianity. He expressed hope that the laity might listen to the social message even if the clergy did not.[28]

The theological rift that had emerged in American Protestantism during the post-Civil War era was clearly referenced in some of the correspondence. Rev. Alford Wishart from Grand Rapids, Michigan, wrote Rauschenbusch to ask if he knew a young man possessing qualifications to be an efficient assistant. "He must be of the liberal school," Wishart concluded.[29] This pastor wanted an assistant who supported the new theological trends in the church, including a commitment to social Christianity. Obviously, Rauschenbusch did not create the great Protestant division of this era. The rise of biblical criticism, the force of Darwin's argument, and the New Theology that emerged to reckon with these powerful changes had met with strong opposition as well as strong support long before Rauschenbusch became an influential voice in Protestantism.

Other correspondents wrote that for some time they had sensed that the church had a social obligation, but Rauschenbusch was able to articulate for them what had been vague in their minds. Other correspondents wrote that they had

---

[24] Frederick I. Bamford to WR, November 1, 1907, box 25, Rauschenbusch Family Papers.

[25] James Mullenbach to WR, June 28, 1907, box 25, Rauschenbusch Family Papers.

[26] Ibid.

[27] Ibid.

[28] F. C. A. Jones to WR, May 13, 1907, box 25, Rauschenbusch Family Papers.

[29] Alford W. Wishart to WR, May 8, 1907, box 25, Rauschenbusch Family Papers.

been convinced of a view similar to Rauschenbusch's understanding of Christian responsibility to society but had never seen it so clearly and powerfully expressed. A pastor from New Hamilton, Iowa, wrote:

> For about twenty years I have been interested in the social and industrial problems that confront the Western World. I have read a good deal and have been amazed at the progress made during the past fifteen years. I have never read a book that at all compares with *Christianity and the Social Crisis* in the clear. .way in which it presents the whole matter in history.... Your discussion of the "right to work"...is the best that I have seen tho' Mrs. Jane Addams in her *Democracy and Social Ethics* puts up much the same plea.[30]

Clearly this minister had been thinking along lines similar to those articulated in *Christianity and the Social Crisis*, but Rauschenbusch cogently argued the urgent need of the church to embrace a social perspective, and his words resonated with this pastor. From Connecticut, Hartford theological student Albert Williams wrote that he was "in reaction to his most individualistic religious environment" and that he previously "had Rauschenbusch's social idea of Christianity, but feebly formulated and expressed."[31] Now it had become clear to him. And layman John Parish described his similar reflections on the social dimensions of Christian responsibility:

> In my untutored way I have been groping along a course similar to that so clearly and logically defined in your great work, saddened by the conviction that neither Church nor State nor industrial system were doing what they could to banish poverty...but feeling also that there was a true religion which required only a faithful priesthood...to bring about the hoped for change in our social systems—which is really the Kingdom of God on earth.... I feel that we have all the materials in hand but are too sodden in greed and pride to go about the building of his Kingdom as we should.[32]

In a similar vein the pastor of the First Baptist Church, Lewiston, Maine, Herbert Bacon Hutchins, wrote, "In a measure I have always held to the ideas here proclaimed...."[33] Here is yet another excellent example of a pastor who already held social views of Christianity though not articulated with the precision and passion for Rauschenbusch. Hutchins's sentiments were commonly expressed by correspondents. Many pastors indicated that they had long felt a responsibility

[30] Unknown (from New Hampton, IA) to WR (the last page is missing), December 30, 1907, box 25, Rauschenbusch Family Papers.

[31] Albert R. Williams to WR, November 4, 1907, box 25, Rauschenbusch Family Papers.

[32] John Parish to WR, October 14, 1907, box 25, Rauschenbusch Family Papers.

[33] Herbert Bacon Hutchins to WR, November 26, 1907, box 25, Rauschenbusch Family Papers.

of service to society that Rauschenbusch had now so clearly and persuasively articulated and legitimated for them. Although other pioneers such as Washington Gladden had already advocated social Christianity, for clarity and force of argument Rauschenbusch's argument was unlike anything readers had ever seen before. Rauschenbusch's persuasive argument and terse style of expression helped clarify the social problem and convince many readers of the truth of the idea of the church's responsibility for society beyond the walls of the churches.

Some older established religion professors offered broad and somewhat bland descriptions of Rauschenbusch's work. Already influential because of his widely used *An Outline of Christian Theology* (1898), Baptist theologian William Newton Clarke noted that the book was a "clear, straightforward, trustworthy view of great realities...a most valuable contribution to the life of the age."[34] Augustus H. Strong, president of Rochester Theological Seminary where Rauschenbusch taught, thought the book would be as influential as Henry George's *Progress and Poverty*.[35] Church historian Albert H. Newman was more pragmatic in his evaluation: he wrote that Rauschenbusch's "semi-communistic teachings are not at all likely to be adopted," but his book should exert "a strong and wholesome influence on Christian readers...[regarding] stewardship in the use of property."[36] Protestant leader Josiah Strong was also specific, if unrealistic, in wishing for the book that "it might be read by every professing Christian who occupies the individualistic point of view."[37] Pioneer of the social gospel Washington Gladden paid a high tribute to Rauschenbusch in person at a joint meeting of Baptist and Congregationalist leaders in 1908. In his address Gladden quoted from *Christianity and the Social Crisis* and described it as an "epoch-making book."[38] This remark was gratifying to Rauschenbusch, who wrote appreciatively to Gladden on December 2, 1908.[39] Four years after the book's publication, John Haynes Holmes wrote one of the most frequently quoted assessments of *Christianity and the Social Crisis*: "Into this book has gone the learning of the scholar, the vision of

---

[34] William Newton Clarke to WR, December 20, 1907, box 25, Rauschenbusch Family Papers.

[35] Augustus H. Strong to WR, June 29, 1907, box 25, Rauschenbusch Family Papers.

[36] A. H. Newman to WR, May 6, 1907, box 25, Rauschenbusch Family Papers.

[37] Josiah Strong to WR, December 13, 1907, box 25, Rauschenbusch Family Papers.

[38] Handy, *The Socialist Gospel in America*, 259.

[39] Ibid., fn.18. The letter reads, in part, "It has been a great satisfaction to meet you thus, and to stand by your side for an hour, for, as I said at the meeting, to me you are one of the veterans who have made it easier for us of the next generation to see our way and to get a hearing. You have done a noble day's work and have lived to see the reapers going out to the harvest which you helped to sow."

the poet, and the passion of the prophet. It is radical without bitterness, uncompromising without fanaticism. It is the first gospel of the New Dispensation."[40] Rauschenbusch's dean, William Arnold Stevens, realized that Rauschenbusch had addressed the conscience of Christians with a formidable argument. He wrote, "You have certainly brought together important facts, and one is made to ask himself, 'What can I do?' Thousands of readers will be forced, as I have been, into serious thought—on conditions now existing in the congested sections of our great cities."[41]

Rauschenbusch's key idea—that the church has a social dimension and responsibility—struck deeply into the religious consciousness of his day. In 1909 John Erickson, a Senate clerk, wrote that Rauschenbusch had produced "a true interpretation of Christianity as a social religion."[42] Moreover, Rauschenbusch was addressing a highly relevant issue in American society and won sympathy for his position beyond the churches. Leighton Williams, reflecting on Rauschenbusch's new book, reported that "our views on economic questions were not original with us—but we found in them an eternal validity as verified for us by this inner light."[43] Although the economic questions were not new, connecting them with the church for a solution was a new challenge for many. Economic problems were obvious. Rauschenbusch wanted the church to be part of the solution to the nation's pressing problems, and some readers seized on his proposal for connecting church and economics. The problem was that Rauschenbusch's agenda did not offer specific steps to alter the economic structure.

All sorts of middle-class people resonated with Rauschenbusch's call to action—students, laymen, women, ministers, and church administrators. Notably missing (with a few exceptions) are letters from the wealthy, the poor, and the very working-class Rauschenbusch proposed to help, which is already a telling commentary. The poor may not have had access to the book, the leisure time to read, or resources of money, time, and confidence to respond. In his New York publishing experience he likewise had very little response. The social gospel appealed to members of the middle class. The churches did not ultimately succeed in changing the economy. Instead, the political reforms of the Progressives led by Theodore Roosevelt and others eventually produced the forty-hour work-week, the universal vote, the end to child labor, and other major reforms.[44] But the churches were made conscious of their social and economic responsibilities by

[40] Cited by Henry B. Robins on p. 2 of "Walter Rauschenbusch: A Prophet of the New Social Order," typescript, box 39, Rauschenbusch Family Papers.

[41] William Arnold Stevens to WR, July 2, 1907, box 25, Rauschenbusch Family Papers.

[42] John Erickson to WR, November 26, 1909, box 25, Rauschenbusch Family Papers.

[43] Williams, "The Reign of the New Humanity," *The Kingdom* (December 1907) np., cited in Hudson, ed., *Walter Rauschenbusch: Selected Writings*, 37-38.

[44] For an assessment of the Progressives, see McGerr, *A Fierce Discontent.*

Rauschenbusch's book. He hoped that they would at least serve as the conscience of the nation regarding economic injustice issues, and many accepted this role. Their awakened consciences did not result in a Christian Socialist party with block voting as it did in several European countries, but the Federal Council of Churches actually adopted the social responsibility of the churches as part of its agenda. Rauschenbusch's writing raised consciousness of the economic issue without offering a concrete solution.

Why then was Rauschenbusch's book successful? In the end, Rauschenbusch's genius is that he successfully reformulated and restated the Christian message for his day. The first and most important answer to this question is found in the content of his message. His argument rang true. Rochester University President John M. Dana wrote that "for moral courage and earnestness, for sustained power, clearness and unity of treatment as well as for breadth of study it easily surpasses any book in its field which I am familiar with."[45] Dana called to mind Walt Whitman's phrase contrasting a mere book with one that "touches" others. He continued, "So with your book to me it thrills with the personal magnetism of its author, and again and again in reading it I was forced to remark this living force of moral and spiritual thought which in its heights seemed prophetic indeed."[46] Dana's compliments were numerous, but the bottom line was that the book moved and persuaded him personally.

When in 1938 Dores Sharpe, Rauschenbusch's first biographer, asked Rauschenbusch's daughter, Winifred, why the book succeeded, she observed, "The way it coincided with the panic of 1907...is of course significant."[47] Here Winifred was referring to a serious economic depression which occurred during the first decade of the century. Moreover, she said that the time of writing was "a period in which the illusion of progress had not yet been destroyed." Rauschenbusch had been optimistic about the growth of the Kingdom, but World War I destroyed his hopeful outlook. Moreover, in 1938, Winifred was writing almost a decade into the worst depression of the nation's history."[48] Winifred Rauschenbusch thus pointed out economic factors and the cultural outlook of the era that might have contributed to the rapid favorable reception of the volume.[49] Making this assessment thirty-one years later and with the advantage of historical perspective, she took into full account external social factors that may have affected the reception as well as Rauschenbusch's argument. But her "illusion of progress" phrase suggests that she viewed his influence as short-lived.

---

[45] John M. Dana to WR, July 14, 1907, box 25, Rauschenbusch Family Papers.

[46] Ibid.

[47] Winifred [Rauschenbusch] Rorty to Dores Sharpe, December 17, 1938, box 50, Rauschenbusch Family Papers.

[48] Ibid.

[49] Ibid.

Rauschenbusch himself was asked in 1918 to explain the overwhelming response to *Christianity and the Social Crisis*. He observed that "the social movement got hold of me just as the social awakening was getting hold of the country. The book came out of a psychological moment and was taken as an expression of what thousands were feeling."[50] His view corresponds to the testimony of his early correspondents. He labeled the simultaneous effect of converging influences "a psychological moment." Robert Handy also noted that the publication was well-timed: "Coming at a time when the progressive movement was rising in popularity and affecting national legislation, it touched a public which recognized the need for social change. It came in a period when liberal theology was winning a substantial following in many churches."[51]

In the next generation, notable pastor Harry Emerson Fosdick wrote that the book "struck home so poignantly on the intelligence and conscience...that it ushered in a new era in Christian thought and action."[52] Charles Strain argued that Rauschenbusch's work was profoundly effective because it exposed two crises. The economy produced grinding poverty, which touched the conscience of many people. Moreover, the church was in crisis because it had failed to respond to the social crisis. Individualized religion marginalized religion from the center of the culture. The church needed to take on social responsibility, and Rauschenbusch had pointed the way.[53] Rauschenbusch was able through the power of his argument to convert many readers to a revolutionary new conception of Christianity. Understanding the American church of this era is impossible without reference to the social gospel. The testimony of the letters reveals that the first and most important reason for the book's success was that ministers felt and accepted the truth and relevance of its message. Rauschenbusch spoke to the consciences of readers.

The second answer to the "why" of Rauschenbusch's success lies in the style of his writing, which in turn was a reflection of his temperament—irenic toward other people but combative toward social injustice. His reception rate was high, in no little part, because of the way he wrote. Strong noted that "the sympathetic spirit of the book is so manifest that its occasional chivalry [which the wealthy Strong defined as siding with the underdog!] is easily pardoned."[54] Rochester resident William Arnold Stevens wrote, "Your kindness disarms criticism. Even those obstructionists, the exegetes and theologians, do not feel much worse for

---

[50] WR, "The Genesis of *Christianity and the Social Crisis*," 53; also quoted in Evans, *The Kingdom Is Always but Coming*, 196.

[51] Handy, *The Social Gospel in America*, 258.

[52] Fosdick, introduction to *A Rauschenbusch Reader*, xiii.

[53] Strain, "Toward a Generic Analysis," 529, 535–46.

[54] Augustus H. Strong to WR, June 29, 1907, box 25, Rauschenbusch Family Papers.

their punishing...so much good nature [is felt]."[55] William H. Boocock, pastor of the First Reformed Church in Bayonne, New Jersey, reported that for years he had been deeply interested in the Christian Socialist movement, and he had apparently been combative in his defense of socialist views. After reading Rauschenbusch and sensing the tone of his approach to persuasion, Boocock wrote to Rauschenbusch, saying that he had resolved henceforth to state his views with more charity to those who did not agree with him on the social dimensions of Christianity. "In my enthusiasm I have not always been discreet. I resolve to be more cautious and tactful," he wrote.[56] Rauschenbusch did not name a single opponent by name in his book; he let the argument speak for itself. Moreover, the tone he conveyed was not harsh and judgmental, but rather his design was to construct an argument that would persuade the conscience of his readers.

Rauschenbusch was charitable, but he communicated his conviction with clarity and force. Many writers were moved by the passion that pervades his writing. Georgia Kendrick, in a letter to A. H. Strong, claimed that Rauschenbusch's book "fairly tingles with vitality and has besides that sympathetic quality which only the very best books have and through which they are able to communicate to their readers not only their ideas but also their fire."[57] "Tingle," "vitality," "fire"; she obviously felt the passion of the writer for his subject. As Paul Minus wrote, Rauschenbusch's message was "delivered with verve uncommon for scholars."[58] Columbia historian Robert Cross, himself a masterful writer, noted that Rauschenbusch had created "a persuasive book" and pointed out the salient characteristics of his writing style:

> [E]ach chapter is a model of clarity put together with the skills of a platform orator. Rauschenbusch wrote in short pithy sentences; when qualifications were necessary, he made them in subsequent sentences, equally terse. He had a remarkable command of metaphor.... He had a nice taste for irony, especially the ironic epigram with which to climax an extended paragraph. The book also fitted into the familiar tradition of clerical jeremiads.... Rauschenbusch made lay acceptance easier, furthermore, by refusing to denounce the villains of the social crisis; he named no names. He wanted his book to be "constructive," and was later to take pride in the fact that even his critics found no hate in it.[59]

Rauschenbusch conveyed deep passion because the subject mattered so much to

---

[55] William Arnold Stevens to WR, July 2, 1907, box 25, Rauschenbusch Family Papers.

[56] William H. Boocock to WR, November 9, 1907, box 25, Rauschenbusch Family Papers.

[57] Georgia A. Kendrick to A. H. Strong, July 18, 1907, box 25, Rauschenbusch Family Papers.

[58] Minus, *Walter Rauschenbusch*, 163.

[59] Cross, introduction to *Christianity and the Social Crisis*, 1964 ed., xvii–xviii.

him.

The fact that Rauschenbusch had written much of this material over a decade earlier and had published selected ideas of his thinking in earlier contexts—especially to the audiences of the Brotherhood of the Kingdom and the Baptist Congress—doubtless gave him the advantage of full command of the message he sought to communicate. In the end, he relied on Scripture, church history, theology, and sociology to create a fervent call for the church to assist in creating a more just society. Minister Charles W. Briggs declared in his letter to Rauschenbusch, "I wish I could tell you how it [the book] has taken hold of my soul and changed my preaching to my people here, and changed my very thinking, and my very self.... The inspiration your book brings to me is more than can be measured...."[60] The comments in this and many other letters suggest that Rauschenbusch's writing brought about a kind of second conversion for many readers—to Social Christianity. If the first reason for Rauschenbusch's success was his message, the second reason was the way he presented it.

People from all over the United States continued to write to Rauschenbusch. Almost two years after publication, Herbert Cash, pastor of the Friends Church in Paonia, Colorado, wrote, "Tho a stranger may I thank you warmly for the great good your book *Christianity and the Social Crisis* has done for me? It has brought a great change into my life as a minister and given me a larger vision...."[61] Oliver C. Horsman, pastor of First Baptist Church, Morristown, New Jersey, was persuaded by reading the argument: "Allow me to thank you out of the fullness of my heart for your book *Christianity and the Social Crisis*, the last page of which I have just turned. Within twelve months I have caught the social vision. It has come to me like a breath of inspiration."[62] Rauschenbusch's friend Octavia Munger expressed her wish for a smaller version of the book—a primer that would more easily reach "the common people."[63] J.B. Gay, a poor farmer, wrote to Rauschenbusch, asking him to write a brief cheaper version that he could share with his friends.[64] Munger and Gay eventually had their wishes fulfilled. In 1910 Rauschenbusch reported to Strong, "A new edition of *Christianity and the Social Crisis* has just been published at fifty cents, in order to reach a different class of readers."[65] Another writer remarked how useful a German translation would be.[66] The book evidently carried its own power to the hearts of many readers. Ample evidence in the letters exists to suggest that simply reading the book was sufficient

[60] Charles W. Briggs to WR, January 22, 1908, box 25, Rauschenbusch Family Papers.
[61] Herbert T. Cash to WR, October 27, 1908, box 25, Rauschenbusch Family Papers.
[62] Oliver C. Horsman to WR, n.d., box 25, Rauschenbusch Family Papers.
[63] Octavia Munger to WR, October 3, 1907, box 25, Rauschenbusch Family Papers.
[64] J. B. Gay to WR, December 17, 1909, box 25, Rauschenbusch Family Papers.
[65] WR to A. H. Strong, April 25, 1911, box 39, Rauschenbusch Family Papers.
[66] Rufus W. Weeks to WR, September 26, 1907, box 25, Rauschenbusch Family Papers.

to change the views of his readers. Harry Emerson Fosdick, perhaps the most successful pastoral author of his generation, saw clearly that "it was through his books [that Rauschenbusch] most influentially reached the churches."[67] But people had to have access to the book. In order to achieve commercial success, publishers had created effective distribution systems. Letters came to Rauschenbusch from all over the country. The institution of the press and the strategies of publishers for advertising, distributing, and selling are also part of the story of Rauschenbusch's success.

Success of *Christianity and the Social Crisis*: The Press and Dissemination Strategies

Rauschenbusch had something to say and said it well. But additional steps were required for successful dissemination of his ideas. The letters clearly reveal the enormous power of print media. Rauschenbusch's publisher, Macmillan, was a sophisticated book company with solid knowledge of the book trade. Book distribution combined with the reading culture of ministers was a third reason for Rauschenbusch's success. Not surprising are the notes of congratulations to Rauschenbusch from acquaintances in Rochester and from academic colleagues in other cities. But judging from the letters, Rauschenbusch's greatest impact was on individual ministers across the United States. They experienced the force of his argument through reading the book. He heard from many people who had never met him, conveying their indebtedness to him. This wide-reaching impact simply could not have happened without the assistance of the power of the press to disseminate his views.

In terms of general church history, the influence of the press is most commonly cited for its role in the success of the Protestant Reformations of the sixteenth century.[68] The mass media is so pervasive in Western culture today that its cultural influence can easily be overlooked. The rate for reprinting the 50,000 copies of the book was remarkable. The flyleaf of the 1912 edition of *Christianity and the Social Crisis* records that the book was printed in March 1907, and reprinted in October and November 1907; April, September, and December 1908; December 1909; January and June 1910; January, March, May, and November 1911; February and March 1912.[69] Not only did the publishers have effective distribution systems, they could also measure demand and keep up with production (hence the fifteen printings in five years).

Dissemination of ideas is difficult to track and more difficult to measure, yet

---

[67] Fosdick, introduction to *A Rauschenbusch Reader*, xviii.
[68] See Eisenstein, *The Printing Press as an Agent of Change*.
[69] WR, *Christianity and the Social Crisis*, 1912 ed., flyleaf.

there is evidence of the effectiveness of additional methods of spreading Rauschenbusch's influence beyond the sheer act of publishing and distributing *Christianity and the Social Crisis*. The earliest letters to Rauschenbusch indicate that ministers were giving reports on the book at associational meetings, which were regularly scheduled gatherings of ministers for their mutual benefit, and a long-established structure for networking. Henry Moehlman, Rauschenbusch's colleague in church history at Rochester, reported that "various ministerial associations are having papers [presented on the book]."[70] In this way pastors in some regions rapidly became aware of the book, and this information doubtless spurred additional purchases. In a printed program, the Woburn Association of Congregational Ministers announced on October 14, 1907, a seminar on Rauschenbusch's *Christianity and the Social Crisis* for their November 19 meeting, and they gave specific reading instructions to prepare for the meeting.[71] Other letters indicate that individual churches had established study clubs or societies in which they conducted studies of Rauschenbusch's book across a period of several weeks. These sessions were often led by the minister. Rochester Dean J. W. A. Stewart and Chicago churchman John Wollett both reported this kind of activity in the local churches.[72] Some pastors used the book as the basis for a series of sermons, usually for their Sunday evening or midweek services. Rauschenbusch was receiving letters from ministers of virtually all of the major Protestant denominations and from Maine to California. It was a phenomenal response. Thus the national dissemination was complemented by organizational promotion of reading and studying the book at the local level.

The book also began immediately to influence academic institutions. Student Beryl Ewald wrote to Rauschenbusch that "Professor [Francis] Peabody has brought [your book] to class and called it an important contribution to the general subject of Christian Ethics and Modern Life. He said it was a superior treatment of the subject.... Your book has been presented in a very favorable light to Harvard students."[73] Ewald did not claim to have read the book, and apparently had not, but for him it was enough that his professor had endorsed it. In December 1909, Walter Fiske, acting dean of Oberlin Theological Seminary in Ohio, wrote Rauschenbusch that "the remarkable book on the Social Crisis has made a deep impression here as elsewhere. I was obliged to purchase for our library this fall

---

[70] Conrad Henry Moehlman to WR, July 8, 1907, box 25, Rauschenbusch Family Papers.

[71] B. Alfred Dumm to WR, November 13, 1907, enclosing a program of the Woburn Association (of Congregational Ministers), announcing the upcoming meeting on November 19 at 2:00 p.m. where a seminar on *Christianity and the Social Crisis* would be held (box 25, Rauschenbusch Family Papers).

[72] J. W. A. Stewart to WR, April 29, 1907, and John Wollett to WR, September 27, 1907, box 25, Rauschenbusch Family Papers.

[73] Beryl Ewald to WR, May 1, 1907, box 25, Rauschenbusch Family Papers.

three additional copies, so great was the demand for it."[74] Vida Scudder, a leading progressive professor of religion at Wellesley, was even more upbeat. She strongly supported the social gospel: she wrote to Rauschenbusch indicating that she had "long been looking forward to the privilege [of meeting him], and I want to thank you from the bottom of my heart for your book."[75] She said that she was reading it with a club of college girls and others as well: "It is helping to put socialism where it belongs as no other book does. Socialism is a deeper passion to me than in the old...days. I'm sure it is to you!"[76] The book was being read among privileged college students, yet another category of readers.

Another influence on the broad dissemination of Rauschenbusch's work was publicity. Printed book reviews and reports of Rauschenbusch's public speeches in the months after the book appeared provided yet another source for stimulating dissemination of the book and its message. These reports were most commonly found in denominational magazines and journals.[77] Reports also reached larger audiences in more general non-denominational publications. One of the more famous of these reports came in 1909 from the already mentioned publication by Ray Stannard Baker, in which he asked ministers what book had influenced them most, and they overwhelmingly cited *Christianity and the Social Crisis.*[78] Within six months or so of publication, Rufus Weeks, *Christian Socialist* editor, encouraged Rauschenbusch to write articles for publications such as *The Independent* and *The Outlook*; he also said that he would then publish them in *The Christian Socialist.* "Anything," he said, "to keep your name in print. We are desired to show the wisdom of the serpent, you know."[79] Weeks's strategy was for Rauschenbusch to keep publishing articles on the social gospel. Countless other editors asked for submissions to their journals in following years.[80] Another factor evident in the popular reception of Rauschenbusch then was the support and promotion of established institutions: ministerial associations, church study groups, universities, and religious journals all contributed to the growing awareness and dissemination of the book.

---

[74] Walter Fiske to WR, December 13, 1909, box 25, Rauschenbusch Family Papers.

[75] Vida Scudder to WR. Rauschenbusch recorded that Scudder's note was written at the luncheon of the Twentieth Century Club, Boston, November 28, 1908, in the 1894–1908 scrapbook.

[76] Ibid.

[77] See, for example, "Christianity and the Social Crisis," *The Watchman* 89/25 (June 20, 1907): 7; "Christianity and the Social Crisis," *The Watchman* 90/6 (February 6, 1908): 7; "The Social Problem," *The Examiner* 85/29 (July 18, 1907): 902.

[78] Baker, *The Spiritual Unrest*, 263.

[79] Rufus Weeks to WR, September 26, 1907, box 25, Rauschenbusch Family Papers.

[80] See John Phillips (*The American Magazine*) to WR, February 8, 1908, box 25, Rauschenbusch Family Papers.

Rauschenbusch did hear from some ordinary laborers and people in financial straits. But the letters do not provide much evidence from lower-class American factory workers. Instead, the letters indicate that the beneficiaries of Rauschenbusch's book were primarily ministers and other religious leaders, and that this was the social class most influenced by Rauschenbusch's vision. Although aimed at assisting the lower class, the actual audience hearing the social gospel was middle-class citizens who populated American Protestant churches.

Immediate Outcomes

Many outcomes of this rapid reception of social Christianity may be identified. Two are most obvious: (1) controversy over the social message and (2) the establishment of national institutional support for social Christianity. Due to the massive publicity of the book, these outcomes occurred quickly.

Rauschenbusch's academic friends occasionally offered critiques of his work. For example, Augustus Strong thought Rauschenbusch "systematically took the side of the underdog."[81] W. R. L. Smith, pastor of Second Baptist Church, Richmond, Virginia, expressed his general agreement with the book, while at the same time he noted that "just how common land tenure and juster distribution of property, and ownership of tools can be brought about you fail to indicate except in a vague and general fashion."[82] Rauschenbusch was an academic; he was not practical enough for Smith. In the *New York Times* Saturday Review of Books, Joseph O'Connor published a long and generally supportive review of the book.[83] However, he also had a serious reservation about Rauschenbusch's failure to propose specific solutions to economic problems. He noted that socialism is an old ideal, but it had not worked because people are selfish, not altruistic. Here the criticism is pragmatic rather than theological: how can the changes Rauschenbusch proposes be implemented? Rauschenbusch thought that if Christians acted in a Christian manner, they would support the causes he identified, such as a living wage, a forty-hour work week, public ownership of utilities, and so forth. He painted a picture of a more just America, but he had no mechanism for bringing about actual changes. Many people raised the question, and Rauschenbusch later wrote another book to address this problem. Friendly correspondents also reported criticisms they had heard. J. W. A. Stewart, Rochester University dean, wrote to Rauschenbusch that he had "not heard of any hostility being excited by [the book], though I believe that some of the well-to-do people in the First Presbyterian Church did not wholly approve of it."[84] F. C. A. Jones had heard the

---

[81] Augustus Strong to WR, June 29, 1907, box 25, Rauschenbusch Family Papers.

[82] W. R. L. Smith to WR, July 22, 1907, box 25, Rauschenbusch Family Papers.

[83] O'Connor, "The Spirit of Discontent."

[84] J. W. A. Stewart to WR, October 10, 1907, box 25, Rauschenbusch Family Papers.

already familiar complaint that "Christ was no social reformer" and social conditions can only by changed by saving souls.[85] Criticism grew sharper in later years. In 1911, I. M. Haldeman, pastor of First Baptist Church, New York City, published *Professor Rauschenbusch's Christianity and the Social Crisis,* which attacked Rauschenbusch's use of Scripture, his view of the kingdom of God, his doctrine of Christ, and his use of sociology.[86] Haldeman concluded, "However skillfully Professor Rauschenbusch may have presented the case for Christian socialism, a faithful analysis of his book will show that it is composed of modified German rationalism (echoes of Wellhausen and Harnack), twentieth century humanitarianism, and the doctrine of a Christ and a Church unknown to Paul."[87] Haldeman represents an early thorough rejection of the social gospel and all of the arguments Rauschenbusch brought to bear to promote it. Haldeman rejected "adoption of the New Theology and a social gospel."[88]

Protestantism was dividing into two theological camps before Rauschenbusch's publication. The attitude people adopted toward the social gospel provided one more marker of one's Protestant identity. The attacks of Haldeman and others pained Rauschenbusch.[89] He did not want people to choose between two types of Protestant Christianity but hoped readers would accept his belief that Christianity rightly understood included both personal and social Christian dimensions of salvation.[90] A short time before his death Rauschenbusch wrote, "My life has been physically very lonely and often beset by the consciousness of conservative antagonism. I have been upheld by the comfort of God."[91] He was saddened by personal attacks on his views.

Whereas some Christians criticized Rauschenbusch's social Christianity, others embraced it and created organizations to assure that social issues received attention of the church in the future. In December 1907, Methodist clergymen established the Methodist Federation for Social Service. This group adopted a social creed that called for "justice for all men…arbitration in industrial dissensions…abolition of child labor…reduction of hours of labor…living wage…and recognition of the Golden Rule."[92] In the following year, 1908, the Methodist

[85] F. C. A. Jones to WR, May 13, 1907, box 25, Rauschenbusch Family Papers.

[86] Haldeman, *Professor Rauschenbusch's Christianity and the Social Crisis.*

[87] Ibid., 42.

[88] Ibid.

[89] Barnes, "Walter Rauschenbusch—His Personal Testimony," 985.

[90] "There are two great entities in human life—the human soul and the human race—and Christianity was meant to save both" (WR, *Christianity and the Social Crisis*, 367).

[91] Barnes, "Walter Rauschenbusch—His Personal Testimony," 985. This statement emphasized his own personal conversion experience and its deep meaning throughout his life. For him it was fully compatible with social Christianity.

[92] Cracknell and White, *An Introduction to World Methodism*, 234.

Episcopal Church adopted the social creed, which historians of Methodism judged to be one of the "crowning achievements" of the denomination.[93] Methodism became the first major denomination to commit itself to support many of the goals of social Christianity; also in 1908 Rauschenbusch was present in Philadelphia when the Federal Council of Churches in Christ "incorporated in its charter a revised version of the Methodist social creed."[94] These events meant that the idea and agenda of social Christianity now had institutional homes. Many additional individual denominations would soon adopt similar organizational structures dedicated to applying Christian principles toward the achievement of a more just society. This was a new departure for American Protestant Christians. The obvious immediate outcome of Rauschenbusch's proposals was a division of opinions, but within one year of the publication of *Christianity and the Social Crisis,* the idea was accepted as part of the framework for future Christian engagement with the nation by the nation's largest Protestant denomination.

Dorrien noted that Rauschenbusch's book converted thousands of pastors, academics, and activists to the social gospel.[95] Relying on letters written to Rauschenbusch chiefly in 1907, it is possible to discover something of the immediate and remarkable popular reception of Rauschenbusch's first major book. He would spend the remaining eleven years of his life spelling out the implications of *Christianity and the Social Crisis.*

Christianity and the Social Crisis made an impact because it offered a convincing and readable understanding of the Christian faith as a social religion. Moreover, it offered ways for ministers to feel a new sense of relevance for their ministry through their attempts to alleviate suffering in their communities and envision a better social order in American society. Many were sympathetic with ministry to the poor; now they had biblical and theological justification for making social reconstruction part of their agenda as pastors. Rauschenbusch offered a new and significant interpretation of Christianity that was accepted by a substantial portion of his generation and which has endured for more than a century. He seems to have probed Christian conscience regarding moral obligation, and he changed many people's understanding of the Christian faith. Rauschenbusch generated motivation to act on his insights regarding the social responsibility of the churches. The accessible and passionate argument of the book made it a persuasive influence for many early readers. The book's compelling presentation has continued to carry conviction to readers in the generations following. Rauschenbusch's compassionate argument calling the church to work for the salvation for society as well as for the individual called for action.

---

[93] Richey, Rowe and Schmidt, eds., *The Methodist Experience in America*, 1:302.
[94] Evans, *The Kingdom Is Always but Coming*, 196.
[95] Dorrien, *Soul in Society*, 41.

The power of the book trade coupled with ministerial reading culture should not be overlooked. These factors represent a pragmatic dimension of the question of the book's success. Many of the book's convinced readers had never heard of Rauschenbusch and would never meet him. Yet the book itself gave them new vision, courage, and an added reason to continue their vocation in ministry. Simply reading this widely disseminated book persuaded many readers that Rauschenbusch's interpretation of Christianity was correct.

The power of print to carry ideas to remote cities and towns is also part of the story. For the reception of Rauschenbusch to succeed as quickly as it did, disseminators needed effective networking and publicity. The churches and associations of ministers promoted knowledge of the program of the social gospel. University professors did their part in informing students. The religious press also was a significant carrier of information. The evidence of the letters shows that a variety of factors were effective agents in the reception of social Christianity during the years immediately following publication of *Christianity and the Social Crisis*. Also significant for the longer term were institutions committed to perpetuating the goals of the social gospel. The idea spread from the Methodists and the Federal Council of Churches and prompted many other denominations to create agencies to work for social justice. Despite criticism of the social gospel from conservative quarters, leaders of major denominations in what came to be called the liberal mainstream believed they could no longer ignore the social obligations of the church. All of these factors came together in contributing to Rauschenbusch's meteoric rise to prominence. The presentation of the message was critical, and so were the dynamics of reception of new ideas. In 1907 and the months following many ministers were prompted to learn more about why and how the church should engage in the world. The message of the social gospel was finding a stronger voice—thanks in large part to the favorable assessment of *Christianity and the Social Crisis* written by this brilliant and dedicated Baptist minister and professor. He had altered the perception of Christianity.

Rauschenbusch had developed the major idea of his life as a young pastor. As a professor he took the opportunity to publish his argument, and he was surprised at the response he received. His conviction that Jesus taught social Christianity was his great insight. This idea affected everything in his life. But he was also more than a literary advocate of social Christianity. We turn next to explore salient dimensions of his vocational life and his contribution to each of them.

PART 2

RAUSCHENBUSCH'S PUBLIC IDENTITIES

Rauschenbusch assumed several identities and leadership roles during his lifetime. He was a pastor, a Baptist leader, a professor of church history, and a public Christian spokesman. In each role he made constructive contributions to American religious life. His advocacy of the social gospel so overshadowed his other work in the minds of later generations that his multiple other contributions have been neglected. They also deserve to be remembered.

Rauschenbusch began his professional work as a full-time minister in New York City. He reflected deeply on the task of the minister, especially in the ordination sermons he preached, and he offered guidance to his readers regarding the education of ministers and principles of ministry. The majority of his congregation appreciated his work, but his ministry was not without conflict. Not everyone wanted to follow the young pastor's lead, particularly on some of his progressive new social ideas. Rauschenbusch's sermons provide a record of his public ministry. They are splendid examples of clarity in organization, biblical exposition, and practical application to life. The sermons are by no means limited to social gospel themes. He addressed a broad range of topics reaching from the meaning of Easter to the imperative of missions and the necessity of temperance. Rauschenbusch also taught a Sunday school class and, recognizing the importance of assisting other teachers, he contracted to write weekly Sunday school lessons throughout much of 1892 for *The Inquirer*, a Baptist publication. To preaching and teaching tasks Rauschenbusch added extensive reading and writing—so much so that he may be viewed as a model of a scholar-pastor. As a pastor he sustained strong commitments both to serving people and to articulating his ideas.

Second, Rauschenbusch embraced his Baptist identity and contributed significantly to his Baptist denomination. He served his own German Baptist congregation and saw it grow in a difficult environment, but it was chiefly through his public speaking and his writing that he influenced other Baptists of the day. He engaged in current debates over issues that arose in the churches of New York City and in the denomination at large. He did not hesitate to offer his opinions. Rauschenbusch networked with Baptist ministers and offered leadership for helping ministers understand progressive positions, especially in meetings of the Baptist Congress. He was a strong believer in Baptist belief and practice and an apologist for kindred Reformation Anabaptists. His series of articles under the rubric "Why I Am a Baptist" captured much of the spirit of the denomination, receiving praise a half century later for its enduring value. His contributions to the denomination were considerable.

Third, Rauschenbusch became a professor at Rochester Theological Seminary, first in New Testament for the German language instruction department and then in church history for the English course of study. He was effective in the classroom. He taught the content of church history, new critical historical methodology, and the perspectives that formed the basis of historical discourse during his era. In the role of professor, he became an apologist for the value of church history. He thought ministers could greatly benefit from the study of history. Students recalled with gratitude the Christian spirit of the man. Rauschenbusch did not do much original archival research or publish technical articles or books on the history of Christianity. However, his writings were informed by a historical perspective. He liked to draw principles and examples from the history of the church and regularly used these in his articles and books.

Fourth, Rauschenbusch served the role as a "public Christian" in American society. During the decade 1907–1918 he was constantly quoted in the newspapers as well as being widely read and heard. His proposal that the church should be involved in establishing justice in the nation appealed broadly to the progressives in American society. The requests for him to speak were more than he could possibly meet, so he had to choose among many offers to make public addresses. There may have been other public voices equally well known and influential, but he was certainly among the best-known Protestant leaders of this decade. Rauschenbusch was a public Christian in the sense that he positioned himself on multiple issues of his day, and he helped give a sense of direction to American Protestant Christianity. To be sure, he was a devoted Baptist, but he was also much more: he transcended his Baptist identity. Rauschenbusch represented a triumphal Protestantism, seeking to establish its influence throughout American society. Along with other Protestant leaders he took a strong position against Roman Catholicism. The tension between Protestants and Catholics was perhaps the most visible conflict in American Christianity of this era. Less discussed, but also pervasive was the problem of unbelief, which he also addressed. He was a great promoter of the foreign mission enterprise and also of cooperative efforts among denominations and religions. The large body of American Protestants was fracturing between progressives and conservatives, and Rauschenbusch offered leadership among mainline progressives. He was also close to many leaders of Reform Judaism.

Rauschenbusch adopted and even led key trends of the dominant Protestant culture. His outlook provides a lens for mainline Protestant self-understanding during the first two decades of the twentieth century. Minister and professor, Baptist and Protestant—these are fruitful professional and confessional sites from which to explore the diversity and range of Rauschenbusch's identity and legacy.

CHAPTER 5

RAUSCHENBUSCH THE PASTOR-SCHOLAR

Following graduation from seminary and negotiations for a position in missions or the pastorate, Rauschenbusch accepted a call from the Second German Baptist Church in Manhattan, a congregation of 125 members. He was twenty-five years old. The church was located on the edge of Hell's Kitchen, a notorious district in New York City.[1] At that time New York's population was 1.5 million; almost 400,000 of these people were German immigrants. The German Baptists numbered 12,500 in 147 congregations across the United States and Canada.[2] Rauschenbusch seriously considered missions as a vocation and supported the foreign missionary enterprise throughout his life, but the first professional opening for him was ministry. In a sense he was engaging in home missions since he devoted himself in ministry to German immigrants. His fluency in both German and English suited him well for this task. Following in his father's footsteps of ethnic ministry doubtless gave added satisfaction to this vocational choice. Rauschenbusch's pastoral work may conveniently be understood in two parts. From 1886 to 1891 he established himself as an effective preacher and pastor and continued to pursue his academic interests. He was unmarried, and his mother and his sister lived with him for a time. In 1891 he took a sabbatical and went to Europe. During the second part of his pastoral ministry, 1892–1897, Rauschenbusch married Pauline Rother. Two of their five children were born in New York City. During this period Rauschenbusch also increased his activity in Baptist organizations and in speaking out on social issues, often in Baptist periodicals. In 1897 Rauschenbusch transitioned from pastor to professor. But the eleven-year pastoral period was formative for him. What was the nature of his ministry? What were his thoughts on the task of ministry? What about his own sermons? He was uniquely positioned by training and location to educate through writing. Moreover, he became an activist, seeking to create a better New York City. As minister he took on several important tasks.

Rauschenbusch plunged into his work as pastor in June 1886, and the church

---

[1] The Second German Baptist Church was located on the lower west side of Manhattan between 9th and 10th Avenues, first on 45th Street and later moved to 43rd Street.

[2] Minus, *Walter Rauschenbusch*, 49.

ordained him in October 1886. He made a strong impression during his ordination interview. George H. Charles, a member of the council, wrote a letter full of praise and appreciation to Rauschenbusch for his responses at the ordination examination:

> I want to take the liberty of expressing to you my utmost hearty and earnest commendation, of the splendid way in which you acquitted yourself at the examination this afternoon...your thorough understanding...of the matters involved very greatly pleased me. During the years past I have attended the examination of not a few young men for the ministry; but none have given to me so satisfactory a statement of truth.... Under God I am sure that you will be a great help to men in their struggles to realize righteousness...and to know God as He wants to be known, i.e., the Father God who loves them.[3]

Rauschenbusch delivered his first sermon in New York under the title "Dein Reich Komme" ("Thy Kingdom Come"), where he announced that until the kingdom comes, Christ's followers must labor for justice and love.[4]

Rauschenbusch engaged the life of ministry at many levels, and he reflected on the nature of his profession. Regular preaching was Rauschenbusch's first and most public responsibility. In addition, he assumed many pastoral tasks in caring for people in need. He also engaged in serious and extended scholarly efforts during his years as a pastor through regular Bible study and through publishing frequently on several topics that sustained his special interest, including missions, social reform, and Baptist life. Additionally, he published numerous Sunday school lessons in the Baptist journal *The Inquirer*. During his busy ministry he functioned as pastor, teacher, scholar, and activist. This chapter examines key elements of Rauschenbusch's life as a pastor.

The Task and Practice of Ministry

In preparation for his seminary work Rauschenbusch had outlined the standard curriculum of study, which he called the mental discipline, and had also reflected on additional ways a ministerial student should prepare for ministry, especially by giving attention to personal spiritual formation, seeking practical experience, and serving in churches.

In several of his sermons Rauschenbusch addressed the task of ministry. Early in his tenure as pastor, Rauschenbusch preached the ordination sermon of

---

[3] George H. Charles, Jr. to WR, October 14, 1886, box 23, Rauschenbusch Family Papers.

[4] WR, "Dein Reich Komme," June 6, 1886, vol. 2:7–37, box 150, Rauschenbusch Family Papers.

his good friend Nathaniel Schmidt.[5] He charged Schmidt on three points: first, the pastor himself must be a man of God. He counseled Schmidt: "Live near to God, then will your conviction rest firm, that there is a living God, and that the mortal man may have dealings with him. Live with God lest your faith become dim; lest the shout of assurance be on your lips but the will of doubt in your heart…let the branch be not severed from the vine."[6] The first task for the minister is to cultivate devotion to God. Second, Rauschenbusch charged Schmidt to "be a prophet of God, proclaiming God's word of life to men. Remember that men have eternal souls with eternal needs, and that no information about the life that now is will instruct a soul about eternal life."[7] Here he emphasized the preaching task of the minister. Third and finally, Rauschenbusch understood the minister's task to be one of standing between God and the people as an intercessor. As a point of leadership, Rauschenbusch told Schmidt that as people came to love him they would also learn to love God. And Rauschenbusch's further advice was to "Be their brother. Stand not aloof from them. Christ did not. He came not to be ministered unto, but to minister…. Be a child of God and a brother of men [so] that you will lead them to their Father who is in heaven."[8] Rauschenbusch designed this sermon to inspire Schmidt on the occasion of the beginning of his ministry, but it also reflected Rauschenbusch's own conception of the identity and the practical tasks of the minister and his prescription for a good ministry.

After ten years as a pastor, Rauschenbusch preached a sermon on "Ministerial Education" to his congregation as part of an effort to generate financial support for Baptist seminaries.[9] Here he once again addressed the nature of ministry, noting the importance of leaders throughout Scripture and church history. "The true minister is the successor of the prophet," he declared.[10] Rauschenbusch felt deeply the importance of the ministry, and he reminded his church of the tasks of ministers. First, they must be "expounders of the Christian tradition, the Bible and church…. [They] need more than occasional reading…. [They need] competent knowledge [of the Bible]."[11] Second, just as he had charged Schmidt, ministers must be "personal examples of the Christian life…dedicated to God."[12]

[5] WR, "Charge to the Candidate" (ordination of Nathaniel Schmidt, First Swedish Baptist Church, New York at 23rd Street, March 22, 1888), vol. 10:54–58, box 150, Rauschenbusch Family Papers.

[6] Ibid., 55–56.

[7] Ibid., 56.

[8] WR, "Charge to the Candidate," 58.

[9] WR, "Ministerial Education," April 12, 1896, vol. 34:97–104, box 151, Rauschenbusch Family Papers.

[10] Ibid., 99.

[11] Ibid., 100.

[12] Ibid.

Third, they must be competent "leaders and organizers, [which is] more important now than ever."[13] Finally, ministers should be "seers of the future."[14] They should acknowledge the failures of the church and recognize the perennial needs of the people. Rauschenbusch was reflecting a concept of ministry similar to what he held at the beginning of his time at the Second German Baptist Church, but after years of experience his language was much more direct, specific, and practical. Rauschenbusch admonished the congregation to support ministers by praying for them and encouraging them, and to avoid engaging in fault-finding. Moreover, he encouraged church members to pray for others to enter Christian service. He concluded with an appeal for members to support the Rochester and Chicago Baptist seminaries.[15]

In Rauschenbusch's farewell "Last Sermon," preached to his church on Sunday evening, July 4, 1897, he expressed thanksgiving for the growth, progress, and spirit of the church.[16] He remembered their affectionate relationship, recalling, "I was different from former ministers... But you made allowances and with few exceptions were ready to believe me genuine.... We have lived in peace."[17] However, Rauschenbusch did not completely sugarcoat his pastoral record. He conceded that problems remained in personal relationships:

> There have been private quarrels, more among sisters than men, and [some were] occasionally angry with me, but [they] didn't last. [I] can't say that I have the same respect and admiration of all, but I cherish no grudge against anybody. [I] have been obliged to hurt some feelings, but [I] hope that if [you] have not forgiven me, [you] will when I am gone.[18]

In this final sermon Rauschenbusch directly addressed some difficulties he had faced in his church. The source of the problem was his authoritarian attitude that had doubtless created tension within the church. He believed that the minister "should have great powers but use [them] as little as possible."[19] Apparently not all members agreed. Rauschenbusch also conceded that the church's growth "had not been so remarkable as hoped, [but] that N.Y. [is] a field where few [churches] even hold their own."[20] He had experienced the struggle of inner city

---

[13] Ibid., 100–101.

[14] Ibid., 101.

[15] Rauschenbusch's support for seminary education was doubtless influenced by his father's career, which was devoted to training pastors at Rochester as well as to his own stellar success in seminary training.

[16] WR, "Last Sermon as a Pastor," July 4, 1897, vol. 39:140–55, box 152, Rauschenbusch Family Papers.

[17] Ibid., 143–44.

[18] Ibid., 145–46.

[19] Ibid., 152.

[20] Ibid., 146–47.

churches. Moreover, the families in this congregation had a deeply contentious history.[21] These were difficulties, but Rauschenbusch also recalled many positive experiences with the church. Church members had been personally kind to him. He had experienced a deep sense of loneliness, due especially to the deafness that began after an illness contracted while engaged in pastoral care.[22] For seven years of his pastorate he had been unmarried, but when he married, the church had welcomed his wife, and "some have almost adopted my children."[23] He reported that the church had grown from 143 members to about twice that size, and he had baptized 207 people during his eleven years as pastor. They had built a new building and had no pressing debt. The church members had provided good financial support and had grown in their missionary interest.[24]

In this final sermon Rauschenbusch cast further light on his understanding of ministry. He listed six principles that had guided his ministry. The first two described his preaching. He said that he had "preached Christ, not self, anecdotes or personal feelings, no small gospel, nor philosophy, nor anything abstract."[25] He had tried to wield influence, but he had neither been sensational nor tried to draw publicity. He had preached simply, clearly, and boldly because he wanted to make things "clear to the simplest mind."[26] With respect to church governance, Rauschenbusch declared his belief in church democracy, and had "high respect in the wisdom and good intentions of my brethren."[27] Rauschenbusch also reminded the congregation that he had supported good relations with other churches.

Regarding pastoral work, Rauschenbusch said he believed that Christianity ought to touch all of life; it should be practical. He specifically mentioned work with the young people and said that he would like to have done more. He would also like to have helped facilitate social progress through the church by offering a cooperative store, summer outings for entire families, and better housing, but he had met much apathy regarding these proposals from his congregation. Finally, Rauschenbusch said that he had kept in mind the notion that following Christ meant bearing his cross. This meant sometimes taking an unpopular stand. He

---

[21] Rauschenbusch collected notes for a nonpublished history of his New York City church. The record of disputes among congregation members is almost continuous. See his notes for "History of the Second German Baptist Church," box 39, Rauschenbusch Family Papers.

[22] Winifred [Rauschenbusch] Rorty to Dores Sharpe, December 17, 1938, box 50, Rauschenbusch Family Papers.

[23] WR, "Last Sermon as a Pastor," 144–45.

[24] Ibid., 146. John D. Rockefeller had provided substantial financial assistance for completing the new church building.

[25] Ibid., 150.

[26] Ibid.

[27] Ibid., 152.

conceded that his assertion of ministerial authority had perhaps run counter to Baptist democracy and his denunciation of materialism had brought criticism from some of his members. Rauschenbusch found solace in the suffering of biblical prophets who had gone before him. Opposition was the price of their calling.

Rauschenbusch closed his long farewell sermon with a lucid and stirring expression of his vision of ministry: "this shall be my joy and crown, if I hear and see you pressing forward in the footsteps of Jesus Christ to whom I have tried to lead you."[28] The theme of leadership looms large in his farewell. He had admonished Nathaniel Schmidt to be a "brother" to his parishioners.[29] Being a brother to members while trying to lead them was not an easy task. Rauschenbusch in actual practice had exercised his authority as pastor and had taken criticism as a result. The tone of the sermon suggests a sense of regret and self-justification as well as celebration of his years as a pastor.

Rauschenbusch's diary provides the clearest insight into the actual daily activities of the young pastor. His Sundays were filled with church activities. For April 1, 1888, he wrote, "Taught class with good interest. Preached with effect on the power of the risen Christ. Led Children's Band in the afternoon and preached at night on the Alpha and Omega. Communion afterwards. Had on the whole a good Sunday."[30] Other regular church activities for the week included teachers' meeting on Wednesday evening. On Thursday evening he led the young people's meeting. During the month he took special collections for missions and for ministerial education. Much of this structure of activity remained familiar in Baptist practice a century later.

Rauschenbusch gave attention to his own regular commitments, including attending a Monday conference of ministers. On Friday his routine was to read the *Standard*, which covered Baptist news, and then spend three hours preparing his Sunday evening sermon. He led a prayer meeting that evening. On Saturday he wrote his Sunday morning sermon and studied late. During the week he often spent time with other ministers discussing biblical and theological ideas. Rauschenbusch also devoted time visiting the sick and the distressed of his congregation.[31] On another day he visited a dying little girl, whom he described as "a lovely little life panting itself out; bright unearthly eyes," and asked the enduring theological question, "what was she here for?"[32]

Rauschenbusch took time to pursue his own non-church interests as well, but these activities often left him with a sense of guilt. He recorded spending time

---

[28] Ibid., 155.
[29] WR, "Charge to the Candidate," 58.
[30] WR, diary, April 1, 1888, box 97, Rauschenbusch Family Papers.
[31] Ibid.
[32] Ibid.

with his sister Emma and also in taking long walks. On Saturday evening he "studied till quite late" and chided himself for being "not very attentive to the [church] work."[33] This comment suggests tension between two noble tasks—intellectual pursuit of his own interests competed with time devoted to his pastoral obligations. Either commitment could, of course, be a full-time occupation. Rauschenbusch revealed the minister's internal struggle in another Monday entry. On this day he went to the ministers' conference. In the evening he began to read the second volume of *War and Peace*, and he read some Latin with Emma in the evening. He concluded, "Had a full day, yet no substantial [religious] good done to anyone."[34] The tension expressed here is palpable.

But was reading Tolstoy not useful to him? His personal reading interests enriched his life immeasurably by igniting his imagination. While reading the last volume of *War and Peace* he wrote that "the experience made me stop and think.... Often one thinks he has the secret of life in his grasp and the scenes are clear. But the hour passes and there is nothing left but a sense of something beyond."[35] The diary reveals both the routines of parish life and his deep personal feelings. His sermons reveal much about his understanding of the message of Christianity, not least of which is the critical shift from his focus on personal to social Christianity.

Rauschenbusch's Sermons

Success in the pulpit is perhaps the single most important criteria for measuring a Baptist minister's effectiveness. Rauschenbusch wrote his earliest sermons predominantly in German mixed with occasional English passages. Within three years the language balance shifted to sermons predominantly in English. The ethnic German congregation was evidently becoming more familiar with the language of their adopted country. As a young minister, Rauschenbusch based most of his earliest sermons on the New Testament with occasional use of the Psalms and the Prophets. The sermons are carefully structured and would be easy for an audience to follow.[36] Thomas Harwood Pattison, professor of homiletics and pastoral theology at Rochester, taught students that every sermon should have only

---

[33] Ibid., April 7, 1888.

[34] Ibid., April 9, 1888.

[35] Ibid., April 16, 1888.

[36] See Rauschenbusch Family Papers, boxes 150–152. Loyde O. Ackerman gave this priceless set to the American Baptist Historical Society. Rauschenbusch's collection of sermons fills 45 volumes and runs from 1886 to 1905. Rauschenbusch prepared a table of contents for each volume. The general pattern is one or two sermons for each Sunday plus special occasion sermons or addresses. Each sermon includes a title or theme and a biblical text. Rauschenbusch usually outlined the sermons; they are handwritten, and they include date and place of delivery (sometimes multiple deliveries). These records reveal a remarkable level of organization and self-discipline by the young minister from the beginning of his ministry.

one theme, clearly presented in direct speech. The sermon should be written out, practiced, and delivered extemporaneously.[37] The focus of each of Rauschenbusch's sermons shows that he followed his professor's guidance regarding themes and clarity. He did not write out his sermons fully but used a modified shorthand system. At the outset of his ministry Rauschenbusch collected sermons and commentaries by leading ministers, professors, and missionaries of his day, including Dwight L. Moody, John Broadus, Henry Drummond, H. L. Hastings, and Hudson Taylor.[38]

Rauschenbusch sometimes delivered exegetical sermons, but usually he chose a topic or theme and analyzed it under three to six headings or key words, making practical applications as he progressed. He delivered a broad spectrum of sermons, including development of doctrinal or biblical themes, guidelines for personal morality and social ethics, celebration of special days of the Christian calendar, special church emphases, and sermons for other special occasions such as funerals. Rauschenbusch's sermon writing is skeletal. His illustrations are usually brief—most often references or mere allusions to biblical events or to current American social conditions.

Review of Rauschenbusch's sermons shows that he began his ministry with traditional Baptist messages emphasizing conversion and the practice of piety or Christian living. Rauschenbusch stressed both themes.[39] The topic Rauschenbusch addressed most frequently in his early preaching was salvation. Six months after he arrived in New York City, Rauschenbusch preached "Salvation by Grace" (Rom 3:23-24) under four traditional headings: (1) Since Scripture declares that all have sinned, the unconverted must be warned not to deny the testimony of conscience, Scripture, and reason. (2) The sinner should be cautioned not try to earn God's approval, but rather throw himself on the mercy of God. (3) A similar warning to a Christian is to beware of delighting in his own goodness. (4) Finally, he offered assurance for Christians: you are safe, he declared; hold on to grace.[40] The sermon has a clear parallel structure and is addressed to the unconverted and converted alike. In this sermon Rauschenbusch drew on the classic Lutheran dis-

[37] See "Dr. Pattison's Lectures on Homiletics," September 1884, box 89, Rauschenbusch Family Papers. Pattison later published his ideas on preaching as *The Making of a Sermon: For the Classroom and Study* (Philadelphia: American Baptist Publication Society, 1898).

[38] See section five of the 1886–1890 scrapbook, Rauschenbusch Family Papers.

[39] These are the two core ideas of German Pietism; they were readily adjusted to American conversionist revivalism and emphasis on Christian living. See Schneider, "Americanization of Karl August Rauschenbusch, 1816–1899," 14.

[40] WR, "Salvation by Grace," January 20, 1887, vol. 4:64, box 150, Rauschenbusch Family Papers.

tinction between law and grace. Later in 1887 he preached on the popular evangelistic text "God So Loved the World."[41] Rauschenbusch gave yet another traditional exposition of the Protestant view of salvation in a sermon on "How to Become Just" (Rom 3:15-24), in which he affirmed that the effort to live a decent life and obey religious laws does not make one guiltless. Hate and impurity are not easily removed from consciousness. The law brings only awareness of sin, not freedom from it. By contrast, justification is a gift of God through Christ. Moreover, it is available to all; it is given freely and may be accepted by all through faith.[42] To the end of his ministry Rauschenbusch continued to preach the traditional idea of personal salvation. Less than six months before he concluded his ministry in New York, his sermon topic was "Saving Souls."[43] His purpose in this sermon was to encourage church members to engage in "soul-saving." He identified two issues in the sermon: why become involved and how to proceed. The reasons for becoming involved in saving souls, included (1) the value of every soul, since all are made in the image of God, and conversion is the starting point of the relationship with God; (2) the joy the event brings to the individual; and (3) the keen awareness that it is easy to ruin a soul, but not so easy to save one. In the second part of the sermon, Rauschenbusch turned to methods that laity should consider for the task. Here he noted that in order to engage in the personal work of soul-saving it is necessary that one have a personal experience of salvation, have the love for another person that opens hearts, and finally, seek opportunity to witness. In this sermon Rauschenbusch combined traditional theology and pragmatic advice in trying to help church members engage in seeking the salvation of others.[44] Clearly, to the very end of his pastorate the personal conversion experience remained foundational for him. The evidence is in the record of his sermons.

Rauschenbusch also devoted many sermons to the traditional theme of personal conduct, with guidelines for ethical living. For example, when he preached on "The Golden Rule" ("Do unto others as you would have them do unto you," Matt 7:12), he interpreted this passage as a general guide to the Christian life. In this sermon Rauschenbusch conveyed the inevitability of relationships, pointing out that we do not live to ourselves; we affect others. The question is, "How shall we act?" He said that we cannot carry around a handbook of duties, but that the "golden rule is a guideline that will help Christians in their relationships with one

---

[41] WR, "God So Loved the World," October 23, 1887, vol. 7:188–92, box 150, Rauschenbusch Family Papers.

[42] WR, "How to Become Just," February 7, 1890, vol. 16:41–47, box 150, Rauschenbusch Family Papers.

[43] WR, "Saving Souls," January 24, 1897, vol. 37:117–26, box 151, Rauschenbusch Family Papers.

[44] Ibid.

another."[45] In putting the rule into practice, he emphasized the importance of honesty, care, fairness, and compassion. In September 1889, at a conference address in Milwaukee, Rauschenbusch preached another sermon on behavior titled "Christian Ethics," with reference to the kingdom of God (Matt 5:20). He began the sermon with the Beatitudes—Jesus' blessings on the simple, humble, crushed, weak, and the seekers of righteousness. He reminded hearers that Jesus said that he came not to destroy the law, but to fulfill it—with the familiar contrasts Jesus drew between murder and anger, between adultery and lust, and so forth. Rauschenbusch identified the virtues of simplicity, honesty, truth, and righteousness as characteristics of life in the kingdom and concluded the address with the declaration that a Christian must be a radical.[46] In this sermon he was moving toward voicing a more revolutionary identity for Christian living. But in other sermons he continued to present traditional treatments of individual commandments, such as "What Shall I Do with my Sundays" (Isa 58:13-14), "The Ninth Commandment" (Exod 20:16), and "The Tenth Commandment" (Exod 20:17).[47]

Rauschenbusch addressed several special-day issues in his preaching. He preached a temperance sermon almost every year. Alcohol abuse was rampant in his city, and it posed serious problems for individuals and families. Problems were acute in the slums of the rapidly growing major cities, and the temperance campaign gathered momentum during the first two decades of the twentieth century. In his 1888 temperance sermon, Rauschenbusch referred to Ezekiel's watchman, whose task it was to warn. He proceeded to list the many ways liquor harmed people: it injures the body, hurts the intellect, diminishes prosperity, threatens morality, and harms spirituality and Christian influence. He concluded that it is the duty of all Christians to be temperate, to abstain entirely.[48] The arguments he raises are largely pragmatic, citing levels of injury to individuals and society. Rauschenbusch also preached sermons appropriate to high points of the church calendar, especially Christmas and Easter. At Thanksgiving he reviewed the blessings enjoyed by the entire nation, and on Decoration Day he explained that the nation honored the war dead because of their sacrifice for all citizens. These were all occasions for specific remembrances.

---

[45] WR, "The Golden Rule," June 9, 1889, vol. 8:82–87, box 150, Rauschenbusch Family Papers.

[46] WR, "Christian Ethics," (Matt 5:20), Milwaukee, September 1889, vol. 16:52–57, box 150, Rauschenbusch Family Papers.

[47] WR, "What Shall I Do with My Sundays?" June 6, 1890, vol. 16:189–96, box 150; "The Ninth Commandment," November 4, 1894, vol. 26:175–78, box 151; "The Tenth Commandment," September 29, 1894, vol. 28:6–14, box 151, Rauschenbusch Family Papers.

[48] WR, "Temperance Sermon" (Proverbs 23:29–31) August 19, 1888, vol. 11:145–49, box 150, Rauschenbusch Family Papers. Five years later he again preached the same sermon (see vol. 21:99–103, box 151).

In an 1895 sermon on "Communion" (2 Cor 11:26), Rauschenbusch developed the idea of the significance of communion as an act of memory, an act of love, an act of faith, and an act of hope. Here he combined the strong sense of memory in Israel's faith with the well-known Christian virtues laid out by Paul in 1 Corinthians 13.[49] His preaching had matured, and this message made the very familiar nonetheless memorable.

Rauschenbusch's sermons occasionally alluded to the work of pastors. In a sermon addressed to missionaries, Rauschenbusch said that the minister must be faithful about visiting and would have to give up time otherwise spent on studies, social life, and other interests. He said that pastoral ministry requires personal sacrifice; it is not an easy life.[50] This appears to be Rauschenbusch's reflection on his own experience. Pastoral responsibility included preparing thoughts of comfort at difficult times, especially funerals. His sermon collection includes several funeral sermons. Among his most memorable was the "Funeral of D. Eisele, child of Daniel Eisele," delivered at the home of the family during his first year as a pastor.[51] His pastoral work is not as well documented as his preaching, but his deep empathy for others in their loss and suffering is evident in this message. He began by reading Psalm 42, followed by his personal comments to the family:

> At such times as these the words of comfort and consolation rise very reluctantly to the lips. Any words a man can speak seem cold and feeble. They fall so far short of the reality of the sorrow.... We would best like to sit still with those who are stricken down, to let our hearts bend with them with the weight of grief and be silent. The love that unites us to the children whom God gives us, is a most sweet bond. It is most like the love that God bears to us. There is no selfishness in it. We do not expect return of services we render them. On the contrary, the more helpless they are, the dearer they become to us. When we hold them in our arms, we feel as if something of our own freshness and innocence were restored to us. Ah, it's not easy to lose them. They are part of us, and part of our life is buried away when we lose them. There is comfort to know you have not lost your boy forever.... There is one who said with great tenderness, "Suffer the little children to come unto me." We shall one day be where he is. Yet this does not satisfy you. You want him now. Your hearts cry out for him now. Your present loss is real, and nothing will undo it. But do take this thought to your heart that you will see your little one again and know him.[52]

---

[49] WR, "Communion," June 2, 1895, vol. 30:168–71, box 151, Rauschenbusch Family Papers.

[50] WR, "Missionary Sermon at Rochester, NY," May 5, 1889, vol. 14:38, box 150, Rauschenbusch Family Papers. The complete sermon is found on pages 33–39.

[51] WR, "Funeral of D. Eisele, child of Daniel Eisele," February 24, 1887, vol. 4:182–87, box 150, Rauschenbusch Family Papers.

[52] Ibid., 182–84.

Rauschenbusch assured the family that they were not alone by reminding them,

> This child had an earthly father and a Father in heaven who loves him. We get a glimpse of the heart of God and what he feels. In all our affliction he is afflicted. Dear friends, when you talk to God about the loss, you do not speak to one who cannot be touched with a feeling of your infirmities.... Tell God your pains. He alone fully understands you.[53]

Offering the assurance that the boy was with God and that the parents would see him again, Rauschenbusch did not deny the pain they felt in their loss. Nothing can undo that pain. This is a remarkable sermon for a second-year minister who had no children of his own.

Rauschenbusch was bold to speak on subjects beyond the traditional topics addressed in the churches, especially after his first three years of ministry. He preached on pressing issues in American society, including "National Salvation" (1889), "Bible and Science" (1892), a "Political Sermon" (1896), and the "Bradley Martin Ball" (1897).[54] In the "Bradley Martin Ball" sermon, Rauschenbusch sharply criticized the lavish expenditures associated with a famous New York City party held on February 10, 1897.[55] This sermon elicited strong criticism. In a personal letter, "Christine" wrote to Rauschenbusch that he should not preach against the rich and their doings:

> You are put in the pulpit to preach the word of God and teach them how to do right instead of sowing hard feelings into their hearts.... How are the institutions, hospitals, homes, orphans, asylums, and such edifices in existence if not for the rich people, especially the 400 of whom you speak so bitterly.... You yourself must be at heart an anarchist and socialist, or you would not express yourself as you have done.[56]

Rauschenbusch criticized excesses of materialism in America's Gilded Age, and he was criticized in return.

Rauschenbusch's understanding of the kingdom of God shifted while he was a pastor. The evidence in his sermons, the newspaper articles he collected, and in

---

[53] Ibid., 186.

[54] WR, "National Salvation," April 28, 1889, vol. 14:25–32, box 150, Rauschenbusch Family Papers; "Bible and Science," September 20, 1892, box 150 , vol. 14:341–47, Rauschenbusch Family Papers; "Political Sermon," preached after the presidential election, November 8, 1896, vol. 36:50–75, box 152; "Bradley Martin Ball," February 14, 1897, vol. 37:175–95, box 152, Rauschenbusch Family Papers.

[55] WR, "Bradley Martin Ball," vol. 37:175–95.

[56] "Christine" to WR, written the week following the delivery of "Bradley Martin Ball," on p. 11 of the 1897–1899 scrapbook. The "400" is reference to the well-known *Social Register* of America's elite during this era.

his published work all point to 1889.[57] A decisive change in his views appeared in his sermons of 1889.[58] When Rauschenbusch had earlier preached on Jesus' central idea, he had used traditional categories such as the growth of the kingdom and progress toward the future kingdom. By 1889 he altered his view of the kingdom by associating the idea with social reconstruction of the present social order. In the sermon on "National Salvation," Rauschenbusch opened with, "Speaking of national salvation, the Old Testament prophets made this their main theme. Yet we neglect it."[59] He celebrated America's resources, her political and religious liberty, the thriving economy, including rapid growth and success in manufacturing, and the nation's widespread support for public education. But he declared that the United States had a duty to the world. He said that we should not live to ourselves, but we should promote political and religious liberty. He reminded his German-American listeners that in Germany Baptists were not granted legal recognition. He addressed specific changes that would benefit the welfare of the nation, including reform of political corruption, genuine separation of church and state, and redress of social and economic injustices. He argued that both individual church members and the church as an institution had the responsibility of being involved and assertive in the nation's political life.[60] Support for workers began to appear in his sermons. Just before he left for Europe in 1891, Rauschenbusch's sermon "Social Problem, Our Problem," foreshadowed his long manuscript, *Christianity Revolutionary*. Here he took on the problem of poverty and described what was being done about it in various nations, including a description of the American situation and suggestions for reform.[61] Rauschenbusch's sermons reveal a strong interest in addressing issues beyond the walls of his Baptist church.

As he wrote *Christianity Revolutionary*, Rauschenbusch focused his theological reflection on Jesus' teachings on the kingdom of God. After returning from his sabbatical and resuming his pastoral role in 1892, Rauschenbusch addressed the idea of the kingdom of God in several sermons, such as "The Great Commission," "The Kingdom of God Among You," and "The Coming of the Kingdom."

---

[57] The kingdom sermons for 1889 are found in volumes 14–16, box 150. In his first scrapbook, Rauschenbusch collected a score of articles on political, economic, and social issues, beginning in 1889. During that year he also published numerous articles on behalf of the workers in the journal *For the Right*.

[58] For a perceptive study of his sermons see Stackhouse, "The Formation of a Prophet," 138. Stackhouse's chief interest was in tracking Rauschenbusch's growing commitment to the social gospel message.

[59] WR, "National Salvation," 25.

[60] Ibid., 29.

[61] WR, "Social Problem, Our Problem," February 11, 1891, vol. 18:159–75, box 150, Rauschenbusch Family Papers. He preached this sermon three more times (November 1891; January 26, 1892; April 4, 1895).

In these messages he further refined his understanding of the kingdom of God.[62] In "The Great Commission" (Matt 28:19-20), Rauschenbusch developed the idea that Christ's purpose was to establish a kingdom of redeemed humanity, characterized by spiritual rejuvenation. Living according to justice and love, Christ's followers would treat each other as brothers with God as their Father and Christ their only King. Christ initiated the kingdom with a few followers who would make disciples by teaching all nations if not all individuals. Rauschenbusch noted that the Semitic, Latin, and Teutonic peoples had all been reached by the gospel, and that now the Chinese and African people were waiting to hear the gospel. He said that the urgent task of the church was not to teach laws, but one law—namely, the spirit of Christ. Rauschenbusch closed the sermon with a reminder of the promise that Christians would be empowered with the promise of the presence of Christ and that this kingdom would endure until the end of time.[63] Protestants had regularly used this passage in Matthew since the nineteenth century to support the world missionary effort. Rauschenbusch also applied it to the social gospel by shifting his emphasis from individual salvation to the making of disciples for the kingdom. He combined the vision of a redeemed humanity with the missionary enterprise.[64]

Two months later, Rauschenbusch developed additional dimensions of his understanding of the kingdom. In "The Kingdom of God among You" (Luke 17:20-21), he said that people generally expected the kingdom to come in the future; Rauschenbusch claimed that Jesus declared instead that the kingdom is here, now, a present reality, not a future hope. He suggested ways the kingdom is present: (1) by voluntary obedience of the individual; (2) by a fuller measure of spirituality; (3) by ending particular faults such as temper and anger; (4) by making every Christian family a little kingdom of God; (5) by greater power of the church, which can itself be a small kingdom; and (6) by a revolution of social life in the way Christians treat others. Through faith, he said, the power of the kingdom is realized. He concluded the sermon by re-emphasizing that the kingdom of God was a doctrine to be appropriated by Christians for the redemption of society now, not something limited to a distant future. Moreover, he proclaimed that the idea of the kingdom is more than an individual experience of God; it includes many levels of social organization as well, such as family and church. In

---

[62] WR, "The Great Commission" (Matt 28:18-20), February 21, 1892, vol. 19:75–78; "The Kingdom of God Among You" (Luke 17:20-21), April 29, 1892, vol. 19:115–18; "The Coming of the Kingdom" (Luke 17:20-21), September 4, 1892, vol. 9: 216–18 (Rauschenbusch preached this sermon in Cassopolis, MI, at the Baptist church of his friend Will Munger); all in box 150, Rauschenbusch Family Papers.

[63] WR, "The Great Commission," 75–78.

[64] Ibid.

his sermons Rauschenbusch was growing bold in his emphasis on social dimensions of the kingdom of God.[65]

A short time later, Rauschenbusch preached "The Coming of the Kingdom" (Luke 17:20-21). This sermon contains much of his mature thought. As in the two earlier 1892 sermons, he stresses the social and national dimensions of the kingdom. To the individual, family, and church levels of the kingdom he added the city of New York. He identified specific political and economic practices that needed to be reformed, and he appealed to justice as his criteria. Then he added a final level of application of the idea of the kingdom—the entire nation. In this sermon he identified the pervasive problems of the liquor traffic and human suffering brought about by economic manipulation. The prophetic preacher said that the nation had put the value of the power of money over human life. He argued that the nation must not wait for a future millennium for its redemption: "If we are ever to live like children of God, now is the time."[66] In his mind and in his preaching the kingdom of God was firmly social, political and economic, as well as individual and spiritual. It was meant for the here and now.

Analysis of the sermons shows that Rauschenbusch was reflecting seriously on the concept of the redemption of society, the idea he had developed the year before in *Christianity Revolutionary*. Now he regularly explored social Christianity in public from the pulpit. *Christianity Revolutionary* had an intellectual genesis; preaching was a forum for nurturing ideas both before and after the writing of the manuscript in 1891. Significant aspects of Rauschenbusch's developing thought may be traced in the sermons. The crucible for *Christianity and the Social Crisis* was the New York pulpit where he proclaimed the faith. He was addressing social problems in 1889, but his sabbatical discovery of Jesus' encompassing view of the kingdom of God now provided theological underpinning for his social message. Rauschenbusch appropriately used the same title and verses for his last Sunday morning sermon at the Second Baptist Church that he had used for his first sermon—"Thy Kingdom Come." But the meaning of this crucial phrase had been largely transformed in Rauschenbusch's mind. The sermons show him espousing first individual and later social Christianity. He now believed in both and preached both.

Pastor as Sunday School Writer and Biblical Teacher

Rauschenbusch was a scholar-pastor. As a student he excelled in his academic responsibilities and won prizes for his achievements. More importantly for the arc of his life, he never abandoned serious intellectual work. He was a keen student of the Bible, and he was thoroughly familiar with Scripture. In January

[65] WR, "The Kingdom of God among You," 115–18.
[66] WR, "The Coming of the Kingdom," 218.

1885, Rauschenbusch purchased a copy of the Revised Version of the New Testament, a new translation that had appeared in 1881. His New Testament is marked throughout. Since it was a new version, he checked the accuracy of the translation and offered his own suggestions for improvement: For Romans 2:13, he wrote in the margin, "the law" in place of "a law." In the margin of Romans 1:22, he substituted "pretending" for "professing." Beside Romans 2:8, he wrote "self-seeking" in place of "factious," and for Romans 2:19 he suggested "confident in thyself to be" rather than "confident that thou thyself." He also added marginal notes for cross-references and additional notes to guide his interpretation of the text.[67]

Although he took on full pastoral responsibilities, Rauschenbusch continued intellectual pursuits such as writing and publishing throughout his eleven years in New York City. The level of his sustained academic work is impressive and critical for understanding his emerging theology. Rather than looking upon completing his seminary degree as an occasion to relax his intellectual effort, Rauschenbusch used it as a springboard for continued intellectual growth. At the outset of his career as a pastor Rauschenbusch had remarked that he had decided that he was committed to work with people for their salvation rather than writing big books. In his "Missionary Sermon" he had counseled young ministers and missionaries that they would have to leave studies behind in order to spend time visiting and getting to know the members of their churches.[68] His diary shows that he did not neglect this duty; however, Rauschenbusch continued to be drawn to scholarly tasks and thrived on them.[69] "Intellectual work," as he called it, remained central to his persona as a minister. He accomplished far more published and unpublished "intellectual work" than was usual or expected for a minister.

Rauschenbusch read broadly in both religious and nonreligious literature. He gained knowledge of the problems of society and human suffering through personal experience, but he also learned the theory and principles of sociology and economics through reading. He had formed friendships with other reform-minded ministers and had begun to publish *For the Right* in order to address social problems of American workers. All of this had roots in his experience with the people of his congregation. Rauschenbusch published twenty-one articles in *For the Right* in sixteen months.[70] It is clear that he sustained a serious work ethic of reading and writing after he left seminary.

When he took his ten-month sabbatical in 1891, Rauschenbusch stayed very

---

[67] WR's 1881 New Testament, box 38, Rauschenbusch Family Papers. He may have made these comparisons while he was a student. The notes are not dated.

[68] WR, "Missionary Sermon," 1889, vol. 14:38, box 150, Rauschenbusch Family Papers.

[69] WR, diary, 1888, box 97, Rauschenbusch Family Papers.

[70] Minus, *Walter Rauschenbusch*, 66.

busy in Germany reading, attending lectures, and putting his ideas together in a 450-page typescript. Looking back he rightly identified this experience as the most transformative year of his life. The transformation would not have occurred had he taken his sabbatical merely as occasion for the pleasures of rest and travel. Instead, he devoted himself to work on writing out his proposals for church and society, and he returned a changed person. Rauschenbusch arrived back in New York from the sabbatical on December 24. The church had prepared a reception for him, including welcoming addresses by fellow ministers. They were pleased to have their minister back. His research and writing had stabilized his transformed understanding of Christianity.

The German Baptist Publishing House in Cleveland offered Rauschenbusch the position of editor of its publications, but his church pressed him to remain as their pastor, and after much deliberation, he determined that he was not yet ready to give up the ministry. The church showed its appreciation for his decision to stay in New York by providing an assistant pastor, which allowed Rauschenbusch more time to study and write. He had written Sunday school lessons before his sabbatical, and in January *The Inquirer* announced that Rauschenbusch would resume his expositions of the Sunday school lessons the following week.[71] Beginning on January 24, and continuing throughout 1892, he published forty-eight lessons, averaging about 2000 words per lesson—or about 100,000 words of Bible study.[72] Judging from the items Rauschenbusch kept in his scrapbook, writing the Sunday school lessons took a large part of his time in 1892. The lessons represented a significant contribution by the pastor to the teaching ministry of the church.

Rauschenbusch's Sunday school lessons share a close affinity with his sermons. The purpose of both was to apply the biblical text to life. Whereas Rauschenbusch's sermons are focused on ideas and applications drawn from the text of Scripture, his lessons offer more historical background and examination of the biblical passages. If the biblical text was a narrative, he often included a retelling of the story in dramatic form. He later counseled ministers to let the biblical stories carry their own weight in their preaching.[73] The lesson selections for 1892 were based on selections from Isaiah, Jeremiah, Psalms, Daniel, and Acts. He chose a uniting theme each week: in five representative lessons he addressed the contemporary religious issues of suffering, materialism, doubt, social responsibility, and missionary expansion. In each of these his primary audience was Sunday

---

[71] *The Inquirer*, January 7, 1892; also in the 1892 scrapbook, Rauschenbusch Family Papers.

[72] All forty-eight lessons are found in the 1892 scrapbook, Rauschenbusch Family Papers.

[73] WR, "The Value and Use of History for Ministers," Summer School of Rochester and Colgate, May 1914, box 22, Rauschenbusch Family Papers. This article was also published that fall in *The Rochester Theological Seminary Bulletin: The Record*, LXI (November, 1914), 31-41.

school teachers. Rauschenbusch always arranged the material logically around three to seven teaching points, easily grasped for lesson presentation.

Analysis of these five sample lessons demonstrates Rauschenbusch's skill in explaining the biblical texts to readers. In the first of these lessons Rauschenbusch presented Jeremiah in an engaging way.[74] Examining Jeremiah's character, Rauschenbusch first wanted to dispel misconceptions: "Poor Jeremiah has been rather roughly handled…his name has been proverbial for the dolorous and mournful in religion."[75] He had been labeled the weeping prophet and was seen as an unhappy and lonely man. Rauschenbusch agreed that Jeremiah did live in a difficult era, and his "times were out of joint." He had been imprisoned, and he lamented the fall of his capital city, Jerusalem. But Rauschenbusch also put Jeremiah in a positive light for students of the Sunday school text: "When we examine Jeremiah's character more closely, we find there a degree of courage and heroism which turns our pity into admiration and reverence."[76] Rauschenbusch closed the lesson with a practical application to life. He noted that just like Jeremiah all people face difficulties in life: "A repetition of Jeremiah's experience is not a thing to be desired. And yet, a repetition of it in some measure is certain for every man who is following his Master…. It is well to know beforehand what portion of the Bible to turn in the dark days. Jeremiah is a good find to a man that is hard hit."[77] In this lesson Rauschenbusch used his biblical knowledge first to correct a popular but erroneous perception of Jeremiah and then to find in the story of Jeremiah's suffering a way to encourage individual readers in coping with their own struggles.

For another week Rauschenbusch based his lesson on Isaiah 55:1-13, "The Gracious Call."[78] The text opens with the familiar invitation, "Ho everyone that thirsteth, come to the waters." Rauschenbusch launches into his interpretation: the water is free; it is a gift. Why will the people of Babylon not come? Rauschenbusch likens the markets of Babylon to the offices in New York City. In both places they toil away, and "they mean to take the results of their toil and buy satisfaction for their souls with it."[79] He paraphrases the text: "Oh men and women of Babylon and America, why do you spend your life's labor for that which is not bread and can never satisfy you?"[80] This statement arrests attention and

[74] WR, "The Weeping Prophet," *The Inquirer*, February 18, 1892; also on p. 12 in the 1892 scrapbook, Rauschenbusch Family Papers.

[75] WR, "The Weeping Prophet."

[76] Ibid.

[77] Ibid.

[78] WR, "The Gracious Call," *The Inquirer*, February 7, 1892; also on pp. 4–5 of the 1892 scrapbook, Rauschenbusch Family Papers.

[79] Ibid.

[80] Ibid.

makes the point of the lesson. He continues: "Does the peace of your heart increase with the fashionableness of your clothes? Is the everlasting hunger of a human heart to be fed with bows and compliments and gaslights and newspaper notices?"[81] A string of biblical quotations and allusions follows: "Perceive that in seeking your life you lose it and though you should gain, not a fraction of the world but the whole of it, it profits you nothing. The meek inherit the earth and not the ambitious.... Jehovah is ready to enter into a new covenant with your soul and mine."[82]

In this lesson Rauschenbusch addressed the problem of materialism, the pervasive obsession of American culture, and the universal quest for happiness and satisfaction. He reminded the readers of Jesus' beatitude blessing the meek, and said that Jesus is forever against selfishness, materialism, and pride. Rauschenbusch notes that although the light comes into the world, not all men become children of the light: "We must urge the wicked to forsake his way...and [it] does not matter a snap of the finger if they are deacons and Sunday school superintendents."[83] He concluded this section with the promise that God will have mercy, but only on those who renounce their sin. Rauschenbusch raised the question of whether the promise of this Scripture will come to pass. Will God actually conquer? Where is the hope of the Messiah's coming? Rauschenbusch was keenly aware of his reading audience and drew them into the lesson: "Discouraged pastor, do you see no fruit in your church? God's word...will not return void. Dejected teacher, are you almost despairing of your class? Still pour out your Christ-love on these young hearts. Force, material and spiritual, is changed in form but it is never lost."[84] This lesson begins with an invitation to think about a meaningful and fulfilled life and offers an alternative to prevailing materialism. Rauschenbusch's diction is direct and clear and also heavily biblical, using some twenty biblical allusions. The tone of the lesson is sermonic; Rauschenbusch calls for repentance from sin and change of life to prove it, and he does not hesitate to place church leaders under the judgment of the gospel. His readers for these lessons were mostly preachers and Sunday school teachers who tried to communicate a biblical message to students each week, but often with no visible results. He addressed them directly and encouraged them by assuring them that their efforts would not be in vain.

In a third selection Rauschenbusch's exegesis for Sunday schools is his lesson

---

[81] Ibid.
[82] Ibid.
[83] Ibid.
[84] Ibid.

on "The Way of Righteousness" (Ps 1:1-6).[85] To introduce this study Rauschenbusch cited the German Pietist leader A. H. Francke who cautioned, "So long as man has not the Spirit of Christ and denies not himself and takes up his cross to follow, he will have not heart for the Psalms."[86] Psalm 1 is a familiar text. The first two verses sketch the character of the righteous man in contrast to the wicked. Rauschenbusch commented on the status of current American religion, noting that skepticism was probably more prevalent than when the psalmist wrote. He offered a thoughtful analysis of doubt, asserting that "doubt is not only permissible but absolutely necessary if we are not to load ourselves with every variety of nonsense at the bidding of any man who assumes an air of authority."[87] But he said that it is also true that a scornful person who is dismissive of tradition is "less adapted to discover the truth."[88] The righteous person is thoughtful about "large concerns of life [such as] duty and conduct."[89] The psalmist likens the righteous person to a flowering tree with a promise that he will flourish. The wicked, however, are depicted as chaff; they are unstable and have an element of decay in them. The conclusion of the psalm is a summary of the two contrasting courses taken in life and an admonition to Sunday school teachers to teach this truth to the present generation.

In his treatment of the "First Christian Church" (Acts 2:37-47), Rauschenbusch described the Pentecost experience of the pouring out of the Spirit of God on the people.[90] In his message Peter demanded repentance and baptism, and he also promised remission of sin and the gift of the Holy Spirit. Rauschenbusch identifies four characteristics of the early church in this text. The first is the teaching of the apostles. The new group was uninstructed and had much to learn about Jesus. Second, they were characterized by the word "koinonia," or "fellowship." Rauschenbusch says that this early Christian characteristic is the opposite of selfishness; it involves a group of people genuinely committed to sharing. A third characteristic is breaking of bread, in Rauschenbusch's opinion probably an early Christian expression for the Lord's Supper. The fourth and final characteristic is prayer. Rauschenbusch not surprisingly concludes his lesson by emphasizing the earliest church's sense of social responsibility. He summarizes, "The text does not say they had all things private," but rather, "they had all things in common."[91]

---

[85] WR, "The Way of Righteousness," *The Inquirer*, April 3, 1892; also pp. 20–21 of the 1892 scrapbook, Rauschenbusch Family Papers.

[86] Ibid.

[87] Ibid.

[88] Ibid.

[89] Ibid.

[90] WR, "The First Christian Church," *The Inquirer*, July 17, 1892; also p. 72–73 of the 1892 scrapbook, Rauschenbusch Family Papers.

[91] Ibid.

In his lesson on Stephen, "The First Christian Martyr" (Acts 6:1-10; 7:54-60; 8:1-4), Rauschenbusch developed the theme of sacrifice for missions.[92] He declared that of all the early Christians, Stephen was the most like Christ. As a deacon and a preacher, he combined the tasks of two early forms of leadership. He was also, in Rauschenbusch's words, "a hero and prophet" who was charged with innovation and was killed for proclaiming that Jesus was the Messiah. Rauschenbusch noted that Stephen is best known in the Christian tradition as its first martyr. He called Stephen "the seed of the church." Following the death of Stephen, widespread persecution of the church caused followers to scatter and preach. Thus Stephen, declared Rauschenbusch, started the worldwide mission of the church. Stephen was a radical who took the Christian faith in new directions. In this year following his writing of *Christianity Revolutionary*, Rauschenbusch showed fondness for the term "radical," applying it to Jesus, to Stephen, and to all Christians he judged to be bearers of "true Christianity." Rauschenbusch wrote many lessons on the book of Acts. Clearly it provided for him a model for the contemporary church.

Interpretation of the Bible to the laity was an important ministry for Rauschenbusch. As a minister, he was a teacher as well as a proclaimer. In these lessons he always included historical context. He noted that the traditional Protestant exegetical tradition had failed to recognize the importance of background. "But the Bible is History," Rauschenbusch insisted. He believed that historical knowledge is essential to accurate biblical interpretation. Otherwise, Rauschenbusch said, the interpretation is just putting our own idea in and taking out what we want, then claiming divine authority of the idea. "Every biblical book," he urged, "originated in a definite historical environment." Its meaning is distorted when taken out of its historical setting.[93]

Rauschenbusch was a competent instructor of teachers. He introduced textual analysis, literary construction, and historical context as he examined the significance of text after text. As a pastor he was concerned to apply the text to contemporary life and society. He combined his preaching and teaching skills with his knowledge of American social life to convey the meaning of the Bible to his generation. These lessons provide a glimpse of Baptist Sunday school lesson material used in many Baptist churches reached by *The Inquirer*. The lessons also reveal Rauschenbusch at work on a sustained project demanding significant time and work. He was a well-informed scholar-pastor, pouring energy and thought into another avenue of ministry suited to his gifts, capping all of this work in 1895

---

[92] WR, "The First Christian Martyr," *The Inquirer*, August 28, 1892; also pp. 89–90 of the 1892 scrapbook, Rauschenbusch Family Papers.

[93] WR, "The Value and Use of History."

with the publication of his *Life of Jesus* for German language readers.[94]

Rauschenbusch's teaching efforts were not limited to publications. In the mid-1890s Rauschenbusch and Leighton Williams worked with the Deaconess program in New York City. The idea was to train nurses who had expressed a commitment to religious work among the poor.[95] In 1895–1896 Rauschenbusch delivered two series of studies on Jesus' parables prepared for the deaconesses of New York City. This is an extensive unpublished work; he addressed the teaching, homiletic, artistic, and doctrinal values of the parables.[96] Not surprisingly he readily connected the parables to the kingdom of God. These studies provide one more piece of evidence for his teaching ministry to inform the laity about the message of the Bible.

Rauschenbusch's daughter Winifred recalled her father saying that "in all of the early writing for periodicals he did, in addressing the smallest kind of meeting, he tried to organize his material and write it in top-notch style."[97] Rauschenbusch found many opportunities for what he called "literary works" during his years as pastor. His public addresses were frequently reported in the newspapers, often with notes of commendation by the reporter. He wrote articles for both German Baptist *Der Sendbote* (*The Messenger*) and also for English-language Baptist journals. The skills of organization and clarity in his writing as well as command of the Bible and contemporary events enabled Rauschenbusch to write effective sermons and Sunday school lessons. Developing a clear, pungent writing style served him well in preparing sermons and lessons and later when he argued for the social message of the gospel in his books.

Pastoral Roles: Counselor, City Leader, and Social Activist

Rauschenbusch and Pauline Rother met at a Baptist church conference in Milwaukee in 1889 and kept in touch thereafter by mail. Their letters are typical love-letters, conveying passion, longing, and mutual love. The wedding took place at Pauline's home church, First German Baptist Church in Milwaukee, on April 12, 1893. Walter and Pauline established a good marriage. Their first two children were born while he was still a pastor. Three more children would follow in Rochester.

Rauschenbusch kept busy with numerous pastoral responsibilities. He worked with the young people of his church and established rapport with them;

---

[94] WR, *Das Leben Jesu.*

[95] Daniel, "Reminiscences of My Friend," NABHC, #820, 17.

[96] See "Notes on the Parables Given to the Deaconesses," New York, 1895–1896, parts 1 and 2, box 16, Rauschenbusch Family Papers.

[97] Winifred [Rauschenbusch] Rorty to Dores Sharpe, December 17, 1938, box 50, Rauschenbusch Family Papers.

consequently, some of them confided in him, enabling him to offer spiritual counseling. Henry Winterer, a young man under Rauschenbusch's influence, wrote a letter to him in January 1893, describing the agonizing stages of his conversion: "On Sunday, January 9, 1893, I began to think if I should die, what would become of me."[98] He tried to put this notion aside but could not. He prayed for help on Thursday and Friday and felt relief. He felt awful for having spoken against God. He told Rauschenbusch that he needed help and hoped Rauschenbusch would pray for him. Rauschenbusch wrote at the top of the letter, "From Henry Winterer, one of my boys. He's going to be a minister yet."[99] Winterer obviously trusted his pastor and confided to him this account of his deepest spiritual struggles. This letter suggests that Rauschenbusch was deeply involved in the lives of the young people of his church. As a young pastor, Rauschenbusch took special care to minister to German Baptist youth by editing the paper designed especially for them, *Der Jugend-Herold* (*The Youth Herald*).[100]

Rauschenbusch kept up his connections with other churches. He participated in the annual missions conferences held in New York City, notably the meetings held at the Amity Baptist Church, organized by the church's missionary society. The object of the April 1893 conference was "to promote an intelligent interest among members of all Evangelical Churches in the subject of Missions, and to provide an opportunity for the free and courteous discussion of current missionary topics."[101] Most of the speakers were ordained ministers, but the program also included presentations by three women.

Rauschenbusch's church addressed some needs of German immigrants. For example, they hosted a musical and literary entertainment evening sponsored by the Abraham Lincoln Club and the Lyceum League of Americans in celebration of Washington's birthday. This event included the singing of patriotic songs (such as "America" and "Hail Columbia"), prayers, and addresses devoted to George Washington's achievements. This event clearly combined religious and political sensibilities with the idea of promoting both in the German-American community.[102] Rauschenbusch devoted much energy to ministry to immigrants. The immigrant community provided lifelong context for his work. He helped

---

[98] Henry Winterer to WR, n.d., box 139, Rauschenbusch Family Papers. Although no date is given on the letter, internal evidence suggests that the recorded conversion process began January 9, 1893.

[99] Ibid.

[100] Sharpe, *Walter Rauschenbusch*, 98.

[101] See the program of the "Third Annual Conference on Missions, held at the Amity Baptist Church/310 W. 54th Street, Monday and Tuesday, April 3 and 4, 1893," box 139, Rauschenbusch Family Papers.

[102] Musical and literary entertainment by the Abraham Lincoln Club, box 139, Rauschenbusch Family Papers.

them adjust to and embrace their new society.

Rauschenbusch lobbied politicians in New York City for social change in the 1890s. One interesting campaign he pursued was establishment of sand piles (sand boxes) for children. He wrote people with influence on behalf of the children, including the Children's Aid Society and the reformer Jacob Riis.[103] Riis said that the sand hill proposal was "first rate." He later informed Rauschenbusch that the law now assured that there would be playgrounds in the small parks of New York City.[104] Children of the tenements needed places to play. The campaign for sand piles was not just practical but also symbolic of a broader campaign to improve amenities for the betterment of society. The young pastor also campaigned against alcohol abuse. He reported to police commissioner Theodore Roosevelt two saloons that were in (non-specified) violation of the law. Roosevelt replied that he had at once given Rauschenbusch's letter to "the chief with instructions to have the two saloons in question carefully looked after."[105]

Rauschenbusch was an outspoken advocate for reforms of all sorts that would benefit the public. In April 1894 he spoke at a conference on good municipal government, advocating the building of bathhouses for use by the city's poor.[106] On November 18, 1895, Rauschenbusch read "New York as It Ought to Be," a paper prepared for the Baptist Ministers' Conference in which he advocated municipal control of gas, buildings for markets, public trams, telegraph and telephone stations, public parks, and sand piles. The *New York Times* reported that the paper was received with "loud applause."[107] The young activist energized fellow Baptist ministers by his speech, and the paper took notice.

The Baptist denomination in New York City struggled to hold its position during this era. William Bitting and other pastors, including Rauschenbusch, produced a report on the churches. In 1892–1893 the total number of Baptists in New York City was approximately 8000. The twenty-nine churches averaged memberships of 280, with attendance averaging 160 on Sunday morning and 215

---

[103] C. Loving Brace to WR, January 28, 1896, 1894–1908 scrapbook, Rauschenbusch Family Papers.

[104] Jacob Riis to WR, January 27, 1896, 1894–1908 scrapbook, Rauschenbusch Family Papers.

[105] Theodore Roosevelt to WR, July 5, 1895, 1894–1908 scrapbook, Rauschenbusch Family Papers.

[106] "Cheap Baths for the Poor: Walter Rauschenbusch Urges the Building of a Model House by the City," *New York Times*, April 16, 1894.

[107] "New York as It Ought to Be: An Address Before Baptist Ministers by the Rev. W. Rauschenbusch," *New York Times*, November 19, 1895.

in the evening. The pastors noted a lack of spiritual vigor and a lack of cooperation with other churches.[108] The national economic depression of 1892–1894 doubtless made growth more difficult because of reduced financial resources. It was the worst economic depression of the nineteenth century.[109] Work as pastor was a challenge.

As early as April 1888, A. H. Strong, president of Rochester Baptist Theological Seminary, had told Rauschenbusch that he wanted to make a place for him on the faculty. Rauschenbusch returned to Rochester periodically for serious discussions with Strong and with his most trusted professors, Webster and Stevens.[110] Strong made an offer; Rauschenbusch negotiated for a better salary. In the fall Rauschenbusch wrote that he had finally decided to decline the offer, but the seminary remained interested. When an opening occurred in 1897, Rauschenbusch's circumstances had changed. He had experienced some difficulty with church members, he had a family to care for, and his deafness was more serious. Rochester and academic life must have had its appeal.

Reception by Fellow Ministers

Baptist leaders gave Rauschenbusch high praise for his work as pastor of a New York City church. He was a friend to many pastors in New York City. In 1890 C. A. Daniel became pastor of the First German Baptist Church in Harlem. He recalled looking up to Rauschenbusch during the six years they ministered together in the city. Rauschenbusch was a source of support to him, writing "Courage brother, and patience.... I was here two and one-half years before I noted the beginning of an upward start. Keep plugging away...."[111] In 1896 Daniel was called to pastor the German Baptist Church in Rochester. The following year Rauschenbusch moved to Rochester where he became a model member of Daniel's church, offering friendship and support for the next eleven years. Daniel expressed profound gratitude for Rauschenbusch's support.[112] Whether serving as pastor, professor, or congregant, Rauschenbusch took seriously his responsibility for the welfare of the church and its ministers.

On Rauschenbusch's tenth anniversary as pastor, the Second German Baptist Church arranged a celebration and included many of his friends on the invitation list. Letters marking the occasion show that Rauschenbusch had made a

---

[108] William C. Bitting, John J. Brouner, Walter Rauschenbusch, Richard Hartley, Leighton Williams, "Report of Committee appointed to 'Consider our Present Condition as a Denomination' and to make suggestions for its improvement," 6 pages, printed, n.p., n.d., here, pages 1–2, box 17, Rauschenbusch Family Papers.

[109] This is the judgment of John Whiteclay Chambers II (*The Tyranny of Change*, 41).

[110] WR, diary, April 1888, box 97, Rauschenbusch Family Papers.

[111] Daniel, "Reminiscences of My Friend," 3–5.

[112] Ibid., 23.

strong and positive impression on Baptist life as a pastor in New York City and beyond. William H. P. Faunce, the brilliant pastor of Fifth Avenue Baptist Church in New York, wrote a glowing tribute to Rauschenbusch, indicating what Rauschenbusch had meant to him personally:

> [N]o minister in this city has been a greater blessing to me personally in my Christian life and ministry than has Walter Rauschenbusch. The first time I met him on coming to the city I was deeply impressed by his sincerity of spirit, his purity of motive and his absolute devotion to the Gospel of Christ, and his keen insight into all the problems of our day. I have never heard him speak without becoming a wiser and better man. He possesses the power, which few possess, of getting at once at the heart of any subject he discusses, and his insight into truth is almost unequalled in our ministry. I have always thought that his life was a visible fulfillment of the promise, "Blessed are the pure in heart, for they shall see…."

Then Faunce commented on his importance as a minister:

> Mr. Rauschenbusch does see as few men have seen, and his influence extends very far beyond his own dear church. His power is felt both by the English and German speaking population throughout large sections of our country…. [He] has gone forward year after year, and all of us are stronger because he had been strong, and braver because he has been brave. There is no minister in New York City to whom I owe more during the seven years that I have lived here, than I owe to Walter Rauschenbusch.[113]

This tribute from a fellow Baptist minister emphasizes Rauschenbusch's commitment to the Christian ministry, his intellectual power, his character, and his courage. Faunce readily acknowledged Rauschenbusch's influence; he was a perceptive observer.

William Newton Clarke, perhaps the leading Baptist theologian of the day, praised Rauschenbusch's personal qualities. He wrote from Hamilton Theological Seminary, "I have learned to hold him in very high esteem, and to think of him with great tenderness. Rarely have I known a man of such strength of mind, such sweetness of spirit, such brightness of humor, such breadth of interest, and such brave earnestness in behalf of whatever is true and holy."[114]

When Rauschenbusch left New York City for Rochester the following year, public evaluation of his service was equally glowing. The editor of *The Examiner*

---

[113] William P. Faunce to Charles A. Bauer, June 2, 1896, box 102, Rauschenbusch Family Papers. Recognized as one of Baptists' foremost intellectual leaders, Faunce was elected president of Brown University in 1899, where he served for thirty years. See "Faunce, William Herbert Perry," 299–301.

[114] William N. Clarke to Charles A. Bauer, May 28, 1896, box 102, Rauschenbusch Family Papers.

wrote,

> We are both glad and sorry to announce that our esteemed friend, Rev. Walter Rauschenbusch, has resigned the pastorate of the Second German Church of this city to accept the professorship of New Testament Interpretation in the Rochester Theological Seminary, made vacant by the lamented death of Professor Schaffer. We are glad because the vacancy in the seminary faculty is so quickly filled by one so peculiarly qualified for the position; sorry because of the loss to our denomination in this city of one of its strongest forces. Mr. Rauschenbusch is a man of marked individuality, an independent thinker, a fearless advocate of whatever he believes to be true, honest and of good report, and a master of strong Saxon English as well as of the parent German tongue.[115]

Members of the Second Baptist Church later placed an inscribed tablet in the church as a memorial to Rauschenbusch. The tribute recalled his central message: "'Thy Kingdom Come,' His Prayer and Passion, His Life and Inspiration, His Memory a Benediction to Multitudes."[116] By the end of his pastorate, Rauschenbusch had achieved much. In addition to his preaching and pastoral responsibilities in the largest German Baptist congregation in the country, he had published dozens of Sunday school lessons and written on many current topics. He had edited *Jungen-Herold,* the magazine for German Baptist young people. He engaged in extensive networking with other ministers. He had helped organize and publish *For the Right.* He was an active participant in the Brotherhood of the Kingdom and in the Baptist Congress. He was also an active participant in the local Baptist Ministers' Association. Clearly Rauschenbusch had made an impact well beyond his local congregation. Had he been content simply to serve his congregation, Rauschenbusch's influence would likely have been hardly noticed. In fact, it seems that the impression he left on Baptists, especially ministers, outside of his congregation was far more impressive and positive than his work with his own church members. His widening influence would not have been possible without his active life of writing, speech-making, and constant engagement in denominational discussions. Rauschenbusch had led a very active life as a pastor, denominationalist, and scholar. He left a strong legacy as a pastor-scholar. Rauschenbusch received many glowing tributes from fellow Baptists for the quality of his spiritual and intellectual contributions as a minister in America's leading city. What was the range of Rauschenbusch's contribution to Baptists? We turn next to exploring his contribution to his own denomination.

---

[115] *The Examiner*, July 1897; located on p. 33 of the 1897–1899 scrapbook, Rauschenbusch Family Papers.

[116] The wording of a tablet, 2nd German Baptist Church, New York City, #1015, NABHC archives.

CHAPTER 6

RAUSCHENBUSCH'S BAPTIST IDENTITY

Shaped by Baptist Principles

Rauschenbusch was a deeply committed advocate for his Baptist tradition. He was personally shaped by Baptist influences at home and church, and later at seminary. He devoted his work as a pastor to promoting Baptist life in his own German congregation, especially among its young people. At the denominational level, Rauschenbusch engaged in numerous debates published in religious journals. These discussions helped shape the Baptist denomination of his era. In addition, during his pastorate he participated actively in the Baptist Congress, a gathering of progressive Baptists. Rauschenbusch regularly stressed his Baptist identity throughout the years of his pastorate, and as a seminary professor he continued to promote the Baptist cause beginning with his 1903 inaugural lecture in the English division of Rochester Baptist Theological Seminary. He held that of all the Reformation traditions the Anabaptists were nearest the spirit of Christ, and he linked the Anabaptist spirit with the Baptists. Rauschenbusch remained an active contributor to the religious press throughout his career, and from time to time he discussed his views on Baptist issues for that audience. In 1905–1906 Rauschenbusch wrote a series of articles under the title "Why I Am a Baptist." These articles present a clear, persuasive, and systematic summary of Baptist principles. He called on Baptists to celebrate their history. Rauschenbusch was proud of his Baptist heritage: he never distanced himself from the denomination of his childhood and youth. He critiqued its weaknesses and took sides on internal debates, but he remained committed to Baptist teaching and practice throughout his life.

After August Rauschenbusch made his decision to become a Baptist, he spent the remainder of his life working for the denomination. He served German Baptist churches, prepared young German Baptist men for ministry at the German department in Rochester Theological Seminary, and researched Anabaptist origins in Switzerland and Germany. Here again his father's influence was decisive for Rauschenbusch. Baptist influences were never far from Walter as a young person. When the family moved to Germany, they worshiped in Baptist churches. Moreover, August sought out other Baptists, including a visit to Johann Oncken, the inspiration for the spread of Baptist churches to Germany and other European countries. While in Europe Walter personally observed features of both Roman Catholicism and Lutheranism and later defended Baptist views in part by analyzing what he considered to be deficiencies of other traditions.

The Rauschenbusch family worshiped regularly at the First German Baptist Church in Rochester. In this setting Walter learned Scripture, absorbed Baptist views, and here he made his profession of faith and was baptized March 16, 1879.[1] The Baptist church was also a catalyst for his vocational choice: he determined to become a Baptist minister. Baptist influences continued to surround Rauschenbusch during his higher education. Rochester Theological Seminary was considered one of the leading Baptist seminaries of the era. Rauschenbusch was deeply devoted to Baptist work during his pastorate in New York City and gave special attention to its foreign mission effort. Later as a professor, he critiqued Baptist thought, observing that it was "rather flat and thin."[2] But as a professor he also understood his responsibility to be the strengthening and promotion of the Baptist tradition through training ministries and publishing in denominational journals. He pursued this goal throughout the course of his professional life. This chapter explores key dimensions of Rauschenbusch's Baptist identity and his advocacy for Baptist belief and practice.

Rauschenbusch and the Baptist Congress

Early in his ministry Rauschenbusch reached beyond his local Baptist congregation to engage with fellow ministers in the Baptist Congress. Organized in 1882, the Baptist Congress was a forum designed for Baptist leaders to address the relation of religion to a wide range of political, economic, social, and religious issues in American society.[3] The full title of the organization was "The Baptist Congress for the Discussion of Current Questions." Current questions included theological topics, but also much more. At the Congress Rauschenbusch found a welcome place to network and explore his new ideas with other progressive ministers. He joined the Congress in 1888.

The Plan of Organization of the Baptist Congress states that "the spirit of the Congress is to promote healthful sentiment among Baptists through free and courteous discussion."[4] The work of the Congress was controlled by a large committee of one hundred or more. Any member of a Baptist congregation could become an Annual Member of the Congress for one year by paying dues. Baptist

---

[1] Minus, *Walter Rauschenbusch*, 17.
[2] WR, "Introduction to Church History" lectures, box 1, Rauschenbusch Family Papers.
[3] Sharpe, *Walter Rauschenbusch*, 77, 97; Evans, *The Kingdom Is Always but Coming*, 75.
[4] "Plan of Organization," xii.

pastors and professors from both the North and the South participated. The annual meetings lasted three days, and the program was divided into six major segments. For each of these sessions one or two people read a paper of not more than twenty-five minutes, another person presented an oral response of not more than ten minutes, and members of the audience offered brief remarks. This structure encouraged focused discussion on diverse topics. Presentations and responses were recorded by shorthand and published in full each year, providing a vast array of reflections by Baptist participants.[5] This format was well suited to Rauschenbusch's analytic approach to issues.

Rauschenbusch addressed a variety of topics at the Baptist Congress meetings. Although he sustained connection with the group after his move to Rochester, he was most active in the Congress during his years as a pastor. From 1888 to 1895 he made several presentations to the Congress. Some dealt with religious topics, others with social issues. Two of the religious topics dealt with the general nature of religion where he discussed "Emotionalism in Religion" (1893) and "Ethical versus Forensic Conceptions of Salvation" (1893).[6] An earlier paper dealt with the traditional Baptist topic of the "Relation of Church and State" (1889).[7] Two additional papers addressed the internal Baptist issues of "Tradition as a Formative Force in Baptist Doctrine and Church Life" (1894) and "Centralization of Baptist Polity" (1895).[8] His remaining presentations discussed social issues, including education, immigration, monopolies, social reform, money power, and semi-public corporations. All these topics presented pressing questions that Rauschenbusch believed should be addressed by the Baptist leaders. He also published many of these papers separately in popular media, especially Baptist newspapers.

At the Providence, Rhode Island, meeting in 1895, Rauschenbusch took up the question of centralization of power in the Baptist mission board. He acknowledged that controversy had arisen because the Mission Board controlled money and designated its use. He conceded that if boards were abusing power, concentration of authority was not a good thing. Many Baptists, protective of local church autonomy, were suspicious of the power of boards who raised money for

[5] The group published *The Proceedings of the Baptist Congress* each year. Each volume is about 220 pages, plus the table of contents and the lists of officers, committee members, and annual members.

[6] WR, "Emotionalism in Religion: Discussion," 33–34; "Ethical versus Forensic Conceptions of Salvation: Discussion," 76–78.

[7] WR, "Relation of Church and State: Discussion," 138–40. Also see WR, "Keep Them Separate," 3.

[8] WR, "Tradition as a Formative Force in Baptist Doctrine and Church Life," 36–39; "Centralization of Baptist Polity," 58.

missions and set their own agendas. But, on the other hand, he noted that "centralization is made necessary by our development."[9] From 1895 to 1914 there was a growing desire among denominational leaders for increased efficiency, including the creation of national boards and eventually the Northern Baptist Convention (in 1907). Here Rauschenbusch was pragmatic, and he supported centralization. He argued that Christianity was "elastic...not framed in any rigid polity...and able to adapt...to meet the needs of the day."[10] He argued that centralization is not necessarily dangerous because the spirit of America and the spirit of Baptists "make for liberty."[11] He said that this spirit of liberty counteracts centralization, and he supported centralization if it was "of the right kind."[12] In this debate he was seeking balance between the Baptist tradition of direct local democratic governance and promise of increased efficiency anticipated by centralization. In short, Rauschenbusch was keen to support the growing missionary program of Baptist life and thought centralization would help achieve its goals.

A decade later Rauschenbusch traveled to Louisville, Kentucky, for the Baptist Congress to present his paper "Does the New Testament Provide a Definite and Permanent Church Polity?"[13] Drawing on his knowledge of church history, biblical text criticism, and logical inferences in his analysis, he noted the absence of a text directly addressing the problem, and he reminded the audience that a single example was not a precedent. Moreover, he suggested that Jewish and Gentile churches came from cultures that traditionally may have practiced different forms of organization and adapted them in their new churches. But he did not leave his audience without direction. He recalled the language of the Gospels: "He that is greatest among you shall be your servant...even as the Son of Man came not to be ministered unto, but to minister and to give his life a ransom for many."[14] He concluded that the spirit of this passage precludes hierarchy in the church. He said that if the church does not look to the New Testament for legal rules and precedents, but rather to the spirit of Jesus Christ, then it will find the "definite and permanent principles for a Christian church polity."[15] He affirmed that "all members [of the church] must be on a level of freedom and equality."[16] Also, he stated that leadership in the churches would emerge based on "natural

[9] WR, "Centralization of Baptist Polity," 58.

[10] Ibid., 59.

[11] Ibid.

[12] Ibid., 60.

[13] WR, "Does the New Testament Provide a Definite and Permanent Church Polity?" 108–15. The Northern Baptist Convention would be formed two years later, in 1907.

[14] Ibid., 114, quoting Matt 20:28.

[15] Ibid., 115.

[16] Ibid.

and spiritual gifts."[17] In this analysis Rauschenbusch returned to one of the leading themes of his writings: the church must discover the "spirit of Christ" and live by it. In both of these addresses on Baptist polity Rauschenbusch stood for seeking the spirit of Christ and recognizing the values of liberty and equality. The melding of biblical texts and American political ideals is clear in these addresses.

In 1892 Rauschenbusch served as recording secretary for the Baptist Congress. In his "Prefatory Note" to the *Proceedings,* he reflected on the value of the Congress. He wrote that "students of current questions will find this [volume] a ready means of reference to some of the best thought of our denomination." Furthermore, "those who follow...the progress of Baptist thought will see the working of the mind of our denomination recorded here with a freedom and accuracy unparalleled, probably, in any other set of documents."[18] This is a bold claim for the independence, integrity, and quality of the Baptist Congress and explains why Rauschenbusch was devoted to its work. The annual conventions of the denominations provided a forum for inspiration, information, and program promotion. But Rauschenbusch much preferred the Congress where the approach was analytical and reflective for Baptists who wanted openly to debate major current topics. The experience of the Baptist Congress was highly valued by other participants as well. Carter Helm Jones wrote rhetorically, "Is this Congress worth having?" He replied, "A Baptist Congress had its finest definition this afternoon in Dr. Matterson's remark that it promoted denominational self-knowledge, and I think that is one of the finest things in the world."[19] "The Baptist Congress," he said, "is a platform where the denomination can express itself."[20] This organization offered thoughtful Baptists a networking structure for likeminded pastors and for critical examination of current issues facing American society and the Baptist denomination. Rauschenbusch was very much at home with this gathering of progressive Baptists.

Baptist Denominational Controversies

Despite efforts toward achieving unity and peace in the churches, the actual state of affairs in American religion is often characterized by conflict over belief and practices and the authority to settle disputes. In Baptist life the problem is exacerbated by local church polity. In the 1890s Baptist congregations faced a number of issues. Rauschenbusch was an independent thinker, and as a young minister he engaged his fellow Baptists in dialogue. In 1892 alone he engaged in public debate over no fewer than four lively controversies among New York City

---

[17] Ibid.

[18] WR, "Prefatory Note," n.p.

[19] Jones, "Comments," 116.

[20] Ibid., 117.

Baptist ministers: the role of creeds, seventh-day worship, the use of the gown in the pulpit, and the problems with the annual meetings of the denomination. He articulated his view of Baptist positions in all of these discussions. The debates did not resolve these questions, but they reveal vitality among Baptists in a rapidly changing society, and they reveal Rauschenbusch as an engaged participant in shaping denominational identity.

One of the most important issues Rauschenbusch addressed was the ongoing tension between the liberty of individual Christians to seek truth and the authority of creeds.[21] He addressed the issue in his article "Heretics in the Truth." He began the article with a quotation from Milton's *Areopagitica,* one of the great seventeenth-century pleas for religious toleration. Milton wrote, "Truth is compared in the Scripture to a streaming fountain. If these waters flow not in a perpetual progression, they sicken into a muddy pool of conformity and tradition. A man may be a heretic in truth."[22]

In his article Rauschenbusch addressed freedom of inquiry in current Baptist theological reflection. He argued that a Christian should adopt Milton's attitude of becoming an open-minded inquirer after truth, rejecting the notion that a received creed or body of doctrine can be fixed for all time. He held that each Baptist ultimately should seek truth for himself or herself rather than passively accepting a borrowed faith without personal reflection. He wrote,

> Baptists reject the authority of creeds in which truth is cut up, dried, neatly arranged, and conveniently labeled, not because we refuse the matter in the creeds but because we believe it is better for a Christian to make an imperfect collection for himself than to have the perfect collection made for him.... And so we prefer to give a man the Bible and bid him search there and in the profundities of his own heart.... In our own denomination it is peculiarly important that this be recognized. For we build not on authority but on truth.[23]

For Rauschenbusch the quest for truth was personal. Authority lies within the experience of the individual, not in a creed, and he continued,

> Therefore when any man eyes with mistrust the free search for truth in any direction, when he tries to choke off discussion by bluster or the ominous shake of the editorial head, he is proclaiming that the foundation of the Baptist denomination is unsafe, and he weans our church members from that free pursuit of truth which alone can make them stalwart and victorious, and trains up a decrepit future generation for our church. Such a man is the real heretic whom Baptists should cry down and read out of the denomination. To quote Milton

[21] See WR, "Heretics in the Truth," *Inquirer*, April 14, 1892; also on p. 34 of the 1892 scrapbook, Rauschenbusch Family Papers.

[22] Ibid.

[23] Ibid.

again, "They are the troublers; they are the dividers of unity...."[24]

In this article Rauschenbusch took a very strong position against creeds and in favor of individual responsibility in searching out the truth. This position mirrored his own training and experience. He wanted readers to understand theology as reflection on religious experience, based on individual pursuit of truth about God, not as a creed adopted in the past and accepted as forever binding all future believers. Avoiding creedalism is a recurring issue among Baptists. Rauschenbusch made his position clear: Baptists must not let themselves be bound by rigid creeds but must affirm freedom to seek truth for themselves. The position of noncreedalism formally remained a cherished Baptist ideal, but not without serious periodic challenges.

A second debate among fellow Baptists centered on the question of Sabbath (Saturday) worship observed by Seventh-day Baptists. Rauschenbusch read his paper "Modern Judaizers" before the New York Baptist Ministers Association, explaining why Baptists need not worship on the Sabbath. He used strong language to argue his point, and Abram H. Lewis, editor of *The Sabbath Outlook*, a Seventh-day Baptist journal, reprinted Rauschenbusch's address with a rejoinder.[25] In the address Rauschenbusch argued that Jesus and Paul rejected religious leaders who insisted on requiring outward observances. He said there was no value in traditions of worship such as having a congregation "rise, sit, kneel" or in observing certain times and days and places for worship.[26] He wrote that just as "the Judaizers insisted on circumcision in Paul's day; the Sabbatarians insist on Saturday worship in our day."[27] Rauschenbusch argued that scriptural guidance called for one day of rest in seven without worrying about which day. He said that the Judaizers mistook the sign for the thing, but that Paul's view of liberty delivered Christians from rigidly following the command to worship on Saturday. Thus Rauschenbusch defended the Christian tradition of Sunday worship in opposition to literal observance of the command in Exodus 20.

For editor Lewis, Rauschenbusch's position was an arbitrary rejection of the requirement of Saturday worship made clear in the Ten Commandments. Lewis insisted in his reply to Rauschenbusch that without holding certain convictions the Baptist denomination would disappear. He held that places of worship do not matter, but time of worship does. It was a command from God and therefore a matter of obedience for Christians. Moreover, he said that if it is "Judaizing" to keep the fourth commandment, it is equally "Judaizing" to keep the fifth or the

---

[24] Ibid.

[25] WR, "Modern Judaizers," *The Sabbath Outlook*, April 1892; also on p. 43 of the 1892 scrapbook, Rauschenbusch Family Papers.

[26] Ibid.

[27] Ibid.

tenth. For Lewis the bottom line was that it is arbitrary to reject the clear guidelines of one of the Ten Commandments. Lewis nevertheless closed his response by commending Rauschenbusch for his good spirit. He said that he personally knew and honored Rauschenbusch but that he must oppose his fundamental error.[28]

Rauschenbusch replied in a sequel to his "Modern Judaizers" article.[29] He stated his position that under Christ the Old Testament law was abrogated, and it was up to the Sabbatarians to prove that this law was an exception. He reiterated that it was not "Judaizing" to keep one day, but it was Judaizing to require a specific day of the week. Rauschenbusch did not give a strong argument for supporting Sunday worship; his father had written a little book on the subject, and it may well be that for him the issue had been settled long before, so Sunday worship needed no further defense.[30] In reply to Lewis's charge that his rationalization would lead to giving up Baptist identity, Rauschenbusch energetically denied the charge. He wrote, "I am a Baptist. I baptize believers only, and by immersion only. I demand of unbaptized believers that they shall be baptized…my position on the law has not yet affected my practice as a Baptist."[31] Lewis held his ground, replying that Jesus kept the Sabbath and that Christians today should not abandon obedience to the Ten Commandments but should follow the example of Jesus and worship on Saturday.

The Sabbath controversy followed the Baptists into the following year. It was the major topic of discussion at the Baptist ministers' meeting in 1893. In *The Evangel and Sabbath Outlook* Lewis described the opinions of the presenters and discussants in the meeting:

> The younger men were mainly silent, and many were troubled and thoughtful. Several of the speakers seemed more anxious to be rid of the whole thing than they did to candidly discuss the paper. It was a strange discussion to occur in such a gathering, among men who so frequently assert that Baptist history and Baptist doctrine show that "The Bible alone is the Baptist standard of faith and practice."[32]

The debate appears in part at least to have been over the fear of losing young

---

[28] Ibid.

[29] WR, "Modern Judaizers," *The Sabbath Outlook*, June 1892; also on pp. 67–68 of the 1892 scrapbook, Rauschenbusch Family Papers.

[30] A. Rauschenbusch, *Saturday or Sunday: Which Should We Observe?*, 96 pages.

[31] Ibid.

[32] Article in *The Evangel and Sabbath Outlook*, December 14, 1893 in the 1893 scrapbook, Rauschenbusch Family Papers. The 1893 scrapbook has no page numbers, but items are arranged in roughly chronological order.

Baptist ministers to a rival denomination.[33] "The Bible alone" was a popular phrase among Baptists, but the Bible requires interpretation, and these Baptist ministers were sharply divided over how it should be interpreted. The resolution of the matter was to agree on no resolution: the two views were accommodated by continuing to maintain two separate denominations. This was a common solution to divisions among American Protestants, including Baptists.[34]

Another minor debate arose over Baptist ministers wearing a gown to lead worship services.[35] The Reverend Dr. Robert Stuart MacArthur, articulate and polished pastor of Calvary Baptist Church in New York City, favored wearing a gown in the pulpit. He thought it added dignity to the worship service in this most affluent of the Baptist churches in New York City. His motivation was to enhance the aesthetics of worship. Rauschenbusch thought MacArthur's innovation warranted discussion because of its implication. Rauschenbusch opposed formalism in religion, and he offered his reasons. His first argument was that there is no desire for a gown in most Baptist churches. Baptist churches were generally plain, and the use of gowns seemed to appear only in wealthy churches. Rauschenbusch appealed to scriptural example. He asked, "Did Jesus and the apostles wear gowns or desire them? Were they for simplicity or elaborateness in the externals of worship?"[36] Looking further to examples in history, Rauschenbusch asked rhetorically whether the leaders of the Methodists, Quakers, and "the Reformation restorers of spiritual religion" encouraged the use of gowns.[37] Rauschenbusch maintained that elaboration of the outward trappings of worship was almost invariably accompanied by decline in spiritual life. Moreover, he objected because he thought the use of gowns sharpened the division between clergy and laity. Finally, Rauschenbusch appealed to a cherished Baptist doctrine: "The churches that hold to the universal priesthood of believers will be found to have the least distinction in the dress of the clergy."[38] Rauschenbusch concluded his argument with the hope that Dr. MacArthur would not introduce the gown into the Calvary pulpit, reasoning, "He will add nothing to his spiritual power. He

---

[33] The First Seventh-day Baptist Church of New York had 141 members at its fiftieth anniversary in 1846. It was one of one hundred Seventh-day Baptist churches in the United States in 1895. See Main, "The Seventh-day Baptist General Conference, 1802–1902," 1:227; 2:698.

[34] For a recent account of the Seventh-Day Baptist denomination, see Sanford, *A Choosing People*.

[35] See "The Gown and the Pulpit" (no journal or date given), p. 46 of the 1892 scrapbook, Rauschenbusch Family Papers.

[36] Ibid.

[37] Ibid.

[38] Ibid.

may lose by it."[39]

Formalism was a growing trend in the worship practices of several American denominations during this era. Worshipers who could afford to do so built more elaborate buildings and included stained glass windows, expensive organs, and professional singers to enhance worship. Other groups, such as the Holiness wing of Methodism, resisted this trend. They stressed the holy Christian life and eventually separated to form new Holiness denominations in the late nineteenth and early twentieth century. The Baptists resolved the issue congregation by congregation. Their polity spared them from requiring uniformity in all churches and therefore avoided division of the denomination over this issue.

A fourth point of Baptist debate focused on current practices in annual conventions of the denomination.[40] Rauschenbusch opened his criticism somewhat cautiously with the statement that the meeting in Philadelphia was good, but it could have been great. He reported that this had been his usual experience at Baptist conventions. He raised the question of the cause of the current malaise in these meetings, asked what could be done to improve the annual meetings, and offered three suggestions. First, he mentioned the problem of "the blight of eloquence," noting that rhetorical polish took precedence over the spiritual depth in the convention preaching. He observed that although the audience applauded the speaker's eloquence at the end of speeches, in the end participants felt empty and disappointed. The convention planners tended to use the same preachers, noted for their eloquence, year after year, but Rauschenbusch suggested that new speakers who conveyed spiritual power were needed to make a convention great. He pressed the issue to the organizers, asking, "Why were some of the retired missionaries not heard? Why did we not hear from some of those just going out? It would have been inspiring for them and for us as well."[41] His second suggestion was to limit the length of sermons and to use a bell, if necessary, to limit long-winded preachers. He was weary of hour-long sermons. By contrast, speeches at the meetings of the Baptist Congress were limited to twenty-five minutes, and the threat of a bell ringing caused all participants to finish on time. "Thirty minutes is enough time for almost any topic," Rauschenbusch declared.[42] Third, he suggested adopting the "federal system," that is, having some plenary gather-

---

[39] Ibid.

[40] WR, "About the Anniversaries," *The Examiner*, June 23, 1892; also on pp. 60–61 of the 1892 scrapbook, Rauschenbusch Family Papers.

[41] Ibid.

[42] Ibid.

ings of all participants alternating with smaller break-out sessions on varied topics.[43] Rauschenbusch thought about many issues, and he was not shy about offering his suggestions for reform on matters relating to church and denomination. His was a stimulating presence for Baptists, as his engagement in these four debates indicates.

During the Progressive era, denominations became preoccupied with efficiency. Books such as Frederick W. Taylor's *The Principles of Scientific Management* (1911) and Clarence Barbour's *Making Religion Efficient* (1912)[44] provided guidance. The largest structural change in Baptist life during Rauschenbusch's lifetime was the organization of the Northern Baptist Convention in 1907. As with the formation of a Mission Board, the debate over the establishment of a convention centered on whether concentration of power in a convention might cause a loss of power for individual congregations. Freedom and authority pose a never-ending issue for Baptists. Rauschenbusch supported the new organization. These debates reveal how engaged Rauschenbusch was not only as a local pastor, but also in joining Baptist discussions at associational and denominational levels. He did not shy away from assuming leadership roles. He took positions and offered reasoned arguments for the positions he believed Baptists should hold.

Rauschenbusch and the Anabaptists

After he had chosen to become a Baptist, August Rauschenbusch spent much time in Germany and Switzerland researching the Anabaptists, understanding them to be kindred spirits with the Baptists. Following his father's lead, Rauschenbusch frequently discussed the Anabaptists, finding in them models of genuine Christianity. When he visited Germany during his sabbatical in 1891, he reported frequent long talks with Dr. Ludwig Keller, who published extensively on the Anabaptists.[45] Rauschenbusch believed that Anabaptist thought and practice had more promise for the future of Protestantism than the teachings of the

---

[43] This convention model is regularly used today for meetings of large Baptist conventions such as the Baptist World Alliance.

[44] Taylor, Frederick A., *The Principles of Scientific Management*; Barbour, Clarence., *Making Religion Efficient.*

[45] WR, diary, November 1891. During the 1880s Ludwig Keller (1849–1915) published books on the Anabaptists, including *Geschichte der Wiedertäufer und ihres Reiches zu Münster* (*History of the Anabaptists and Their Kingdom at Münster*), 1880; *Ein Apostel der Wiedertäufer* (*An Apostle of the Anabaptists*), 1882; *Die Reformation und die älteren Reformparteien* (*The Reformation and an Alternative Reformation Party*), 1885; and *Die Waldenser und die deutschen Bibelübersetzungen* (*The Waldensians and the German Translation of the Bible*), 1886. Later Rauschenbusch highly recommended Henry Vedder's *Balthasar Hubmaier: the Leader of the Anabaptists* (1905). See Smucker, *The Origins of Walter Rauschenbusch's Social Ethics*, 150, n. 25.

magisterial reformers.[46] When Rauschenbusch gave his inaugural lecture as church history professor in the English division to the Rochester Seminary audience on September 14, 1903, he chose as his subject "The Prophetic Character of the Anabaptist Movement."[47] He was not only informing the audience; he was attempting to demonstrate to Baptists the relevance of knowing church history and the importance of knowing the Anabaptist heritage. He listed many reasons for his approval of the Anabaptists. Rauschenbusch said the Anabaptists were prophetic in the sense that they represented an "advance movement" in the "process of spiritual emancipation."[48] By "advance movement" Rauschenbusch meant that the Anabaptists were right to demand that the established church end its practice of abuse of tithes and also its ceremonialism in worship. Moreover, they adopted new understandings of baptism and the Lord's Supper.[49] Third and most importantly, Anabaptists taught that the personal experience of Christianity was "the only essential" of the faith. Whereas Luther had formulated the doctrine of salvation by faith alone, the Anabaptists improved on Luther by their insistence on personal religious experience.[50] Fourth, the Anabaptists gave far more emphasis to ethical conduct than to doctrine. Instead of seeking the pleasures of the world, they sought to raise standards of morality.[51] Fifth, the Anabaptists "undertook to organize a church of believers."[52] This was their reason for rejecting infant baptism. Moreover, as a church Anabaptists shared their goods with needy brethren.

Sixth, the Anabaptists repudiated compulsion on behalf of religion. Many of their members had suffered brutal punishments or death for their beliefs, and they advocated separation of the church from the state.[53] Seventh, the Anabaptists emphasized the activity of the Holy Spirit in the heart of the individuals. "The Spirit is the principle of freedom," Rauschenbusch wrote, "and hence of progress."[54] Here again Rauschenbusch identified American Protestant cultural

[46] WR, diary, November 1891, box 97, Rauschenbusch Family Papers.

[47] WR, "The Prophetic Character of the Anabaptist Movement: Address at the Opening of the Seminary, September 14, 1903," typescript, box 5, Rauschenbusch Family Papers.

[48] WR, "The Prophetic Character," 2. In Rauschenbusch's view, the church advanced as it became freer and more democratic.

[49] Ibid., 6–8.

[50] Ibid., 8–9.

[51] Ibid., 10–11.

[52] Ibid., 12.

[53] Ibid., 15. Moreover, Rauschenbusch emphasized that this separation had become part of American religious practice.

[54] WR, "The Prophetic Character," 17.

values with Anabaptist interpretation of Christianity. Finally, Rauschenbusch affirmed that the Anabaptists believed in "a religious transformation of social life."[55] He wrote that whereas Luther distrusted the masses of people, the Anabaptists embraced the masses. Rauschenbusch saw Anabaptist Christians as people who possessed "prophetic power"; in short, they were an "ideal" expression of Christianity.[56] Modern scholars offer a far more analytical view of Anabaptists, but Rauschenbusch's praise is unstinting and uncritical because he found in them ideas and practices for the modern American church to emulate.[57]

Rauschenbusch emphasized Anabaptist traits he especially valued such as spiritual rather than ceremonial religion, experiential rather than doctrinal religion, and ethical conduct rather than intellectual orthodoxy. They stood for religious liberty. For Rauschenbusch, the Anabaptists were "prophetic" in their more comprehensive rejection of the past and its false forms of Christianity and because they represented the direction of the Christian future. Rauschenbusch clearly appropriated from history what he wanted to use to articulate as his conception of genuine Christian practice in the present. He thought in terms of a normative Christianity by which modern churches should be measured. He used both Scripture and Baptist/Anabaptist criteria and added his own criteria of freedom and progress to show that the Anabaptists had advanced beyond other Reformation forms of Christianity. In 1905 Rauschenbusch translated and commented on two letters from Conrad Grebel and the Zurich Anabaptists to Thomas Münzer. He concluded that they were "moving steadfastly and bravely toward realist [Christianity because] they fend off any substitute for personal experience in religion."[58] Key criteria of a genuine church for Rauschenbusch included emphasis on personal experience of Christ, democratic authority in the structure of the local church, and religious tolerance based on separation of church and state. All of these traits were expressions of growing democracy.[59] Anabaptists and Baptists shared these beliefs, and he found both movements to be true expressions of the

[55] WR, "The Prophetic Character," 18. Rauschenbusch is here affirming Anabaptist support for his belief in the social character of Christianity.

[56] WR, "The Prophetic Character," 20, 1.

[57] In the twentieth century Mennonite and other scholars made great strides in recovering Anabaptist history in its original context. Modern scholarship was early summarized by Williams, *The Radical Reformation*.

[58] WR, "The Zurich Anabaptists and Thomas Münzer," 106.

[59] WR, "A Baptist Reinterpretation of Church History," 1, 5–8, typescript, box 21, Rauschenbusch Family Papers.

spirit of Christ.[60] In his view, the Reformation was an "unfinished movement."[61] Rauschenbusch regularly employed examples from sectarian church movements to serve as benchmarks for setting standards for the present church, and the Anabaptists most nearly met his criteria before the emergence of the Baptists.[62]

Why I Am a Baptist: Rauschenbusch's Summary of the Baptist Tradition

When asked as a minister to speak to young students, Rauschenbusch often took the occasion to inform them and try to inspire them to cherish their Baptist heritage. His address "Baptists in History" is a good example of this effort.[63] He told his young Baptist audience that their history should be a cause of pride. The Baptists had "cut loose from the past" when the church needed reform. Rauschenbusch drew an important contrast between the religious practice in the United States and Europe. Baptists do not claim to embrace the whole of society as state churches do, he said, but admit only those who make a conscious choice to belong to the church. Rauschenbusch was also proud to report that Baptists had no dark record of suppressing dissent or forcing conformity as other traditions did. This comment was a not so subtle jab at other denominations, especially Roman Catholicism. He was proud of the Baptist heritage of religious liberty. Regarding baptism, he noted that after the Reformation appeared it "did not take long to discover that infant baptism was not in the New Testament."[64] The Anabaptists rejected infant baptism. Contrary to a successionist belief of some Baptists that Baptist history could be traced to the era of the New Testament, Rauschenbusch believed that Baptists had no traceable historical continuity to the first century. He thought that Baptists nevertheless carried the spirit of biblical Christianity, and he told the students that they were fortunate to be part of a tradition that held the idea of personal spiritual experience as the basis for church membership. He wanted Baptist youth to be informed and proud of their heritage.

Rauschenbusch shared his convictions about the Baptist heritage with enthusiasm on many occasions, not only to student gatherings, but also to his own

---

[60] He is, of course, not engaging the question of Baptist origins, widely debated by historians in the twentieth century. Instead, he is affirming that both groups embraced what he considered to be key tenets of genuine Christianity. He saw them as a model for the present American church.

[61] WR, "A Baptist Reinterpretation," 9.

[62] C. H. Moehlman, Rauschenbusch's successor at Rochester, confirmed that Rauschenbusch "presented a very sympathetic approach to left-wing movements" (see Smucker, *The Origins of Walter Rauschenbusch's Social Ethics*, 150, n. 25).

[63] WR, "Baptists in History," May 1, 1903, at the meeting of the Baptist Young People of New York, Address 2 (1902–1903):140–52, box 152, Rauschenbusch Family Papers.

[64] Ibid.

church members and to associational meetings of Baptist churches in New York and beyond. At the meeting of the Rochester Baptist Social Union in 1903, Rauschenbusch addressed the Baptist insistence on the concept of a believer's church. He noted that all churches believe their church members are Christian, "but the heart has been cut out of the doctrine by the belief that baptism regenerates, resulting in a baptized membership instead of a regenerate one."[65] He claimed that "of the three traditional bases for church membership—ritual, creed and experience—Baptists recognized experience, the soul's encounter with God, as the only true basis [for church membership]."[66] Here Rauschenbusch articulated this Baptist foundational belief by contrasting it with almost all other denominations. Baptists insisted that a person express belief and trust in Christ for salvation before baptism, and this set Baptists apart from most modern American denominations. Rauschenbusch was a strong Baptist advocate, and he was always prepared to celebrate central Baptist convictions.

Baptist identity is elusive, and it has been defined in many ways. Rauschenbusch contributed his own reflections to this discussion. He affirmed the importance of the Baptist heritage most fully and most directly in "Why I Am a Baptist," a five-part series of articles published in 1905–1906 by *The Rochester Baptist Monthly*.[67] This was his most thorough and systematic attempt to define, summarize, and vigorously argue for Baptist thought and practice. His audience was the general Baptist community, and these articles amount to a brief Baptist manual. In his introductory article Rauschenbusch described two models of becoming a Baptist. He confessed with disarming frankness that he was Baptist because his father was a Baptist; moreover, he observed that this is the experience of most Baptists. But Rauschenbusch declared that his father was Baptist by choice: August "found in [Baptist] teachings the truths that he had been grasping for, and under great loss of position and trouble of soul, became a Baptist."[68] Walter set these two models against one another to emphasize the Baptist position that each person born into a Baptist family must individually decide whether to become a Christian. He drew a simple parallel, noting that just as citizens are Americans by birth, they also should become Americans by conviction; similarly, children born into Baptist homes must adopt their Baptist views through personal

[65] The report on Rauschenbusch's speech "Regenerate Church Membership" appears in *Rochester Baptist Monthly* 17/7 (March 1903): 52.

[66] Ibid.

[67] WR, "Why I Am a Baptist," *The Rochester Baptist Monthly*, "Why I Am a Baptist: Prelude," 20/2 (November 1905): 2–3; "Why I Am a Baptist: My First Reason," 20/4 (December 1905): 85–88; "Why I Am a Baptist: My Second Reason," 20/5 (January 1906): 106–108; "Why I Am a Baptist: My Third Reason," 20/6 (February 1906): 134–36; "Why I Am a Baptist: My Fourth Reason," 20/7 (March 1906): 156–59.

[68] WR, "Why I Am a Baptist," *The Rochester Baptist Monthly* 20 (1905–1906): 2.

conviction. The analogy is imprecise, but his intent is clear: he affirmed the necessity of personal choice to commit to Christ.

Following this brief preface, Rauschenbusch wrote four full articles and developed four major categories of reasons for being Baptist. His first reason for being Baptist was that the Christian faith, as Baptists hold it, sets spiritual experience boldly to the fore as the one great thing in religion.[69] He said that Baptists call each person to conscious repentance from sin to faith in Christ. If someone wants to enter a Baptist church, said Rauschenbusch, the only criterion is evidence of such experience. Rauschenbusch explained that the point of religion is to put people in contact with God.[70] How is this accomplished? Rauschenbusch called on his knowledge of church history to draw contrasting claims among Christian traditions. He noted that the Catholic Church emphasized sacraments and rituals and that the Lutherans stressed catechism and confirmation to make this connection. But Baptists relied on experience as the bedrock of their faith. Rauschenbusch believed that making personal experience the starting point of faith had significant implications. He observed, for example, that "the great mass of men take their religion at second hand," but he argued that this is not true religion. The essential point of religion is that it be experienced by each individual.[71] Rauschenbusch conceded that not all Baptists recognize experience as the core of their faith. Some Baptists insist on "immersion in a purely legal and ritualistic spirit."[72] Others "would be only too glad if we had an iron-clad Baptist creed."[73] And he recognized that "experience" can be merely a "shallow emotion" for some.[74] Nevertheless, Rauschenbusch clearly embraced voluntary personal experience as the foundational Baptist principle that for him made religion true and vital. This belief is, of course, the historic basis for Baptists rejecting infant baptism. It is fully compatible with the practice of the revivalism Baptists embraced during the First and Second Great Awakenings in the mid-eighteenth and early nineteenth centuries and for many waves of revival thereafter. Baptists have maintained the idea that each individual must make the personal decision to trust in God, and that no one can do that for another person. Rauschenbusch's first reason for embracing the Baptist path is that true religion is personal and experienced.

Rauschenbusch organized his second argument around Baptist social expression and organization. He had begun the series with his very strong emphasis on individual experience. Next he turned to its corollary. He wrote, "But religion

[69] WR, "Why I Am a Baptist: My First Reason," 85.
[70] Ibid., 85–86.
[71] Ibid., 87.
[72] Ibid.
[73] Ibid.
[74] Ibid.

is not a purely individual matter. Nothing in life is. We are social beings, and all elements of our life come to their full development only through social interchange and cooperation."[75] Baptist social organization has several important implications according to Rauschenbusch. He developed three in particular. First, Baptist churches admit only people "who deliberately apply" for membership and who seek to distinguish themselves from "the world."[76] They have an emphasis on living the Christian life. Second, Baptist churches are "Christian democracies." The congregation is the locus of authority, and it confers power on its ministers and officers. Rauschenbusch declared that the "democracy of the Baptist churches is something to be proud of." He thought the apostolic churches were democratic, and in modern Baptist life, "each church is sovereign in its own affairs."[77] Finally, regarding the church's legal position in society, Rauschenbusch affirmed that Baptists "decline all alliances with the state. They accept no dictation from the State in their spiritual affairs. They ask no favors from the State...."[78] Despite his affirmation of these goals in theory, Rauschenbusch was a realist. He accepted that the principles he had set forth were not always practiced, and he cited ways Baptist practices had subverted their own democratic principles of organization. But he affirmed the importance of having democratic principles "in their very constitution in all of these many levels of social arrangements."[79]

In developing his third category of reasons for being a Baptist, Rauschenbusch focused on worship. His strategy for this point was to discuss a variety of alternate forms of worship and to critique them. He noted that primitive religion was based on seeking such rewards as good harvests, health, and protection.[80] Rauschenbusch observed that many forms of Christianity had also adopted "superstitious ideas" in the way they understood the sacraments of the church. He rejected belief in the power of sacraments alone to save. He said that Baptists are radical Protestants when it comes to an understanding of baptism and the Lord's Supper.[81] Moreover, Rauschenbusch concluded that real worship, "the only kind that God cares for, is a Christ-like life." Jesus' prayer, Rauschenbusch declared, was meant to teach "utter simplicity."[82] He rejected sacramentalism as the essence of the meaning of worship and instead emphasized living out the Christian life.

Rauschenbusch's final article on Baptist identity addressed the intellectual component of religion, affirming that "religion appeals to the whole of man

---

[75] WR, "Why I Am a Baptist: My Second Reason," 106. See footnote 67, above.
[76] Ibid., 107.
[77] Ibid.
[78] Ibid., 107–108.
[79] Ibid., 108.
[80] WR, "Why I Am a Baptist: My Third Reason," 134.
[81] Ibid., 135.
[82] Ibid., 136–37.

and...there is an intellectual element in all religions" because people seek answers to the eternal questions of how the world originated, why there is suffering, and what comes after death.[83] Rauschenbusch observed that Baptists rejected the authority of creeds and confessions of faith, but they do have statements of faith, which are non-binding.[84] In Rauschenbusch's view Baptists have always recognized the Bible as their sole authority. He was clearly aware that Baptists had experienced problems relating to authority. He acknowledged again that some Baptists had "turned the Bible into one huge creed" by insisting that everyone accept their interpretation of Scripture, and that other Baptists had paralyzed the Bible by turning it into a law book and a collection of proof texts.[85] By contrast he asserted that at their best Baptists had "sought the adjustment between Freedom and Authority" by rejecting creeds while trying to learn from the Bible how to guide their lives.[86] In a postlude to this series of articles Rauschenbusch expressed the hope that readers might have a clearer understanding of "their own faith and the nature of our denomination."[87] In these concluding remarks Rauschenbusch expressed his reservation about accepting the invitation to write this series on Baptists' identity. He wrote, "I should do harm if I give to Baptists the impression that 'we are the [only] people and there are no others.'"[88] He readily conceded that Baptists are capable of being narrow in their views and that there are also fine qualities in other denominations.[89] While advocating Baptist views, Rauschenbusch did not want to be guilty of the arrogance of religious exclusivism.

Reception of Rauschenbusch's interpretation of Baptist identity was strong during his lifetime and also a half century later. These articles were reprinted in *The Baptist World* in 1913[90] and in *Canadian Baptist* in 1912–1913[91]; they were also translated into French.[92] Rauschenbusch received praise from new readers of the essays: William Braisted wrote, "Having just finished reading the third of your statements...[on] 'Why I Am a Baptist,' I cannot resist the impulse to thank

[83] WR, "Why I Am a Baptist: My Fourth Reason," 156.

[84] Ibid., 158.

[85] Ibid.

[86] Ibid., 159.

[87] Ibid.

[88] Ibid.

[89] Ibid., 159, 106.

[90] See J. N. Prestidge to WR, January 4, 1913. In this letter Prestidge tells Rauschenbusch that it gave him much pleasure to republish "Why I Am a Baptist." On January 5 Rauschenbusch replied that although he was unaware that Dr. Prestidge was republishing it, he was happy for him to do so (box 32, Rauschenbusch Family Papers).

[91] See "Why I Am a Baptist—II" (in *Canadian Baptist*).

[92] "Pourquoi je suis baptiste:" traduit por G. Brabant, Pasteur, 2nd ed. (Paris: n.p. ,n.d), referenced in the card catalogue of the ABHS.

you for these timely, clear, vital declarations...."[93] Henlee Barnette, professor of ethics at Southern Baptist Theological Seminary from 1952 to 1977, found Rauschenbusch's statement of Baptist principles so compelling that he republished them in 1958 for Southern Baptist readers in *The Baptist Leader*. In a brief assessment of Rauschenbusch, Barnette wrote glowingly:

> He was a man of great tenderness, strength of mind, sweet reasonableness, and brightness of humor. Few of his enemies could resist the graciousness of his spirit. He was "so humble that he knew not that he was great, so truly a follower of the Master that he was all unconscious of his own leadership." Scholars place him alongside such leaders as Martin Luther, John Calvin, Roger Williams, Jonathan Edwards, and John Wesley. A Baptist of such spiritual and intellectual stature deserves serious study on the part of all Christians, especially those of his own church affiliation.[94]

Barnette continued with his rationale for republishing this series:

> Rauschenbusch's vital statement will help everyone of the Baptist persuasion to clarify in his own mind the basic reasons for his church affiliation and it will serve to build a bridge of fellowship between North American Baptists and Baptists around the world. Baptist pastors, teachers, and denominational leaders constantly need a clear and cogent statement of the Baptist position to put into the hands of the people to whom they minister. This statement admirably meets such a need. It can be presented, also, with a sense of pride, to non-Baptists who ask about basic Baptist principles.[95]

Although he had a strong sense of unity of the church, Rauschenbusch reflected on Baptist principles throughout his career and on many occasions offered a spirited defense of the Baptist tradition. Articulation and defense of the Christian tradition in its Anabaptist and Baptist expressions mattered deeply to Walter Rauschenbusch.[96] That his articulation of Baptist identity accurately reflected essential Baptist convictions was evident: his essay was reprinted to guide Baptist readers in both the North and the South as well as in Europe.

---

[93] William F. Braisted to WR, January 13, 1913, box 27, Rauschenbusch Family Papers.

[94] Barnette, "Walter Rauschenbusch: Baptist Thinker and Leader," 17. Barnette was keenly enthusiastic about Rauschenbusch's understanding of Baptists and thought it could be widely useful. Note: the inside quotation marks are not identified by Barnette.

[95] Ibid.

[96] For his own understanding of Baptists Rauschenbusch relied on Henry Vedder. At the end of his career, speaking of Vedder, Rauschenbusch wrote, "There is no one to whom we owe more for his contributions to the literature of Baptist history" (WR, "Commencement," typescript, May 1917, 3, box 22, Rauschenbusch Family Papers).

Addresses to Baptist Conventions

Rauschenbusch was a famous figure during the last eleven years of his life, and he was in constant demand to speak at individual churches and also at conferences and conventions.[97] What did he have to say to major gatherings of Baptists? Three speeches demonstrate his keen passion for Baptists to open themselves to the challenge of responding to the social crisis.

Rauschenbusch was invited to address the meeting of the Baptist World Alliance at Philadelphia in 1911.[98] This was a rare opportunity since the Alliance met roughly only every five years. Program personnel introduced Rauschenbusch as one of the foremost authorities in the world on the subject of sociology.[99] Addressing representatives of Baptists around the world, he chose the theme most important to him, "The Church and the Social Crisis." He identified the problem and challenged Baptists to respond to it. Employing his usual analysis, Rauschenbusch explained the social crisis as a conflict between a privileged class who held political and economic power and the nameless working class that toils endlessly but never escapes poverty and insecurity. But he warned that the workers were growing in numbers, education, democracy, and self-respect and that they demand "a fair share in the proceeds of the common toil."[100]

Rauschenbusch believed that American society was changing dramatically. Speaking to this assembly of world Baptists, he declared, "Our age has outgrown its old order...." He recalled his observation of nature when he was a boy to make his point: "I once saw a...locust...climb a tree...and pass through its metamorphosis from a chrysalis to a mature locust in an hour. It burst its old shell down the back and spread its untried wings to the air to dry. We are passing through a similar process."[101] Society had passed from the feudal age and was currently undergoing revolutionary economic change "from capitalism to collectivism, from industrialism and autocracy to industrial democracy."[102] Rauschenbusch then raised his question to the Alliance audience: "This is the present crisis. How is the church concerned in it?"[103] He painted a bleak picture, reporting, "Today

---

[97] C. A. Netting wrote in 1912 asking Rauschenbusch if he could speak at Woodward Avenue Baptist Church in Detroit, noting "[I] know the appreciation and high esteem in which you are held in the city" (C. A. Netting to WR, December 6, 1912, box 27, Rauschenbusch Family Papers).

[98] The Alliance met first in London in 1905. Rauschenbusch spoke at the Second Congress, which met in Philadelphia, June 19–25, 1911. For full background consult Pierard, ed., *Baptists Together in Christ 1905–2005*.

[99] WR, "The Church and the Social Crisis," 372.

[100] Ibid., 373.

[101] Ibid.

[102] Ibid., 374.

[103] Ibid.

country churches are left high and dry, and in downtown churches it is hard to establish contact with the rubble of human beings." Although suffering people turn to the church for help, sadly "the church is impotent" to respond to them.[104]

He argued that the problem for the churches was made worse "if the masses feel the church is antagonistic toward them."[105] Rauschenbusch warned that the spirit of Christianity is "a timeless force for progress, but the church is a very conservative institution."[106] Whereas the Roman Catholic Church developed in a feudal despotic age and had fought the rise of democracy and individualism, Protestantism had grown up with the new commercial class and supported freedom and individualism. Rauschenbusch saw the current danger to be that it would now "turn against the collectivist thought of the new working class."[107] In his view, both Roman Catholics and Protestants had demonstrated limited views of social responsibility. The church must consider its task anew. Rauschenbusch was implicitly asking Baptists to embrace progressive new paths rather than hanging on to a conservative past.

In this speech Rauschenbusch painted history with broad strokes. Coming to his main point, he declared that the church must speak to the current generation and its problems. He wrote, "If the church opposes a cause that is manifestly just, it creates bitterness and anarchy plus hatred for religion."[108] He asserted that churches exist to establish justice, peace, political liberty, and brotherhood, but the churches had, in fact, held back these causes. He summarized his judgment for the Baptist audience declaring, "This has been the greatest scandal in Christendom."[109] He then challenged the Baptist leaders, proclaiming, "We Baptists are called to reverse this attitude."[110]

Rauschenbusch appealed to history as the source of Baptist identity and inspiration, pointing to key themes in the Baptist heritage. According to Rauschenbusch Baptists are heirs of the medieval sects, which held convictions of democracy and fraternity and were persecuted for their social principles as well as their religion:

> We are heirs of the glorious Anabaptist movement of the Reformation which embodied the religious and social hopes of the common people and was trodden down in blood for that combination. We are directly descended from the most radical party of the English Revolution. We have embodied the principles of democracy in the congregational organization of our churches. We have exalted

[104] Ibid.
[105] Ibid.
[106] Ibid.
[107] Ibid.
[108] Ibid., 375.
[109] Ibid.
[110] Ibid.

individual liberty in making religion a free act of the soul and repudiating all coercion in religion."[111]

Here he reminded this international gathering of Baptists of their radical past, noted that Baptists had always flourished most among the common people, and declared that Baptists "have always been the friends of young democracy in all nations" and should never be the foe of liberty.[112]

Rauschenbusch ended his message by declaring that Baptists had repeatedly taken action to express sympathy with the cause of workers. But in the present social challenge "Baptists have not equaled Congregationalists, not remotely equaled Presbyterians, and have allowed our old-time rival, the Methodists, to snatch the leadership by their remarkable action in the General Conference of 1908," when they went on record supporting the cause of the American worker.[113] Whereas these other denominations had officially recognized the problem and taken a position by 1911, Baptists needed to wake up to their social responsibility—otherwise they would lose the opportunity. Rauschenbusch felt a sense of urgency for Baptists. He was keenly aware that opportunities do not remain open indefinitely, and he insisted that, like the original Baptists, Baptists of the present urgently needed to take a radical new path. Rauschenbusch closed his message with a passionate challenge for Baptists to accept social Christianity, declaring, "There is more religion, more of the spirit of Jesus and the prophets in the little finger in the cause [of the social gospel] than in the thigh-bone of most of the theological controversies of the past. To side with that cause is the spirit of religious faith." He promised that this cause would "open vast opportunities of moral and spiritual service to our peoples and also offer the chance for a great spiritual enlargement and quickening for our own religious life."[114] This was an opportunity for Baptists to show that faith was relevant to society's needs. They must not ignore it.

Rauschenbusch was doubtless chosen to speak at the World Congress because of his high profile in American Baptist life. On this occasion, he was a Baptist speaking to Baptists, a minister delivering a challenging sermon, and a leader of a new vision for Christians. Rauschenbusch called for a broader view of Christianity when he urged all Christians, including Baptists, to embrace a social as well as an individual gospel. Baptist identity itself changed significantly during the twentieth century. Baptists devoted increased energy to new trends such as missions and denominational organization. They also had to decide where they stood on the social gospel. Baptist identity has not remained static, least of all in

[111] Ibid., 375–76.
[112] Ibid., 376.
[113] Ibid.
[114] Ibid.

Rauschenbusch's era. Rauschenbusch was a driving force of the social gospel, and he challenged these Baptists from around the world to ponder social responsibility.

Rauschenbusch also responded to calls to speak to the national gatherings of his own denomination. At the meeting of the Northern Baptist Convention in 1910 Rauschenbusch spoke on "The Freedom of Spiritual Religion." He had his Baptist audience very much in mind when he made these remarks. His starting point was his critique of law and authoritarianism, whether in the New Testament or in modern Protestant practice. True religion, he argued, is free and ethical and practiced in brotherhood and justice. Reiterating a familiar theme, he asserted that this form of Christianity is best found in Anabaptist and Baptist life. He illustrated his point by his reference to Roger Williams who, he said, perceived all coercion as "the poison of true religion."[115] Rauschenbusch probed the devastating effects of the church's use of punishment or execution to coerce conformity. Most accounts of persecution seek to elicit sympathy and admiration for martyrs. However, Rauschenbusch shifted perspective, arguing that the deadliest influence was not on those killed, but those who dodged death because "either consciously or half-consciously they suppressed or altered their conviction."[116] In this analysis Rauschenbusch showed how religious coercion corrupts the whole society by denying the conscience of the majority. He concluded that Baptist protest against religious coercion was a protest against dishonesty.

Addressing this gathering chiefly of Baptist ministers and leaders, Rauschenbusch revisited familiar themes: he told them that America was in social and economic transition and that the denomination needed to respond with revolutionary new measures in ministry. This was a thinly-veiled plea for them to embrace the message of the social gospel. He reminded the audience that the Baptists and Anabaptists before them were radicals of the radical.[117] They adopted the most progressive views of the church and baptism of any of the heirs of the Reformation. He often used this rhetorical ploy to generate pride in the past and a dare not to be constrained by current practices. He was trying to persuade Baptists to break with tradition and adopt radical attitudes that would empower them to engage in the social gospel. Thus he wrote, "When the Baptist movement was in its cradle, nobody ever expected that baby to sit on the brakes of the chariot of progress."[118] "We were for a reformation without tarrying."[119] Both of these comments are references to the radical character of Baptists in their infancy, which

---

115 WR, "The Freedom of Spiritual Religion," 8.

116 Ibid.

117 Ibid.

118 Ibid., 12.

119 Ibid., 13. The reference is to Robert Browne's famous separatist tract, "A Treatise of Reformation without Tarrying for Anie" (1582).

Rauschenbusch contrasted with their current conservative character and failure to take on new initiatives, especially social ministries.

Rauschenbusch closed his address with a positive summary of what Baptists had achieved. They had experienced numerical growth and had exercised major influence on American society through promoting separation of church and state, democratic organization, and recognition of a conscious spiritual experience as the great aim of religion.[120] He emphasized that the principle of freedom had nurtured Baptist success. Baptist principles were more than a list of "distinctives" for Rauschenbusch. This sermon shows Rauschenbusch taking Baptist principles to heart and explicating them in an attempt to persuade fellow Baptists to become activists.

The Northern Baptist Convention leaders asked Rauschenbusch to address them again at their national meeting on May 22, 1915, in Los Angeles. He chose the topic "American Christianity and National Life." The topic was Rauschenbusch's great passion, and he took the opportunity once again to present his social views to this Baptist audience. The question he put to them was, "What has Christianity done for our nation in the past? What can it do in the new needs that are upon us?"[121] He reminded the Baptists of the message of the gospel, noting that the gospel of Jesus Christ stands for "great principles [that] represent the highest spiritual convictions of the race." He called for listeners to recognize the preciousness of every life, but also the need of all for salvation before God. The gospel stands for the duty to surrender selfishness and to be ready to serve. Finally, it stands for "the law of love...community [and] brotherhood."[122]

Rauschenbusch once again began his speech by complimenting the church on past great achievements of shaping the Christian character of citizens. He discussed how society forms the ethics of individuals: "Individuals take notions of right and wrong, the admirable and the contemptible from the society in which we live."[123] And it is the institution of the church that has been instrumental in shaping the ethical life of the nation. Rauschenbusch further noted that "the religious organizations of our country have had such enormous vitality and propaganda that they have nearly kept pace with the settling of the country."[124] He called the church's past achievement of helping Christianize the nation a "social miracle."[125] No one, he said, should underestimate the achievements of the churches.[126] Rauschenbusch conceded that the churches were never ideal. Some,

---

[120] Ibid., 14.

[121] WR, "American Christianity and National Life," 5.

[122] Ibid.

[123] Ibid.

[124] Ibid.

[125] Ibid.

[126] Ibid.

he said, had gone stale. Some "fluttered madly in the cyclone of emotionalism in some professionalized revival."[127] Nevertheless, he paid tribute to the past: "No matter how crude and ignorant the pastor may have been in generations gone by, there was always some saving power in them."[128] These ministers taught each generation moral values and the message of regeneration. Baptists worked especially among the "plain people."[129]

Rauschenbusch's rhetorical strategy was to praise fellow Baptists for past accomplishments and then to challenge his hearers to work to create a more Christian nation now. In order to do this he said the churches must first move toward unity, to love one another. Second, they must "steady the emotional life of the nation: it has lost self-restraint and we must restore sobriety and moderation. Third, we need to work for a more just society."[130] Hearers doubtless expected his emphasis on the social gospel. Rauschenbusch delivered that word, but not before providing substantial rationale for it. The speech demonstrated excellent balance. Rauschenbusch essentially said, "You have kept up your responsibility to the nation in the past. The nation has changed. Now you have new responsibilities to apply principles of the gospel to the new social and economic realities of the nation." As he had done five years before, Rauschenbusch once again made the case for the social gospel on the national platform of the annual Northern Baptist Convention.

Rauschenbusch remained a devoted Baptist until the end of his life, but he took criticism from other Baptists. J. W. Porter, editor of the Southern Baptist Kentucky *Western Recorder*, wrote to Rauschenbusch, "You have no right to do or say anything that is calculated to belittle or destroy the denomination you serve.... In my judgment the decadence of Baptists in your own section of the country is the best commentary on the liberality of yourself and others in this country."[131] Rauschenbusch wasted no time in responding. As for liberal views being the cause of decline, Rauschenbusch assured Porter that "the great majority of pastors and people are untouched by them." Porter said that pointing out failures "belittles in the denomination." Rauschenbusch replied, "Are you prepared to say that the Baptist denomination is so exceptional that it alone has committed no serious mistakes? How about doctrinal wrangles, opposition to foreign missions...."[132] Further, "Should a professor of history, teaching Baptist students, keep them ig-

[127] Ibid., 6.
[128] Ibid.
[129] Ibid.
[130] Ibid., 6–7.
[131] J. W. Porter to WR, March 27, 1915, box 27, Rauschenbusch Family Papers.
[132] WR to J. W. Porter, March 29, 1915, box 27, Rauschenbusch Family Papers.

norant about [failures], in a state of illusion and unprepared to meet similar dangers today?"[133] Finally, Rauschenbusch assured Porter that liberalism was not the problem, but rather the "city life, industrial conditions, mammonism which would reach the South in sixty years."[134] He told Porter that his writings contributed to the strength of Baptists, and he included a sermon, a resolution, and a concluding argument, "I fear many sticklers for the denomination have so little of the true Baptist spirit and historical inheritance that they do not recognize it when they see it. They are much closer to the Roman Catholics in their mental attitude than they are aware of."[135] Rauschenbusch's response was in keeping with his understanding that the true Baptist spirit was revolutionary. A Rauschenbusch Baptist was far more progressive than many fellow Baptists.

Rauschenbusch was deeply loyal to Baptists. When his close friend Leighton Williams left the denomination for the Episcopal Church, he was somewhat bewildered, writing, "There is a good deal of tragedy in the whole thing. You have always sought to understand and set forth what is essential and noble in the Baptist position, but the actual forces have been against these things, and now you turn away."[136] By contrast, Rauschenbusch remained committed to what he found essential and noble in the Baptist position.

Contributions to Baptist Denominational Life: Father and Son

August Rauschenbusch is still recognized as the major founding figure among German Baptists in the United States, now called the North American Baptist Convention, whose seminary is located in Sioux Falls, South Dakota. His autobiography records how he became a Baptist and defended Baptist principles among German immigrants. In addition, it reveals many ways in which he provided leadership to the denomination. His contributions began with his missionary spirit. He became aware of the situation of the Germans in America and left Germany for an uncertain future in America. His initial employment was with the American Tract Society where he corrected older German tracts and wrote new ones as well. For a while he served as pastor of a small German Baptist congregation at Mt. Sterling on the Missouri frontier, west of St. Louis. He moved to Rochester Theological Seminary in 1857 and headed the German department for thirty years, providing instruction to a generation of German pastors, including the capable figures who would become outstanding leaders of the denomination. Augustus wrote books and tracts offering guidance on matters such as Sunday observance, temperance, and the characterization of the women of the Bible.

---

133 Ibid.
134 Ibid.
135 Ibid.
136 WR to Leighton Williams, June 16, 1917, box 27, Rauschenbusch Family Papers

As a church historian, he was passionate about dissenters in the Middle Ages and especially about the history of the Anabaptists and Baptists. Recognizing the importance of congregational singing for worship, Augustus devoted time to assist in creating hymnals for the denomination. When the International Sunday School lesson program began in 1873, he recognized its significance and wrote parallel lessons in German, printed for German Baptists by the German Publishing House in Cleveland, Ohio—another service for an entire denomination. August did much to shape the German Baptist denomination during the critical era of its early development as these new citizens were learning the meaning of being Baptist and being American.[137]

Comparing the activities that occupied Walter Rauschenbusch with those of his father reveals remarkable parallels. In point after point similarities emerge, including keen awareness of their immigrant roots and their responsibility to the German-American community, the high values they placed on education, and not least, in their overall contributions to Baptist life. Walter also served as minister and professor, articulated and defended Baptist thought and practices, worked on production of hymnals, and wrote scores of Sunday school lessons. He was a prolific author who published in both German and English religious publications, and especially in Baptist papers. Both men had a lifelong commitment to missions, and as a church historian, Walter shared his father's interest in dissenters and sectarians, particularly Anabaptists and Baptists. He differed from his father theologically and struck out in new directions with his social Christian emphasis. Like his father before him, Walter made impressive contributions to German and English-language Baptists. Although both men are honored by the denomination, German Baptists took a conservative direction whereas the North American Baptist Convention fully adopted the challenge of the social gospel. Commitment to justice remains to this day a strong emphasis at Rauschenbusch's old seminary in Rochester. Both men devoted much of their lives to the welfare of Baptists.

Rauschenbusch was shaped by his Baptist influences in home, church, and higher education. He affirmed the Baptist tradition throughout his life. He was not only shaped by Baptists; he became a shaper of Baptists. He ministered to the immigrant population of Baptists in New York City for eleven years. He was also active in the life of his denomination, providing leadership through preparing papers for the Baptist Congress and in publishing his opinions on current debates in denominational papers. Rauschenbusch moved from pastoral ministry to seminary teaching in order to train Baptist ministers. Moreover, convinced that his

---

[137] August Rauschenbusch's life is summarized in *Life and Ministry*. Completed by Walter Rauschenbusch and translated by Donald H. Madvig. Sioux Falls, SD: North American Baptist Heritage Commission, 2008.

Baptist faith was the best path for Christianity, he carefully articulated an extended explanation and defense of the Baptist tradition. Rauschenbusch's natural audience was the Baptist community. He also contributed to *Der Sendbote*, a Baptist denominational paper for Germans.[138] At the end of his life the *Watchman-Examiner* reported, "It is not too much to say that he is the most widely read of all the Baptist authors of our generation."[139]

As a scholar Rauschenbusch made an impact on his own generation and beyond. He reached audiences well beyond the Baptists with his message. But he may also be seen as contributing to awareness of new principles being adopted by Baptists in the twentieth century: he was a strong advocate for Baptist efforts toward social responsibility and Christian unity, as well as their already well-established enterprise of foreign missions. He embraced all of these trends. Baptists fiercely debated their social responsibility in the century following Rauschenbusch's publications. He so effectively presented his argument that he could not be ignored and helped keep the issue before the churches to the present day. Rauschenbusch thereby added a new dimension to Baptist identity. The programs of the Baptist World Congress in 2010 and 2015, a century after Rauschenbusch's addresses, attest to the overwhelming importance of social justice for Baptists worldwide today. In many ways social justice has taken center stage for this gathering.[140] Baptists may rightly cherish Rauschenbusch for adding significant depth to their Christian theological tradition by articulating the social gospel for all Christians. Many Baptists today are happy to be identified as Rauschenbusch Baptists. He not only perpetuated the Baptist tradition, he enriched it. Or as he would have said, he encouraged his seminary students to adopt "an enlarged vision" of Christianity. He looked to the Baptists of the present and the future and called them to social responsibility. But he also relied heavily on the Baptists of the past to define his own Christian identity.

---

[138] *Der Sendbote* was the German Baptist publication from 1866–1971. Its original editor and publisher was Rev. Phil Brickel. In 1874 the weekly paper was enlarged to eight pages. During Rauschenbusch's era it was published in Cleveland by the German Baptist Publication Society.

[139] "Dr. Rauschenbusch Passes Away," 983.

[140] See, for example, Baptist World Alliance, *Congress Program Guide*. The Baptist World Congress was held in Honolulu, HI, July 28–August 1, 2010. Social issues were prominently featured throughout the meeting.

CHAPTER 7

RAUSCHENBUSCH AS PROFESSOR OF CHURCH HISTORY

Following eleven years as a pastor, Rauschenbusch's profession took a new direction. He accepted an invitation to become a seminary professor at Rochester Theological Seminary where he served for twenty-one years. His enthusiasm for work as he began his task as professor knew no bounds. His words passionately express the urgency he felt to fulfill his life in service:

> A life of service is a holy duty. Yes, and a blessed privilege too. How swiftly life spins away! I count myself among the young men, yet half of the allotted three score and ten is gone for me. And sometimes as I listen to the racing of the years, I feel a terrible catch of the heart, not at the coming of death, but at the passing of life. So much to be done, and as yet so little accomplished: I want to work, to serve in the redemption of the world from wrong, to help my Master save humanity. It is a glory, a privilege, and I want much of it. I fear lest my life pass away and I have not slacked my thirst for the service of God. This life can be so full, so noble, so blessed to us, so useful to others. And so often it is empty, vapid, trivial, discontented, useless. Which is the real privilege, to serve or to be idle? Which is the real burden, to live for self or to live for the Kingdom of God?[1]

For his first five years at Rochester (1897–1902), Rauschenbusch trained young German-speaking ministers in the German department.[2] When the Rochester Theological Seminary Church historian Benjamin True died suddenly, the school's president, Augustus Strong, invited Rauschenbusch to take the post of professor of church history. He accepted the offer and held this position from 1902 until his death in 1918. Rauschenbusch published all of his major works on the social gospel while also teaching church history in the seminary. In 1912

---

[1] WR, "The Workers," *The Baptist Union*, February 26, 1898.

[2] Many of these students had neither college nor high school training. Rauschenbusch was obliged to offer a variety of courses such as introductions to science and politics in order to inform them about modern society (see Ramaker, *The German Baptists of North America*, 86). In 1901 he completed and embellished his father's autobiography, *Leben und Werken von August Rauschenbusch* (*Life and Work of August Rauschenbusch*), and in 1902 he published a guide to the working of the American political system, *Die Politische Verfassung Unseres*.

Rauschenbusch described his discipline as "historical studies which are my professional duty and my intellectual satisfaction."[3] But the social gospel preoccupied Rauschenbusch so fully that he did not publish a book in the field of church history—as he had hoped he might.[4]

Nevertheless, church history was Rauschenbusch's profession for sixteen years and provided the context for his work. What did he teach? What did he emphasize in his teaching? How did his understanding of church history influence his social gospel writings, and how did his passion for social justice shape his teaching of church history? The major sources for recovering this dimension of his life are Rauschenbusch's own unpublished lecture notes as well as remembrances of students. In his very first lecture as professor of church history in January 1903, Rauschenbusch revealed several lines of his thinking as he took up his new teaching responsibilities. He told students that he was glad to return to the room where he sat as a student. He admonished them "that we must always work while it is day." He announced that he was aware of his own deficiencies; he asked the students' forbearance, saying that he would work to catch up. Regarding his perspective as a scholar, he said that he would "be candid and truthful, yet teach with reverence for Christ."[5] The focus of this chapter is Rauschenbusch's reflection on his work as historian of Christianity rather than his role as pastor, theologian, or modern social prophet.[6]

---

[3] Rauschenbusch, *Christianizing the Social Order*, vii.

[4] Although Rauschenbusch's publication of original historical research is rare, his article on the Anabaptists, published early in his career as a church historian, demonstrates superlative historical and analytical skills. See WR, "The Zurich Anabaptists and Thomas Munzer," 91–106. For a study of Rauschenbusch's critical historical work on the Anabaptists, see Pitts, "Rauschenbusch and the Reformation," 32–46.

[5] The sources for studying Rauschenbusch in the classroom are plentiful. Rauschenbusch and his family kept much unpublished material, including many of his lecture notes for church history classes. The material from his lectures includes notes from his opening lectures, which address introductory matters such as values and methods in the discipline, the origin of Christianity, and proper attitude of the beginning student of church history. The collection contains notes from his courses on both European and American church history and also a list of study questions for one of Rauschenbusch's exams. Boxes 1–6 and 18–22 of the Rauschenbusch Family Papers contain his church history lectures. The lecture notes begin on p. 1 of box 1.

[6] This chapter omits discussion of Rauschenbusch's personal life. In addition to his professional responsibilities, Rauschenbusch attended Rochester's German Baptist Church and devoted time to painting and to his five children. He believed in ongoing adult education and was a leader in the People's Sunday Night Forum and the Rochester Lyceum. He had many hobbies, including wood carving, music, camping, and horticulture. He was deeply devoted to his family. He bought a summer home in Bobcaygeon, Canada, for extended summer stays with his family for hiking, camping, canoeing, and writing (Sharpe, *Walter Rauschenbusch*, 423–24).

Rauschenbusch benefitted from many resources for his work in church history. The study of the church's history has a long heritage, including monumental works by Eusebius, Bede, Flacius, Baronius, and in the modern world, Mosheim and his successors. Rauschenbusch was deeply influenced by Neander. But more importantly, the modern critical scholars who shaped the discipline in Rauschenbusch's era were Adolph Harnack in Germany and Philip Schaff in the United States. Among his contemporary historians, Rauschenbusch expressed special admiration for Hans von Schubert's survey of church history.[7]

Rauschenbusch in the Classroom: Apologist for the Value of Church History

Rauschenbusch was conscious of his responsibility as a seminary professor to prepare ministers for service in the church. His notes for his introductory lectures in church history indicate that he took great care in explaining to his students both the methods and content of church history. He was especially concerned to convince students of the relevance of church history in their curriculum of study and for their lives as ministers. He gave extensive attention to the connection between the spirit of Jesus and the history of Christianity, the appropriate spirit students should adopt for interpreting church history, and the many values provided by studying the history of the church. In published articles Rauschenbusch examined the critical method employed by historians and the growing importance of church history in the educational preparation of future ministers. He thought it important that ministers approach church history from the perspective of modern historical presuppositions including modern biblical criticism, which had allowed scholars to recover new insights on Jesus and the kingdom of God, as well as the original message of the early church. Rauschenbusch told his church history students that there are two types of men: "those who read history and those who don't."[8] By this he meant to affirm that church history would give these prospective ministers an informed perspective they could not otherwise achieve. He believed that knowledge of history would offer a fuller perspective on life: it would help readers understand reasons for human actions and also provide moral guidance in life.

Rauschenbusch also explained the procedures he would follow. He would

---

[7] Rauschenbusch lists titles of many works he consulted in both German and English. For an account of major developments in writing the history of Christianity in Europe see Meinhold, *Geschichte der kirchlichen Historiographie*, and for development in the United States, consult Bowden, *Church History in the Age of Science*.

[8] WR, "Introduction to the Study of Church History," box 1, Rauschenbusch Family Papers.

use the lecture method. He would give students extended time for their examinations if they needed it. He required them to write a paper for the course and to memorize the chronology of church history.[9] He assigned A. H. Newman's two-volume textbook as well as selected primary sources for them to read.[10] Rauschenbusch followed a traditional breakdown of major themes in church history, including missions, organization, worship, Christian life and morals, doctrine, and religious life. He concluded his introduction to the course with an explanation of the traditional divisions of church history into the ancient, medieval, and modern periods. These opening comments to students were meant to provide a rationale for the study of church history, to win their confidence that Rauschenbusch would be demanding while being fair in accommodating the needs of students, and finally to inform them about the nature of the subject by identifying its major content categories.

Rauschenbusch recognized that he faced a major challenge in convincing students of the value of church history. In the introductory remarks to his course, Rauschenbusch freely conceded that church history is not as obviously practical for the minister as are courses in elocution, homiletics, or pastoral theology. Nor does the content of church history carry the same sense of sacredness and authority as the Bible.[11] He observed that students "bring to the seminary a deep reverence for the Bible—in theory at least—and a desire to study it." But as for church history, students tended to view it as a "disciplinary burden which the inscrutable counsel of boards and faculties imposes on those who mean to be scholarly preachers."[12] Rauschenbusch therefore believed he had to address the problem directly and to work diligently to demonstrate to his students the relevance of the study of church history for their work as future ministers.[13] He believed that knowledge of the story of 1900 years of the church's experience might help the minister understand the church of today and provide the student with clearer vision and purpose in ministry. He warned that church history should not be studied merely for sermon illustrations. Instead, studying the story of the church as an institution provided breadth of awareness not only of the church but also of

---

[9] Ibid.

[10] WR, first lecture as professor of church history, 4, box 1, Rauschenbusch Family Papers. Newman was a Baptist and a church historian who had achieved national recognition, especially through his general textbook, which enjoyed fourteen printings by 1931. See Newman, *A Manual of Church History*. For an assessment of Newman, see Jonas, *A Critical Evaluation of Albert Henry Newman*.

[11] WR, "Influence of Historical Studies on Theology," 112.

[12] Ibid.

[13] WR, "Introduction to the Study of Church History."

the larger society. This broad knowledge would be a valuable component of pastoral formation.[14] In his own experience, close study of the New Testament and of modern theologian Albrecht Ritschl had offered new vistas of the nature and purpose of the church. Historical studies had opened for him the theological implications of Jesus' understanding of the kingdom of God.

Rauschenbusch was fully aware that he was addressing Baptist students. He thought they could learn by comparing Baptists with other denominations and often used this strategy in his teaching. He observed that Baptists traditionally had less interest in church history than Anglicans or Lutherans because of traditional Baptist individualism, yet he assured the seminarians that Baptists had achieved much in their history. Rauschenbusch thought they should celebrate their democratic tradition and the remarkable growth they had achieved since they began as a denomination. But the other side of the coin, according to Rauschenbusch, was that history showed that Baptist theological perception "is rather flat and thin," and Baptists "do not fully realize their mission and status in the whole story of Christendom."[15] The result of this neglect, Rauschenbusch told his students, was that "We [Baptists] lack self-consciousness and lack common memory," and this situation "puts us at a disadvantage."[16] On a positive note, he assured students that the Baptist denomination had no "hoary wrong" to live down; instead, Baptists could take pride in a long tradition of prophetic "revolutionary protest."[17] In terms of size, Baptists were already a leading denomination. Church history could help Baptists overcome their provincialism by developing awareness of the many strengths of their historical heritage. In short, knowing church history was crucial in the formation of an informed Baptist minister and was therefore a vital part of Baptist seminary training. Finally, and significantly, Rauschenbusch held that church history should inspire ministers to be prophetic. By this he meant that he wanted Baptist ministerial students to develop a revolutionary mentality that was willing to challenge the status quo. He later wrote that "the scribe sees [God's] will as written law; the prophet feels it as a living force and fire in his bones."[18] Here Rauschenbusch appealed to a positive image of Baptists as reformers—an image he used over and over and that doubtless reflected his view of his own task as a reformer in the life of the church. As a professor, Rauschenbusch was a committed advocate for the values of studying church history.

---

[14] Ibid.

[15] Ibid.

[16] Ibid.

[17] WR, "Values as Baptist Leaders," box 1, Rauschenbusch Family Papers. Rauschenbusch repeated these arguments when addressing young Baptist audiences and also when addressing large Baptist conventions.

[18] WR, *The Social Teachings of Jesus*, typescript, box 1, Rauschenbusch Family Papers.

Testimonies to Rauschenbusch's success in the classroom abound. For example, F. W. C. Meyer wrote, "He was a wonderfully versatile and inspiring teacher. Keen in insight, broad in sympathies, uncompromising in correct conclusion, still he never lacked that sparkle of humor and fervor of heart which [kept] students and colleagues alike...under the spell of his genius."[19] Many former students expressed similar sentiments.

Moving to the Center: Church History and the Seminary Curriculum

Not only did Rauschenbusch defend the value of the study of church history, he also believed it was enjoying increasing importance in the seminary curriculum, and he was right. In 1907 he published a long article in which he contended that "the rise of history to a dominating position in the theological curriculum and the present powerful influence of historical studies on scientific theology are both of recent origin."[20] Rauschenbusch structured his essay around the four classical divisions of seminary courses: historical, biblical, theological, and practical studies. His purpose in this article was to show how significantly the recent rise of historical studies had influenced the other major divisions of the seminary curriculum. The article served as his affirmation for the importance of church history in ministerial training: he was an apologist for the study of the history of Christianity.

Rauschenbusch observed that whereas theology had prevailed in ministerial training of the Roman Catholic Middle Ages, during the Reformation the focus shifted to biblical studies, and thereafter exegesis achieved a central position in ministerial training among Protestants. There was good reason students came to seminary already devoted to biblical studies since this is where the emphasis was placed in Baptist homes and churches, but understanding of the Bible was changing. Rauschenbusch described the revolutionary transition in biblical studies that had transpired during the nineteenth century and was reshaping views of the Bible at Rochester Seminary and elsewhere. He wrote that the common perception before the widespread adoption of biblical criticism was that:

> The high theories of inspiration set the biblical books apart from all other historical records.
>
> They were divine; all other records were human. The apostles had an infallible teaching authority. What was taught and practiced while they presided over the church was true and authoritative; whatever came after was human frailty and error. Thus the apostolic age was cut off from all subsequent church history as

---

[19] Meyer, "Rauschenbusch Aflame for God!" 305.

[20] WR, "The Influence of Historical Studies on Theology," 111.

sui generis.[21]

In recent years, however, things had changed. He observed,

> All recent developments in the biblical sciences have taught us how intimate and organized were the relations between the biblical books and the contemporary life in which they originated...a biblical book gets its significance only in connection with its historical development.... On the most important questions of historical criticism of the New Testament no one is competent to speak unless he knows the second century as well as the first.[22]

Rauschenbusch argued that without historical context, "exegesis is likely to see itself in fruitless minutiae, cutting out tidy proof-texts for theology and pretty sermon texts for homiletics, but never gaining a living comprehension of the Bible which it claims to expound."[23] This was a bold statement, but he was fully convinced of the necessity of providing historical context for interpreting biblical texts. This great shift in biblical studies rested on understanding and accepting the historical character of the Bible. The modern historical-critical method had transformed modern understanding of the Bible.

Next Rauschenbusch turned to theology. He noted that the current approach to natural science recognized the development of all life, and that this idea had great force in modern thought.[24] The notion of development of thought transformed modern views of theology; Christian thought had not been immune to change and was not static. It was now clear to modern interpreters that Christian doctrine had developed in history: "Whatever is new in theology has slowly come to be," Rauschenbusch wrote, "[thus] the sense of continuity and development held by historical studies is one of the most necessary equipments for a religion."[25] Theology, he declared, is the slowest of all departments to change, but it is imperative that it be informed by being aware of the best thought of its age—including "contemporary secular life...exegesis...history...and natural science."[26] He thought that the study of history could offer theologians additional critical facility, above all, the perspective that institutions and ideas, including Christian dogma had all developed. Theologians could not ignore historical development; they must reckon with change. History was transforming theology as well as biblical studies.[27]

Rauschenbusch turned next to examine what history could contribute to

[21] Ibid., 112.
[22] Ibid., 113.
[23] Ibid., 115.
[24] Ibid., 116.
[25] Ibid., 117.
[26] Ibid., 118–19.
[27] Ibid., 119.

practical studies. He warned ministers against continuing to preach old interpretations now discredited and citing "facts that aren't so" in sermons.[28] The aim of the minister in reading history should be to understand human experience. To reach this goal "a vital comprehension of present-day life is the prime requisite; the study of church history is next to it."[29] The two go hand-in-hand in his view. This combination provides knowledge essential for an informed minister to be able to communicate the gospel to the modern world.

Rauschenbusch concluded that "history...revitalizes and balances all other departments of theology."[30] The growth of modern historical study and its influence were unparalleled during Rauschenbusch's lifetime. In the early twentieth century the eleventh edition of *Encyclopedia Britannica* appeared (Cambridge University Press, 1910–1911), and has since been judged the finest collection of articles ever achieved by this distinguished publication. The writing of the history of Christianity also flourished in Europe and in the U.S. as evidenced by the prolific publication of church histories, encyclopedias of religion and ethics, and the great French dictionaries of liturgy, theology, and archaeology. Both Catholic and Protestant scholars published critical studies. These impressive academic achievements were based on the idea that essential facts should be collected to provide basic information on all subjects. In addition, nineteenth-century historians began to assemble vast collections of primary sources, especially collections of government documents. Similarly, church historians began to publish source collections and write historical narratives and critical monograph studies on the history of the church based on primary sources. The goal was to learn all that was possible about the church's past. This most fertile era for the establishment of the discipline of church history saw the beginning of the Weimar Edition of Luther's collected works in 1883. The era produced highly influential church historians such as the Roman Catholic Ignaz Döllinger (Munich). Rauschenbusch admired the work of Adolph Harnack (Berlin), whom he called the greatest living church historian. Harnack and Reinhold Seeberg notably recast Christian theology in terms of its historical development.[31] In the United States Philip Schaff accomplished landmark work for church history, editing English translations of the *Fathers*, and writing his own massive history of Christianity with its emphasis on the early church and the Protestant Reformation.[32] Rauschenbusch called him a

[28] Ibid., 120.

[29] Ibid., 121.

[30] Ibid., 127.

[31] Harnack, *History of Dogma*; Seeberg, *The History of Doctrines*.

[32] See Schaff, *History of the Christian Church*; *Ante-Nicene Fathers*; *Nicene and Post-Nicene Fathers*.

"church historian of the first rank."[33] Schaff also helped establish the American Society of Church History in 1888, devoted wholly to the study of the history of Christianity. Rauschenbusch's generation inherited this halcyon era of church history studies; they placed much confidence in the perspective provided by informed historians to guide their studies.

Historical Critical Method and Church History

Rauschenbusch made his bold claims for history in part because of what he saw as "the powerful influence" of the new historical methodology.[34] Just as science created its much-discussed methods of inquiry, nineteenth-century historians refined historical criticism, their methodology for close reading of texts, evaluating sources, exposing forgeries, and sorting out what happened in the human past. Rauschenbusch "thought of history and science jointly as the distinctive hallmarks of modern intellectual life since the sixteenth century."[35]

Rauschenbusch emphasized the historical method in his seminary classes. He created a list of study questions for his first examination of the course. One of the questions he told students to prepare for was "Why is criticism necessary, and what is meant by it?" For the actual exam that he gave on September 22, 1908, he asked students to (1) give a chronological outline of church history (brief), (2) mention the large works in Church History (name only), and (3) explain the nature and need for historical criticism.[36] Clearly, only the third question required the students to do more than report from memory; it required thought. It was the essay question for the exam and reflected Rauschenbusch's belief that grappling with the historical critical method was the most important concept to be taught in the early phase of church history studies. He was intent on students learning and being able to apply this method to their reading of all history. Stevens had taught him the importance of historical criticism for reading the New Testament. This method both revolutionized Rauschenbusch's understanding of the Bible and church history and became foundational to his own methodology. He thought understanding the new method was one of the most important ideas that he could leave with his students.[37]

In 1914 Rauschenbusch published "The Value and Use of History."[38] The lecture was originally written as an "address he delivered at a special session of

---

[33] WR, "The Contributions of Germany to the National Life of America," commencement address to the German Department, typescript (1903), box 92, Rauschenbusch Family Papers.

[34] WR, "The Influence of Historical Studies on Theology," 111.

[35] Barnes, "Walter Rauschenbusch as Historian," 256.

[36] WR, "Introduction to Church History."

[37] See Stevens, "Biblical Criticism," 13–17.

[38] WR, "The Value and Use of History," *The Record* (November 1914): 31–41.

Rochester-Colgate Theological Seminaries meeting at Rochester, May 1914."[39] In this address to students and faculty, Rauschenbusch developed his defense of the use of criticism. His point was that since it is a tool that seeks to "separate truth from falsehood," those who denounce the use of historical criticism "ask us to accept the assertions of past generations without testing them[40] He declared that fear of criticism opened people to seduction of all kinds of false claims in books, errors that had been repeated over and over. Rauschenbusch illustrated his point with an example from critical study of the Bible. He observed that people objected to the Revised Version translation "because it seemed to tamper with the inspired King James Version."[41] He wrote that at first glance it appeared that this respectful treatment of the King James Version of the Bible was based on deep piety and reverence for the antiquity of the King James Version. But in the long run, this misplaced devotion undermined an accurate understanding of the Bible because it promoted intense loyalty to a translation that included known erroneous passages based on inferior manuscripts.[42] Rauschenbusch advocated historical analysis of the context of each book of the Bible since the background for each book was different.[43] Text without context would lead to faulty interpretations. Rauschenbusch had studied biblical texts closely in seminary and also in writing Sunday school lessons. He also understood the importance of the method for recovering the history of the church. The critical approach to texts was a source of worry in many churches because it overturned some cherished interpretations; nevertheless, many seminaries adopted the new approaches to biblical interpretation during this era because the faculty were increasingly convinced of the validity of the method.

Rauschenbusch believed that one of the key explanations behind the acceptance of the critical method was a huge cultural shift in presuppositions: "Observation of life has created the scientific attitude.... It has taught accuracy and truthfulness and changed life from a static to a dynamic thing. This has been one of the greatest psychological changes in modern times."[44] The newer historical view of things emphasized that human life and history were best understood in terms of development. This meant that doctrine, although assumed by many to be set in stone for all the ages, actually had a history. Historical critical study showed that Christian doctrine had in fact developed out of rival positions and debates that occurred earlier in the history of the church. This was quite clear in

---

[39] This is Rauschenbusch's description in "The Study of Church History," box 1, Rauschenbusch Family Papers.

[40] WR, "The Value and Use of History," 38.

[41] Ibid.

[42] Ibid., 36.

[43] Ibid.

[44] Ibid.

Harnack's magisterial history of key doctrines, including the doctrines of the Trinity and the person of Christ.[45] The Bible, likewise, developed from various sources in different environments. It thus became clear that doctrine and scriptural interpretations were dynamic in their formation. Awareness of historical perspective, though unsettling at first when it discredited unfounded views, in the end provided a clearer and more accurate understanding of the role the church played in shaping its Scripture and its doctrine.[46]

In Rauschenbusch's view, proper understanding of Scripture had enormously important implications for individuals and for the church. He wrote as an example that "if a minister indoctrinates people with the premillennial scheme… he therewith sterilizes the intellect of his congregation." He labeled premillennial interpretation as "salvation by catastrophe," and claimed that Jesus did not teach this viewpoint.[47] This teaching was particularly objectionable to Rauschenbusch's personal agenda for the church: "I believe this [view of the imminent end of a wicked world] is one of the most powerful obstacles to all social effort."[48] Rauschenbusch believed that the church had taught wrong ideas in the past. He did not hesitate to condemn what he thought were false claims about the church's history, such as the papal claims to authority in Catholicism, the claim to apostolic succession held by the Church of England, and the teaching of some Baptists that they could trace their history all the way back to the New Testament. Students should have accurate information about church history so that they could make their own critical judgment about the truth or falsehood of claims made by churches. Rauschenbusch believed that historical criticism was a powerful corrective tool that could help eliminate errors of historical interpretation and also shed new light on Christian origins. And in Rauschenbusch's case, the method enabled him to recover early social dimensions in the message of the Old Testament prophets, Jesus and the primitive church, thus forming solid biblical and historical support for his major interest—the re-establishment of social Christianity in church and society.

---

[45] Harnack, *History of Dogma*.

[46] Rauschenbusch was fond of creating memorable, down-to-earth apothegms. He wrote, "A friend asked me recently, 'Why do all the evangelists hold the old views of the Bible?' I replied, 'Why do all the great teachers hold the new views of the Bible?'" (WR, "The Value and Use of History," 32.)

[47] WR, "Our Attitude toward Millennialism," *The Examiner* (September 24, 1896) (also cited in Hudson, ed., *Walter Rauschenbusch: Selected Writings*, 94).

[48] WR, "The Value and Use of History," 40.

The Critical Path to the Church's Past: Rauschenbusch and Döllinger

Rauschenbusch developed a strong admiration for a fellow church historian, Ignaz Döllinger, largely because they shared a common historical critical approach to the task of doing church history. Johann J. I. von Döllinger (1799–1890) was professor of church history for almost a half century at the University of Munich. Döllinger was Roman Catholic, and despite Rauschenbusch's general hostility to Catholicism, he was so drawn to Döllinger's work that he wrote a lecture on this great church historian and delivered it on nine separate occasions.[49] Döllinger's commitment to the truth led him to defy the papacy for making false claims about the papal past. Although an intensely devoted Roman Catholic, he took exception to the Vatican I Council ruling of papal infallibility, and for this reason the church excommunicated him. Döllinger's resistance made him the celebrated symbol of opposition to this new papal dogma.

Döllinger was ordained a priest in 1822; he soon secured an appointment as professor of church history at Aschaffenburg (1823–1826) where he published *The Teaching of the Eucharist in the First Three Centuries* in 1826. On the strength of this publication, Döllinger was called to the University of Munich, where he served for the remainder of his academic career (1826–1873). Döllinger's early work was characterized by vigorous defense of Catholic belief and polemical anti-Protestant studies, including his study of *The Reformation* (3 volumes, 1846–1848) and *Luther* (1851).

In 1848 revolutionary fervor inspired a nationalist movement in Germany. Prompted by this political ferment, Döllinger voiced his support for the independence of the German Catholic Church from papal control. On April 5–6, 1861, Döllinger lectured in Munich on "The Roman Question"—whether the papacy should yield the papal states to the movement for national Italian unity or defend its right to territory. Döllinger argued in these lectures that the pope's spiritual role would continue even if he lost the papal states to Italian unification. Döllinger had publicly sided with Italian unification, thereby undermining claims of temporal power by the papacy. Historian Lord Acton said that this was a "first unconscious, unpremeditated step in the process of detachment" by Döllinger, and that in it "the historian has begun to prevail over the divine."[50] Döllinger had

[49] WR, "Review of the Life of Döllinger," typescript of lecture. Rauschenbusch dated the nine occasions on which he delivered the lecture. See Rauschenbusch's cover letter, "Döllinger," box 18, Rauschenbusch Family Papers. Eventually he published the lecture as an extended book review of Johannes Friederich's *Ignaz von Döllenger* (see WR, "Review of *The Life of Döllinger*," 733–43). In the article he adds a general assessment of the book before proceeding to the narrative of Döllinger's life.

[50] See Acton, "Döllinger," 701; emphasized by Boudens, introduction to *Alfred Plummer*,

published *Hippolytus and Callistus* (1853) where he noted that Hippolytus had denounced Callistus, the bishop of Rome, as a heretic. It was clear to Döllinger that the papacy had erred in the past; it does not speak infallibly.

In the nineteenth century the papacy faced growing challenges to its authority in European society. In addition to impending loss of territory, the emergence of powerful new intellectual ideas challenged traditional Christian views, and the growing authority of national states exercised increased controls over education and marriage. Pius IX responded by asserting his own authority with three historic teachings. He issued the doctrine of the Immaculate Conception of the Blessed Virgin Mary in 1854. In 1864 he produced *The Syllabus of Errors,* a set of eighty theses condemning views current in modern life such as rationalism, socialism, secret societies, and liberalism, all opposed by the papacy.[51] But his boldest claim to authority was his declaration of papal infallibility issued at Vatican Council I in 1870.

Döllinger brought a historical perspective to bear on these issues. Historical study convinced Döllinger that these pronouncements had no place in Catholic tradition. These innovations were a departure from the faith and should therefore be rejected. For example, when Pius IX declared the doctrine of the Immaculate Conception, Döllinger responded that the new Roman doctrine was "contrary to the tradition of the first thirteen centuries, according to which the church claimed that only Christ was conceived without sin."[52]

Döllinger's immediate and enduring fame rested on his rejection of Vatican I's 1870 teaching affirming papal infallibility. In 1871 Archbishop Scherr of Munich demanded that Döllinger and church historian Johann Friedrich, Döllinger's colleague and future biographer, submit to the new dogma by March 15. Both refused. Döllinger explained the reasons he could not accept papal claims to authority:

> as a *Christian*, because it contradicts the plain words of Christ and the Apostles, nor as a *theologian* because it contradicts the whole of the true tradition of the Church, nor as a *student of history*, because the contention for it has cost Europe rivers of blood, degraded nations, and corrupted Churches, nor as a *citizen* because it will lead to ruinous disputes between Church and State....[53]

On April 23 both men were formally excommunicated. Döllinger lived another twenty years following expulsion from the Council. He accepted the infallibility of the church, but not of the papacy. In 1880 he bitterly remarked, "Rome

---

xviii.

[51] For an outline of the categories of condemned ideas see "Syllabus Errorum" in *Oxford Dictionary of Christian Church.*

[52] Döllinger, quoted in Boudens, introduction to *Alfred Plummer*, 107.

[53] Ibid., 18.

does not ask for faith; she asks for obedience."[54] In short, this church historian had, by critical study, tried to steer the church away from dogmatic decrees he believed had no foundation in history—and foundation in history was essential for Döllinger. Boudens's judgment is that Döllinger was the first Catholic historian who relied on historical criticism in his approach to the history of the church.[55] He was certainly the most influential Catholic historian of his era.

Rauschenbusch was clearly fascinated by Döllinger's story. His usual anti-Catholic feeling gave way to admiration. Three reasons suggest why he looked so favorably on this Catholic. First, Rauschenbusch wrote that "one of the most instructive elements of the biography of Döllinger was the "evidence given of the repression of intellectual liberty."[56] Among the most painful betrayals of conscience for Döllinger was acceptance of the doctrine by Bishop Karl Joseph Hefele, the great historian of the ecumenical councils, who, according to Döllinger "does not believe his own interpretation of the dogma."[57] In reviewing Döllinger's life, Rauschenbusch found further evidence that papal repression persisted into the present. Rauschenbusch saw in Döllinger a Roman Catholic church historian calling his own church to remain faithful to the past, suffering the consequences of challenging the church, and refusing to obey what he believed to be false teaching. Rauschenbusch and Döllinger prized freedom of conscience and independent moral judgment. They were willing to defy authority.

Second, these historians shared a common view of the nature of Christianity. Both men sought to shift the focus of their understanding of Christianity from theology to history. Thus they viewed Christianity as more than a set of beliefs. Both men shared the notion of Christianity as a force for good in the lives of individuals and the church. Christian doctrine and canon law must take second place to the goal of transformation of lives and societies. Moreover, theology cannot make legitimate claims if grounded on historical error.

A third factor drawing Rauschenbusch to Döllinger was the new historical worldview they shared. Döllinger reported that he regretted wasting ten years before he discovered and adopted modern historical methodology. Rauschenbusch encountered the critical method in biblical courses during his days in seminary. Both men abandoned pre-critical perspectives and embraced the validity of the historical critical method. The method was more than a technique of investigation. It opened them to a new worldview. Historical criticism provided the basis

---

[54] Ibid., 190–91.
[55] Boudens, introduction to *Alfred Plummer*, xix.
[56] WR, Review of *The Life of Döllinger* by Johannes Friedrich, 739.
[57] Boudens, introduction to *Alfred Plummer*, 26.

for Döllinger's rejection of the historical credibility of the Pseudo-Isidorian Decretals and other forged documents used to support inflated papal claims.[58] He held that neither the immaculate conception of Mary nor the infallibility of the pope was a teaching of the early church. Historian and theologian Adrian Hastings has asserted that "the inter-involvement of history, conceived in modern terms, and belief may constitute the most central and persistent theme in Christian thought throughout the 19th and 20th centuries."[59] Acton summarized the force of this revolution on modern understanding when he asserted, "The ecclesiastical history of his [Döllinger's] youth went to pieces against the new criticism of 1863."[60] But Döllinger reconstructed his intellectual framework. As his close friend Lord Acton perceptively wrote, Döllinger was touched by two major intellectual currents of the day: scientific methods of history and the theory of development.[61]

A similar dynamic was at work in Rauschenbusch's experience. Historical criticism was the key instrument in opening new perspectives on Scripture; he wrote that "it is interesting that the idea of the Kingdom of God should never have come in for any real investigation till the latter half of this century…[and moreover] the work of historical criticism is working up the raw material for recovering the idea"[62] Regarding Döllinger's work, Rauschenbusch noted that the thirteenth paragraph of the *Syllabus of Errors* upheld scholastic methods and rejected the new methods.[63] Rauschenbusch observed, "Thus the church was driving in one direction and simultaneously his studies were pushing Döllinger in the opposite direction."[64] The historian of science and religion John Hedley Brooke judged the historical-critical method to be profoundly influential in changing the outlook of the era. He discussed the thought and massive impact of Lyell on geology and Darwin on biology, but nevertheless concluded in deft phrase that "the most radical challenge to biblical authority came not from the history of science

---

[58] The decretals are a collection of canon law documents, ascribed to St. Isidore of Seville (c. 560-636) but actually compiled about 850. This collection contains spurious documents claiming papal supremacy over all the church.

[59] Hastings, "History," 301.

[60] Acton, "Döllinger," 734.

[61] John Emerich Edward Dalberg, first Baron Acton, was the leading British Catholic historian and was a close friend of Döllinger. He planned but never completed writing a history of liberty. He also planned and wrote the introduction to the *Cambridge Modern History* (12 vols., 1901–1911). At the time of Döllinger's death, Acton produced a notable review and analysis of Döllinger's life and work. (See Acton, "Döllinger," 701.)

[62] WR to Will and Mrs. [Munger], July 11, 1896, box 50, Rauschenbusch Family Papers.

[63] WR, "Review of *The Life of Döllinger*," 742.

[64] Ibid., 741.

but from the science of history.... The science of history had created a watershed."[65]

From modern critical studies Rauschenbusch learned that Jesus' central message was "the kingdom of God," thus providing the scriptural basis for his claim that Jesus proclaimed salvation for society. Rauschenbusch believed that Jesus' original message of redemption was aimed not merely at individuals but also at society. To be faithful to the message of earliest Christianity meant restoration of a social gospel. The path to this insight came through the method of careful historical study. The new method profoundly altered the perception of the past for both Döllinger and Rauschenbusch and for countless historians since. Rauschenbusch's appreciation for Döllinger illustrates how deeply significant the historical method was for the modern world.

The Content and Use of the History of Christianity

Rauschenbusch's various reading lists of church histories show that he was familiar with the leading works in the discipline. He was so exuberant in his praise of Hans von Schubert's superb *Outlines of Church History* that he began translating it himself.[66] His lectures clearly demonstrate that he was teaching the classical story of the internal history of the church. His list of lecture topics followed the standard curriculum so that students were introduced to the essentials of ancient, medieval, Reformation, and modern church history.[67] Johann Mosheim (1694–1755) was perhaps the most influential church historian of the early eighteenth century. From his time forward the question of the external history of the church as well as its internal content had also been recognized. German scholarship employed both categories, but external factors were generally treated as a secondary issue by church historians, and Protestant church historians followed German leadership.

Among Protestant historians in the twentieth century, Kenneth Scott Latourette was a pioneer in broadening the subject matter of church history. Latourette included the criteria of influence of the environment on the church and the influence of the church on the environment among the topics to be considered. Environment was a broad, non-specific category, but he understood that context was essential for understanding the Christian mission. He was interested in chronicling the history of missions where these mutual influences were readily evident, and context was clearly different from Europe or the United States. He

---

[65] Brooke, *Science and Religion*, 270.

[66] See Schubert, *Outlines of Church History*.

[67] In addition to the standard survey, Rauschenbusch prepared notes for separate courses on American Christianity, Christian unity, the history of church property, and the rise of democratic religion. See notes in box 7, Rauschenbusch Family Papers.

consciously adopted the language of the *History of Christianity* (1953) in his major textbook while rejecting church history as too narrow.[68]

In the United States the study of the history of Christianity has undergone massive changes during the last half century. In 1997 Harry Stout and Robert Taylor documented a major shift in the historiography of the discipline.[69] They noted that church historians had traditionally worked in seminaries and occupied themselves with the institutional topics such as doctrine, hierarchy, devotion, missions, and worship. However, the Stout and Taylor study showed that scholarship after the 1960s had increasingly shifted to universities where the discipline attracted both historians and sociologists. By the 1970s the term "religious studies" grew in popularity. The focus shifted to the impact of religion on the broader culture rather than on the internal life of institutional churches.[70]

Rauschenbusch operated at both levels of the study of the history of Christianity. While he taught formal courses in traditional church history at Rochester, he also included in his lectures his interest in the relationship of the church to society. He wrote that the history of Christianity was "larger than Church History."[71] When he shifted to publishing his books, the internal practices of the churches often became a secondary story to his call for the churches of the present to seek redemption of society by pursuing justice. The study of the internal history of the church was important, but its external influence was even more important.

Rauschenbusch had in mind significant uses of church history that went beyond traditional textbook treatments of the internal life of the church. He had appropriated current trends of thought in his own intellectual and spiritual formation, and he sought to convey these to his students and to his readers. His teaching notes and his major publications reveal that he gave special emphases first to the place of Jesus as the foundation of the church, both historically and in the present. Second, Rauschenbusch's lectures referred to solidarity, social awareness, ethics, and justice in church history—themes at the heart of the social gospel he had already appropriated for himself and wanted to instill in young ministers.

---

[68] See Latourette, *A History of Christianity*, xxiii, and *A History of the Expansion of Christianity*, 1:xii–xvi.

[69] Stout and Taylor, "Studies of Religion in American Society," 15–47.

[70] Because of attention to the cultural impact of religion, many historians now prefer to use "history of Christianity" rather than "church history." For the shift to "history of Christianity" see Cherry, *Hurrying toward Zion*, 112–19, esp. 116.

[71] Barnes, "Walter Rauschenbusch as Historian," 255. Here Barnes acknowledges in an endnote that this quote comes from the Fetter manuscript, a set of classroom notes taken in the years 1911–1913 by George Fetter, one of Rauschenbusch's church history students. The manuscript is another valuable source of information on Rauschenbusch's understanding of church history. It is found in Box 141 of the Rauschenbusch Family Papers.

Finally, study of church history would be useful by providing ministers with specific examples of right and wrong—signs of the presence and absence of the kingdom of God; events and patterns in church history (as he called it) could help provide guidance for discerning the spirit of Jesus at the church's origin, throughout its history, and in its challenge for the present.

Jesus and Church History

For Rauschenbusch Jesus was the source of Christian origins and the standard for its evaluation throughout history. The church had for centuries emphasized the divinity of Christ, but the nineteenth century saw the beginnings of an unprecedented effort to discover the historical Jesus as well. The new theology adopted this emphasis: leaders of this school did not deny the divinity of Jesus Christ but did seek to recover and emphasize the true humanity of Jesus, which had been marginalized in traditional Christian thought. This meant that it was important to find ways to stress the impact of the person of Jesus in world history. Understood as a historical figure, how could his influence be described? A common approach, also adopted by Rauschenbusch, was to focus on Jesus as a "new force" released in history, which had brought about profound changes in society from the first century to the present.

Rauschenbusch was fully aware of the importance of authority in religion. In the typescript for his book *The Social Principles of Jesus*, he wrote, "The Spirit of Christ is peculiarly the authority and pride of modern Christianity; we need authority. No intellectual emancipation will ever carry us beyond that need. It is fundamental in human society."[72] Rauschenbusch contended that "none of the accepted authorities of the existing social order will serve us, for we are not seeking the justification of things as they are, but their overthrow and renewal."[73] Rauschenbusch was using revolutionary language when he wrote these lines. He was calling readers to change church practice. He identified a variety of sources of authority that had appeared in church history, including councils, creeds, the Fathers, papal definitions, the Bible variously interpreted, and the original generations of Christians when "the Lord had a unique authority." But he concluded that "modern theology everywhere is laying a new stress on the Spirit and consciousness of Jesus, and finding in that the living soul of Christianity, the divine and permanent light within the Bible."[74] This interpretation was very much in keeping with the attitude of the new theology toward authority grounded in the presence of Jesus in the world as a "force."

Rauschenbusch understood the continuation of the "force" in terms of the

---

[72] WR, *The Social Principles of Jesus*, 3, typescript, box 1, Rauschenbusch Family Papers.
[73] Ibid., 4.
[74] Ibid., 5.

"Spirit of Jesus." Jesus' guidance through his spirit offered the path to genuine Christianity. Rauschenbusch helped his readers of *The Social Principles of Jesus* by identifying ten specifics in Jesus' thought: first, Jesus showed indifference to traditional religious concerns such as the Temple at Jerusalem and its sacrificial ritual;[75] second, he showed compassion for human suffering;[76] third, he showed "a sense of solidarity with the common people. He was a plain man, a carpenter, and never turned his back on his class."[77] Fourth, Jesus "had a deliberate faith in democracy."[78] Fifth, "a further work of the Spirit of Jesus is his distrust of the influence of private riches."[79] Sixth, Jesus' faith "in human nature seems...another important element in his spirit."[80] Seventh, Jesus expressed "faith in love as a basis for human society."[81] Eighth, Jesus taught a reversal of values. He was suspicious of selfish aristocracies.[82] Ninth, "The fighting temper" is one of the marks of the Spirit of Jesus.[83] Finally, Jesus expressed faith in the initiative of the individual.[84] This interpretation of Jesus reflected a mix of New Testament witness combined with Rauschenbusch's own biases and interest in politics, economics, and society. He found in Jesus a kindred spirit, ready to challenge the status quo. He wanted readers to be informed by the spirit of Jesus and the best of church history, and to adopt this spirit for their own lives. He conceded that "it is most difficult to estimate accurately the historic influence of religious ideas. They are subtle and hard to trace."[85]

For Rauschenbusch, then, the origin of Christianity began with the life of Jesus and his influence in history. He believed that the real canon for judging the church is the "spirit of Jesus" as it is applied to the church's organization, ethics, theology, and worship throughout its history and in the present. By studying church history, he believed that we can see how Jesus' ethical emphasis was changed from its original intent to an "insistence on orthodoxy and ritual in the church."[86] The pressing issue for him was the current response to Jesus' message. Rauschenbusch wrote, "But still the question remains how clearly the student

[75] Ibid., 15.
[76] Ibid., 24.
[77] Ibid., 27.
[78] Ibid., 33.
[79] Ibid., 40.
[80] Ibid., 55.
[81] Ibid., 57.
[82] Ibid., 63.
[83] Ibid., 67.
[84] Ibid., 68.
[85] Ibid., 10.
[86] WR, "The Ultimate Qualification for the Study," introductory lecture, box 1, Rauschenbusch Family Papers.

himself has apprehended the Spirit of Jesus."[87] How should the student achieve his goal? The student apprehends the Spirit of Jesus through "physical closeness to Christ, absorption of his personality entering into his point of view." Moreover, he wrote, "the illumination of the intellect by actual following of Christian life is the ultimate qualification for useful study of church history."[88] For Rauschenbusch, understanding the spirit of Jesus could come only through full commitment to him; the study of church history was more than an intellectual pursuit. Neander's influence pervades Rauschenbusch's sentiment: the key to history was to understand individuals, and the beginning point for understanding was the heart rather than the head. Jesus' "force" in history was the power to change people when they adopted his spirit, according to Rauschenbusch. He was deeply immersed in New Testament studies from his seminary days, and he wrote at the end of his life: "Jesus has been to me the inexhaustible source of fresh impulse, life and courage."[89] Rauschenbusch was also influenced by Shailer Mathews's *The Social Teachings of Jesus* (1897) and Francis Greenwood Peabody's *Jesus Christ and the Social Question* (1900). Both of these American scholars interpreted Jesus' view of the kingdom in more social terms than European scholars.[90] In Rauschenbusch's view Jesus' life was the ultimate religious biography. Jesus provided the origin and the driving force of all church history. The church historian must always begin here and reckon with the influence of the spirit of Jesus. The ongoing spirit of Christ serves both as the motivation and center for the church today.

The Social Gospel and Church History

Rauschenbusch is not remembered as a historian of the church, but rather as an original thinker whose greatest impact on the church was to articulate what he saw as a neglected dimension of Jesus' message of the kingdom of God, and to call the church to its responsibilities to redeem the world around it. Yet his view of the kingdom of God was tied to his identity as a church historian.

As a professor of church history, Rauschenbusch regularly addressed social issues in his lectures. He believed that he should inspire ministerial students to learn more than facts of history of Christianity. Their studies should motivate them to help create a more just society. Rauschenbusch's list of lectures followed standard chronological development of key topics.[91] However, as components of

---

[87] Ibid.

[88] Ibid.

[89] "Letter to Dr. Lemuel Call Barnes, Field Secretary, American Baptist Home Mission Society, May 10, 1918."

[90] Evans, *The Kingdom Is Always but Coming*, 151.

[91] WR, first lecture as professor of church history, 1903. See List of Lectures for different periods in boxes 1–6, Rauschenbusch Family Papers.

individual lectures, he regularly inserted discussions of ethical issues. He wanted students to begin to think in solidaristic terms. Rauschenbusch therefore communicated his perspective and his convictions about the social gospel to his church history students.[92] He also offered students specific guidelines from Jesus' social teachings. For example, he pointed out that "in his [Jesus'] description of the Great Judgment there is no word of church or creed. The damning fact for some is simply that they have been indifferent while other men suffered."[93] Rauschenbusch also drew out the social implications of Jesus' words. He wrote that if indifference condemns individuals, "will it not condemn a nation if it permits whole social classes to be ill-fed, ill-clad, ill-housed?"[94] Rauschenbusch also prepared outlines for new courses such as "The History of Church Property" and "The Rise of Democratic Religion."[95] He did not limit himself to traditional curricula, but pursued themes relating the church to economics and politics.

In 1914 when reflecting with ministerial students on the value and use of history, Rauschenbusch urged them boldly to call the nation to justice. He declared that the church needed prophetic leaders, people with "moral will, forward movement...."[96] Rauschenbusch wanted students to become minister-prophets—in short, to seek justice for the nation that he envisioned. He argued that the world and the church are in constant need of renovation. Rauschenbusch thus combined the dual values of knowing church history and speaking a prophetic word to the church. He said that the minister without benefit of historical wisdom was more likely to be either a fanatic with narrow vision, or a church leader simply content with the present.[97] He told students that the minister needs moral courage to act and needs wisdom of the past to guide decisions regarding renovation of church and world. He believed that knowledge of church history would make students aware of the church's relation to society in general, and this knowledge would enhance their conviction of the church's social obligation. Church history must be about more than creeds and ceremonies and its own internal history; it must also seek social redemption.

In Rauschenbusch's view, in order to prepare for ministry, students must be informed about current conditions in America. In 1904, soon after his move from teaching German language seminary students a wide variety of subjects to focusing on church history for English language students, Rauschenbusch investigated how other seminaries were addressing social problems in America. He gathered

[92] WR, "Introduction to the Study of Church History."

[93] WR, *The Social Teachings of Jesus*, typescript, 24–25.

[94] Ibid.

[95] WR, "The History of Church Property," and "The Rise of Democratic Religion," box 7, Rauschenbusch Family Papers.

[96] WR, *The Social Teachings of Jesus*, typescript, 24–25.

[97] WR, "The Value and Use of History," 41.

information and wrote out comparative curricula requirements for the seminaries at Andover, Rochester, Oberlin, and Cobb. He found the curriculum across the usual three years to be similar in all of these seminaries. Students took courses in Bible, historical and practical theology, church history, and elocution each year.[98] But along with these disciplines Rauschenbusch noted that Andover Theological Seminary offered "Social Economics: The Outline of an Elective Course of Study." The Andover course had been referenced in an article published in the *Christian Union* (October 18, 1888), and an inquirer had asked Rauschenbusch about its content and value. This course was intended as an analysis of American social issues for current seminarians, but it was also designed to inform the previous generation of ministers who had not been instructed on a Christian view of social issues during their formal training. They would have to work through the subject on their own. The syllabus for the course was therefore detailed. It offered suggested readings of general books, and outlined a curriculum devoted to three major topics: (1) Labor and the Social Evolution of Labor, (2) The Treatment of Crime and the Criminal Classes, and (3) The Treatment of Pauperdom and Disease. Each of these divisions was in turn subdivided into twelve topics. Rauschenbusch devoted his interest chiefly to labor and poverty, but he also occasionally addressed problems of disease and crime. Throughout his career he wrote extensively about labor, including most of the specific twelve labor topics addressed in the Andover syllabus: "The Relation of Society to those who have not been fully incorporated into it, with special references to the present aims and demands of the Laboring classes."[99] Although not yet part of standard seminary curriculum, the social problems were pressing enough that some of the seminaries began offering courses in sociology, and soon their numbers would grow. Social ethics would become a staple of the curriculum in many schools. The topics were clearly designed to inform students about current social problems. The thirty-six topics addressed in this curriculum provided ample material for a full-length course. Rauschenbusch had already worked extensively on many of these problems as a young minister and wrote much to inform the church about the intersection of human need and how the church might respond. This course was not about the

---

[98] WR, handwritten notes, box 102, Rauschenbusch Family Papers.

[99] The section on labor included the study of twelve topics:(1) The Transition from Slavery to Serfdom, (2) Workmen of the Free Cities, (3) The English Laborer at Rise of Industrialization, (4) The Factory System, (5) Chartism and Trade Unions, (6) English Labor Relations, (7) The Political Relations of Democracy to Laboring Classes, (8) American Labor as Affected by Slavery and Immigration, (9) American Labor as Affected by State Systems of Education, (10) Wages and Profits, (11) What Constitutes a Working Day: The Use of Leisure, (12) Socialism in America Compared with Socialism in Germany and England in its Present Aims and Demands. See "Social Economics: The Outline of an Elective Course of Study," typescript, box 102, Rauschenbusch Family Papers.

church in the past. It was a companion study of society and analysis of the role of the church in the present. Rauschenbusch believed that knowledge of both was essential for the well-prepared contemporary minister.

Moral Evidence for the Kingdom of God: Discerning Good and Evil in Church History

Rauschenbusch also looked to church history to help identify characteristics of the Kingdom of God. The Kingdom was found in practices that matched the spirit of Jesus or the will of God. He believed that the church had failed at many points in interpreting the spirit of Jesus and putting it into practice, but it had succeeded on other occasions. Knowledge of church history could make successes and failures clearer and could thereby provide guidance to the young ministers in their task of working toward establishing the kingdom of God. It could provide instruction in moral judgment by studying examples of decisions taken in the past.

Rauschenbusch stressed the moral dimensions of church history. He wrote that "religious history is an effort to arrive at true value judgments about the fundamental facts of life."[100] In his view people must make moral judgments: they must name wrong wherever they find it. For example, he criticized the medieval Inquisition's use of force; but he also criticized the readiness of modern Christians to break labor strikes by the use of violence. Here he was judging practices of the churches by their responses to moral problems. Church history revealed many missteps in the past: the church had wrongly assumed political power and held views that were patently false. Rauschenbusch also commended select people and movements in church history that for him demonstrated positive features in the church's history, including the fight to end slavery and alcoholism.

As a Baptist and a church historian, Rauschenbusch had great admiration for the Baptists and Anabaptists.[101] He explained why he thought the Anabaptists should be emulated. The Anabaptists emphasized ethical conduct over doctrine and ceremony; they emphasized personal experience of Christianity, they rejected infant baptism, and they opposed state compulsion in religion.[102] He loved to promote American democracy and found Baptist Roger Williams a great champion of the correct relationship of church to state. Rauschenbusch was not work-

---

[100] WR, "A Baptist Reinterpretation of Church History," presented at the Baptist Seminary Faculties Union, University of Chicago, April 1913, box 21, Rauschenbusch Family Papers.

[101] See the more complete discussion of his views on Baptists and Anabaptists in chapter 6.

[102] See WR, "The Prophetic Character of the Anabaptist Movement," an address at the opening of the fall term Rochester Baptist Theological Seminary, September 14, 1903, box 4, Rauschenbusch Family Papers.

ing to reconstruct a nuanced understanding of the complexity of historical Baptists. Instead, he was looking for patterns of Christian life and practice that, in his view, modeled the "spirit of Christ" and also those that failed to strive for the spirit. In his mind the Anabaptists and Baptists most nearly expressed the spirit of Jesus and the practice of the early church: these Christians embraced principles of the kingdom of God.[103]

Rauschenbusch also gave attention to the American religious experience.[104] He often drew contrasts between European and American Christianity, notably in his lecture "The Historic Genius of the American Culture."[105] He was fully conversant with German church histories and noted that they gave almost no attention to the United States.[106] Nevertheless, he thought the American churches had much to offer the "older churches" of Europe.[107] In this lecture he gave most attention to "distinctive qualities of American churches" and stressed separation of church and state, democracy, and the involvement of lay men and women as positive features. The values he noted closely reflected his interpretation of the Anabaptists. He believed that the churches could function as "a unique asset in the social transformation of our nation."[108]

Rauschenbusch described the fulfillment he found in his own teaching vocation. His goal as a church history professor was to serve the church by recovering a vision of apostolic Christianity. In his Döllinger lecture Rauschenbusch wrote that Döllinger was filled

> with the desire to set forth that early life of the Church and so help to create it in his day. It was really...that effort to repristinate the church and to approximate apostolic conditions which has been one of the great reformatory forces in church history. Döllinger hoped to aid it by teaching history, thus bringing the Church to a consciousness of its best self and organizing its sluggish blood with the fresh breath of ideas and ideals. That is the contribution which the scholar

---

[103] Ibid.

[104] Henry Warner Bowden studied Rauschenbusch's contribution to the new discipline of American church history. He based his analysis on the class notes taken by George Fetter in 1912. See box 141, Rauschenbusch Family Papers for Fetter's notes; also see Bowden, "Church History and the Social Gospel," 170–95.

[105] WR, "The Historic Genius of the American Churches," box 4, Rauschenbusch Family Papers.

[106] Ibid., 1–2, 5. He noted that Kurtz, which he identified as the most widely used textbook in Germany, gave only seven pages of its four volumes to America. Baptists and Methodists received seven lines each. Whereas Europeans held the grand narrative in the writing of church history, Americans largely produced denominational chronicles.

[107] WR, "A Baptist Reinterpretation of Church History," box 21, Rauschenbusch Family Papers.

[108] WR, "The Historic Genius," 1, box 4, Rauschenbusch Family Papers.

can make to practical life.[109]

Church history points the way not only to the spirit of Jesus but also to the spirit of the earliest church; both provided a benchmark for the life of the church in the present. Rauschenbusch declared that study of the church would correct religious individualism, provide awareness of the church universal, and heighten tolerance and gentleness through acquiring a more dispassionate outlook on others while adopting a more humble distrust of one's own infallibility.[110] Rauschenbusch's description of the well-informed minister was in many ways a reflection of his own personality and tastes. The informed minister must "combine clear and even passionate convictions about right and truth with tolerance and sympathetic insight into the thought life of a given age.... [We should] beware of trying to assert or deny facts that do not fit with what we regard as right or fitting."[111] The minister with the historian's perspective should have a tolerant outlook in order to understand an age, but also be prepared to have the integrity to criticize and reject anything that seems untrue or morally wrong in the church's history.

Modern church historians have not placed high on their agenda the task of searching out the good and the bad in the church history for praise or condemnation. Instead they tend to follow Rauschenbusch's other admonition to strive for sympathetic insight, tolerance, and distrust of their own infallibility.[112] But for Rauschenbusch, history also had moral purpose. Since Plutarch wrote his *Parallel Lives* (second century CE), history has been used by many instructors to teach by example.[113] Modern Christians have been drawn to favorite charismatic figures such as St. Francis, Albert Schweitzer, or Mother Teresa as models for inspiration and imitation. Modern historians have wrestled with how to approach moral judgment of historical events. Moreover, they realize they cannot help but make judgments on people, institutions, and events of the past—if in somewhat more subtle fashion than Rauschenbusch employed. Rauschenbusch found in church history a pragmatic tool for understanding society. He believed the minister and the lay person inevitably would be confronted with moral questions and that church history provided indispensable guidance for ministers charged with leading the churches of the next generation to make good moral choices. It was filled with lessons of resisting or welcoming the coming of the kingdom. Rauschenbusch later wrote, "Church history would...furnish illustrations of sermons more

---

[109] WR, "Ignatius von Döllinger," box 18, Rauschenbusch Family Papers. See p. 7 of the lecture.

[110] WR, "VIII. Values" (in first day of lecture notes), box 1, Rauschenbusch Family Papers.

[111] WR, "Introduction to Church History."

[112] WR, "VIII. Values."

[113] Breisach, *Historiography*, 70–71.

cogent than any argument. It could proclaim in tones of thunder that sin will wreck both men and nations...when men or churches say to the Lord, 'Depart from us,' not even the Almighty can do anything for them."[114]

Student Reception of Rauschenbusch as Professor

Rauschenbusch received high praise from former students. Edwin T. Dahlberg, later president of the American Baptist Convention and of the National Council of Churches, was Rauschenbusch's student for four years (1913–1917) and also served as his secretary. Dahlberg spoke on Rauschenbusch at a seminary convocation and later gave an oral interview in which he offered his recollections.[115] Rauschenbusch's secretaries typed his correspondence and chapters of his books, and because of his deafness they also had to assist at public functions when he was lecturing, in chapel services or in public forums. The students took notes while speakers talked in order to show Rauschenbusch what was being said. In question-and-answer sessions following Rauschenbusch's lectures they performed a similar service: the student secretary briefly wrote the question on a notepad and handed it to Rauschenbusch so that he could respond with little delay.[116] Dahlberg recalled Rauschenbusch with deep fondness:

> The picture of this tall, kindly brown-bearded man, with his noble forehead and twinkling eyes will remain with many forever.... Primarily, we remember him as a follower of Jesus Christ—a man who personified everything we think of when we think of Christ: greatness of soul, integrity of intellect, and overwhelming dedication to the Kingdom of God.[117]

This admiring student further recalled that those "who knew him best will always think of him as the most Christ-like man we ever met: a man who literally made the life of the Savior his daily example."[118] "The students called him 'Rauchie,'" Dahlberg said. "He was my greatest teacher."[119] Rauschenbusch made a similar impression on the future professor Henry Burke Robins, who recalled,

> Had you been living in Rochester more than twenty years ago, you might have seen him, almost any day, walking down East Avenue, from his house on Portsmouth Terrace to his lecture room on Alexander Street. Tall, erect, bearded, possessed of a piercing brown eye which saw right through you. Gifted with the power of logical analysis and an equally impressive sense of humor. Stone deaf,

---

[114] WR, "The Influence of Historical Studies on Theology," 120.

[115] See Dahlberg, *Walter Rauschenbusch*, leaflet, and "Edwin Dahlberg in Conversation," 209–18.

[116] Dahlberg, *Walter Rauschenbusch*, 210.

[117] Ibid., 10.

[118] Ibid., 3.

[119] Dahlberg, "Dahlberg in Conversation," 209, 212.

> but so much alive that little went on in his immediate environment or in his world that escaped him.[120]

Robins also noted Rauschenbusch's public life in Rochester, recalling his leadership of the People's Sunday Evenings, organized meetings that addressed all manner of social issues from a religious perspective.[121] Robins said that Rauschenbusch's greatest contribution to his students was not what he taught them about history, but rather his religious spirit, characterized by "a passionate yearning for genuine kinship of spirit and experience with Jesus Christ which suffused his whole bearing...."[122]

Dores R. Sharpe, also a former student and secretary, and Rauschenbusch's first biographer, met Rauschenbusch in 1908. In 1939 at Rochester, Sharpe delivered the Rauschenbusch Fellowship lecture, "A Great Good Man."[123] He recalled how Rauschenbusch inspired students to think for themselves: "He is great who shocks you, probes you, arouses you, unsettles you...until you are jostled out of your wonted ways...."[124] Sharpe praised Rauschenbusch for his free and independent spirit. He described Rauschenbusch's father as a person who was "afraid of upsetting things theologically...and this fear froze his freedom."[125] By contrast, Sharpe described Rauschenbusch as free and original in thinking, one who challenged the status quo. In Sharpe's vivid image Rauschenbusch was "a piece of ecclesiastic nebula thrown off by the Baptist denomination as it moved through time in its orbit to complacency."[126] Sharpe was deeply devoted to his professor, and his praise was effusive. He found in Rauschenbusch a balance between intellect and heart, a capacity for thinking united with a capacity for loving. He found him "free from all cant, prejudice, hate and ill will.... [and] on the whole...the best man I have ever known."[127] Sharpe emphasized Rauschenbusch's independent thought and the way he unsettled students by probing their thinking. This was stimulating and memorable classroom teaching.

Rauschenbusch loved the Rochester seminary students, and they were drawn to him. Rochester faculty member Cornelius Woelfkin recalled Rauschenbusch's powerful influence: "In his professional work he was a magnet for students. Many

---

[120] Henry Burke Robins, "The Contribution of Walter Rauschenbusch to World Peace," *The Bulletin* (Rochester: Colgate Rochester Divinity School, May 1940, 149.

[121] Ibid., 149–50.

[122] Robins, *Rochester Seminary Bulletin*, 1918, 34, cited in Sharpe, *Walter Rauschenbusch*, 433, n. 13.

[123] The speech appears as ch. 19 of the biography (Sharpe, *Walter Rauschenbusch*, 420–40).

[124] Ibid., 420.

[125] Ibid., 421.

[126] Ibid., 422.

[127] Ibid., 426.

men who came to our seminary felt the lure of his presence and came because he was there. All students came to feel the power of his message and were inspired by his challenge to undertake tasks requiring sacrifice and courage."[128] In this tribute Woelfkin captured the impact on his students of the charismatic professor. C. A. Daniel, pastor of the First German Baptist Church in Rochester (founded in 1851) and Rauschenbusch's pastor, also recalled Rauschenbusch's influence on his students. He wrote, "When I think of Walter's work and handicap in hearing I am astounded how he influenced and molded the characters and minds of the German students. He stepped down to listen to their recitations and answers with his ear close to the mouth of the student."[129] Rauschenbusch's dealing with his deafness was heroic in the eyes of many, including his pastor. One of these students, Albert W. Beavan, who was later president of Colgate-Rochester Divinity School, recalled the deep impression Rauschenbusch made on him during his student days at Rochester Theological Seminary. He wrote,

> I sat in his classroom and had the privilege of frequent informal conferences with him. He opened all the windows of life that looked out upon the struggle and heartache of the children of men, but he always helped me to see in the midst of that agony the striving of people for the best, their quest of the God who was near, and the answer to their needs in the message of Christ in whom he believed.... Above all, however, is the impression which he left of a man of Christ-like spirit.[130]

The testimonies of these former students and colleagues recall Rauschenbusch's striking presence, his physical handicap, his intellect, and his dedication to the kingdom of God. But the most profound impression left with these young students was the spirit of the man. This is what enriched their lives in the long term and was their most important takeaway from knowing Rauschenbusch: they felt they had met a man who exemplified the spirit of Christ. The influence of the professor on these students was unforgettable.

As a church historian assigned to regular teaching, Rauschenbusch became an apologist who articulated many reasons to his students for the value of studying church history. He also encouraged colleagues in other seminaries to promote the value of historical studies and thereby to secure a firm place for church history in the seminary course of study. Rauschenbusch used his knowledge of church history to critique the contemporary church and to place his arguments for the social gospel in historical context. His class notes show that he urgently wanted to train

---

[128] Cornelius Woelfkin, "Rochester Theological Seminary Bulletin: The Record," November 1918, 22, cited in Sharpe, *Walter Rauschenbusch*, 438, n. 25.

[129] Daniel, "Reminiscences of My Friend," 26.

[130] Albert W. Beavan to Dores Sharpe, 1941, box 39, Rauschenbusch Family Papers. Cited in Sharpe, 408.

prophetic ministers. A large part of his goal was driven by the idea of instilling in the young students the will to change—to be revolutionary in outlook rather than accepting the status quo. Behind this goal was his hope to orient students toward becoming leaders of society, working to create a better nation. He sought to give them larger goals for their work in the church. In the context of the classroom, Rauschenbusch was devoted to conveying the idea of the spirit of Jesus—how it had both flourished and diminished in various eras of the church's history, and how it could be appropriated by the students as a guide to their lives.

Rauschenbusch sought to motivate students to be prophetic and to give them a vision of a better nation; in his relatively brief contact with the students Rauschenbusch wanted to plant in them the historical method as a key component of his teaching. He believed he was providing them with a tool that would serve them throughout their lives as discerning readers, ministers, and interpreters of the Christian faith. In teaching them Christian history and a method for evaluating the church's past, he was preparing students to encounter their world critically and to minister in it. Rauschenbusch the church historian contributed through his teaching to the formation of ministers with a modern outlook for service in the contemporary church. He thought critical analysis of church history would help future ministers be able to better detect and promote the spirit of Christ as they analyzed contemporary American society.

As a professor at Rochester Theological Seminary, Rauschenbusch made his living teaching church history. He was a Baptist historian, but he was not primarily a historian of Baptists. He was a church historian with responsibility to his students for the grand narrative of church history. His purview was the worldwide church with its long history, examined critically. Rauschenbusch always wanted to write church history. However, his greatest passion was Christian social justice, and after publishing his first book on the subject, he was constantly asked to address the question of the social gospel. Overwhelmed with the urgency of this massive task of reform in the current church, he responded with numerous lectures and publications, mostly on social issues, and he made a powerful impact on Christian thinking.

Although he did not research and write church history, it is plausible to argue that Rauschenbusch's historical perspectives were a crucial component in forming his creative insights into the American church and society of his era. As a teacher he included the broad sweep and the method of church history and added to that a strong emphasis on the person and spirit of Jesus. Moreover, he insisted on the church's obligation to society and the use of education to inform moral choices. He employed pragmatic applications of the story of the church to its current situation. Both in his work as a church historian and as a social gospeller, Rauschenbusch's life work demonstrated to the students his conviction of the relevance of studying the history of Christianity.

CHAPTER 8

RAUSCHENBUSCH: PUBLIC PROTESTANT

During the final decade of his life, Rauschenbusch emerged as one of the most significant religious voices in America. By speaking frequently and writing voluminously, he sustained his position as a highly visible Protestant leader. While he was deeply devoted to his Baptist denomination, Rauschenbusch was also an enthusiastic supporter of American Protestantism more broadly and hoped that Protestantism would become the religion of the nation. This chapter explores Rauschenbusch's leadership role in progressive American Protestantism during the period 1907–1918.

Several lines of evidence point to Rauschenbusch's role as a leading Protestant voice in the decade before World War I. Rauschenbusch's former student Edwin Dahlberg compiled a list of prominent figures of the day who sought Rauschenbusch's counsel. The list included political figures such as David Lloyd George, Theodore Roosevelt, Woodrow Wilson, and Eugene Debs. He also corresponded with social reformers such as Jacob Riis, Zona Gale, and Vida Scudder. But Rauschenbusch's influence was felt most directly by people already committed to traditional Christianity. Dahlberg noted that many religious leaders took inspiration from him, including Christian activist Kagawa of Japan, Baptist minister Harry Emerson Fosdick, Unitarian minister and social activist John Haynes Holmes, Methodist Bishop Francis J. M. McConnell, and others.[1]

He managed to attract a wide public reception.

Rauschenbusch appealed to many audiences; he was in constant demand to lecture and to write after 1907. He was often on the move, using the modern Pullman cars on the efficient train system and speaking to audiences of the Northeastern U.S. and beyond. He wrote frequently for religious journals and his work was noticed in the secular press. He published his major volumes during a ten-year span. Through speaking and publishing he reached an increasingly wide audience and influenced multiple sectors of society.

Rauschenbusch's stature in the religious life of the nation during this decade was indeed impressive. In 1937, two decades after Rauschenbusch's death, Henry Pitney Van Dusen, professor and later president of Union Theological Seminary, offered high praise for Rauschenbusch. He wrote, "It is clear, it seems to me, that

---

[1] Dahlberg, *Walter Rauschenbusch*, 2.

the greatest single personal influence in the life and thought of the American Church in the last fifty years, was exerted by Walter Rauschenbusch."[2] Historian Charles Hopkins wrote, "The classic statement of American social Christianity is that of Walter Rauschenbusch, whose works were undoubtedly the most significant religious publications in the United States if not in the English language in the first two decades of the new century."[3] These estimates of Rauschenbusch's impact were doubtless due to the impact of the social message of Christianity articulated by Rauschenbusch, which stimulated a new dimension for theological reflection and for activist ministry. He challenged the churches to examine their identity and reshape their practice accordingly.

American Protestantism in 1900

American society in the period 1890–1914 was characterized by its variety and complexity. America's many diverse populations—Native Americans, African Americans, Asians, Hispanics, and Europeans—carried their own religious identities, but American history of this era was still heavily shaped by European culture.[4] People came from many countries and brought their language, ethnicity, and religion with them: the United States was indeed a nation of immigrants. Rauschenbusch's German background placed him in an ethnic minority. His own commitment was deeply Christian; however, he recognized the growing problem of discontent with the church and rapid secularization in Europe. Religiously, European culture was overwhelmingly Christian with a small minority of Jews. However, large numbers of Europeans were only loosely committed to church life or were no longer engaged in regular religious observance. A small percentage were crusading atheists; many non-believers were baptized as infants but were now indifferent rather than overtly hostile to religion. American ministers and churches would have to confront a growing attitude that the church was irrelevant to American lives; still, Rauschenbusch's goal was to Christianize the nation.

The American religious scene was dominated by separate groups of affiliated

---

[2] Henry Pitney Van Dusen made this statement when he gave the Rauschenbusch Lectures at Colgate Theological Seminary in 1937. See box 106, Rauschenbusch Family Papers. His lecture was published in *Church and State in the Modern World* (New York: Harper and Brothers, 1937). Van Dusen's statement also appeared on the front of the printed invitation to the "Rauschenbusch Day" at the Colgate Rochester Divinity School, September 11, 1957, celebrating the fiftieth anniversary of the publication of Rauschenbusch's *Christianity and the Social Crisis.* See "Rauschenbusch Day" in the book of the Enoch Pond Lectures, 922.6, qR189M, ABHS.

[3] Hopkins, *The Rise of the Social Gospel in American Protestantism*, 216.

[4] For a helpful survey that includes the intersection of both ethnic and religious history of the U.S. during this era, see Marty, *The Irony of It All*, vol. 1, 93-149.

churches identified as denominations.[5] Local churches affiliated with a denomination shared common traditions so that it was easy when moving from one community to another to associate with like-minded believers. The Orthodox family of Christians was small. Likewise new religious movements flourished but attracted limited numbers of followers when compared with the dozen or so largest denominations. The Roman Catholic presence was large and growing. However, the religious landscape was largely Protestant, and Protestants exercised cultural leadership in the religious outlook of the nation.[6]

While Protestants shared Reformation patterns of thought, they were already fracturing into two opposing parties between traditional conservative and progressive new theology patterns. This division dominated the story of Protestantism in the twentieth-century United States. Martin Marty narrated the religious story of the 1893–1915 era as the pursuit and triumph of modernity in culture and religion. However, he also included counter-modernism, the conservative resistance to new thinking. Whereas the new theology adopted modern historical critical study of the Bible, conservative Protestants rejected it and claimed biblical inerrancy as the basis for their views. The new theology had also accommodated religious belief to science, specifically to the questions raised most recently by Darwin. The conservatives condemned evolutionary theory and its implications for understanding God, humanity, and the world. The Bible and science were two critical points of difference in the two diverging camps of American Protestantism and would remain so throughout the following century.

The two factions also viewed history very differently. The new theology adopted as a presupposition the belief that things in the present are best understood by studying their development in history. Liberal thinkers tended to be optimistic and to believe in the possibility of human progress. Relying on a literal reading of Genesis, the conservatives believed the history of the earth and humanity was brief. They gave more credence to divine causation in history than to the processes of human history. This difference also emerged in intense and unresolved debate over religious interpretation of the future, specifically how to understand the future triumph of Christ. Whereas the progressives tended to assume a bright future and envisioned redemption of society, the conservatives generally affirmed that the future was dark indeed. They constructed arguments around the notion of the millennium, insisting on the imminent end of history, which in turn served as motivation for evangelism and missions. Thus the debate over Christ's future reign became the center of a major theological battle of the

---

[5] See the classic analysis of the nature of denominations in the United States in Mead, *The Lively Experiment*.

[6] Asian immigrants were beginning to introduce additional religious practices, but their numbers and influence remained miniscule.

era.

In his role as a public Protestant spokesman, Rauschenbusch's commitment to the new theology clearly placed him in the liberal modernist camp. As a child, he held more conservative views; as he grew, he adopted new views and modified his earlier positions. Rauschenbusch inherited powerful traditions in American Protestantism, including conversionist Christianity, the long crusade for temperance, and the traditional Protestant opposition to Roman Catholicism. As leader of a new generation, Rauschenbusch also embraced newer Protestant trends. During his student years Rauschenbusch had championed the emerging new theology. He enthusiastically promoted a theology that valued each person as an individual and affirmed that the center of religion was relationships—with God and with others. This personalism was a popular way of presenting theology during Rauschenbusch's era. He strongly supported the foreign missionary enterprise, another important trend. Yet another movement was the new emphasis on working with people of other denominations in the pursuit of Christian unity, which developed into the ecumenical movement. In addition to these trends, he added his own passion for a social gospel in which the church worked to transform society. Rauschenbusch thus represented what would in the twentieth century be referred to as mainline Protestantism. The liberal wing of the great Protestant division exercised cultural power and influence into the 1960s when it began to lose ground to increasing secularization and conservative Christianity, and also to reformulate itself to support new forms of liberation Christianity.

Rauschenbusch and Older Traditions of American Protestantism

Rauschenbusch was not a reclusive professor who remained confined to his study and classroom; rather, he was a very public leader of Protestant Christians in the United States. In his brief survey of American Protestantism, Winthrop Hudson called the era of 1890–1914 "the halcyon years" of the movement.[7] John Higham added that Protestantism of this era provided the nation's leadership in politics, culture, business, and philanthropy. Higham contended that the nation's universities, museums, and architecture rivaled the best in Europe. The nation promoted programs of public health, public parks, and literacy. Protestant political influence was particularly evident under President Woodrow Wilson, and during this period church membership flourished.[8] In his analysis of this era, Robert Handy noted a strong impetus among Protestants to "Christianize and *civilize*" society. In effect, this meant widespread adoption of Protestant religious values and national aspirations toward freedom and liberty. The proposal to

[7] Hudson, *American Protestantism*, 124–27.
[8] Higham, "Ethnicity and American Protestants," 253.

Christianize was urgent in Rauschenbusch's thought.[9] In the decade prior to World War I, Rauschenbusch interacted with many trends, sometimes supporting, sometimes opposing, and sometimes innovating on the vast Protestant landscape. Rauschenbusch inherited several older perspectives from American Protestantism, including personal conversion, the Prohibition Movement, and anti-Catholicism.

Revivalism/Conversionism

Revivalism has been a vital feature of American Protestantism since the eighteenth century. The revivals of that century, collectively called the Great Awakening, spread to all of the American colonies, thanks in part to the great English itinerant George Whitefield, but also through the efforts of many other preachers and evangelists. Jonathan Edwards, theologian of the revival, reflected deeply on the nature of the will and its transformation, concluding that religion was a matter of religious affections. Individuals were changed by their experience of God. Considered the work of God's spirit, Edwards believed that revivals could not be humanly planned or summoned at will. Revivals were characterized by an extraordinary number of conversions. Moreover, they passed as mysteriously as they appeared, prompting the notion of "seasons of revival."[10] Although sharply criticized by Charles Chauncy in his *Seasonable Thoughts on Religion,* revivalism flourished again and again, notably on the American frontier during the nineteenth century, where it became the agent of thousands of conversions in what is termed the Second Great Awakening. The revival stimulated unprecedented growth for Methodists, Baptists, and Presbyterians on the frontier and in the South. Revivals succeeded not only in rural camp meetings but also in America's cities under the leadership of Charles G. Finney, the most notable pre-Civil War evangelist of the nineteenth century. Finney announced revival meetings, advertised, and preached for several weeks in one place, thus establishing the tradition of the professional revivalist. Revivalists increasingly relied on human powers of persuasion for success. Walter's father, August Rauschenbusch, was a Pietist Lutheran who was not content with baptism as the essential characteristic of a Christian, but also preached the necessity of conversion. When he moved to the United States, he adapted his Pietism to the revivalism practiced by many denominations. Walter grew up in this conversionist tradition.

During the second half of the nineteenth century the most influential American evangelist was Dwight L. Moody. He and singer Ira Sankey conducted successful revivals in Britain and returned to acclaim in the United States in 1875, where they spent subsequent years conducting revivals. Moody had no formal

[9] Handy, *A Christian America,* ix-x and 82-100.

[10] For a summary of characteristics of revival, consult McClymond, "Revival," 308–12.

theological training. His simple, direct message connected with audiences and elicited huge responses. Moody was the dominant evangelist during Rauschenbusch's life. As a young minister Rauschenbusch collected and saved several of Moody's sermons as models for his own preaching, but he realized that he did not possess the revivalist's gifts of pulpit persuasion. Nevertheless, he contributed to a German edition of Sankey's *Gospel Hymns*, and he valued the work of this revival team. Later in life he looked back with favor on the work Moody and Sankey had accomplished.

At the same time Rauschenbusch believed that many revivalists had cheapened the message of salvation. He scathingly wrote concerning revivals, "Some produce skin-deep changes. Things have simmered down to signing a card, shaking hands, or being introduced to the evangelist."[11] Walter often referred to the importance of his own conversion experience.[12] But whereas traditional evangelists had tended to reduce the whole gospel to personal conversion, Rauschenbusch viewed this as only a half-gospel. It was this revivalist reduction of Christianity to a single event that Rauschenbusch battled throughout his life. He affirmed this great American Protestant tradition and built on it. Yes, the individual must be redeemed. But now the church must realize that the society was also in need of redemption.

The Prohibition Movement

Protestants campaigned against alcohol consumption throughout the nineteenth century. Many counties and eventually state after state passed laws regulating the sale of beverage alcohol. Only after Rauschenbusch's death did this movement lead to a Constitutional amendment prohibiting alcoholic beverage use, ratified in 1919 and put into effect at the national level in 1920. Several Protestant churches supported this movement, notably the Methodists, Presbyterians, and Baptists. Because of different cultural heritages, Episcopalians, Lutherans, and Roman Catholics were less enthusiastic about supporting Prohibition.

Rauschenbusch identified alcoholism as a curse on society. He wrote an article summarizing this issue for a conference paper he presented in Berlin in 1910.[13] In the article he argued that the United States had advanced farther and faster than other nations. He attributed this fact chiefly to "the type of religion

---

[11] WR, *A Theology for the Social Gospel*, 97, 1997 ed.

[12] "Letter to Dr. Lemuel Call Barnes, Field Secretary, American Baptist Home Mission Society, May 10, 1918," 38–40, provided Rauschenbusch's clearest affirmation of the importance of his own personal conversion.

[13] WR, "The Movement against Alcoholism in America," 588–99. A pamphlet version is also found in box 19, Rauschenbusch Family Papers.

and to the efficiency of the churches of America."[14] Rauschenbusch counted the advancement of the Prohibition cause as "one of the most important chapters in the Church History of America."[15] He briefly traced the history of the movement, indicating that cider and wine were commonly consumed during the colonial period, and there was little sentiment against their use. He marked a major change with the Revolutionary War era when importation of wine was reduced and Americans turned to distilled liquors—rum and whiskey. These were the popular forms of alcohol that accompanied frontiersmen on their westward movement. Thus about 1800 churches turned their attention to the problem. By the 1830s Americans had organized thousands of local temperance societies, and by the 1840s public drunkenness was stigmatized and churches began to teach total abstinence even though the term "temperance" was still commonly employed. The Civil War interrupted this reform movement.

Following the Civil War, the churches revived the campaign, now under the leadership of women. Rauschenbusch saw the women's leadership as critical for the success of the temperance campaign. The Woman's Christian Temperance Union (organized in 1874) secured membership of hundreds of thousands. Rauschenbusch noted, "The economic interests of the saloon and the movement were directly antagonistic. The misery created by alcohol has to be borne by the women, and they know it and hate it."[16] Rauschenbusch explained to his European audience the legal arrangement of local options whereby counties and states controlled consumption of alcohol by adopting prohibition or repealing it by popular vote. He explained that currently only about half of the population lived in "dry" areas that voted against the sale of beverage alcohol. But demand for and consumption of alcohol persisted, especially in the cities. When local governments permitted saloons to operate, the alcohol licenses provided significant revenue to their budgets. Economics played an important role in the debate over beverage alcohol.

Rauschenbusch was concerned with this issue throughout his life. His father had a drinking problem, and Walter also had observed the effect of saloons during his ministry in New York City. He said that alcoholism was "one of the most important questions of popular welfare" in the nation.[17] He agreed with three-time presidential candidate William Jennings Bryan that alcohol was a powerful factor in the corruption of politics.[18] Furthermore, he saw the economic power of greed at work in alcohol sales. In 1910 Rauschenbusch was convinced that the

---

[14] Ibid., 588.

[15] Ibid.

[16] Ibid., 591.

[17] Ibid., 596.

[18] Ibid.

fight against alcoholism was being won, but he was aware of many difficulties in the campaign. This issue was important in his life because he viewed it as part of the ethical responsibility of Christianity "to destroy both the effects and the cause of sin, and to transform the life of humanity into the Kingdom of God."[19]

Rauschenbusch's Anti-Catholicism

In 1900 Protestants still differed sharply with Roman Catholics. The Roman Catholic denomination grew rapidly in the United States, and by the mid-nineteenth century it was the nation's largest denomination, a position it has never relinquished. Rauschenbusch's statistics showed that 36.7 percent of the total U.S. church membership in 1906 was Roman Catholic.[20] Only in unity did Protestants collectively outnumber Catholics. The Catholic Church therefore represented the largest religious obstacle to achieving the Protestant vision for the United States. A dominant denominational narrative for Rauschenbusch and other Protestant denominations of this era was rejection of Roman Catholic teaching and influence.

With a few notable personal exceptions—such as Johann Joseph Ignaz von Döllinger, who shared Rauschenbusch's confidence in the historical method and exposed false claims about the church and its past; John Ryan and other strong Catholic defenders of social Christianity; and his connection with Ed Hanna, a childhood friend who entered the priesthood—Rauschenbusch's view of Catholicism was generally strongly negative. His anti-Catholic sentiment was in keeping with the general tenor of Protestant attitudes at the turn of the twentieth century. The same sentiment was clearly expressed, for example, by Josiah Strong in *Our Country,* one of the most influential Protestant publications of Rauschenbusch's generation. Strong viewed Catholicism as a "peril" to society, because they teach that everyone must be subject to the Roman pontiff, they do not believe in separation of church and state, they demand censorship of the press, and they oppose the public school system.[21]

A variety of sources contributed to Rauschenbusch's negative attitude toward Roman Catholicism. As a child in Germany Rauschenbusch was exposed to the mutual animosity between Catholics and Lutherans. He said the children in the Protestant and Catholic schools tormented each other. He did not remember the name of the Catholic "war-hymn," but recalled that the Protestant ditty describing Catholics ended in "fried in butter, stirred in flour, led to the devil."[22] He said that as children they really felt the evil character of Catholics and the

[19] Ibid., 595.

[20] Rauschenbusch, *Christianizing the Social Order*, 25.

[21] Strong, *Our Country*, 59–88, here 61, 71, 74.

[22] Minus, *Walter Rauschenbusch*, 9.

righteousness of the Protestants. Throughout his writing Rauschenbusch castigated the medieval Catholic Church for several reasons. The Church claimed to be the only path to salvation, teaching that the sacraments (the means of grace) were necessary for salvation, and only the Church could dispense them. Because of its claim to control their salvation, the church thereby exercised unwarranted influence over individuals.[23] The Church harshly punished heretics, and by its "terrible display of powers" the Church severely limited freedoms.[24] He criticized its monasticism and ascetic practice. Later the Church controlled thought by placing books on the *Index of Prohibited Books*. In his last major writing Rauschenbusch did not temper his view; quite the reverse, he declared: "The medieval papacy was a great international power, rich, haughty, luxurious, domineering, commanding the police power of the state for its coercive purpose."[25] Rauschenbusch argued that the church claimed too much for itself—substituting the Church for Jesus' message of the kingdom of God. He noted that Luther wrote against the "masses, processions, crosses, holy water and relics of the church."[26] Rauschenbusch interpreted this as a critique of "outward performance," and he joined the general Protestant criticism of "ceremonialism" in the Roman Catholic Church.[27] He found parallels in Jesus' criticism of established religion of his day, with its focus on laws and ceremonies. Both represented external forms of religion.

When Rauschenbusch considered the Roman Catholic Church in the United States, he found hierarchical patterns developed centuries before still in place, despite the advance of democracy. The Roman Catholic structure remained monarchial, while Rauschenbusch insisted that American political life was based on democracy, as was the spirit of American Protestantism. The church was still focused on sacraments, ceremonies, and rituals rather than personal relationships. Services were conducted in Latin, unintelligible to most worshipers.[28] Rauschenbusch judged Catholicism "a foreign body [lodged] in the midst of our mutual life" of the nation.[29] He thought it un-American, chiefly because it was anti-democratic, and he cited numerous expressions of denial of liberties by the Catholic Church. In the political life of the U.S. Rauschenbusch reported that Cardinal Gibbons, the leader of American Catholicism, condemned proposed moves toward political democracy such as initiative, referendum, judicial recall, and direct

---

[23] WR, *Righteousness of the Kingdom*, 164.
[24] WR, *Christianizing the Social Order*, 25.
[25] WR, *A Theology for the Social Gospel*, 89, 1997 ed.
[26] WR, *Righteousness of the Kingdom*, 270.
[27] Ibid., 271.
[28] WR, *Christianizing the Social Order*, 34.
[29] Evans, *The Kingdom Is Always but Coming*, 155.

election of U.S. senators.[30] These were precisely the political changes Rauschenbusch supported to move the nation towards democracy. Because of abuse of power in the past, Rauschenbusch declared that "the best service that can be rendered to a church is to keep it out of power."[31] Here he expresses his Baptist heritage of separation of church and state. Because he was a great proponent of the public schools, Rauschenbusch criticized Catholic-sponsored parochial schools as an effort to promote Catholicism, and argued that their education policies undermined "the common spirit of the nation."[32]

Rauschenbusch did applaud Catholic Christian social practice. He praised some priests as admirable examples of true Christianity—living with the poor and giving themselves in service. These, he declared, were "splendid incarnations of personal democracy."[33] And he also singled out for praise the Roman Catholic professor and social gospeller John A. Ryan for advocating social reform of many injustices.[34]

Rauschenbusch was a strong advocate of a Protestant America, and his attitude was almost entirely negative when he turned to modern Roman Catholic doctrine. In his *Theology* Rauschenbusch insisted that where "doctrine becomes rigid and is the pre-eminent thing in religion, 'faith' means submission of the mind to the teaching and guidance of the Church."[35] In short, the Roman Catholic Church limited liberties related to marriage, schooling, voting, and so forth, and for Rauschenbusch the American experience was all about affirming and increasing freedom and democracy. The influences of revivalism, temperance and anti-Catholicism were vital current Protestant traditions rooted in the nineteenth century. Protestants were also exploring new trends.

Rauschenbusch and Newer Traditions in American Protestantism

Foreign Missions

One of the dominant themes of Christianity during the late nineteenth century was the surge of foreign missions from Christian centers in the West into vast areas throughout the world. Protestant missions abroad began in the eight-

---

[30] WR, *Christianizing the Social Order*, 26. All of these legal practices give more power to ordinary citizens to challenge the power of the incumbent office holders.

[31] WR, *Righteousness of the Kingdom*, 163.

[32] WR, *Christianizing the Social Order*, 442.

[33] Ibid., 26.

[34] Ibid., 27. Ryan's list is very close to Rauschenbusch's and other social reformers: he advocated minimum wage, eight-hour work-day, relief for the unemployed, and so forth.

[35] WR, *A Theology for the Social Gospel*, 101, 1997 ed. He would apply this critique to doctrinaire Protestants as well.

eenth century but reached a new level of interest and activity during the late nineteenth and early twentieth centuries.[36] For many, it had become the darling of the Protestant enterprise. Rauschenbusch, along with many others, was enthusiastic for missions and remained devoted to the movement throughout his life. Kenneth Scott Latourette, Yale church historian who chronicled the expansion of Christianity throughout history, called the nineteenth century "The Great Century" of Christian missions. His phrase "never before" emphasized the magnitude of the new missionary effort and its success. In 1886 college students gathered at Moody's Northfield summer conference, and one hundred committed themselves to the foreign mission enterprise. This was the beginning of the Student Volunteer Movement (SVM) for foreign missions, the spearhead of the movement. Under the leadership of Methodist layman John R. Mott and Presbyterian Robert E. Speer, they adopted the motto, "the evangelization of the world in this generation," resolving to take the Christian message throughout the world. Before World War I they had recruited some 20,000 university students to fulfill this task.

The Christian mission was part of the expansion of Western influence throughout the world during the nineteenth and twentieth centuries. Later criticized for often confusing or combining the spread of Western civilization with the spread of Christianity and for its triumphal spirit of conquest and superiority, foreign missions was one of the most significant energizing and uniting forces among Protestants during this era. Impelled by the biblical injunction to go into the world and make disciples, and motivated by their own conversion experiences, missionaries went by the thousands to convert new followers around the globe. The height of this phase of the missionary impulse reached its peak during Rauschenbusch's adult life.

Rauschenbusch's own Baptist denomination was intensely enthusiastic about promoting missions. A number of young seminarians chose this path of service, including those at Rochester Baptist Theological Seminary where President A. H. Strong sustained a life-long interest in supporting the project. More than one hundred of his students became foreign missionaries. From 1892–1895 Strong served as president of the American Baptist Missionary Union and was often called on for missionary sermons and addresses. He and his wife toured the mission field in 1916–1917, an experience that provided the basis for his book *A Tour of the Missions: Observations and Conclusions.*[37]

As a young pastor, Rauschenbusch collected articles and sermons by and

---

[36] Mission leaders during Rauschenbusch's era included John R. Mott, Robert E. Speer, and Rufus Anderson. Foreign missions flourished during this era of American expansion and imperialism. See Hutchison, *Errand to the World*, 91–124.

[37] See "A. H. Strong," 142–43. Also see Strong, *A Tour of the Missions.*

about Hudson Taylor, the well-known founder of the China Inland Mission.[38] While he was a pastor Rauschenbusch addressed in print many issues that especially interested him, and the foreign missionary enterprise was prominent among them. He regularly preached on the topic. He had considered missions as a profession, and his sister, Emma, engaged in foreign mission work in India. Following significant academic achievement of her own, Emma married the director of the Telegu Mission in India, John Everett Clough, in 1894.[39] Rauschenbusch's contribution to missions was reflective and motivational. In 1892 Rauschenbusch gave two lectures on missionary theory at a Missionary Conference in Springfield, Massachusetts. The thesis of his first lecture, "Conceptions of Missions," was that "there is a need for emphasizing the evangelical conception of missions."[40] He also affirmed the value of secondary conceptions of missions, especially education. He insisted that while philanthropic work was also accomplishing much good, interest in helping people in physical difficulty must not displace the hope of seeing individuals converted. Rauschenbusch rhetorically asked, "What do I mean by that [evangelical Christianity]?"[41] His answer was that it was not any specific type of doctrine, but "the extension of faith in the crucified and risen Christ who imparts his spirit to those who believe...and transforms them.... That is the primary aim of Christian missions."[42]

In the companion lecture, "Conceptions of Missions II," Rauschenbusch reaffirmed his central theme.[43] Then he explained how the ideas of evolution and progress had created an unwarranted optimism among some religious thinkers. Evolution might work in nature, he wrote, but "a new element enters in when it reaches the ethical nature of man."[44] In this article he affirmed that the ethical direction of humanity was downward. Thus a new force was needed, and it entered human history "by the coming of the spirit of the risen Christ, transforming individuals, fusing them into a new society."[45] Therefore the first requirement of

---

[38] WR, 1886–1890 scrapbook, Rauschenbusch Family Papers.

[39] Emma Rauschenbusch-Clough wrote *A Study of Mary Wollstonecraft and the Rights of Woman* (London: Longmans, Green & Company, 1898); a publication announcement is found on p. 28 of the 1899–1901 scrapbook, Rauschenbusch Family Papers. Reviewers noted that it was an entirely admirable work, exceedingly well-written, and an important contribution to the history of the modern advancement of women. Her husband, J. E. Clough, made Telegu Mission famous by bringing thousands of outcasts into the churches in the Telegu area.

[40] WR, "Conceptions of Missions I," 1; also p. 144 of the 1892 scrapbook, Rauschenbusch Family Papers.

[41] Ibid.

[42] Ibid.

[43] WR, "Conceptions of Missions II," 1; also pp. 144–45 of the 1892 scrapbook, Rauschenbusch Family Papers.

[44] Ibid.

[45] Ibid.

missions was spiritual, namely, to preach "faith in the power of the risen Christ."[46] Rauschenbusch declared, "Nothing exceeds the value of regeneration of the individual soul."[47] These two articles represented Rauschenbusch's analysis of the Christian foreign mission enterprise, marked with clarity of analysis and presentation. The religious press reported favorably:

> The missionary conference hosted speakers and subjects including Professor Walter Rauschenbusch's paper "The Evangelical as Distinguished from Secondary Conceptions of Missions" which was regarded as one of the most luminous essays of the occasion and a rich treat to hear.[48]

The resounding message of these lectures was the young pastor's passionate assertion that the primary goal of missions is the conversion of individuals. Everything else is secondary. When it came to foreign missions, Rauschenbusch sounded the note of individual conversion loud and clear.

Amity Church, located near Rauschenbusch's Second German Baptist Church, hosted an annual missions emphasis meeting, and Rauschenbusch regularly participated in this event, organized for the community of churches by its pastor and Rauschenbusch's close friend, Leighton Williams.[49] The year after his Conceptions of Missions articles, Rauschenbusch spoke at the Conference on Missions held at the Amity Church. The reporter wrote, "Rev. Walter Rauschenbusch, of New York, gave a clear, vigorous address on 'Discipling vs. Proselytizing,' which was spoken of as the 'gem' of the meeting."[50] Rauschenbusch was already building a reputation for excellence in communication very early in his career. Reporters repeatedly singled out his presentations for praise. Two years later in a sermon on "Foreign Missions," Rauschenbusch declared to his congregation that missions was one of the great causes of the day. He reported to his audience that he had almost enlisted as a missionary.[51] In this sermon he declared that the goals of missions were biblical, and they included salvation of souls, education of children, penetrating our national life with the spirit of Christ, and

---

[46] Ibid.

[47] Ibid.

[48] *The Inquirer*, November 27, 1892; also on p. 113 of the 1892 scrapbook, Rauschenbusch Family Papers; another report of this conference appeared in *The National Bulletin* (Philadelphia), November 24, 1892.

[49] See Third Annual Conference on Missions held at the Amity Baptist Church, April 3 and 4, 1893; Rauschenbusch's topic was "Discipling vs. Proselyting" (box 139, Rauschenbusch Family Papers).

[50] Newspaper report of the Conference on Missions, n.p., 1893 scrapbook, Rauschenbusch Family Papers. The name or date of the newspaper is not attached. A copy of the printed program of this conference is available in box 139, Rauschenbusch Family Papers.

[51] WR, "Foreign Missions" (Isa 52:10), February 3, 1895, vol. 29:23–33, box 151, Rauschenbusch Family Papers.

extension of Christianity to heathen realms. He concluded that missions "is God's will for this era."[52] In this sermon he emphasized both personal conversion and the transformation of society. The young minister could hardly have been more enthusiastic for the missionary enterprise. He believed that through the agency of missions the gospel would be planted throughout the world, thus extending the kingdom of God as never before. Rauschenbusch noted how the world had changed, creating conditions favorable for missions. In the past missionaries had been kept out of several large countries, but these were now open. Whereas Catholics had engaged seriously in foreign missions since the sixteenth century, Protestants had seriously joined the movement only in the nineteenth century. Languages had been harder to master in the past; many of them had not had written form. But, Rauschenbusch reported that people now heard God's word in 250 languages, that missionaries were planting schools, that most denominations now supported missions, and that people were offering financial support for the enterprise. The mood of optimism was palpable from missionary leaders of the era, and Rauschenbusch clearly shared the general Protestant enthusiasm for foreign missions. It was a major Protestant venture. However, missionary leaders such as Mott feared that the window of opportunity was limited, and Rauschenbusch echoed that sentiment: the church must act now. As a spokesman for current American Protestant trends, Rauschenbusch was a passionate supporter of foreign missions.[53]

Cooperation with Other Traditions

The World Parliament of Religions was an exposition held in Chicago in 1893 whose purpose was to provide a platform for spokespersons representing the world's major religions. Although some publications had appeared on the subject in the post-Civil War era, this was the most notable event of the nineteenth century for calling attention to the presence of non-Christian religions in the United States. Rauschenbusch was a pastor in New York at the time of the 1893 meeting and did not attend. But his participation in the National Morals Mission meeting in 1900 is evidence of his eagerness to work with other faith traditions. Appropriate to the diversity of this meeting, he addressed aspects of religion common to all, in this case the question of worship. The meeting in New York City included speakers from Hinduism, Judaism, and Christianity, and featured papers on the possibility of common worship as an expression of common life.[54] Because of Rauschenbusch's passion for the welfare of all humanity, the *Universalist Leader* later praised Rauschenbusch in a glowing obituary. Why, it asked, should

---

[52] Ibid., 23.
[53] WR, "Foreign Missions," 32.
[54] "State Conference of Religion to be Held Next Week."

a Universalist eulogize a Baptist? The answer was:

> he was a world citizen. His was a vision of that unity of the human race in which justice and love were to prevail in all relations, from individual to international.... It is true that he was a member and a minister of the Baptist Church, and loved and honored that fellowship, but even more was he in fellowship with the whole household of God.... [He] went beyond the bounds of mere tolerance. He sensed the significance of others' yearning to reach God.[55]

Rauschenbusch was not restricted by religious boundaries; this was a clear expression of his affirmation: "Nothing that is human is alien to me."[56] He welcomed opportunities to work with leaders of non-Christian religions, but they represented a tiny percentage of the U.S. population. Rauschenbusch had much more to say about Christian unity and other denominations.

Rauschenbusch worked with leaders of many denominations. He was an advocate of religious cooperation, and he was read and appreciated by members of many denominations. In 1900 he participated in the New York State Conference of Religion. This meeting was held at the United Charities Building and attracted participants from a variety of denominations, including The Church of the Holy Communion (Episcopal), All Souls (Unitarian), and Brick (Presbyterian). On this occasion Rauschenbusch addressed the conference on "Religion, the Life of God in the Soul of Man."[57] He was actively engaging in interdenominational activity before the modern ecumenical movement was launched.

Of the three great Christian traditions—Orthodox, Roman Catholic, and Protestant—the Protestants were the Christians who had fragmented into numerous denominations during the Protestant Reformation. Protestants recognized the need to come together to speak with a common voice. The American Protestant clergy took on the problem of bringing churches together and devoted much effort to the vision of Christian unity. Recognizing the vast task of changing an entire society, Rauschenbusch joined the call to the churches to work together. He did not, however, seem to spend much effort on the actual tasks of institutional unification. Those, in fact, would flower later. Rochester professor Henry Robins judged, "I am under the impression that he cared little for organic union but much for the spirit of mutuality, which he everywhere attempted to arouse and conserve."[58]

---

[55] "The Passing of a Great Leader," 2.

[56] WR, *Christianizing the Social Order*, 94.

[57] *New York Times*, October 22, 1900.

[58] Henry B. Robins to Mrs. [Winifred] Rorty, September 16, 1929, box 39, Rauschenbusch Family Papers.

Rauschenbusch addressed the issue of Christian unity in an extended annotated outline and also in a formal commencement address.[59] He thought the financial and doctrinal competition sustained by denominations was wasteful. Moreover, it created an attitude of Christians looking down on other Christians.[60] The move toward unity had already made tentative steps during the nineteenth century, but it made huge steps forward through the foreign mission field effort and the organization of the Federal Council of Churches in 1908. Rauschenbusch surveyed denominational unions currently under consideration. He thought it was "a very remarkable tribute to the Christian and practical spirit that actual efforts toward church union are everywhere being made."[61] He cited examples of discussions in Canada and in the United States where dialogue was under way among the Baptist, Methodist, and Presbyterian families. Also discussions were proceeding between Baptists and Disciples and between Congregationalists and other denominations.

The event that triggered his interest most was the Episcopalian House of Bishops' invitation in 1886 for others to join them. However, their criteria for reunion, formally adopted in 1888 as the Lambeth Quadrilateral, included (1) the authority of the Bible, (2) the Nicene Creed, (3) the practice of baptism and the Lord's Supper and (4) the historic episcopate. Rauschenbusch sternly opposed the fourth point because the Episcopal Church did not recognize the validity of the ordination of other ministers. He insisted that unity must be based on equality and acceptance of others. He rejected the Episcopalian proposal, but he rightly predicted that "the next twenty years are certain to bring striking developments."[62] For the present he envisioned cooperation along the lines of the Federal Council of Churches.

Another approach to positioning Rauschenbusch as Protestant spokesman is found in his relationship with other denominations outside the purview of Christian unity. He had little patience for New Religious Movements such as Mormonism, Spiritualism, or Christian Science. He occasionally attacked aspects of these groups. For example, he believed the Mormons, like the Roman Catholics, were "a dangerous power within the state . . . [because of their] large vested wealth and semipolitical power."[63] Sometimes he dismissed them: "they are of

---

[59] WR, "Course of Christian Unity," undated typescript, box 7, Rauschenbusch Family Papers; WR, "Commencement," typescript, May 1917, 33 pages, box 22, Rauschenbusch Family Papers.

[60] Rauschenbusch saw this attitude as a "manifestation of original sin [and] a serious spiritual loss" (WR, "Commencement," 7–8).

[61] WR, "Course on Christian Unity." Manuscript partially typed and partially in long hand, box 7, Rauschenbusch Family Papers.

[62] Ibid.

[63] WR, *Christianizing the Social Order*, 273.

interest only to the statistician and the church historian, but practically negligible in summing up the real religious forces of the nation."[64] But he also provided his reasons for rejecting them. In his view Mormonism was syncretistic, blending traditional religious ideas with superstitions and relying on an additional "divinely given book."[65] Similarly, Christian Science relies on another book "by which the essentially Christian tradition is interpreted, modified, and overpowered."[66] Regarding efforts toward unity, he concluded, "I am hopeless about the Roman Catholic Church, Mormonism, and Christian Science. I simply leave them out."[67]

Rauschenbusch was sympathetic with the emerging holiness movement. He expressed deep appreciation for *The Tongue of Fire* (1856) by William Arthur, an Irish Methodist minister. This book emphasized Wesley's teaching on sanctification or holy living. Rauschenbusch supported the holiness movement's emphasis on devotion to a holy life, but he was less enthusiastic about emerging Pentecostalism. In his 1917 *Theology* he addressed the doctrine of the Holy Spirit in less than two pages.[68] Whereas Pentecostals saw the gifts of the Spirit as a second level of blessing after conversion, the point Rauschenbusch made is that the "tongue of fire" had become the common property of the entire assembly at Pentecost. In that event the Spirit of God was poured out like "tongues of fire" on each person.[69] Rauschenbusch's attitude toward Pentecostal expressions is mixed. Interpreting Paul, on the one hand he saw speaking in tongues as "a communion with God...a gift of the Holy Spirit."[70] It was "proof of the power with which the spiritual life had taken hold of these new converts."[71] On the other hand he noted that Paul "does not encourage public exercise of it.... It shows these people were conscious of direct contact with God.... But it is evident, too, that the church at this point was dangerously near the verge of mental aberration."[72]

Rauschenbusch identified six major denominations that, in his view, constituted the "true American Church": Baptists, Presbyterians, Reformed, Disciples, Methodists, and Congregationalists.[73] He differentiated these from Lutherans, who relied too heavily on confessions of faith, and Episcopalians, who relied too

---

[64] WR, *The American Church*, 4.
[65] WR, "Commencement," 25.
[66] Ibid., 26.
[67] Ibid., 27.
[68] WR, *A Theology for the Social Gospel*, 1997 ed., 188–89.
[69] Ibid., 189.
[70] WR, "Speaking in Tongues—What Was It?" 1251. A copy of the article is in box 94, Rauschenbusch Family Papers.
[71] Ibid., 1252.
[72] Ibid.
[73] WR, "The American Church," *The Congregationalist* (October 23, 1913): 562.

heavily on their polity.[74] The select six were unified by their common emphasis on increasingly democratic polities, similarities in worship, evangelistic appeal, religious experience, methods of teaching the young, internal organizations in the local church, and social meetings for cultivating the spiritual life.[75] Rauschenbusch concluded: "The great family of Christian people which I have outlined constitutes the true American church if there is any."[76] Rauschenbusch's expansive inclusiveness is more evident when he speaks of individuals rather than denominations: he pronounced, "I am a Baptist, but I am more than a Baptist. All things are mine whether Francis of Assisi, or Luther, or Knox, or Wesley; all are mine because I am Christ's."[77]

The movement for unity continued to gather strength in the early twentieth century. In May 1917 Rauschenbusch gave the commencement address at Rochester Theological Seminary and chose the topic of unity.[78] He told the graduates that "creating unity out of division was one of the greatest problems of religious leadership, and was surely to confront the men of the graduating class throughout their ministry."[79] Despite many obstacles, unity was an important goal for the church:

> Every denomination has stood on guard over some fragment of tradition, often so petty that to outsiders it looks silly and pathetic. And meanwhile the modern world is losing its religious conscience. It has no clear sense of God or a divine law anymore. In thousands of Christian homes the candle of family worship has gone out, and the children never hear the voice of father or mother uplifted in prayer.... In the industrial centers the working people have dropped out of connection with the Protestant churches.[80]

Rauschenbusch insisted that the challenge of the churches should not be denominational competitions but rather the challenges presented by the growing secularization of society. He was deeply devoted to the Baptist denomination, but he also recognized the importance of the churches working toward religious unity.

Growing Protestant Division

Theologically, Rauschenbusch was progressive. Protestantism was a large and diverse movement in the United States. Despite adoption of newer trends by

---

[74] Ibid.
[75] Ibid., 5–6.
[76] Ibid., 8.
[77] WR, "Why I Am a Baptist: My Fourth Reason," 159.
[78] WR, "Commencement."
[79] Ibid., 2.
[80] Ibid., 32.

some Protestants, emerging mainline Protestantism experienced strong opposition by conservatives. Rauschenbusch was by disposition an irenic person. He much preferred to avoid conflict. He was also a man of convictions, and he was outspoken. As a student at Rochester Theological Seminary, Rauschenbusch openly disagreed with his professor, A. H. Strong, on the doctrine of the atonement. Rauschenbusch's father feared that Walter might not pass his ordination because of his strongly held views on the Bible. He was denied a missionary appointment because of his liberal religious views on Old Testament interpretation. Although he preferred to address issues rather than individuals, he could not avoid criticism by conservative Protestants who sharply disagreed with him. This was a source of personal pain for him. Controversy plagued him to the extent that in his brief personal theological statement he included his desire to show God's love to all.[81]

Conservative critics took exception to Rauschenbusch's adoption of the new theology, with its acceptance of modern methods of biblical interpretation, the theory of evolution and modern views of atonement. Rauschenbusch defended aspects of his new theology views at various times throughout his career. As he developed his social gospel conviction, he spent much of his intellectual energy defending his view that original Christianity included both individual and social redemption. Here again, he met opposition from traditionalists who argued that salvation was an individual matter; only through conversion of individuals would society be transformed. Other critics regularly charged Rauschenbusch with substituting socialism for Christianity. The debates grew into a full-fledged theological struggle between liberalism and fundamentalism and produced institutional battles during the 1920s within the Northern Presbyterian and Baptist denominations.

A variety of debates contributed to growing division among Protestants long before the emergence of actual struggles to control denominations. One of the most significant points of debate for Rauschenbusch centered on the understanding of the millennium, the one-thousand-year reign of Christ described in Revelation 20:1-10. Conservative millennialists generally gravitated to the interpretation that the condition of the world was getting worse. Christ would have to intervene and judge the world before his one-thousand-year reign; hence, this position is called pre-millennial. This view received support in the nineteenth century writings of John Nelson Darby who interpreted Christian history in terms of dispensations or eras. Cyrus I. Scofield incorporated this idea into his comments published in the Scofield Reference Bible (1909), and both men affirmed their belief in the imminent return of Christ. On the other hand, interpreters devoted to reform and to progress in society believed that the world was growing

[81] WR, "An Affirmation of Faith," typescript, n.d., 1, #1022, NABHC archives.

better rather than worse, and they believed in Christ coming to reign at the end of a long era of progress; this optimistic position referred to as post-millennialism, was adopted by social gospel leaders.[82] Still other interpreters—amillennialists—rejected both of these views, holding that this passage is not to be understood as predictive of centuries in the future, but was meant for the generation of the original audience—first-century readers of the book of Revelation. Rauschenbusch did not enter this elaborate debate without cause. He rejected the growing premillennial view because it negated his belief in the possibility of redemption of American society. He took up this contested issue numerous times during his career, notably as a pastor in 1896 and again as a professor when he summarized his position again in a chapter of his *Theology*.[83]

Rauschenbusch's approach affirmed that religion needs an eschatology since religion by its very nature looks to the future destiny of the individual and of the human race. He challenged the conservatives who were obsessed with eschatology and the liberals who marginalized it. He complained that pre-millennialists seemed best pleased when humanity was defeated.[84] He countered with his strong belief that science and the social gospel could affect the future for good.[85] Rauschenbusch reminded readers of the Old Testament promise of the Day of Yahweh, a day of judgment that anticipates a future when oppression is overthrown.[86]

The millennial debate was further grounded in opposing understandings of the nature and the interpretation of Scripture. Conservatives adopted the view that God was the author of the Bible. Therefore they could draw from any part of it to erect an elaborate scheme of the end of the world, including a rapture, multiple judgments, and so forth. Liberals who adopted the historical method insisted that Scripture was shaped by human authors, and the context of a passage must always be taken into account in making an interpretation. Thus views of the origin and nature of Scripture were critical in shaping two different Protestantisms emerging during Rauschenbusch's era. Rauschenbusch personally struggled with what the evidence of Scripture actually revealed. He distinguished between biblical eschatology, which he accepted, and apocalyptic, which he associated with premillennial dispensation. He wrote that adherents of apocalyptic had created little diagrams which map the history of the human race, and these are deterministic. Moreover, they rely on catastrophe to resolve problems, and they distort the meaning of Scripture by relying on a theory of verbal inerrancy and opposing historical methods of interpretation. They select texts from various

[82] Stein, "Millennialism," 220.
[83] WR, "Our Attitude Toward Milleniarism" and *A Theology for the Social Gospel.*
[84] WR, *A Theology for the Social Gospel*, 1997 ed., 211.
[85] Ibid.
[86] Ibid., 212.

places and piece them together like a mosaic.[87]

For Rauschenbusch, patching together a picture of the end of the world in this manner was a gross distortion and misuse of Scripture.[88] He pointed out that a careful look at Scripture actually revealed a variety of views about the future—envisioning in some places a new heaven and a new earth, in others the end of the world and death. Rauschenbusch claimed that we should honestly recognize this variety and not "mangle" the text.[89] For reasons of sustaining legitimate biblical exegesis, retaining the integrity of the historical method and his own theological interests, Rauschenbusch vigorously rejected apocalyptic premillennial views.

Following Bushnell, Rauschenbusch advocated shifting from Protestantism's model of placing total emphasis on one personal emotional crisis in understanding one's relationship with God to a model that emphasized lifetime Christian nurture.[90] Furthermore, Rauschenbusch's model of the kingdom is one of ongoing development of relationships with other people and with God. This, he believed, is what Jesus taught. But conservatives were not convinced. Rauschenbusch's views on eschatology, millennialism, and apocalypticism already put him at odds with traditional views. Within his own denomination, I. M. Haldeman, pastor of First Baptist Church, New York City, launched a sharply worded critique of Rauschenbusch, rejecting his conclusions.[91] Haldeman's response was not a welcome reception of a fellow Baptist, but rather a hostile and decisive rejection of Rauschenbusch's views, and many Protestants shared Haldeman's views. Rauschenbusch argued for historical context of Scripture, for a positive view of human freedom, and for a hopeful eschatology as a basis for the transformation of American society. It would be contradictory for him to work simultaneously for the transformation of society and at the same time affirm its imminent end.

Religion and Poverty

Christian churches have sought relief for the poor for centuries, but the new industrial system exposed poverty as never before. England and the United States shared common economic conditions and common social problems. The new industrial economy inspired humanitarian efforts on a scale not seen before. The nineteenth century saw efforts at prison reforms and care for the blind, the deaf, and people suffering mental disease. Some humanitarians promoted abolition of

[87] Ibid., 216.

[88] Ibid., 190–92.

[89] Ibid., 218.

[90] Ibid., 226. See Bushnell's classic treatment in *Christian Nurture.*

[91] Haldeman, *Professor Rauschenbusch's Christianity and the Social Crisis.* This is a printed 42-page pamphlet.

slavery and others reform of factory practices. A broad range of human suffering prompted response by humanitarian activists. Rauschenbusch had strong opinions on some of these social ills. He wrote that our prisons were "cut off from all that exercises a saving influence on their lives—the love of wife and child and home, work and play, contact with nature, hope, ambition, [and instead] only fear and coercion are in full force."[92] The purpose of incarceration should not be vindictive punishment, but remedial, aiming at the social restoration of the offender. He reminded Christians to remember "the divine worth of 'the least of these.'"[93]

Several reform movements were closely associated with the church or were led by people motivated by religious sentiment. Rauschenbusch was especially sympathetic with innovations that addressed needs of the poor. The settlement house movement provided refuge for the indigent. Its most famous site was Hull House in Chicago (founded in 1889), led by Jane Addams. The Y.M.C.A. (1844) organized in England by George Williams and soon established in the United States, along with the Y.W.C.A. (1866), addressed the needs of young people migrating to cities and looking for jobs. This organization became a major forum for Rauschenbusch's delivery of many public lectures. The Y.M.C.A. defined its purpose as providing a "home away from home" and improving the "spiritual and mental condition of young men."[94] This agenda matched Rauschenbusch's interests. Y.M.C.A. secretaries welcomed him and were instrumental in promoting his *The Social Principles of Jesus* for their study groups. Dores Sharpe recalled that Rauschenbusch also admired the work of the newly formed holiness Salvation Army in London (founded in 1865), and according to Sharpe he came close to joining them. Years later, however, Rauschenbusch judged that "When the Army moved from the barracks to the citadel they followed the churches and became high hat."[95] Sharpe says that Rauschenbusch even considered starting a similar movement but "felt he was not eloquent or dynamic enough to lead such a movement."[96] Rauschenbusch recognized the vision of ministry to the poor as close to his own understanding of Jesus' intent. These humanitarian relief organizations were designed to alleviate the suffering of various groups of people. They were established institutions, and they brought welcome reliable relief to people. Although limited in scope, their services were an improvement on random charity. However, in the end this approach was not enough for Rauschenbusch.

Rauschenbusch was interested in eliminating systemic causes of suffering he

---

[92] WR, *A Theology for the Social Gospel*, 1997 ed., 214.
[93] Ibid., 214–15.
[94] Hopkins, *History of the Y.M.C.A. in North America*, 17–18, 36.
[95] Sharpe, *Walter Rauschenbusch*, 427.
[96] Ibid.

identified in the economic structure. His position represented a more thoroughgoing reform. He used the comparison that as a physician might alleviate pain with repeated pain-killing medication, the better solution was to eliminate the cause of the pain. Likewise, Rauschenbusch wanted to eliminate the sources of injustice in the economic order that brought relentless suffering to the poor year after year. To this end Rauschenbusch devoted time and effort to informing the people of Rochester about current trends in American life. Rauschenbusch and Presbyterian minister Paul Moore Strayer along with the Rochester Labor Council organized a Public Sunday-Evening Movement. The organizers invited speakers, including Rauschenbusch, to speak on current social trends and problems, followed by question-and-answer sessions. They met for fifteen to twenty weeks during the winter. Strayer reported that the greatest interest was generated by a debate format in which speakers and audience discussed such themes as, "Who can do more for society, a religious or a materialistic socialist?"[97] Rauschenbusch led many of these Sunday evening services. He was modeling what religious leaders might do to shape opinion.

Rauschenbusch was well connected to Protestant social gospel leaders who had preceded him—such as Washington Gladden and Josiah Strong. He worked with contemporaries such as W. D. P. Bliss, and he encouraged emerging leaders of the coming generation such as Harry Emerson Fosdick. Emphasis on the social gospel was relatively new, and people were made aware of it by Gladden, Ely, and others, but especially through the work of Rauschenbusch. The social gospellers saw this as the new task of the church, and they were persuasive. The proposals he made in his books resonated in the churches and propelled him into a position of Protestant leadership. In Rauschenbusch's thought, missions, Christian unity, a theology adapted to the present, and a new social vision converged with earlier traditions to define the changing American Protestant identity of his era.

Religion and Society

European liberal theology of Rauschenbusch's era stressed the value of each individual soul as the most important of all values in human existence. Rauschenbusch also often wrote that nothing was more significant than the value of each person since everyone was made in the image of God. Harnack summarized Jesus' message in three statements: the kingdom of God and its coming, God the Father and the infinite value of the human soul, and the higher righteousness and the commandment of love.[98] Many thinkers constructed theologies that centered on the concept of the value of each individual. Personalism of several varieties

[97] Henry B. Robins to Mrs. [Winifred] Rorty, September 16, 1929, box 39, Rauschenbusch Family Papers.

[98] Harnack, *What Is Christianity?*, 19–77.

emerged in a new wave of theological reflection. Rauschenbusch, along with many progressive Protestants, invoked the image of God and stressed the notion of the infinite value of human soul as a central tenet of the Christian faith. He wrote, "Every new soul presents a new problem of redemption. The souls filled with the life of God are the fountain from which all life-giving impulses flow out into the life of society. But a human soul is of eternal value for its own sake."[99] This religious affirmation matched closely Americans' long held cultural value placed on individuals and their liberties.

The older Protestants had preached the value of the individual and the centrality of conversion, and the new liberalism stressed the infinite value of the individual. Both of these formulations could easily reduce understanding of religion to individual redemption. What Rauschenbusch added to the general liberal formulation was a new emphasis on redeeming society. A religion of relationships for him meant not only conversions but conscious solidarity with others and a total effort to redeem society and nation. Evil permeates society. The church cannot sit back and ignore how society has changed dramatically and now threatens the lives of many people. Unjust structures must be challenged. Humanity always exists in social relationships that are simply inescapable, and these structures affect individuals for better or worse. It is not possible to claim that individuals are unaffected by their social interests. By insisting that society is sinful and that the church must work to redeem it, Rauschenbusch's message represents a separate trajectory from the liberalism developed by European theologians. The American social gospel offered a new dimension of Christian reflection, and many in the American public recognized Rauschenbusch as its significant spokesman.

From the standpoint of the modern reader, Rauschenbusch's vision of social justice was severely flawed. He failed to address inequities with women and the violence perpetrated against other groups—especially African Americans. His failure to address racism and gender injustices is clear; his vision was limited. It would take another half century for the culture and the church to become sensitive to their failings on these major issues. It is indeed telling that critics of his own day did not fault him on his failure to address inequalities in these two areas. Rauschenbusch was a product of his time, and his focus was on the workers.

Reception of the Prophet for the Social Gospel

Each generation produces its spokesmen and women, whose influence generally rises for a time and then usually wanes, whereas the influence of a few has survived for generations. The most visible Protestants in Rauschenbusch's gener-

---

[99] WR, "Religion in the Life of God and the Soul of Man," pamphlet #10 in the *Brotherhood of the Kingdom* series, a bound volume in the ABHS.

ation included leading ministers, evangelists, historians, theologians, social critics, and missionaries. In Rauschenbusch's day the best-known ministers were Henry Ward Beecher in New York City and Phillip Brooks in Boston. The role of the press was important in creating spokespersons—whether through regular newspaper reporting of their work and associated controversies or through the influence of the author's own writing. Beecher, for example, became the most well-known minister in the country because his sermons were printed in syndication each week, but a charge of sexual misconduct brought a different kind of notoriety. Printed books carried much influence in religious circles—from translations of Harnack's many works to the publications of influential American writers such as theologian William Adams Brown. Many other individuals also served as Protestant spokesmen of the Rauschenbusch era. Well before Rauschenbusch's public recognition, Josiah Strong's *Our Country* (1885) set out a Protestant agenda that made him one of the most influential religious writers of his era. Following Rauschenbusch, Harry Emerson Fosdick, by virtue of his location at Riverside Church in New York City, his prolific accessible writings, and his controversies with fundamentalists, became the nation's best-known Protestant minister. During the era immediately before Rauschenbusch, Dwight L. Moody was certainly the nation's best-known evangelist. Spanning the eras of Moody, Rauschenbusch, and Fosdick, John R. Mott, leader of the modern foreign missionary movement, exercised vast influence among young Christians in a cause cherished by most Protestants of this era. Both Moody and Mott were wholeheartedly focused on a single dimension of the American Protestant experience—conversions at home and abroad. Rauschenbusch and Fosdick took a broader view of religion that included added responsibility for society.

Because of Rauschenbusch's vigorous critique of injustices in America, contemporary readers and journalists identified him as a prophet. He was recognized as the most eloquent, persuasive and influential exponent of social Christianity. His approach challenged the status quo in church and society. In his *Theology* Rauschenbusch wrote, "Genuine prophecy springs up where fervent religious experience combines with a democratic spirit, strong social feelings, and free utterances. Some sense of antagonism between the will of God and the present order of things is necessary to ignite the spirit of the prophet."[100] Rauschenbusch's analysis of the Old Testament prophet matches his own self-understanding. He set himself the task of reconciling "the present order of things with the will of God," and for this reason his readers often referred to him as "prophet." Rauschenbusch devoted himself to analyzing causes of injustices and speaking truth to power, applying the Christian gospel to society. After he published his proposal in *Christianity and the Social Crisis* (1907), people wanted to hear the famous man speak

[100] WR, *A Theology for the Social Gospel*, 1997 ed., 195.

and to read more from him. It was natural that he most often chose to address topics related to the theme of the social gospel. This was his passion, and this is what audiences came to hear. He was occupied for the remainder of his life with articulating this long-neglected dimension of Christianity—whether speaking at the local Rochester Lyceum, to students gathered at Y.M.C.A. centers across the Northern United States, or at national and international gatherings of Baptists.

As Rauschenbusch recalled toward the end of his life, his articulation of the social responsibility of the churches came at a "psychological moment" when the time was right—and before World War I undermined the country's underlying optimism. The success of the Progressive Party agenda and the election of 1912 suggested a strong sentiment for political reform at the national level. Roman Catholic and Jewish leaders articulated their versions of the social gospel. During this time, American religious leaders acknowledged the need to address social ills more systematically, and many looked to Rauschenbusch as their spokesman.

Rauschenbusch was regularly asked to speak to churches, associations, gatherings of the Y.M.C.A., and at other venues. In his annual summary of activities for 1911 he reported having delivered eighty-seven sermons and addresses plus organizing and speaking at several of the twenty meetings of the People's Sunday Evening in Rochester with an average attendance of over one thousand. He declined forty-seven invitations.[101] By 1913 he was receiving at least $75 for a lecture.[102] But by then he was declining most invitations, indicating in correspondence that he was keeping summers free and was committed to "literary work [because] I feel that I can do more good by writing for thousands than by speaking to hundreds."[103] A half year later he wrote, "I am keeping my winter free this year for special research work and declining practically everything."[104] As public spokesman for Protestantism he used both voice and increasingly, his pen.

Rauschenbusch was not only a writer; he was also a deeply involved activist and worked tirelessly for reform in Rochester, particularly in the city's public education.[105] He was a leader of the Rochester People's Sunday Evening and the Rochester Lyceum. Both of these gatherings were created to inform Rochester's citizens about current social trends in American society, but his influence also extended to the national level. Early in 1914 the *New York Times* published a major article on the formation of the Religious Citizenship League in New York

---

[101] WR to A. H. Strong, April 25, 1911, box 27, Rauschenbusch Family Papers. He missed no classes except for the week he presented the Merrick lectures at Ohio Wesleyan University.

[102] WR to R. A. Hoover, December 26, 1913, box 27, Rauschenbusch Family Papers.

[103] WR to W. D. Weatherford, December 5, 1913, box 27, Rauschenbusch Family Papers.

[104] WR to Mr. Alger, July 18, 1913, box 27, Rauschenbusch Family Papers.

[105] Evans, *The Kingdom Is Always but Coming*, 205.

City, a new organization that proposed to bring together individual church members throughout the nation to support specific social reforms through legislation. Lamenting the church's loss of influence, the League offered a long list of progressive reforms, mirroring the goals Rauschenbusch had often articulated. The idea originated with social reformer W. D. P. Bliss, and Rauschenbusch was named president. The *Times* article carried large pictures of its five major leaders: Rauschenbusch, Bliss, Josiah Strong, and Methodist bishops Francis J. McDowell and E. R. Hendrix. Other notable religious leaders enlisted included Washington Gladden, Jane Addams, Henry S. Coffin, and Rabbi Stephen S. Wise.[106] Clearly Rauschenbusch sought to remain personally involved in implementing his vision. As president of the organization, Rauschenbusch's picture was the largest. He was the face of the Protestant social gospel.

Despite his herculean effort, Rauschenbusch's influence was undercut by conservative ministers, and his immigrant origins created complex identity problems. Highly patriotic on the one hand, he strenuously resisted American entry into World War I because of his love for Germany, a position viewed by many as disloyalty to the United States. This, too, undercut his influence.

Rauschenbusch's loyalties were torn. He defended Germany for its creativity and cultural leadership. He published his opinion in an article, "Be Fair to Germany," which was not well received.[107] He implored the U.S. to remain neutral in this European fight. This article drew a strong response from Aberdeen professor James Stalker, who criticized him for failing to recognize and condemn German aggression and the suffering it brought to Belgium and other countries. In 1915 Rauschenbusch took another tack in his argument against the war. With Congregational minister Charles Aked, he wrote a manifesto, "Private Profit and the Nation's Honor," which was published in July.[108] In this text he and Aked argued that the nation was making huge profits selling arms for the war. Once again, his efforts generated negative public opinion. A third level of Rauschenbusch's defense for American neutrality was his growing commitment to peace. He believed that the New Testament and the example of Jesus modeled nonviolence.[109] Rauschenbusch suffered criticism for his stance—not merely in the general press, but also in Rochester and from people who had been friends. Martin Leuschner recalled the pain of this experience, leading Rauschenbusch to despair of ever experiencing happiness again. Leuschner reported he had read fierce denunciations written in bitter hatred toward Rauschenbusch by five close friends

[106] Bliss, "Seeks to Make Religion a Legislative Force."

[107] WR, "Be Fair to Germany."

[108] Sharpe, *Walter Rauschenbusch*, 373.

[109] The stages of Rauschenbusch's argument are summarized in Evans, *The Kingdom Is Always but Coming*, 263–73, 286–89.

because of his pro-German stance. Rauschenbusch wore a black armband; his students saw a man whose spirit of optimism and progress was broken by war. The grand vision of national reconstruction appeared to Rauschenbusch to have failed. Rauschenbusch's wife, Pauline, told Leuschner that Rauschenbusch had "died of a broken heart" because of the terrible disillusionment that came to him in those dark days.[110] Rauschenbusch had been caught up in this moment of reform and made an enduring contribution to it, working diligently for a more just society with the goal of welcoming influences of the kingdom of God in America. But his pro-German stance discredited him in many people's eyes. His influence waned; he died in 1918, but his influence survived and flourished in following generations.

That Rauschenbusch was perhaps the most visible Protestant leader for a decade is a tribute to the vitality he brought to a new message for the church. Judging from the letters Rauschenbusch received, his ideas excited attention because of their relevance. The churches recognized the problems in society but had not found sufficient motivation or ways to deal with them although they had certainly tried. Rauschenbusch awakened the churches to their role in creating a better society. Prompted by conscience and the desire for a just society, he aroused Christians to address social injustices. This was a new challenge, and his argument left no doubt that it was incumbent on the churches to work for the salvation of society, not merely for themselves. Rauschenbusch believed this was not optional for the churches; rather, it was the core of Jesus' teaching expressed in announcing the coming of the kingdom of God. Rauschenbusch's vision of American society was inclusive: his vision reached beyond his own denomination. Henry B. Robins remarked on "the circle of his influence. Into his home there came men of the most diverse types—earnest souls in quest of the best, capitalists and socialists, Protestant, Catholic, Jews and free thinker—all persuaded by something in the man.[111] The published reviews of his books and reporters' accounts of his speeches as well as the letters he received from readers of his books attest to the powerful reception Rauschenbusch continued to received as public Protestant leader. In the century following his death, his message was alternately denied and attacked or accepted and implemented. But he could not be ignored.[112]

---

[110] Pauline Rauschenbusch, cited in Leuschner, "Walter Rauschenbusch and Our Day."

[111] See Henry B. Robins, "Walter Rauschenbusch: A Prophet of the New Social Order," 4, typescript, box 39, Rauschenbusch Family Papers.

[112] See chapter 12 for a survey of Rauschenbusch's influence during the century following his death.

PART 3

THREE PATHS OF CHRISTIANITY AND A CENTURY OF LEGACY

In the course of their long history, Christians have employed numerous ways of defining, expressing, and living out their faith. In the last decade of his life Rauschenbusch published books that explored three ways of understanding Christianity: the path of Christian spirituality, the path of Christian ethics, and the path of Christian thought. The breadth and variety of dimensions in Rauschenbusch's own personal Christianity is often overlooked, but his books demonstrate the wide range of his Christianity as well as his creativity. These also should be recognized as significant Rauschenbusch legacies. Each of the next three chapters explores a key distinctive dimension of Rauschenbusch's understanding of Christianity.

In *For God and the People: Prayers of the Social Awakening* (1909) Rauschenbusch approached Christianity from the standpoint of articulating people's needs through prayer. These prayers are direct, pragmatic, and accessible. Rauschenbusch remained attuned to the inner spiritual needs of Christians and sought to give these sentiments expression. In today's language Rauschenbusch's prayers fall under the category of Rauschenbusch's spirituality. He made a strong impression on contemporaries through the genre of prayer-writing and thereby addressed inner longings of many ordinary Christians. In the past, many Christians have viewed their faith in terms of a spiritual quest for God, and for many people today this approach has become the paramount meaning of religion. Rauschenbusch contributed richly to this strand of Christian understanding and practice. His pastoral touch was appealing to readers.

On another level, Rauschenbusch was keen to continue to show how the principles of the Christian faith could be applied in practice to transform American society. Washington Gladden, Rauschenbusch's social gospel predecessor, favored the term "applied Christianity." This language was also used to designate the chair later held by Reinhold Niebuhr (Dodge Professor of Applied Christianity) at Union Theological Seminary in New York City.

The discipline of social ethics achieved a major role in twentieth century American Christianity, and Rauschenbusch contributed significantly to this development. Recognizing a wide range of Christian relationships to society, Gladden, Rauschenbusch and both Niebuhrs all adopted activist positions supporting the notion of the church as an agent of transformations of society. For them a Christianity limited to the individual was incomplete Christianity. Most Christians throughout the history of the church have affirmed the value of church as a community of worship and moral support. Beyond the ecclesiastical dimensions, the social Christian thinkers sought to apply the principles of Christianity to the structural reordering of the entire American society. Some sort of relation to the larger society is inevitable for individual Christians and churches, and Rauschenbusch took a vigorous line of approach to this question. In his 1912 book, *Christianizing the Social Order,* Rauschenbusch directly addressed the relationship of Christianity to the United States. In this book Rauschenbusch offers concrete proposals for the redemption of the nation. *Christianizing the Social Order* represents Christianity as activism—working to change life for the better. In 1916 Rauschenbusch wrote *The Principles of Jesus*, which gave him opportunity to focus on Christ and on current understandings of his life and message and to apply his teachings to social ethics.

Third, Rauschenbusch explored his faith through theological reflection. Invited to present the Taylor Lectures at Yale Divinity School, Rauschenbusch took this occasion to develop Christian theology from the perspective of the social gospel. In this last book Rauschenbusch gave the topic his careful attention by writing *A Theology for the Social Gospel.* While he employed some of the traditional categories of systematic theology, his basic plan was to address the twin themes of sin and redemption. Combining *The Theology* with the *The Principles*, Rauschenbusch offered a theology that sought to address the Christian faith to the needs of the society of his day. Reflection on belief is inevitable and desirable. Rauschenbusch gave careful attention to this dimension of the faith.

Recognition of Rauschenbusch's serious treatment of several dimensions of Christianity complicates our understanding of the nature of the man. He was not one-dimensional, and his Christianity cannot be reduced to the single theme of social gospeller. He embraced and articulated multiple dimensions of Christianity. Some Christians focus on spirituality, others on action, and still others on reflection. In Rauschenbusch's view, Christian practice was not limited exclusively to a single category, but rather involved multiple enriching layers of experience. Each of the next three chapters summarizes and analyzes Rauschenbusch's books published from 1910 to 1917 and reception by the earliest readers of those volumes.

Rauschenbusch's influence on Christianity in America has been enduring and significant. A century after his death it is clear that he recognized a new dimension of the faith and successfully called attention to it. His argument is persuasive and significant. His idea cannot be ignored, and his contribution appears to be permanent. The final chapter is devoted to sketching decade by decade the ongoing importance of Rauschenbusch in the hundred years following his death. Disrupted by World War I and its aftermath, the ideas of the social gospel rebounded thereafter. Reinhold Niebuhr criticized Rauschenbusch's optimism, but he nevertheless made justice in American society central in his own theological reflection. Niebuhr's influence remained powerful only to be superseded by liberation theologies, which also have affinities to Rauschenbusch. It is fitting to extend reflection on the early reception of Rauschenbusch to a summary of his long-term legacy.

CHAPTER 9

RAUSCHENBUSCH'S CHRISTIAN SPIRITUALITY

The name Walter Rauschenbusch calls to mind the prophetic advocate of the social gospel. But Rauschenbusch also experienced a deep quality of spirituality, which he expressed in three major genres of his writings—hymns, poetry, and prayers. His daughter wrote that Rauschenbusch "was a good deal of a real st...as well as very personally a mystic."[1] As a service to the German Baptist community, Rauschenbusch translated hymns of revivalist Ira Sankey. He wrote that Lutheran Pietist hymns had been especially meaningful to him throughout his life. Rauschenbusch also tried his hand at creative writing. In novels such as *Hard Times* Charles Dickens had indelibly impressed into the minds of readers the plight of the poor in Industrial England, and Rauschenbusch also attempted to write stories that narrated the struggles of the poor. These efforts did not enjoy much success. Much more successful were some of his poems that directly addressed his personal relationship with God, especially "The Highest Battle," and "The Little Gate of God," both written near the end of his life. The most influential of his spiritual writings were his prayers, probably the most common act of devotion for all Christians. Rauschenbusch originally gave his book of prayers the title *For God and the People*; he later changed the title to *Prayers for the Social Awakening*. In some later editions the two titles are joined as title and subtitle. This book represents Rauschenbusch's chief contribution to the heritage of Christian spirituality. In this book he sought to turn the human spirit toward God through the familiar medium of brief addresses to God.[2] Of his many writings he said that *Prayers for the Social Awakening* was his favorite book.[3]

In the minds of many observers social activism is understood as the opposite of Christian spirituality. This chapter asserts the opposite for Rauschenbusch. In his view, spirituality is the essential foundation of and complement to his social message; he could not conceive of a Christianity apart from both spirituality and action. This chapter briefly considers current interest in spirituality; it then ana-

[1] Winifred [Rauschenbusch] Rorty to Dores Sharpe, December 17, 1933, box 50, Rauschenbusch Family Papers.

[2] See WR, *For God and the People* and *Prayers for the Social Awakening*.

[3] Minus, *Walter Rauschenbusch*, 166.

lyzes Rauschenbusch's major writings devoted to spirituality and assesses reception of his contribution to this dimension of Christianity. Rauschenbusch left a deep legacy of spirituality to the church.

The Heritage of Christian Spirituality

Consciousness of the centrality of spirituality in religion has increased markedly in recent decades. The term "spirituality" is fluid and has no clear consensus definition. Broadly defined, Arthur Holder suggests that spirituality is "human experience in daily life of that which is perceived to have ultimate meaning."[4] David Scott affirms that Christian spirituality commonly refers to an individual's personal quest for the divine, the dimensions of Christianity that emphasize the personal experience of ongoing encounters with God.[5] Philip Sheldrake, a leading authority, defines spirituality as "the theory and practice of the Christian life."[6] The New Testament itself speaks of Christianity as "The Way" and gives much attention to discipleship by followers of Christ.[7] Modern accounts of the history of Christian spirituality focus especially on traditions of public worship (including Eucharistic prayers, hymns, and sermons) and on the personal practice of devotions (most notably through prayer and living out the Christian life). In this broad sense, spirituality has always been a part of the corporate life of the church and of the individual's quest for God. Traditional Christian spirituality affirms the centrality of experienced faith, expressed in worship and devotion. According to spirituality scholar Gordon Wakefield, Roman Catholic scholar Phillipe Pourrat identified spirituality as a separate category of Christian theology, thereby creating heightened awareness of spirituality.[8] In Pourrat's view spirituality should be understood as a third category of Christian reflection in addition to the two traditional categories of dogmatic and moral theology. By naming spirituality as a distinct and important branch of theology in its own right, thanks to the work of Pourrat, the idea of three conceptual dimensions of Christianity emerged more clearly.[9]

Among Protestants, the twentieth-century Methodist spiritual writer R. Newton Flew argued in *The Idea of Perfection in Christian Theology* (1934) that spirituality was not derived from the rational formulations of dogma and ethics,

---

[4] Holder, "Christian Forms of Spirituality," 1183–84. The quotation is from Holder. He concludes that this topic is so big that "no typology could ever encompass the wide range of Christian forms of spirituality" (1184).

[5] For recent definitions and introductions to spirituality see Scott, "Spirituality," 1137.

[6] Sheldrake, *Spirituality and History*, 40. Sheldrake devotes a full chapter to the question, "What Is Spirituality?" (40–64).

[7] Sheldrake, *A Brief History of Spirituality*, 14, 32–33.

[8] See Wakefield, "Spirituality," 361–62; also Pourrat, *La Spiritualité Chrétienne*, 4 vols.

[9] Wakefield, "Spirituality," 361–62.

but rather spirituality provided the original source of spiritual energy, and thus provided the foundation for Christian thought and morality. In his view spirituality becomes the center of Christianity; theology and moral teaching are derivative and secondary concerns.[10] In this thinking, spirituality assumes primacy among all categories: it is the heart of religion. Similarly, Sheldrake elevates spirituality to the center: he argues that spiritualities arise from human existence and are not merely second-order practices logically derived from pre-existing belief systems and doctrines.[11] Whereas early Protestantism focused on justification by faith and the authority of Scripture, in the seventeenth and eighteenth centuries Protestantism shifted emphasis to personal conversion plus the practice of piety. Pietism, Methodism, and American revivalism all gave priority to the conversion experience and Christian practice. Spirituality emphasizes the lifelong quest for a sense of the presence of God in everyday experience. In his study of recent American spirituality, sociologist Robert Wuthnow notes shift in models of spirituality, but also sees the quest for the spiritual as a persistent part of the American identity.[12]

Rauschenbusch understood that prayer is at the heart of personal Christian longing for God. Often defined as communicating with God, prayer is commonly understood to comprise several elements, including confession of sin, praise to God, specific thanksgivings, petitions for help, and intercessions for others. All these elements appear in Rauschenbusch's book of prayers, *For God and the People.*

Protestant consciousness and appropriation of spirituality as a Christian discipline has grown rapidly during the last half century.[13] This new awareness is readily discernible at many levels, including clerical, lay, and academic experience. In recent years Protestant seminaries have begun addressing spiritual formation of clergy as well as providing training in the traditional academic disciplines and practical studies. The spirituality of one called to the ministry had been assumed. But conscious awareness of spiritual health during seminary training and throughout the minister's life is now recognized as an important dimension of training for future ministers, reflected in curriculum changes that address spiritual formation not merely as a single course of study, but rather as a parallel program of study and practice pursued for a year or even throughout the seminary training. Some of the inspiration for this movement came from increased contact between Protestants and Catholics, especially following the Second Vatican Council (1962–1965).[14] In the past, the Protestant ethos traditionally has been perceived

[10] Ibid.

[11] Sheldrake, *A Brief History of Spirituality*, 25.

[12] Wuthnow, *After Heaven*, vii, 3–18.

[13] Scott, "Prayer," 963.

[14] Church historian Glenn Hinson, for instance, pioneered recovery of Christian devotional classics for Baptist ministers in the South, the largest Protestant denomination in the

as activist rather than contemplative, and seminary training was shaped accordingly. Currently Protestant ministerial training is giving new affirmation to the importance of cultivating sensitivities to spirituality.

Second, at the level of lay perception and practice of religion, research of sociologists during recent decades has documented an increasingly important distinction between the notions of "religious" and "spiritual." They have noted that many people make a conscious distinction between the two categories, and many prefer to identify themselves as "spiritual," suggesting affirmation of belief in God, belief in a spiritual realm and the notion of life as a spiritual quest.[15] At the same time this research found widespread disenchantment or outright rejection of the importance of traditional religion understood institutionally as denominational structure with accompanying battles over authority, dogmatic theology, or ethical absolutes. Many Americans since the 1960s have embraced the self-description of "spiritual" rather than "religious."

Third, academics have also devoted serious attention to spirituality, especially since the 1980s. Louis Bouyer's *A History of Christian Spirituality* was already a landmark work from the 1960s.[16] In the 1980s a splendid three-volume study of Christian spirituality appeared.[17] Also in the 1980s scholars began publishing major primary materials in *The Classics of Western Spirituality: A Library of the Great Spiritual Masters.*[18] Added to *Western Spirituality* is the publication of the impressive *Spirituality in the Modern World: Within Religious Tradition and Beyond.*[19] In short, spirituality is currently a favored path of scholars for affirming the constructive and positive dimension of religion as an ongoing quest for discerning the presence of God.[20]

Many current studies understand spirituality in terms of the broadest welfare

---

nation. He traced his interest in spirituality to a personal encounter in 1960 with Catholic Trappist monk Thomas Merton, who changed Hinson's mind by simply saying to him, "I believe in prayer." Hinson offered seminary students courses on spirituality and later reflected that although seminaries had offered courses in classical theological disciplines and practical studies, spiritual formation had been missing (see Hinson, *A Miracle of Grace*, 125, 135–40, 157–70).

[15] See Roof, *Spiritual Marketplace*. English studies include Carrette and King, *Selling Spirituality*, and Heelas and Woodhead, *The Spirituality Revolution*.

[16] Bouyer, *A History of Christian Spirituality*, 3 vols.

[17] McGinn, Meyendorff, and Leclercq, eds., *Christian Spirituality*; Raitt, ed. *Christian Spirituality*; Dupré, Saliers, and Meyendorff, eds. *Christian Spirituality.*

[18] Payne and Furina, eds., *The Classics of Western Spirituality*. Simultaneously an ambitious companion series appeared that was devoted to *Spirituality in World Religions*. A third series was devoted to *Sources of American Spirituality*, ed. by John Furina.

[19] Heelas, ed., *Spirituality in the Modern World.*

[20] For a survey of spirituality in a variety of traditions see Beversluis, *Sourcebook of the World's Religions.*

of the entire human community. This view of spirituality stresses the quest for ending violence and injustice, for promoting peace among different races and political systems, and for caring for the ecological interests which affect everyone on the planet.[21] These goals involve shaping economic policy and the exercise of political will to achieve justice as well as promoting interreligious understanding and acceptance of the necessity of curtailing violence and war. Broadly put, the goal of this understanding of spirituality is to build a satisfactory future for human flourishing.[22]

During Rauschenbusch's era, William James and Rudolf Otto searched for language to probe the core of religious experience.[23] Rauschenbusch looked to different sources but also sought to grasp the nature of the human experience of God. Rauschenbusch also reflected systematically on the nature of religion in formal papers, notably in addresses before the Baptist Congress.

Rauschenbusch's Spiritual Formation with Fellow Pastors

Rauschenbusch's own experience of spirituality was shaped by his early Christian training and practice. However, he also identified powerful influences during his early ministry—especially friendships and reading—which affected his core spirituality. In 1887 Rauschenbusch formed a close connection with fellow Baptist ministers Leighton Williams and Nathaniel Schmidt. They gathered to discuss strategies for ministry in New York City, but "at the same time they were cultivating their inner devotional life."[24] This self-proclaimed "Society of Jesus" met on Sunday afternoons to discuss devotional literature and also to spend time in "reflection, contemplation and prayer, followed by communion."[25] Their readings included Augustine's *Confessions*, *The Imitation of Christ*, John Bunyan's *Pilgrim's Progress*, Richard Baxter's *The Saints' Everlasting Rest*, Philip Doddridge's *The Rise and Progress of Piety in the Soul*, accounts of St. Francis's life, and Henry Scougal's *The Life of God in the Soul of Man*. Scougal (1650–1678) was a Church of Scotland minister and a professor at King's College, Aberdeen. In *The Life of God in the Soul of Man* (1677), Scougal says he will lay out the foundation of religion. He begins by identifying mistakes people make. Some say religion is a matter of opinion; others, duties such as worship and poverty relief; still others, ecstatic devotion. According to Scougal, all of these have the "resemblance of piety...shadows and false imitations of it, but true religion is a Union of the Soul

[21] King, *The Search for Spirituality*.

[22] King, *The Search for Spirituality*, 63.

[23] See James, *The Varieties of Religious Experience*, and Otto, *Das Heilige*.

[24] Hudson, ed., *Walter Rauschenbusch: Selected Writings*, 21.

[25] Ibid., 18–19.

with God—a real participation of the Divine Nature, the very Image of God!"[26] Rauschenbusch adopted a similar view of the meaning of religion, and on several occasions he used the phrase "the life of God in the soul of man" to describe the essence of religion. These books are all classics of Christian spirituality, and these Sunday gatherings focused on practicing devotion, including prayer and communion.[27]

Rauschenbusch also referred to a variety of more recent authors who affected the shaping of his core convictions, including Frederick Robertson, Leo Tolstoy, and Giuseppe Mazzini. The three young pastors also read together William Arthur's *The Tongue of Fire*. Influential in the dawning Holiness movement, Arthur emphasized the power of the spirit as an energizing force. Rauschenbusch published an excerpt from Arthur in the August 1890 issue of *For the Right*.[28] Arthur's book provided an extended exposition of the place of the Holy Spirit in the book of Acts and evidence of power conveyed by the Spirit, notably at Pentecost. Throughout the book Arthur pointed to the vitality of the early church and saw it as a model for the present church. He wrote, "My desire is to lessen the distance between my own life and ministry and those of primitive Christians."[29] Arthur advocated "vital religion" and "holy living."[30] He asserted that there can be no Christianity without the power of the Spirit. Rauschenbusch's later references to *The Tongue of Fire* suggest that he adopted Arthur's dictum that "a religion without the Holy Ghost...would certainly not be Christianity."[31] A sense of the presence and power of the Spirit of Christ pervaded Rauschenbusch's Christian life.

Historian Winthrop Hudson, who edited selected writings of Rauschenbusch for the series, *Sources of American Spirituality*, confessed after studying the spiritual dimension of Rauschenbusch's life, "I thought I knew him well from the vantage point of a direct line of academic succession. But when I was called upon to view him from a fresh perspective, I discovered I had not fully known him. There were aspects of his life and thought that were unknown to me, and I was much the poorer for my lack of exposure to them."[32] Although Hudson did not elaborate, he made these remarks to open a study of Rauschenbusch from the perspective of spirituality. Spirituality is indeed another dimension to Rauschenbusch's Christianity often overlooked. Rauschenbusch articulated the quest for spirituality in a variety of ways, including his first major address to the young seminary students at Rochester, through his memorable collection of prayers, and

---

[26] Scougal, *The Life of God in the Soul of Man*, 3–5.
[27] Hudson, ed., *Walter Rauschenbusch: Selected Writings*, 17.
[28] Ibid., 17. See "From *Tongue of Fire*" in *For the Right* (August 1980), 6.
[29] Arthur, *The Tongue of Fire*, ix.
[30] Ibid., 102, 104.
[31] Ibid., 109.
[32] Hudson, ed., *Walter Rauschenbusch: Selected Writings*, 1.

in poetry composed near the end of his life.

Counsels to Young Ministers on Spiritual Reflection

During his ten years as pastor, Rauschenbusch addressed the theme of spirituality in several sermons. In this context he drew guidelines and applications from both the biblical text and life experiences. His goal was to assist church members with daily practice of their faith. When he moved in 1897 from pastor in New York City to professor in Rochester, Rauschenbusch was asked to deliver a commencement address for graduates of the Rochester Seminary German department. In this address to the young ministers, Rauschenbusch reflected on spirituality, and he later published "The Culture of the Spiritual Life," in which he outlined his views on central elements of spirituality.[33]

Rauschenbusch first argued for the priority of the realm of the spiritual in human experience. He built his argument by noting that a human life has physical, intellectual, and spiritual dimensions, and that people create goals or aims for each. He reminded listeners that people have bodily strength, but some animals have superior strength and speed; nevertheless, "we are their masters."[34] A second level of human development is the intellectual. Rauschenbusch said that people "admire the wrestler and the runner, but they reserve their higher homage for the men of thought, the poet, artist, orator, and statesman. The culture of the mind is more important than the culture of the body."[35] In Rauschenbusch's hierarchy of values, the spiritual is the third and most important level of human experience and exceeds even intellectual genius: "To do right," he wrote, "is greater than to be strong. To be good is worthier than to be clever. The spirit outlasts the body and the mind.... It is the one thing in life that lasts...the one thing that God will ask for."[36]

Following this introduction Rauschenbusch then turned to his major theme—the methods for cultivation of the spiritual life. Rauschenbusch drew on a simple analogy to make his case: just as a plant needs careful tending, so does the spiritual life. He suggested that the spiritual life exists in a "hostile climate." "Compare," he says, "our sensuous impulses with the fragile growth of our Godward aspirations."[37] Rauschenbusch wrote that listeners in his audience may hold opposite views of how human nature is formed. Some may have adopted a traditional view that people are "fallen and corrupted by sin." Others may have adopted

---

[33] WR, "The Culture of the Spiritual Life," 17.

[34] Ibid.

[35] Ibid.

[36] Ibid. Arthur cites a similar trope (Arthur, *The Tongue of Fire*, 81–84). Rauschenbusch has made it his own with his vivid illustrations.

[37] Ibid.

a more modern notion that people are "slowly mounting from animal to spiritual."[38] For Rauschenbusch's purposes it does not matter which view of life is adopted. The point he makes is that, however it is formed, "the spiritual life is very feeble in humanity."[39] Like a frail plant, it needs careful nurturing if it is to flourish.

Rauschenbusch then proceeded to offer four suggestions for cultivating this fragile spirituality. First, the listener in his audience should be aware of living in the presence of God. He argued that "if this visible world fills your horizon, if you live for its pleasures and riches, bow to its laws and are swayed by its desires, you are in that measure a child of the world, whatever your creed or your church relations may be."[40] By contrast, the child of God will have thoughts of the living God, live as a child of God and possess the spiritual life. He concluded, "Therefore practice the presence of God. Bring him to mind in prayer.... Apply the social instinct to the best companion of all, to your Father."[41] For Rauschenbusch the first step in the spiritual life was to contribute a keen consciousness of the presence of God in one's life.

Second, Rauschenbusch counseled the young German pastors to "seek the fellowship of God's people."[42] He described with unsettling honesty powerful anti-religious dimensions of American life in 1897. He said, "There is a dry atmosphere of unbelief in the world, in its conversation, its aims, its literature. It saps our own faith. Men live as if there were no God."[43] Therefore he counseled his audience to associate with fellow believers. Here he affirmed the importance of the experience of community and interaction with fellow Christians in the church.

In the third place, Rauschenbusch asked hearers to reflect regularly on their goals, motivations, and actions. He stressed the importance of constantly assessing and correcting one's definition of life's purpose. The fundamental problem, he warned, was that selfishness and pride "steals insidiously into everything we do." In prayer, however, "we can see how things are."[44] Regular prayer and honest reflection are important spiritual exercises for Rauschenbusch. They create an ethos for critical and ongoing honest assessment of life's goals.

Rauschenbusch's fourth and final guideline for spiritual growth was obedience to the Spirit of God. By this he meant that followers of Jesus should both pursue the virtues of the Christian life and also "let go what the Spirit of God

[38] Ibid.
[39] Ibid.
[40] Ibid.
[41] Ibid.
[42] Ibid.
[43] Ibid.
[44] Ibid.

despises."[45] He returned to the analogy of tending plants. Plants need watering, but also weeding. "The spiritual life is fostered," Rauschenbusch noted, "by removing obstacles."[46]

Rauschenbusch's devotion to the spiritual life that he described in this commencement address is palpable in his conclusion:

> But the main thing is to have God; to live in Him; to have Him live in us; to think His thoughts; to love what He loves and hate what He hates; to realize His presence; to feel His holiness and to be holy because He is holy; to feel His goodness in every blessing of our life and even its tribulations; to be happy and trustful; to join in the great purposes of God and to be lifted to greatness of vision and faith and hope with him—that is the blessed life.[47]

Rauschenbusch sought to persuade his audience of the importance of cultivating a spiritual life. The rhythms and cadence of his speech suggests that he felt deeply what he proposed. It was a sermon that grew out of eleven years of recent pastoral experience. He conveyed his message with passion, and he recorded that the speech made "a deep impression" on the audience.[48]

In his speech Rauschenbusch took a fairly simple and well-established approach to his subject. He employed the traditional categories of God, others, self, and world. The first two are straightforward. Rauschenbusch affirmed the importance of devoting time to the presence of God and fellow believers. The third and fourth are more cautionary in tone: he warned against temptation to justify personal ambitions and to pursue worldly pleasures. Rauschenbusch opened and closed his speech to the young ministers with a warning of the fragility of the spiritual life.

In Rauschenbusch's view, Christian spirituality does not begin automatically with baptism. His plant analogy suggests that spiritual growth in life requires cultivation. Moreover, this effort is lifelong. It must be sustained in order for the Christian spiritual life to flourish. This commencement address is both pastoral and practical. For his sources Rauschenbusch turned to church history, both distant and recent. He appealed by name to the English spiritual writer Jeremy Taylor's (1613–1667) "Holy Living" and by phrase to Brother Lawrence (1614–1691) when he counseled above all "to practice the presence of God."[49] The language of

---

[45] Ibid.

[46] Ibid.

[47] Ibid.

[48] WR, handwritten comment on the back of the typescript of "The Culture of the Spiritual Life," 1897, box 102, Rauschenbusch Family Papers.

[49] Rauschenbusch here relies on the language of the seventeenth-century devotional writers Brother Lawrence (Nicholas Herman, 1614–1691) and Jeremy Taylor (1613–1667). Brother Lawrence's chosen title, *The Practice of the Presence of God* (1692) is an enormously influential phrase. It captures the essence of spirituality. Taylor is especially known for *Holy*

Rauschenbusch's closing words—"The main thing is to have God; to live in him; to have him live in us"—echoes Puritan Henry Scougal's *The Life of God In the Soul of Man* (1676).[50] In this address Rauschenbusch offered a practical guideline to seminary graduates and to a broader reading audience. He drew on great traditions of Christian spirituality. In his view spirituality is the practice of the presence of God, the indispensable starting point for the Christian life.

For Rauschenbusch, spirituality addresses the believer's personal daily relationship with God; it complements religious reflection by focusing attention on a sense of an ongoing encounter with God and on responsible daily ethical decisions and choices. Rauschenbusch devoted much of his life to creating a more Christian society, but he believed that the necessary commitment for this work was nurtured in personal spirituality. This pastoral commencement address is a strong indicator that Rauschenbusch gave serious thought to spirituality early in his career. This well-crafted address provides both rationale and guidelines for cultivating spirituality, but it was Rauschenbusch's prayers that were to make his most powerful impact on a large reading public seeking spiritual guidance and comfort.

The Pastoral Intercessor: Prayers for the Social Awakening

In 1910 Rauschenbusch published *For God and the People.*[51] It is a small volume, but it made a powerful impression. He noted the uniqueness of the genre of a book of prayers, acknowledging that prayers attempt to express the most intimate spiritual thoughts of people. But he hoped that in writing these prayers, he as the writer might "in a measure be the voice of all."[52] In this book he set for himself the task of articulating prayers for American people living in the first two decades of the twentieth century and took on the task of spiritual intercessor. As his original title suggests, he was especially concerned to write these new prayers "for God and the people" in ways that gave voice to the ordinary needs of ordinary people.

At the outset Rauschenbusch recognized spiritual and intellectual problems posed by the modern temper and frankly acknowledged that many people had given up praying because of philosophical doubt about religion or because they felt prayer was not effective. But he firmly believed in the value of prayer. He

---

Living (1650) and *Holy Dying* (1651), titles that reflect and summarize the spiritual quest of the Christian throughout life.

[50] This language appears in later works of Rauschenbusch, notably in his article, "Religion: The Life of God in the Soul of Man."

[51] WR, *Prayers.* For this study I have used the 1925 edition, which includes nine additional prayers not published in the original 1910 edition.

[52] Ibid., 11.

believed that public prayer articulating the emptiness of America's materialist goals at least might prompt some people to embrace a vision of life that is more just and more merciful.[53] But he also affirmed much more the belief that prayer might well push beyond the skeptics' view that it merely affects only human consciousness. He believed that prayers may, in fact, move God and find fulfillment: "if there is a center of the spiritual universe in whom our spirits join and have their being; and if the mysterious call of our soul somehow reaches and moves God, so that our longings come back from him as a wave of divine assent which assures their ultimate fulfillment—then it may mean more than any man knows to set Christendom praying."[54] Rauschenbusch believed that public prayer could move both God and individuals in the critical effort to transform society.

By 1910 Rauschenbusch had been a professor for over a decade, and he was now famous, but he had not forgotten his earlier pastoral experience. In publishing this book Rauschenbusch affirmed the importance of Christian spirituality. The Christian faith and life find many forms of expression—individual and social, theological and practical, spiritual and material. Following the massive impact of *Christianity and the Social Crisis,* Rauschenbusch did not immediately publish another hefty volume on the social gospel. Instead, the next dimension of the faith he turned to was Christian spirituality, expressed in this little book of prayers.

In *Prayers* Rauschenbusch's tone shifts to match the genre. In this book he is not making an argument on exegesis of Scripture, the theological and intellectual traditions of the church, and current sociological insight so much as he is articulating through prayers fundamental spiritual aspirations of people of his day. For Rauschenbusch, spirituality and action are linked. He wrote, "Prayer is the most distinctly religious act. Morality is the outcome of religion; it is the test of religion; but it is not religion itself. A man may be a just and loving man, but if he does not pray, he lacks something in the sight of God and he lacks something in the depths of his own consciousness."[55] He held this conviction to the end of his life. In his last book he wrote, "I believe in prayer and meditation in the presence of God."[56] The prayers represent Christian practice "from below." Rauschenbusch does not use theological language of the seminary, but rather his prayers address God in common prose readily understood by lay readers.

Rauschenbusch uses these prayers to intercede through petitions addressed to God on behalf of the people. Some of these prayers were published in religious journals or read from pulpits and thereby served the purpose of public worship. Some people used them for family devotions. However, the format of the pocket-

---

[53] Ibid., 12.
[54] Ibid., 12–13.
[55] Ibid., "Thoughts on Prayer," 1.
[56] WR, *A Theology for the Social Gospel*, 1997 ed., 17.

sized book was designed especially for the benefit of individual readers. Some would find that Rauschenbusch had expressed their own desires. Others would become more aware of the practical needs of ordinary Americans working in a broad range of vocations and professions. This little book enjoyed substantial sales. Moreover, Rauschenbusch invited people to "reprint [individual] simple prayers in newspapers, church programs, and secular publications...."[57] He was not interested in enforcing strict copyright restrictions from this book. Instead, he wanted the prayers to benefit as many readers as possible. Writing this book was in a sense a pastoral gift to church and society.

Rauschenbusch began this little book with an exegesis of the Lord's Prayer, which in the history of the church has been the central prayer of the New Testament. He declared that "the mind of Jesus...conveys the atmosphere of his childlike trust...and gives proof of the peace of his soul."[58] At the outset he asserted the compatibility of spiritual Christianity and social Christianity, asserting that the Lord's Prayer is "the charter of all social prayers."[59] Rauschenbusch observed that when he taught people to say "Our Father," Jesus spoke from "that consciousness of human solidarity which was a matter of course in all his thinking."[60] Solidarity of all people was a key goal for Rauschenbusch since good will toward others was essential in moving American society from its condition of struggle and competition to a society of service and cooperation. In Rauschenbusch's interpretation, the "our" that opens the prayer supports his claim about Jesus' thinking: he did not say, "My Father," but "Our Father." Christianity is social, and Christians are to stand in solidarity with each other in their address to God.

Rauschenbusch declared that in this foundational prayer of Jesus, "There is no request here that we be saved from earthliness and go to heaven which has been the great object of churchly religion."[61] Instead, Jesus called for "transformation of humanity both in its personal units and its corporate life."[62] For Rauschenbusch the focus of salvation in the Lord's Prayer is not a safe escape to heaven beyond, but transformation of life here and now. Rauschenbusch declared that "Jesus was never as 'spiritual' as some of his followers. He never forgot or belittled the elemental needs of men."[63] Rauschenbusch pointed out that the model prayer addresses practical everyday needs, and the petition for bread is the clearest evidence that Jesus recognized "the economic basis of life."[64] He claims

[57] WR, "Thoughts on Prayer," *Prayers*, 13.
[58] Ibid., "Introductory: The Social Meaning of the Lord's Prayer," 15.
[59] Ibid., 17.
[60] Ibid.
[61] Ibid., 18.
[62] Ibid.
[63] Ibid., 19.
[64] Ibid.

that Jesus' concerns were not exclusively spiritual, but material as well. In explaining this prayer, he argued that spirituality is impossible if social responsibility is forgotten: "In these prayers for the inner life, where the soul seems to confront God alone, we should expect to find only individualistic religion. But even here the social note sounds clearly."[65] Rauschenbusch reminds readers that the prayer "will not permit us to ask for God's forgiveness without making us affirm that we have forgiven our brothers and are on a basis of brotherly love.... We shall have to be socially right if we want to be religiously right. Jesus will not suffer us to be pious toward God and merciless toward men."[66] For Rauschenbusch, Christianity was never about a relationship with God alone. He presented a strong exegetical argument for the physical dimension of Christianity in Jesus' model prayer itself. In this collection of prayers he especially had in mind people in the daily tasks of their work.

The Subjects of the Prayers: People, Their Work, Their Condition, and Their Future

Rauschenbusch's prayers are filled with reminders of ethical guidelines for daily living, admonitions to practice the presence of God, and counsel to be attentive to the daily directions of the voice of conscience. Rauschenbusch addressed a great range of topics. How should Christians deal with common difficulties such as greed or anger? How should they develop relationships with family members in their roles as mother, father, children? What does the faith say about disease, aging, and death? Rauschenbusch groups the prayers into three major categories: the ordinary rhythms of life, prayers for various groups of workers, and prayers for the progress of humanity. Each prayer is brief and focused on specific groups of people or specific problems.

Prayers for Ordinary Occasions

Rauschenbusch's first group is daily prayers for morning, evening, and mealtime. His morning prayers are designed to prepare readers with attitudes and relationships in the workplace. He wrote that colleagues should be treated not as "servants to our will, but as brothers equal to us in human dignity."[67] Many phrases from these prayers are reminders about good behavior in the daily interchanges with other people, including specific warnings such as avoiding "sudden anger or secret hate."[68] He cautioned against greed and pride as motivating factors

[65] Ibid., 21.
[66] Ibid.
[67] Ibid., "Morning Prayers," 27.
[68] Ibid., 25.

in work.[69] Rauschenbusch had much to say about constructive approaches to each day. He reminded readers that people can cheer the suffering by sympathy; he encouraged readers to help ungrudgingly when asked to assist at work.[70] Moreover, he appealed to conscience and petitioned God to guide readers "by the voice within."[71] Finally, Rauschenbusch invoked the central Christian virtue of the bond that arises "in the tender ties of love."[72] The key words and phrases of these daily prayers—"conscience," and "the voice within"—counsel the individual reader to look inward for daily guidance.

Rauschenbusch stressed the importance of duty, crucial to interaction with others, in these prayers. He said that as Christ had a spirit of duty, so should we: "Give us a simple eye for duty," he wrote.[73] Similarly he counseled, "In the press of life may we pass from duty to duty in tranquility of heart."[74] Here he is reminding workers that a sense of accomplishment and fulfillment is the reward of work well done. In his view, work that fulfills the demands of duty forms an essential part of spiritual growth.

Anticipating coming hours of rest in the evening prayers, Rauschenbusch petitioned for refreshment of sleep in preparation for the next day. He also reflected with readers on assessing the day's work. He expressed the ever-present sense of incomplete and imperfect work attempted and the desire to make life count: "Thou knowest [the] imperfection [of our work], and we know."[75] He valued highly the aspiration for work well done: "grant that ere our life is done we may under thy tuition become true master workmen, who know the art of a just and relevant life."[76] The idea that work in some sense defines life itself is a natural expression of spirituality for Rauschenbusch. He was personally devoted to his work and was enormously productive. Rauschenbusch found that evening prayers were both an occasion for reflection on work and an opportunity for taking positive moral action, especially the act of forgiving those who had wronged us during the day.[77] Likewise he wrote that evening prayers were an appropriate occasion to be grateful to those who had shown kindness toward us. His prayers articulate Christian teachings often left unspoken.

Prayers before meals are among the most common occasions for prayer in

---

[69] Ibid., 29.
[70] Ibid., 28.
[71] Ibid., 30.
[72] Ibid.
[73] Ibid., 27.
[74] Ibid., 29.
[75] Ibid., "Evening Prayers," 33.
[76] Ibid., 34.
[77] Ibid.

the daily routine of Christian life. In "Grace before Meat" Rauschenbusch expressed gratitude for food and for those who gathered it, while also expressing keen awareness of others in want: "O God, we thank thee for the abundance of our blessing, but we pray that our plenty may not involve want of others."[78] Rauschenbusch sought to instill awareness of the condition of all humanity each time people sat to eat the food that sustained them. The prayers written for mealtime express solidarity and compassion for all people and a clear recognition that Jesus' petition for daily bread is a universal need. Rauschenbusch anchored the basic human need for food in Jesus' model prayer.

Prayers for Specific Vocations

Rauschenbusch devoted the largest section of his prayers to individual workers and their daily tasks. Many of these prayers were devoted to people particularly affected by the nation's industrial economic structure. Ever conscious of growing class distinctions, he was keenly aware of both those without power and those who held economic leverage. For those in privileged positions he prayed, "May we not unknowingly inflict suffering through selfish indulgence or the willful ignorance of a callous heart."[79] His commitment to justice and brotherhood appeared frequently. He wrote, "Grant us wisdom to deal justly and fraternally with every man and woman whom we face in the business life."[80] He noted the powerful temptations faced by businessmen to "slip and fall" into deceitfulness and dishonesty in the "struggle for wealth."[81] To bankers Rauschenbusch wrote, "Since the wealth and savings and welfare of our nation are controlled by our business men, save them from betraying the interests of many for their own enrichment."[82]

Rauschenbusch reserved his deepest expression of compassion for classes of suffering workers. The pathos in his descriptions is deeply moving. He asked for blessing on the children of the earth, but especially for those denied love and protection. He wrote, "Be good to all children who long for human love.... But bless with a sevenfold blessing the young lives whose slender shoulders are already bowed beneath the yoke of toil, and whose glad growth is being stunted forever. Suffer not their little bodies to be utterly sapped, and their minds to be given over to stupidity and to vices of an empty soul."[83] Then he asked employers to have

[78] Ibid., "Grace before Meat," 39.
[79] Ibid., "For the Fatherhood of God," 45. This prayer did not appear in the 1910 edition.
[80] Ibid., "For Consumers," 65.
[81] Ibid., "For Men in Business," 63.
[82] Ibid., 63–64.
[83] Ibid., "For Children Who Work," 51.

"hearts to refuse enrichment at such a price."[84] His prayer voiced a plea to God for working children and also implicitly a plea to employers to end child labor. Rauschenbusch lamented the fact that women were of necessity leaving home to earn a wage in factories, and he pleaded, "Save them from the terrors of utter want."[85] These prayers reveal Rauschenbusch's perception of how industrial America could damage the lives of vulnerable children and women.

To working men Rauschenbusch counseled unity; to unions, "patience and prudence in disputes, and fairness to see the other side...and wisdom resolutely to put aside the two-edged sword of violence."[86] He refused to condone violence but did support workers' rights to create unions and efforts to achieve their goals of healthy working environments, reasonable hours of work, and better wages, and he expressed prayer support for these specific, tangible goals.[87] Immigration levels into the United States reached a peak from 1880 to 1914. Immigrants formed an especially vulnerable sector of the working class. In his prayer "For Immigrants," Rauschenbusch expressed gratitude for the labor of immigrants and hope that they would experience full freedom "in a nation dedicated to liberty."[88] Both Rauschenbusch and his immigrant father had spent much of their energy ministering to German immigrants, and he supported them throughout his life. The distress of those without work did not escape Rauschenbusch's attention and compassion. He composed a prayer for those who "seek honest work in vain, but in idleness suffer humiliation and despair."[89] These prayers reveal Rauschenbusch's understanding of the impact of current industrial conditions in America on ordinary lives.

Rauschenbusch's prayer for employers voiced the hope that since they held power they would exercise it "justly and with love, as older brothers and leaders in the great fellowship of labor." He pleaded with them to muster the resolve to put "human health before profit."[90] The worker-employer relationship was at the forefront of Rauschenbusch's concerns. Tensions repeatedly arose and remained in American society during this era because of owners' desires for industrial profit and workers' demands for a greater share of profits. With awareness even for global workers, Rauschenbusch prayed about goods made abroad, urging that we would wear nothing produced by exploiting the weak. "Save us," he wrote, "from unconscious guilt."[91]

---

[84] Ibid.
[85] Ibid., "For Women Who Toil," 55.
[86] Ibid., "For Workingmen," 57.
[87] Ibid., 58.
[88] Ibid., "For Immigrants," 59–60.
[89] Ibid., "For the Idle," 101–102.
[90] Ibid., "For Employers," 61.
[91] Ibid. "For Consumers," 66.

When he shifted from economic struggles to address the wielders of political power, Rauschenbusch sustained his theme of resisting the use of power to oppress people. Instead, he pleaded for people in authority to support "the liberation of the people in order and stability."[92] For lawyers and legislators, he voiced the prayer that they would be conscious of their calling to see justice done and to defend the poor and weak from oppression.[93] Rauschenbusch observed that public officials wielded much power, and he prayed for them to oppose oppression, to support "the new spirit of democracy" and to "purge our cities and states and nation of the deep causes of corruption…."[94] Rauschenbusch articulated a prayer that democracy would grow in the United States. In his view, growing democracy combined with economic justice was the path that must be taken if the United States were to approximate the kingdom of God on earth.

After prayers relating to economics and politics, Rauschenbusch turned his attention to traditional professionals who sought to serve society. He expressed gratitude for doctors and nurses and for knowledge and skill that brought relief from suffering and healing of the body.[95] Addressing a particular health scourge of his day, Rauschenbusch wrote "A Tuberculosis Prayer," a particularly poignant plea that opens, "O God, we pray thee for all whose vigor is being drained by slow and wasting illness. Strengthen their powers as they battle for their life…."[96] With gratitude for their search for truth and their faithful efforts to inform people, Rauschenbusch singled out "Writers and Newspaper Men." He noted that each profession had its temptations—generally related to love of money—and the same was true of the media: "Since the sanity and wisdom of a nation are in their charge, may they count it shame to set the baser passions of men on fire for the sake of gain."[97] Rauschenbusch believed that the media had a critical responsibility for the health of the state: "Cause them to realize that they have a public function in the commonwealth, and that their country may be saved by their courage or undone by their cowardice and silence."[98] For ministers in churches Rauschenbusch petitioned for "the leaping fire and joy of a new conviction," and "dauntless courage to face the vast needs of the future."[99] He detailed tasks of teachers and reminded them of the lasting influence they would have into the future.[100]

Rauschenbusch's imagination was broad. He included special prayers for

---

[92] Ibid., "For Kings and Magistrates," 67–68

[93] Ibid., "For Lawyers and Legislators," 75.

[94] Ibid., "For Public Officers," 79.

[95] Ibid., "For Doctors and Nurses," 81.

[96] Ibid., "A Tuberculosis Day Prayer," 83.

[97] Ibid., "For Writers and Newspaper Men," 84.

[98] Ibid., 85.

[99] Ibid., "For Ministers," 87.

[100] Ibid., "For Teachers," 88–89.

discoverers and inventors, artists and musicians, prisoners, mothers, lovers, and babies. He was keenly aware of the unique trials and suffering of all people. One of his more moving prayers was addressed to all people at the time they face death.[101] He focused his prayers on others in their present need, later writing, "prayer ought to be a keen realization of our own fellows, and not a forgetfulness of the world."[102] In his prayers Rauschenbusch constantly linked spirituality and social action. Here he advocated in petitions to God what his conscience led him to ask for his nation.

Prayers for the Future

The "Progress of Humanity" forms the final section of Rauschenbusch's collection of prayers. The title of this section demonstrates his optimism and expresses his hope for the future of the nation. He projects his vision of a Christianized country and offers prayers for various dimensions of this imagined redeemed community.

In his prayer "For the Kingdom of God" Rauschenbusch voiced his keen desire for the urgent agenda of the church. He equated the kingdom with God's righteous will, observing that "we have treasured thy words, but we have forgotten their meaning...."[103] In one of his arresting parallelisms, Rauschenbusch wrote, "As we have mastered Nature that we might gain wealth, help us now to master the social relations of mankind that we may gain justice and a world of brothers."[104] Rauschenbusch placed his hope for the progress of mankind on the foundations of righteousness and love.[105] He included "A Social Litany" in the book. This prayer originally was prepared for a mass meeting of the Episcopal Church in New York City in 1913 but also was included in later editions of *Prayers*. "A Social Litany" provided a list of social conditions that needed to be addressed: class bitterness, racial hatred, government corruption, unemployment, child labor, and ill-paid work. The prayer then shifted to his goals for American society: peace, industrial justice, honorable labor relations, health, love of neighbor, reconciliation, and the kingdom of God.[106] According to Rauschenbusch, if humanity is to progress, these goals must be addressed. When he prayed, "For Those Who Come after Us," Rauschenbusch addressed his generation with a prayer for conservation, warning against leaving a world of "wasted resources, sunless houses

[101] Ibid., "Morituri Te Salutant," 203–205.

[102] WR, *Christianizing the Social Order*, 465.

[103] WR, "For the Kingdom of God," *Prayers*, 119.

[104] Ibid.

[105] Ibid., 120.

[106] Ibid., "A Social Litany," 121–23. This litany was used "at a Mass Meeting under the auspices of the Joint Commission on Social Service and the General Convention of the Protestant Episcopal Church, New York 1913" (121).

and poisoned air" (which he believed was already occurring in the tenements).[107] He pled with readers to leave a healthy legacy for the children who would form the next generation.[108]

A closely related topic is the personal guilt people carry for the harm they have inflicted and cannot undo. Rauschenbusch wrote, "Our Father, we look back on the years that are gone and shame and sorrow come upon us, for the harm we have done to others rises up in the memory to accuse us."[109] His prescription for guilt and regret was contrition coupled with efforts to redeem as many souls as we have caused to stumble or fall.[110] Realistically naming remorse, he noted that "all our prayers can never bring back the past, and no tears can wash out the red marks with which we have scarred some life."[111] He expressed the hope that people could learn from the past and be redeemed: "Change us by the power of thy saving grace from sources of evil into sources for good."[112] In the prayer for those who come after us Rauschenbusch addressed damage we might do to the world that would harm unknown people in future generations. But in this prayer, he also asked readers to confront the harm they had done to people they know where a "scarred life…stands before our memory."[113] Rauschenbusch was here probing universal human experience. He addressed the problem of guilt with spiritual counsel to assist in cure of the soul.

Rauschenbusch also offered prayers for some of society's most well-established institutions. Of the church he wrote,

> We remember with love the nurture she gave to our spiritual life in its infancy…[and] the steadfast power for good she has exerted. When we compare her with all other human institutions, we rejoice, for there is none like her. But when we judge her by the mind of her Master, we bow in pity and contrition…. Bid her cease from seeking her own life, lest she lose it.[114]

The church nurtured him and stood for the right, but he warned that it too could fail by pursuing its own self-interest rather than the good of others.

Likewise, he said that the institution of the city provided shelter, commerce, factories, and beauty, but that these values were combined with the vices of fear,

---

[107] Ibid., "For Those Who Come after Us," 124–25.
[108] Ibid.
[109] Ibid., "Oh the Harm We Have Done," 126.
[110] Ibid., 127.
[111] Ibid., 126–27.
[112] Ibid., 127.
[113] Ibid.
[114] Ibid., "For the Church," 134–35.

greed, and corruption and therefore the cities stood in need of justice and brotherhood.[115] The city, too, needed correction. For the nation, Rauschenbusch gave thanks for the opportunity of freedom, achieved at last for many immigrants. But still these free men lived in tenements. Fear of want remained despite the great wealth of the nation. He expressed a vision of the state that will be a "cooperative commonwealth," in which both government and industry should be of the people, by the people, and for the people.[116] Here he used the moving phrases of Lincoln's rhetoric to express goals for the economic as well as the political future of the nation.

Rauschenbusch was a gifted writer. His direct style expressed short petitions cogently. His ability to write penetrating redemptive prayers appropriate to such a large range of individual professions and experiences of life is astonishing.

Leading Themes in the Prayers

Several themes emerge in this collection of prayers, especially the ideas of brotherhood, solidarity, and social unity.[117] Achievement of brotherhood was Rauschenbusch's version of the millennium: it was his hope, his goal for the nation. Rauschenbusch declared that we are all members of one great family.[118] Out of this conviction, he prayed, "Help us to make the welfare of all the supreme law of our land so that our commonwealth may be built strong and secure on the love of all its citizens."[119] Reflection on the contributions of inventors caused Rauschenbusch to think in terms of the common humanity people share, their common inheritance, and their service to one another.[120] He affirmed that discoveries and inventions should be shared for the benefit of everyone. The sense of humanity's interconnectedness also provided a strong argument for Rauschenbusch's prayer against war: "O Thou strong Father of all nations show all thy great family together with an increasing sense of our common blood and destiny, that peace may come on earth at last, and thy sun may shed its light rejoicing on a holy brotherhood of peoples."[121] In Rauschenbusch's view, the goal of solidarity was best expressed through establishing democracy. He prayed for democracy "in the firm edifice of a cooperative commonwealth...."[122] His vision of the Christian future was of a time when people would "stand side by side in equal worth and real

[115] Ibid., "For Our City," 136–37.

[116] Ibid., "For the Cooperative Commonwealth," 139–41.

[117] For example, see references to brotherhood and solidarity in *Prayers*, 70, 83, 98, 110, 120, 140.

[118] Ibid., "For Use by Women's Associations," 98.

[119] Ibid., 120.

[120] Ibid., "For Discoverers and Inventors," 70.

[121] Ibid., "Against War," 110.

[122] Ibid., "For the Cooperative Commonwealth," 140.

freedom...[recognizing God as] the Father of all."[123] His vision was of a society that is democratic in both politics and economics.

Second, Rauschenbusch's spirituality included both the material and the physical dimensions of life. A tendency in Western popular culture has been to understand the concept of "spiritual" in contrast to "material" things. As a consequence of this traditional separation of realms, religious concerns have often been associated exclusively with the spiritual realm and material subjects with nonreligious or secular concerns. This dichotomy remains a widespread popular assumption. But the Rauschenbusch prayers fully address the material side of life as well as the spiritual. This is perhaps one reason the prayers seemed fresh and relevant to Rauschenbusch's generation. In these prayers he dealt with food, poverty, jobs—tangible material goods. When he developed his views on the kingdom of God, he regularly emphasized the phrase "on earth," found in Jesus' prayer.[124] In the later twentieth century, religious scholars affirmed the importance of the material realm to the understanding of religion, expressed in a variety of ways. Some religious scholarship has embraced the language of "wholeness" or "holistic" and has found support in health and medical studies. Theologians and historians have also produced extensive studies of the role of "the body" in the Christian tradition, showing conceptions of the body are firmly grounded in incarnational and eucharistic theologies. In short, Christian spirituality today has embraced the notion of the redemption of the whole person—spirit, mind, and body. These are now regularly seen not as separate entities but as mutually influencing each other. Virtually all of his prayers address concrete problems and practical requests to meet ordinary but absolutely essential physical needs, such as health and safety, provision for food, and care of the environment for future generations. Rauschenbusch also advanced proposals for structural changes in society to remedy endemic problems. In short, Rauschenbusch's spirituality implies the redemption of all of life, including the material realm. He believed that failure to adopt this perspective would lead the church to losing its relevance, and he often warned the church about this great danger.

Third, Rauschenbusch constantly articulated the tension between the way things are and the way they should be. Despite good achieved by both the church and the city, neither had fulfilled its highest calling. This eternal ethical tension led him to identify both present reality and ideal goals as a constant component of his analysis of society. In composing these prayers Rauschenbusch drew many contrasts. For example, in his prayer for the church Rauschenbusch affirmed what it has already accomplished, yet the church needs to do so much more—to express compassion, proclaim the gospel, and stand with the causes of the people rather

123 Ibid., 140–41.
124 WR, *Christianizing the Social Order*, 373.

than serving herself.[125] In praying for the city, he expressed love and pride for the beauty, commerce, factories, and homes afforded by the city; yet he appealed for justice of the city's laws and expressions of brotherhood. The city had not overcome cunning and greed; consequently Rauschenbusch articulated the alternatives—his view of "a city of justice where none shall prey on others; a city of plenty, where vice and poverty shall cease to fester; a city of brotherhood where all success shall be founded on service."[126] The tension between the ideal and the reality occurred repeatedly in his writings because he was calling for reform. He wrote, "Christ has kindled in us the passion for brotherhood, but the social life we have built denies and slays brotherhood."[127] He set himself the task of speaking to church and nation, urging pursuit of the kingdom of God. In these prayers he offered many specifics of what that would look like. His next book would continue this theme and spell out in much greater detail what might be done to Christianize the social order.

Responses to Rauschenbusch's Book of Prayers

Well before publication of *Prayers* Rauschenbusch had already affirmed the centrality of prayer for the Christian.[128] He established a personal balance between spirituality and commitment to social reform and found both essential to Christian faith. During the same year that Rauschenbusch published *Christianity and the Social Crisis* (1907), he expressed his personal faith in the publication of his prayer "Father, thy child comes to thank thee" in *The Watchman*. Henry W. Brown, vice principal in the department of science at New Hampton Literary Institution, wrote a deeply felt letter of appreciation for this prayer:

> Dear Sir:
> We read in our morning devotion your beautiful contribution to *The Watchman* beginning, "Father thy child comes to thank thee." The spirit of your prayer has been with me all day, and I want to thank you for the spiritual uplift your words have given. Such a prayer can come only from a beautiful Christian character; and the world is richer in the possessor of such revealers of the soul's highest and best emotions. Oh, for such sincerity in prayer! May God bless you.
> Sincerely yours,
> Henry W. Brown[129]

---

[125] WR, "For the Church," *Prayers*, 134–35.
[126] Ibid., "For Our City," 136–37.
[127] Ibid., "For the Cooperative Commonwealth," 140.
[128] WR, "Thoughts on Prayer," 1.
[129] Henry Brown to WR, November 26, 1907, box 25, Rauschenbusch Family Papers.

The book of prayers embodied a singular concept. Rauschenbusch realized that people needed practical spiritual support for their lives and that their concerns were largely shaped by their daily work. As he later wrote, "In my *Prayers for the Social Awakening* I have tried to connect the social consciousness with the devotional life by prayers envisioning social groups and movements."[130] He wanted people to feel that the church's message dealt with "the workaday doings of the great noisy world where men seek a living."[131]

Prayers for the Social Awakening elicited responses on a number of levels.[132] Reactions to the *Prayers* book appeared in published reviews as well as in private letters to Rauschenbusch. The letters convey a deep sense of gratitude. Miss L. M. Morden, a business owner living in Waterbury, Connecticut, wrote to Rauschenbusch to express her thanks that the sentiments of his prayers were "from the heart and not from the head merely."[133] A Rochester teacher found helpful "the thoughts of devotion uttered in the form of prayer."[134] Rauschenbusch's success in conveying the spiritual dimensions of life is clear in these letters from readers. His Pietist heritage emerges in the prayers: he was attentive to the heart as well as the head.

The prayers attracted the attention and won the highest possible praise and support from Josiah Strong, president of the American Institute for Social Service in New York City and one of the nation's notable religious leaders. Strong wrote to Rauschenbusch that he had just written the publishers as follows:

> Please accept my thanks for the copy of Dr. Rauschenbusch's *For God and the People.* Prayers written for publication are usually very offensive to me. Their artificiality and smell of oil are with me fatal to devotional feeling, but these prayers are breathed out of a beautiful soul as naturally and sweetly as fragrance rises from a flower. In this warm spiritual atmosphere the heart opens and the devotional spirit is kindled.... These prayers are saturated with the social spirit which is the essential spirit of Christianity. The book is an important contribution to the literature of Social Christianity.[135]

In his personal comments to Rauschenbusch, Strong added: "Your volume is filled with the spirit of the master, and apart from the Scriptures themselves, I have never read anything that so aroused me in the devotional spirit.... They are

---

[130] WR, *A Theology for the Social Gospel,* typescript, box 154, Rauschenbusch Family Papers.

[131] WR, "Introduction to the Gates Lecture of Grinnell College 1914," box 22, Rauschenbusch Family Papers.

[132] Rauschenbusch received several requests for a cheaper edition and a number of requests for single sheets of specific prayers for group distribution.

[133] (Miss) L. M. Morden to WR, June 10, 1912, box 26, Rauschenbusch Family Papers.

[134] John G. Allen to WR, February 23, 1911, box 26, Rauschenbusch Family Papers.

[135] Josiah Strong to WR, November 30, 1910, box 26, Rauschenbusch Family Papers.

far more winning than a syllogism."[136]

Like Rauschenbusch, Strong had adopted a powerful social passion. Rauschenbusch's writing was enormously persuasive for Strong, who praised the prayers for their deeply devotional spirit, even likening the book to Thomas a Kempis' *Imitation of Christ.* His contrast between the comparative influence of logic and prayer in religious discourse is telling; he was clearly moved by reading these prayers.

Reviewer poet Edwin Markham remarked on the lofty and fervent spirit of the prayers for workers in every walk of life. He was especially drawn to the plight of working women. His review appeared two years after the book was published, prompted by a tragedy in American history. On March 25, 1911, fire broke out in a garment factory in the Triangle District of Manhattan, taking the lives of 146 workers (mostly young Jewish and other immigrant women). The doors of the factory had been locked, making emergency escape impossible. Markham noted, "In this hour of the nation's mourning for the hundred working women cruelly betrayed to their death in the heart of America's richest city by the careless forces of graft and greed, this 'Prayer for Women Who Toil' has a new solemnity of meaning."[137]

The reviewer in *The Universalist Leader* thought the title struck the right balance: he noted that "'For God and the People' reflected Jesus' thought in summing up the law by calling for love of God and neighbor."[138] This anonymous reviewer continued, "While the prayers are directed toward real genuine human needs, they are addressed to a very real and genuine God. That is, they are prayers and not advisory essays."[139]

On a lighter note and from a different class of readers, Rauschenbusch told his church history class the story that on return from a trip to Europe, a customs officer puzzled over the name on his trunk. "Walter Rauschenbusch, Rauschenbusch, Rauschenbusch, where have I heard that name before?" Rauschenbusch replied, "Possibly in the *American Magazine*—the prayers called 'For God and the People'?" "That's it!" exclaimed the customs man. "Damn fine prayers, too!"[140] A

---

[136] Ibid.

[137] Edwin Markham, review of "For God and the People," *New York City Magazine*, April 1, 1911, box 94, Rauschenbusch Family Papers.

[138] Anonymous, "For God and the People," *The Universalist Leader*, February 25, 1911, box 94, Rauschenbusch Family Papers.

[139] Ibid.

[140] Dahlberg, *Walter Rauschenbusch: Prophet of Social Christianity*, 9. Dahlberg indicates that much of the material in his article is "derived from personal reminiscences" (11). Rauschenbusch told the same story to a friend. See WR to Mr. Philips, September 9, 1910, box 92, Rauschenbusch Family Papers.

half-century later English Baptist leader Ernest A. Payne attributed the mass appeal of the book to the fact that it "recalls prayer from confession of easy unitemized sins and egocentric personal petitions to active sympathy with the sorrow and sufferings of others."[141] French reviewers were also effusive in their praise. M. Reboul-Mounod wrote of "the fire and emotion of religious thought of Rauschenbusch."[142]

Rauschenbusch also had critics of his approach to prayer. His lawyer friend, Mornay Williams, praised the beauty and helpfulness of the prayers, but took issue with Rauschenbusch for even introducing the possibility that prayer may not go beyond personal desires and the "call of our soul" might not "reach or move God."[143] Williams regretted that Rauschenbusch even entertained the question of religious doubt, but both cultural historian A. N. Wilson and science historian John Hedley have contended that doubt was in fact a pervasive spiritual problem in Victorian England and in the American Gilded Age.[144] Rauschenbusch perceived that some Americans were struggling with belief. Rather than dodging challenges to belief, Rauschenbusch acknowledged the reality of agnosticism in modern life. W. H. P. Faunce, president of Brown University and long-time friend of Rauschenbusch, wrote, "Our generation gives little time to praying, and your prayers will recall them to what President Eliot [of Harvard University, 1869–1909] again and again called prayer 'the highest exercise of the human spirit.'"[145] However, Faunce suggested that there are older and newer conceptions of prayer, and that he and Rauschenbusch seemed to differ in their views. Whereas Faunce saw his own understanding [the older conception] focused on "communion with God," he said that Rauschenbusch's "published prayers came sharp against my conception. In your prayers is it fair to say that the consciousness of humanity is stronger and more obvious than the consciousness of the supreme being?... Some day I should like to talk this out with you.... [I] started out only to say thank you for your beautiful and helpful volume."[146]

Clearly Faunce disagreed with Rauschenbusch on the purpose and impact of prayer, but also appreciated Rauschenbusch calling attention to its importance. Despite holding a different view of the object of prayer, he remained a good friend, eager to pursue future conversation about the nature of prayer. Another correspondent later wrote, "One woman who entertained me last Sunday said,

---

141 Payne, "The Prophet of the Social Gospel," 6.

142 M. Reboul-Monod, "Review of Walter Rauschenbusch's *Prayers*," *Foyer Protestant*, January 16, 1914, box 92, Rauschenbusch Family Papers.

143 Mornay Williams to WR, November 23, 1910, box 26, Rauschenbusch Family Papers.

144 See Wilson, *The Victorians*, 167–71, and Brooke, *Science and Religion*, 270.

145 W. P. Faunce to WR, December 14, 1910, box 26, Rauschenbusch Family Papers.

146 Ibid.

'What can I do to get back my religion? I am unhappy. What proof is there that I will live after death? I don't love anybody!'"[147] She sharply questioned the message and the promises of Christianity, yet she also longed to have her faith restored. One strategy of the churches was to ignore the doubters. A bolder one acknowledged and addressed the difficulty of belief.

The sharpest critic of the prayers objected to Rauschenbusch's claim that Christianity has a social purpose. For this anonymous traditionalist reviewer, "the religion of Christ is spiritual and its appeal is to the individual soul and conscience of each human being."[148] The reviewer took exception to the idea of associating prayer with ordinary human needs, insisting that prayer should be limited to the realm of the divine only. This author also wrote that some of the prayers were very beautiful and found much to admire in the book. While conceding helpful insights and beauty in the prayers, however, the reviewer resisted combining the concepts of "Christianity" and "social."

With war looming Rauschenbusch composed "A Prayer for Peace" for the cover page of *The* [Baptist] *Watchman Examiner* for September 10, 1914.[149] Failing the achievement of peace, Rauschenbusch wrote "A Prayer in Time of War," opening with the impassioned plea, "O God, we call to thee out of the darkness."[150] The prayers had a lasting impact on readers. Early in 1918 Hamilton Holt, editor and publisher of *The Independent* Baptist paper, wrote to Rauschenbusch, "We have not had an article from you for a long time. I wonder if we could not have one of those little prayers or a little short prose poem that we could print in a box somewhere in *The Independent*?"[151] Positive responses to his prayers followed Rauschenbusch for the rest of his life, and following his death the editors of *The Watchman* published Rauschenbusch's "A Prayer for Friendship" beside his obituary.[152]

Reading Rauschenbusch's prayers brought awareness of the many needs for the welfare of an entire nation in all its diversity. Asked how he prepared the prayers, Rauschenbusch replied, "When travelling a railway train alone I used to meditate on the life problems of the people I saw. I then would shut out of my mind everything else but the needs of those people. I imagine that my prayers

---

[147] J. D. Stroops to WR, February 3, 1918, box 32, Rauschenbusch Family Papers.

[148] Anonymous, "New Books," *Rochester (N.Y.) Post Express*, December 9, 1910, box 94, Rauschenbusch Family Papers.

[149] WR, "A Prayer for Peace," *The Watchman Examiner*, September 10, 1914, box 40, Rauschenbusch Family Papers.

[150] WR, "A Prayer in Time of War," *Independent*, October 5, 1914, box 40, Rauschenbusch Family Papers.

[151] Hamilton Holt to WR, January 14, 1918, box 32, Rauschenbusch Family Papers.

[152] WR, "A Prayer for Friendship," *The Watchman*, March 16, 1919.

were the fruitage of a real mystical withdrawal into communion with God."[153] He articulated needs and hopes of many common people and pleaded with the powerful to act with Christian charity. Intercession has always been recognized as a major dimension of prayer. By writing this book, Rauschenbusch, the scholar with a pastor's heart, added the specific practice of intercession to his own spirituality. He took up the task in a very public way. He prayed for major groups in American society to come together to create a more just and more Christian society. He prayed for both physical and spiritual needs, and he expressed hope for a better future for the nation. Reading these prayers reveals Rauschenbusch's deep interest in the transformation of American society. His readers responded largely with gratitude.[154] A half-century later, pastor-scholar Carlyle Marney judged that Rauschenbusch "prays like few saints have prayed and with more effect than most."[155]

Hymns and *The Little Gate to God*

Rauschenbusch found lifelong spiritual strength and nurture from hymns of the church. In a note of instruction for his funeral Rauschenbusch wrote that three Pietist hymns had been especially dear to him and asked that they be sung at his service. He wrote that Paul Gerhardt's "Commit Your Way to God" "has been unspeakable comfort to me." This hymn expressed his faith in the guidance and mercy of God and sustained him "in darkness and loneliness."[156] Another favorite hymn was "I Worship the Power of Love" by Gerhard Tersteegen, who was a friend of his grandparents. Rauschenbusch wrote that this hymn "expressed the intimate feelings of my heart for Jesus, whose saving love has been everything to me."[157] The third hymn he recalled was Gabriel Voigtlaender's "Under the Lilies Comes Every Joy," a favorite of his grandmother and his father, "and I too have loved it."[158] Throughout his life Rauschenbusch expressed gratitude for the spiritual comfort and meaning that hymns of the church provided.[159]

In addition to the hymns of others Rauschenbusch occasionally condensed his own thoughts into poetic form. In 1918 during his terminal illness, he wrote

---

[153] Cited in William P. Lovett, "Church and Its Work," March 18 (no book, journal, or year given), box 39, Rauschenbusch Family Papers.

[154] Five years after publication it remained a "good seller" in New York bookshops. See Rufus Weeks to WR, December 29, 1914, box 26, Rauschenbusch Family Papers.

[155] Marney, "The Significance of Carlyle Marney for Today," 21.

[156] WR, "Instructions in case of my death," box 106, Rauschenbusch Family Papers.

[157] Ibid.

[158] Ibid.

[159] Rauschenbusch died during World War I. Pauline reported that anti-German sentiment was so intense that these favorite hymns could not be sung in German at the funeral (see Leuschner, "Walter Rauschenbusch and Our Day," 3).

a beautiful and moving poem, expressing his reflections on his relationship with God. This might well be the finest personal expression of spirituality he ever wrote:

The Little Gate to God
In the castle of my soul
Is a little postern gate.
Whereat, when I enter,
I am in the presence of God.
In a moment, in the turning of a thought,
I am where God is.
This is a fact.

This world of ours has length and breadth,
A superficial and horizontal world.
When I am with God
I look deep down and high up.
And all is changed.

The world of men is made of jangling noises.
With God it is a great silence.
But that silence is a melody
Sweet as the contentment of love.
Thrilling as a touch of flame.

In this world my days are few
And full of trouble.
I strive and have not;
I ask and learn not.
Its joys are so fleeting,
Its pains are so enduring,
I am in doubt if life be worth living.

When I enter into God,
All life has a meaning.
Without asking I know;
My desires are even now fulfilled,
My fever is gone
In the great quiet of God.
My troubles are but pebbles on the road,
My joys are like the everlasting hills,

So it is when I step through the gate of prayer
From time into eternity.

When I am in the consciousness of God,
My fellowmen are not far-off and forgotten,
But close and strangely dear.
Those whom I love
Have a mystic value.
They shine, as if a light were glowing within them.
Even those who frown on me
And love me not
Seem part of the great scheme of good.
(Or else they seem like stray bumble-bees
Buzzing at a window,
Heads the wrong way, yet seeking the light.)

So it is when my soul steps through the postern gate
Into the presence of God.
Big things become small, and small things become great.
The near becomes far, and the future is near.
The lowly and despised is shot through with glory,
And most of human power and greatness
Seems as full of infernal iniquities
As a carcass is full of maggots.
God is the substance of all revolutions;
When I am in him, I am in the Kingdom of God
And in the Fatherland of my Soul.

Is it strange that I love God?
And when I come back through the gate,
Do you wonder that I carry memories with me?
And my eyes are hot with unshed tears for what I see,
And I feel like a stranger and a homeless man
Where the poor are wasted for gain,
Where rivers run red,
And where God's sunlight is darkened by lies?[160]

[160] WR, "The Little Gate to God," typescript, box 40, Rauschenbusch Family Papers; also in Hudson, ed., *Walter Rauschenbusch: Selected Writings*, 46–48.

Rauschenbusch acknowledged that his days "on earth had been" few, painful, and full of trouble. Moreover, as he wrote these lines, he knew his days on earth were numbered. But when he entered the presence of God through the "gate of prayer" and was "where God is…all is changed." He concluded with the question, "Is it strange that I love God?" These lines reveal a sense of Rauschenbusch's intimate relationship with God. Appropriately, his daughter Winifred spoke of his mystical strain.[161] Even in this most private and personal moment of crisis Rauschenbusch could not forget those with whom he had lived and worked all his life. Coming back from God's presence through the postern gate of prayer made him "feel like a stranger and a homeless man" where he saw "the poor are wasted for gain" and "where rivers run red." His quest for justice for the poor had not been achieved in the United States, and now young men were dying on the devastating battlefields of World War I. Rauschenbusch was at once deeply spiritual but never forgetful of his solidarity with all others. Baptist historian Winthrop Hudson wrote that this moving poem "illumines the spiritual pilgrimage of Walter Rauschenbusch.… Nothing could express more beautifully, in the midst of personal pain…the solace he found in intimate communion with God."[162] His sense of the presence of God was the foundation for Rauschenbusch's other Christian work.

Rauschenbusch found cultivation of spirituality one of life's most important pursuits. He pointed students in this direction, and he drew personal strength from sentiments expressed in earlier spiritual writings, in Christian hymns, and from his own poetic reflection on entering the presence of God. In his hands the written prayer was a flexible tool that communicated specific needs of people across the nation he loved and he voiced their desires succinctly and eloquently. Rauschenbusch possessed an uncommon gift for putting himself in the place of others and articulating their yearnings. Rauschenbusch's prayers were used in private devotion and in public worship. His attention to devotion extended far beyond the formal weekly hour of the worship of God in churches. His spirituality included love for neighbors in their daily conditions of want, disease, despair, and guilt as well as their aspiration for growing sense of the presence of God. Rauschenbusch said prayer was the central religious act. In his little book of prayers he spoke of the individual's communing with God. He asked for forgiveness of his own failings. He addressed specific concerns of individual social groups—children, women, working men, ministers, businessmen—each with special needs. He gave thanks for much that had been achieved. In the final days of his life he imagined in poetry a personal encounter with God.

---

[161] Winifred [Rauschenbusch] Rorty to Dores Sharpe, December 17, 1938, box 50, Rauschenbusch Family Papers.

[162] Hudson, ed., *Walter Rauschenbusch: Selected Writings*, 44, 46.

Spiritual sensibilities remained at the center of Rauschenbusch's practice of Christianity. At the end of his life Rauschenbusch wrote, "Heart religion is always a cry in need," such as "prayer for a sick child, prayer to shake a morbid passion, prayer for forgiveness of an evil deed."[163] Earlier he had written, "a person without prayer lacks...something in the depths of his own consciousness."[164] He lamented that Christianity "came to mean largely creeds, rituals, rules, holy buildings and priests—a sort of religion at second hand with a reflected light and warmth. But in the first generation it came over men as a power direct from the unseen world."[165] Rauschenbusch is rightly linked to the notions of "the social gospel" and "the kingdom of God," and both are enormously important concepts in modern Christianity. But Rauschenbusch was not only an advocate for the social gospel. If Newton Flew's observation regarding spirituality is right, ideas of the social gospel and the kingdom of God are both ultimately grounded in something more basic—in spirituality, the experience of the sense of the divine. A closer look suggests that spirituality remained at the center of Rauschenbusch's life. The starting point and the core dimension of Rauschenbusch's Christianity was his spirituality.

Conclusion: Rauschenbusch's Legacy to Spirituality

From the time of his early pastorate to his last months, Rauschenbusch demonstrated in his writings the importance of an awareness of the presence of God. One of his favorite phrases was, "The Life of God in the soul of man." This brief line summarized for Rauschenbusch the heart of religion. When he began his pastorate, Rauschenbusch read classic texts of spirituality with Leighton Williams and Nathaniel Schmidt. When he spoke to young ministers, he implored them to "practice the presence of God" in prayer. His circle of influence in practicing prayer vastly increased when he published for lay people accessible prayers addressing their concerns directly to God. He also identified hymns that meant most to him. Rauschenbusch's own poetry imagines flight to the presence of God when everything is transformed: "When I am in him, I am in the Kingdom of God and in the Fatherland of my soul."[166] For most people Rauschenbusch's explosively revolutionary idea of a social gospel obscured other dimensions of his Christianity, yet at its core Rauschenbusch's faith was deeply rooted in his profound spirituality. Without that anchor he might have been a conscientious social reformer, but he believed that his devotion to God was the source of power that impelled him to seek a better world. He anchored his thought and life in a sense

---

163 WR, *A Theology for the Social Gospel*, 1997 ed., 17.
164 WR, "Thoughts on Prayer," 1.
165 WR, *Dare We Be Christians*, 11.
166 WR, "The Little Gate to God."

of the presence of God.

Protestant America is characterized by its energy and enterprise, which have produced massive numbers of conversions, impressive buildings, world-wide mission programs, and so forth. It is an activist form of Christianity, especially in its Baptist and Methodist expressions. A rich practice of spirituality is missing in much of Protestant life. As the importance of spirituality gains more traction and Protestants recover its history, they can look beyond the Puritans to figures like Rauschenbusch for direction.

It is ironic that Rauschenbusch is so well known for articulating the social gospel and so little known for the spirituality that produced it. It may be argued that spirituality is always present where there is vital faith. If so, it often remains latent. With Rauschenbusch spirituality is explicitly affirmed as the core of his faith. Spirituality is a legacy of Rauschenbusch yet to be fully recognized by his Protestant descendants.

CHAPTER 10

CHRISTIANIZING AMERICA: CHRISTIANITY AS ACTION

Rauschenbusch returned to Rochester in 1897 and spent the remainder of his life there. The city population in 1904 was 170,000, one-fourth of whom were foreign born. Low wages presented a serious problem for many. While the 14,157 engaged in trade and transport averaged a salary of $1004 per year, the 25,315 employed in manufacturing averaged only $498 per year for men and $267 for women.[1] By comparison, although Rauschenbusch began his ministry in New York City in 1886 at $600 per year, by the early 1900s his salary at Rochester Theological Seminary was $2500 to $3000. Low wages had serious social consequences. The 1900 census of Rochester reported that 29 percent of men and 28 percent of women between the ages of twenty-five and forty-four were unmarried. Also, an investigation committee blamed the practice of semi-professional prostitution (i.e. occasional) on the low wages of working girls.[2]

From the 1890s forward, a myriad of organizations formed to improve the Rochester community. Various churches sponsored Boys Clubs and Girls Clubs.[3] The Salvation Army and a rescue mission served the poor, and the Y.M.C.A. served the youth and the city. The churches worked together and established interfaith organizations.[4] A Labor Lyceum was created in 1896 for Sunday afternoon discussions of topics of interest to working people.[5] In 1908 Paul Moore Strayer organized The People's Sunday Evening (1908–1916), which focused on exploring religious topics.[6] Rauschenbusch provided leadership for both the Labor Lyceum and People's Sunday Evening. His involvement with these local organizations shows Rauschenbusch's desire to contribute personally to social reform in his home city.[7] In these difficult economic times speakers at these gatherings sometimes considered the merits and failures of both socialism and

---

[1] McKelvey, "Walter Rauschenbusch's Rochester," 12.
[2] Ibid., 13.
[3] Ibid., 5.
[4] Ibid., 8.
[5] Ibid., 6.
[6] Ibid., 18
[7] Ibid., 15.

capitalism. Rauschenbusch's proposal was to follow a third path—to serve as a spokesman for a Christian socialism. As McKelvey observed, Rauschenbusch was "ever ready to pit the spiritual power of the social gospel against the materialism of either capitalism or socialism."[8] Rauschenbusch was keenly aware of the economic difficulties of people in his city, and he was actively engaging in providing help for them. These experiences formed the backdrop for Rauschenbusch's motivation to write *Christianity and the Social Crisis* (1907) and *Christianizing the Social Order* (1912).

The United States in 1912

Rauschenbusch's broad vision of Christianity gave attention to multiple dimensions of the faith. His book of prayers focused on the ordinary needs of common people, but Rauschenbusch had a far more ambitious goal. Along with other outspoken leaders of his era, he looked outward from the church and envisioned the whole of America transformed into a Christianized society. If spirituality and prayer is one way of being Christian, another way of being Christian follows the path of action or applied Christianity. Rauschenbusch published his fullest proposals for redeeming the nation in *Christianizing the Social Order*. The nation was experiencing continued growth. The larger cities grew at especially accelerated rates. Rauschenbusch noted that the nation's population reached ninety million by 1910, and that industrialization had transformed the economy.[9] He believed that the church should recognize how society had changed and should adapt its message of hope and redemption accordingly. Heretofore the church had focused its attention primarily on personal redemption and personal morality. Now it was increasingly clear to Rauschenbusch that the sources of evil were systemic and institutional. Accordingly, he set himself the task of sorting out what he called the American "Semi-Christian Social Order."[10]

The American political system experienced profound changes over the course of the first two decades of the twentieth century. One of the most evident shifts was the new power assumed by the government to regulate big business and its willingness to do so. This shift was a major part of the agenda of the Progressive political party. The term "Progressive" came into use about 1910; in his book *The Progressive Movement* (1915), Benjamin P. DeWitt wrote, "the individual could not hope to compete.... Slowly Americans realized they were not free."[11] The problem was that economic power combined with political control left citizens feeling helpless.

---

[8] Ibid., 21.

[9] WR, *Christianizing the Social Order*, 286.

[10] Ibid., 123.

[11] DeWitt, *The Progressive Movement*, quoted in Foner, *Give Me Liberty*, 2:584.

The agenda of the Progressives included specific legislation to support workers' rights, including the forty-hour week, minimum wage, an end to child labor, suffrage for women, and public control of utilities. In addition to these economic goals, the Progressives sought to address widespread political corruption. If the abuses of the economic system were to be reformed, the nation would have to begin the reform with changes in the political structure. Only government legislation would be powerful enough to control economic structures. Historian Lewis Gould traces the roots of the Progressive movement to the 1890s and argues that "during the early months of 1905 the outlines of progressive politics in the United States began to take shape."[12] He says, moreover, that by 1914, "the public life of the United States had undergone changes that shaped the domestic agenda of the nation for the rest of the twentieth century."[13] Federal government intervened to shape economic policy. This mood of reform was the background for the dramatic presidential election of 1912, when four candidates ran for office—William Howard Taft, Theodore Roosevelt, Woodrow Wilson, and Eugene V. Debs. The more conservative Taft stressed traditional economic individualism. Debs, the Socialist Party candidate, recommended a radical overhaul of the economic system, but he attracted a relatively small following.[14] The real contest was between Wilson and Roosevelt. Both men believed government action was necessary. They represented competing strands of Progressivism.[15] Wilson won the election, and government was in position to advance reform. In Rauschenbusch's view, this was a notable year in the American experience. His summary recalls numerous political demands articulated during this era:

> The entire upheaval in the political alignment of 1912, the demand for direct primaries, for direct legislation, for the recall of judges, for the popular election of senators, are an expression of the profound and durable conviction of the nation…that our whole political organization, as it stood ten years ago, had been turned into an instrument to victimize the people on behalf of private interests.[16]

What reformers sought in 1912 was legislation that would set limits on the power of the rich and powerful. Progressives proposed systemic changes that were simply too vast to be addressed by entities smaller than the federal government. Political Progressives supported these systemic reforms as did Walter Rauschenbusch. He called on the church to join this effort, to be the conscience of the well-being of the nation.

In 1912, the same year that the nation voted for a program of significant

[12] Gould, *America in the Progressive Era, 1890–1914*, 37.

[13] Ibid., ix.

[14] Foner, *Give Me Liberty*, 2:616.

[15] Ibid.

[16] WR, *Christianizing the Social Order*, 282.

political reform, Rauschenbusch published his fullest analysis of American society. His title, *Christianizing the Social Order*, reflected his deeply held hope for the nation. Already in *Christianity and the Social Crisis* he had issued his manifesto articulating and defending the idea that Christianity in its original form was both individual and social. Rauschenbusch had presented the church with a clear challenge. In *Christianizing the Social Order*, he turned to more specific guidelines for creating a more just society. He supported reform efforts of the press and the government. However, he spoke from the perspective of religious conviction and sought to enlist religious motivation and arguments for building a more Christian social order. He believed that when the Gospel writers articulated Jesus' message of the kingdom of God, they believed that Jesus envisioned a new society. Rauschenbusch thought the church should build on this insight and offer support for reform, and he therefore made his proposals with conviction. Because of the convergence of the nation's voting for political reform proposed by the Progressives and the publication and wide reception of Rauschenbusch's ideas in *Christianizing the Social Order*, 1912 is often seen as the high point in the history of the social gospel.[17]

Origin of *Christianizing the Social Order* (1912)

Christianizing the Social Order had its origin in two university lectureships. Following publication of *Christianity and the Social Crisis*, many organizations invited Rauschenbusch to give lectures, and he met a number of these requests, including those from universities. The lectures served as the nucleus of *Christianizing the Social Order*. Herbert Welch, president of Ohio Wesleyan University, invited Rauschenbusch in mid-1910 to give the Merrick Lectures. He wrote, "We feel sure that you must by this time have written another message ready for utterance."[18] Rauschenbusch thanked Welch and proposed using the materials he had used for the Earl Lectures in Berkeley in April 1910.[19] He wrote, "It would probably be as mature and effective as anything which I could give in that field at present." He summarized the theme of his work: "The main thought was that by turning its forces toward the task of Christianizing social life and institutions Christianity is entering a new epoch of its history. Christians who have added the social enthusiasm to the total of their religious aims and motives, constitute a new

[17] See, for example, Handy, *The Social Gospel in America*, 11.

[18] Herbert Welch to WR, June 25, 1910, box 25, Rauschenbusch Family Papers. An extended exchange of letters documents the process of negotiation leading to the publication of *Christianizing the Social Order.*

[19] The Berkeley Lectures were given the year before Rauschenbusch by the English historian Ambassador Lord James Bryce, author of *The Holy Roman Empire* (1871), and the year after by former president Theodore Roosevelt (see "As Lectures Fill Many Engagements Professor Rauschenbusch Not Able to Meet All Demands").

type of Christian character."[20] Rauschenbusch thought in terms of a new era for Christianity. His task was to map proposals for this new phase in the history of Christianity. He offered a description for the six lectures—a study of the relation between "the Church" and the "kingdom of God," reprising a familiar theme:

> Christianity began with the hope of proclamation of the Kingdom; in a short time that central thought of the Gospel was almost completely displaced, distorted or forgotten, and the church filled the horizons of Christian Theology and of practical work. In modern times that process is being reversed. The conception of the Kingdom has been rediscovered, is beginning to dominate all the new movement in Christianity...and it is in the great process of Christianizing Christianity.[21]

In fascinating follow-up correspondence, Rauschenbusch and Welch negotiated the terms of publication and royalties. Rauschenbusch was skeptical of a three-way arrangement with a publisher and the university and explained that if the book had sales anything like *Christianity and the Social Crisis*, the royalties for one year would repay the university all it had paid to Rauschenbusch, and all sales thereafter should be clear profit for him. Ever the campaigner for justice, including for his own personal financial position, Rauschenbusch wrote acerbically to the university president, "I really do not think the University should be placed in the position of exploiting its lecturers."[22] Welch replied to Rauschenbusch's candid letter, assuring him that things could be worked out. They negotiated a suitable arrangement and proceeded with the publication process.[23] In January 1911, Rauschenbusch wrote the publisher, "If you have not yet printed the title..., I should like it changed to "Christianizing the Social Order."[24] He was delayed in finishing the re-writing of his lectures for publication but wrote in July 1912 that "the work is now going on well and my hope is that I shall have the MS completed by the end of August—God willing."[25] In November he wrote to Welch with relief, "'Christianizing the Social Order' is out—at last. I have just received the first advance copy a moment ago. It has taken almost as long as Kingdom Come, and I fear you have become impatient."[26] Rauschenbusch reported that in the first four months about 8000 copies of the book were sold at $1.50 each.[27]

---

[20] WR to Herbert Welch, July 2, 1910, box 25, Rauschenbusch Family Papers.

[21] Ibid.

[22] WR to Herbert Welch, August 10, 1910, in box 25, Rauschenbusch Family Papers.

[23] Herbert Welch to WR, October 17, 1910; WR to Welch, November 7, 1910; Welch to WR, November 8, 1910, box 25, Rauschenbusch Family Papers.

[24] WR to Welch, January 30, 1911, box 25, Rauschenbusch Family Papers.

[25] WR to Welch, July 13, 1912, box 25, Rauschenbusch Family Papers.

[26] WR to Welch, November 21, 1912, box 25, Rauschenbusch Family Papers.

[27] WR to R. Hirase, July 2, 1915, regarding translation of the volume into Japanese

Structure of the Book

In the foreword to *Christianizing the Social Order* Rauschenbusch described the background for writing the book. He declared that when he published *Christianity and the Social Crisis* he thought that he had said all he had to say on the American social problems "so I went to Europe for a year and devoted myself to...historical studies."[28] However, when he came home, he found that the "social awakening of our nation" had set in like a storm.[29] The book had won wide popular support, and people wanted Rauschenbusch to continue his interpretation of Christianity. Rauschenbusch reflected,

> Naturally my mind worked on problems which had been raised in my book, but had not really been taken in hand there. I had urged a moral reorganization of social institutions, a Christianizing of public morality. Men asked: What must we do? And what must we undo? What social ideal should guide us? What methods can we safely use in realizing it?... Without the...stimulus of others this book would never have been written.[30]

When criticized for essentially publishing much the same book again, Rauschenbusch denied the charge and sharply challenged his critic, saying he had done the hard work of writing the book.[31] The reviewer was right that both books address social problems from the Christian standpoint. However, Rauschenbusch argued that whereas the first book was a call to action, the second gave more attention to analysis of specific topics. Sometimes Rauschenbusch addressed problems by citing current sociological research. More often he was interested in offering moral analysis of society and guidelines for Christianizing it, seeking to answer questions such as "What makes a Christian society? Where have we gone wrong and why? How can we have such good intentions and still produce evil? How can we change this situation?"[32] Rauschenbusch noted that few church members themselves realized the importance of what was occurring in their churches. In order to address social and economic issues in a substantial way, Rauschenbusch wrote his longest book, which extends to 493 pages. He concluded his introductory remarks with his statement that the book's "purpose is not denunciation. It is wholly constructive.... My sole desire has been to summon the Christian passion for justice and the Christian power of love and mercy to do their share in redeeming our social order from its inherent wrong."[33]

In the early pages of his book Rauschenbusch reported on the current status

---

[28] WR, *Christianizing the Social Order*, vii.
[29] Ibid., vii.
[30] Ibid.
[31] WR to Francis Peabody, December 14, 1912, box 26, Rauschenbusch Family Papers.
[32] WR, *Christianizing the Social Order*, viii.
[33] Ibid., ix–x.

of the nation and its churches. He celebrated especially the fact that the numerous denominations affiliated with the Federal Council of Churches (1908) had recently embraced a social service document declaring that they "deem it the duty of all Christian people to concern themselves directly with certain practical industrial problems."[34] The declaration enumerates many specifics, including support for "equal rights and complete justice for all," regulations protecting all workers with reasonable hours of work and a living wage, and reducing poverty in the nation.[35] Adoption of the document by the FCC meant that the social gospel was not limited to a professor's ivory tower proposal. Implementing a social dimension of the gospel would now be adopted as part of the structural agenda of many churches. Conscious adoption by American churches of a social responsibility would be a new step for organized Christianity in the nation. If the Progressive movement created a legacy throughout the twentieth century, so did the social gospel.

Christianized America

Rauschenbusch's proposal was far-reaching: he wanted to see the entire United States become more Christian. Interestingly, he contended that "large domains of our social life have come under the sway of Christian law in the spirit and in their fundamental structure...[but there are] portions of the social order which are still unchristianized."[36] He judged American society to be neither fully Christianized nor fully unchristian. He described the status of current American society as "semi-Christian."[37] Some sectors (or "orders" in his language) had made great strides forward and could be labelled semi-Christian.

In defining what he meant by "Christianizing" Rauschenbusch assured readers that he did "not mean putting the name of Christ into the Constitution...that would only be one more act of national hypocrisy."[38] Nor did he mean any sort of theocracy that would make Christian belief and worship compulsory.[39] That would violate his strong defense of the Baptist tradition of religious freedom guaranteed by separation of church and state. Rauschenbusch had long before written, "Keep them Separate."[40] He did not want the state ever to violate conscience by imposing religion on people. On the other hand, he did not want to separate

---

[34] Ibid., 14–15.
[35] Ibid.
[36] Ibid, 123.
[37] Ibid.
[38] Ibid., 124.
[39] Ibid.
[40] WR, "Keep them Separate," 3.

religion from culture: he hoped Christian values could permeate and reshape society. For Rauschenbusch Christianizing the social order meant "bringing it into harmony with the ethical convictions which we identify with Christianity."[41]

He observed, "An unchristian social order can be known by the fact that it makes good men do bad things. It tempts, defeats, drains, and degrades, and leaves men stunted, cowed, and shamed in manhood."[42] On the other hand, "A Christian social order makes bad men do good things. It sets high aims, steadies the vagrant impulses of the weak, trains the powers of the young and...leaves people with the consciousness of a broader and nobler humanity as the years go on."[43]

In introducing his discussion of the social order Rauschenbusch draws attention to both spirit and structure. Rauschenbusch claimed that several key institutions of American society—family, church, education, and politics—had already become Christianized. This rhetorical strategy produced one of the more memorable dimensions of his book. Critics found this aspect of the book an easy target since Rauschenbusch is so openly optimistic about the level of Christianization achieved in American society by 1912. He contrasts the ancient patriarchal structure with the modern family in Western society. In the former the father exercised despotic power to the detriment of other family members, and he cites the examples of Abraham, Jacob and David, all major figures in the Hebrew Scriptures. But these biblical figures also had disastrous family relations, which Rauschenbusch traces to patriarchal social structures and practices. Roman life was also patriarchal, but during the Empire Christianity introduced a new pattern of family life. He argues that the institution of the family passed through an ethical transformation under Christian tutelage whereby women were accorded more personal rights. Rauschenbusch's argument is that by becoming more democratic, the Christian family has transformed the nature of family; moreover, the structure will be perpetuated because "every Christianized family leaves tradition in the hearts of its children...[and] by such precedents public opinion and custom are formed."[44] He believes that the influence of structures could go either way—toward promoting habitual wrong or habitual right. Rauschenbusch makes his historical arguments in broad strokes. His criterion for Christianization is the growth of democracy, giving voice to the rights of wives and children as well as to fathers. For him democracy is a key expression of the spirit of Christ.

Second, Rauschenbusch traces a similar history for the church, which has

---

[41] WR, *Christianizing the Social Order*, 125.
[42] Ibid., 127.
[43] Ibid.
[44] Ibid., 135.

not always been "Christianized." For example, during the early modern era monarchs and aristocrats ruled the church and used its resources to enrich themselves; they coerced belief and extorted tithes—in short, they degraded the church.[45] Rauschenbusch contrasts the pre-Reformation era with current conditions of the church in the United States, where the assumption is that ministry is an honorable profession of people who seek to serve. He says that in the United States the church offers salvation freely to all; most churches have a democratic structure where authority and governance are shared, and the people voluntarily offer financial support to sustain the churches. In Rauschenbusch's view, all of this means that the church in modern America has become a Christian institution. He concludes that the church, like the family, was Christianized when it abandoned despotism and exploitation and came under the law of service.[46] Here again the criteria of democratization and service are critical for Rauschenbusch.

The third institution that comes under Rauschenbusch's favorable review is education. He describes inequities of the past when education was reserved as a privilege for aristocratic society and when Negro education was prohibited. In Rauschenbusch's telling of the history, these inequities have given way to a more democratic education in public schools in the United States where the financial support for the public-school system is derived from taxation. Under this system the entire community is taxed, and all citizens may benefit from access to education. This was the theory of public education. Rauschenbusch was not concerned with describing actual practices of education in the United States. Had he done so, he would have found much evidence of discrimination and inequity towards women, the blacks, and the poor, as his modern critics have noted. Rauschenbusch was making an argument that the American system, unlike European education, was inclusive in theory and intent.

As he develops his argument, Rauschenbusch's criteria for Christianizing in all of these institutions emerges—a service orientation, a democratic spirit, and a structural/legal change that guarantees the opportunity of broad participation by most citizens of the nation in family, church, and school. Rauschenbusch writes that while democracy is not the same as Christianity, he firmly insists that Christianity supports equality for all. When democracy undermines hierarchy and social class divisions, new opportunities open to all.

Fourth, Rauschenbusch claims that even the political sphere has been Christianized. He recognizes that "to Americans this may seem a staggering assertion, for of all corrupt things surely our politics is the corruptest."[47] Rauschenbusch asserts that "the fundamental redemption of the State took place when special

[45] Ibid., 137.
[46] Ibid., 141.
[47] Ibid., 147

privilege was thrust out of the constitution and the theory of national government; privilege was replaced in principle by personal liberty and equal rights."[48] So, for Rauschenbusch the U.S. Constitution, based on principles of freedom, justice, and democracy is what legitimized the American system of government and qualified it as having been "Christianized"—potentially, at least. He conceded that in practice it still had a long way to go to fulfill its promises. Rauschenbusch found further evidence of the righteousness of the political system in that the judicial system was based on the assumption that rich and poor alike have justice meted out to them: "it is felt to be an outrage and a betrayal of the spirit of our institutions" if the courts fail to uphold this principle.[49] He reminds readers that this was affirmed by the U.S. Constitution.

Rauschenbusch did not whitewash harsh and unjust American political realities; he wasn't naïve. The actual practice of politics in the United States did not match the ideals of the Constitution. In fact, American political life was full of corruption. He wrote,

> The rich and the poor are not equal before our Constitution. The real decisions in politics are made by small cliques, and except in seasons of popular revolt the votes of great numbers of citizens count for almost nothing. In actual practice the administration of public affairs is full of favoritism to the powerful, and even more full of damnable neglect for those things which are vital to the common people.[50]

But he sustains his argument by calling all of these practices "derailments" of justice. In his imagery "the railroad bed and the trackage are still there, even when the train is ditched."[51] The critical point of his argument is that the fundamental law in the Constitution supports human rights of liberty and justice for all. Rauschenbusch argues that in spite of its failings, the American political system is based on equity. Again, in practice he was blind to political rights of women and African Americans, but he argued that political life is structured for the common good of all. By contrast, political life in Germany was still stratified into class divisions and privilege. He thus defends political democracy when assessing the institutions of American life.

On the surface Rauschenbusch's claim that the American political sphere had been Christianized seems ridiculous because of widespread evidence of political corruption during his era—and he constantly writes against political injustices—yet here he wants to affirm his faith in the ideal of democracy. Rauschenbusch thus concludes that four great sectors of the American social order—family,

---

[48] Ibid., 148.

[49] Ibid.

[50] Ibid., 151.

[51] Ibid.

church, education, and political organization—have passed through systemic institutional changes that have made them to some degree semi-Christian. He writes that this analysis should create "immense hopefulness...the larger part of the work of Christianizing our social order is already accomplished."[52] Christianity has already achieved much of its social task.

Rauschenbusch has often been ridiculed for excessive optimism, and this is the passage usually cited. However, subverting the claim that his optimism is naïve at best or at its worst delusional, he offered reservations and disavowals. His critics have tended to ignore that all of his claims are conditional. Families must work at cooperation; few achieve their potential of living for each other. Likewise, the churches have failed to serve others and instead are often self-serving. Public education was just now reaching large numbers and was experiencing problems as well. Rauschenbusch often cited examples of political failure in other writings. What he sought to do here was not to claim full Christianization, but to indicate that the structures of all of these social orders now rested on democratic principles. These four institutions were only semi-Christian, but they were not plagued with systemic injustice that appears in societies with constitutions that privilege selected individuals or social classes. European immigrants were still arriving in record numbers. They believed life would be better in the United States.

Rauschenbusch was clearly hopeful. His positive evaluation of four key orders made his next step all the more memorable. He moved in the next part of the book to develop his claims for the non-Christian character of the American economic system. Purposely overdrawing the contrasts of two models in society, Rauschenbusch set up an effective rhetorical strategy, affirming the Christianization of virtually all of American life with only one great exception. What he does find wrong is the U.S. economic structure.

The Unredeemed Economic Order

Rauschenbusch devoted two-thirds of this book to the American economic system. He analyzed its structure, critiqued its failings, and offered alternative paths for "Christianizing" this dimension of the social order. His writing was bold and direct. By the time of this writing he had lived half a century. He had benefited from his professional life in the United States and was appropriately grateful. But conscience would not let him ignore the suffering of fellow Americans—especially workers in the urban industrial economy.

Rauschenbusch begins with the assumption that the nation's "business life is the seat and the source of our present troubles.... It is in commerce and industry that we encounter the great collective inhumanities that shame our Christian feeling such as child labor and the bloody total of industrial accidents.. and the

[52] Ibid., 155.

source of sex prostitution, poverty, and political corruption."[53] His approach is pragmatic. He wrote, "Just as an experience of typhoid fever would call for analysis of the water supply, so these chronic conditions call for a moral analysis of the economic order and justify the presumption that it is fundamentally unchristian. In discussing the American economy, Rauschenbusch's tone clearly shifts from optimistically and cheerfully upbeat to searchingly critical. He observes that the economic system is not understood by lay people in the Christian churches or by their leaders. Rauschenbusch's central task in this book is to explain the system and to demonstrate its social failings. As he puts it, "The church should make a moral analysis...of the relationship of economic life to labor laws and values of humanity."[54]

Rauschenbusch's major goal was to Christianize the American economy. Through personal observation and extensive reading, he appeared well informed on his topic.[55] He frequently cited government studies of the American economy and its workers. In addition, he was thoroughly versed in social theory. Added to his research was his on-site observation of social structures in Britain and Germany, which provided important sources of national comparisons in his book.

Rauschenbusch continued to study and write about Christianity and social issues with energy and urgency. In the last year of his life Rauschenbusch published "Justice and Brotherhood," a study of the history of labor. He read the paper to the Council of Women for Home Missions, who had decided their members would study the conditions of labor. This text admirably enhances his arguments in *Christianizing the Social Order* and is employed in this analysis.[56]

Rauschenbusch was struck by the contrasts between the traditional economy of his boyhood in the 1870s and the economy of 1912. As a youth, he had enjoyed summer work on a farm near Williamsport, Pennsylvania, and had also observed the work of a master tailor while living in Altena, Germany. He described these economies as self-sufficient and self-sustaining and designated them "pre-capitalist." By contrast, industry in America had built large factories, streamlined organization of people, and employed steam power to run engines. All of this had

---

[53] Ibid., 156.

[54] Ibid., 158.

[55] Rauschenbusch said that he was not an expert in the field of economics, yet by 1912 he had read extensively in the fields of economics and sociology. In an unpublished and undated list of readings, he cites seventeen volumes on sociology, six on economics, and eight novels devoted to reform themes. See Rauschenbusch's unpublished "The Social Aspects of Christianity," box 90, Rauschenbusch Family Papers.

[56] WR, "Justice and Brotherhood," 165–87. I cite this text in the following pages as well as *Christianizing the Social Order*.

created hitherto undreamed levels of production, and he saluted this great technical achievement.[57] But his moral objection was that the system of ownership and control had concentrated power in the hands of a few who exercised too much power over their fellow men.

Rauschenbusch identifies three stages in the history of economics—from pre-capitalist to capitalist to what he hopes will emerge as the collectivist pattern. He notes that each stage is different in ethical spirit and philosophy of life: whereas cooperation generates good will and solidarity, competition produces selfishness and jealousy. He reports with optimism current evidence of an emerging cooperative spirit, indicating that Western society may well be on the cusp of accepting the third (collectivist) model of economics. Rauschenbusch is keenly aware of the risks of using the term "socialism" because, in its most radical form, it was associated with violence, sexual libertinism, and atheism, all of which went against prevailing social norms[58] He, of course, rejects these more radical dimensions of the movement, but he accepts the basic economic goal of socialism, which seeks to benefit all members of society.[59] Since Christianity has contributed much to moral life in America culture, and socialism seeks the well-being of the entire society, he contends that socialism and Christianity should be allies and not opponents in the quest for bringing in the kingdom of God.[60] But the progress of an economic cooperative spirit was very slow.

Capitalism was ascendant in 1912. Rauschenbusch said that capitalism had created two classes, employers and wage earners, who were each dependent on the other, but their interests were opposed to each other.[61] He believed that the moral problem for the age was that the capitalist exercised "all power" over the workers.[62] Whereas the nation had checks and balances written into the political system, there were none for economic power exercised over others, which, according to Rauschenbusch, undermined our humanity.[63] He noted that the power of the corporation was the reason for numerous labor strikes that were in progress while he was writing in 1911.[64] He was fully conversant with the dynamics of American economics and included analyses of labor disputes and reasons for

---

[57] WR, *Christianizing the Social Order*, 162.

[58] For discussion of the many dimensions of socialism, see Zinn, "The Socialist Challenge" in *A People's History of the United States*, 321–57, esp. 321, 331, and 334. Rauschenbusch directly rejects what he calls the "cruder type of socialism," which is skeptical of Christian belief and Christian moral teaching (see WR, *Christianizing the Social Order*, 397).

[59] WR, *Christianizing the Social Order*, 395–97.

[60] Ibid., 398–99.

[61] Ibid., 180; also WR, "Justice and Brotherhood," 178.

[62] WR, *Christianizing the Social Order*, 180.

[63] Ibid., 181.

[64] Ibid., 184–90.

them. He pointed out, for example, that some men worked seven days per week and others had to take twelve-hour shifts. He observed sympathetically that, at $10 per week, workers could barely pay their bills.[65] Rauschenbusch thought workers had shown restraint in their actions because they were slow to violence and orderly in their protest.[66] The problem was not only the exploitation of labor; there was the deeper spiritual/psychological question of human dignity. In Rauschenbusch's language, underlying the material demand was "the spiritual demand for a fuller and freer manhood."[67] Whereas workers experienced a sense of equality in many aspects of their lives, this did not hold for industrial relations: "they have tasted democracy and are not content with any relation that denies it to them."[68] The nation needed economic democracy.

The Churches and the Economy

The underlying problem for American society was its obsession with money. Rauschenbusch concluded that American society is committed to profit above everything else; this goal undermined both the workers' security and also the morality of the businessman. Rauschenbusch recalled from his years as a pastor a young man who told him he would not choose to become a Christian because as a salesman he was instructed to misrepresent his product. He told Rauschenbusch flatly, "I have to lie too much."[69] In Rauschenbusch's view, obsession with profit had subverted Christian morality in the nation.

Rauschenbusch thought that the churches should be more aware: if profit is "so much the dominant force in our economic life and social order, it is of highest importance that every religious teacher and leader understand the moral nature of Profit."[70] In the existing system employers alone provided what was most important to workers—a job and a living. They were therefore the most powerful group in any industrial community.[71] Rauschenbusch demonstrated how business controlled natural resources, property and rent, transportation, and banking—all economic products essential for life. For Rauschenbusch, it was immoral to support a system that produces unearned profit or charged more than something is worth. He noted that for the sake of profit 15,000 persons were killed annually in accidents, and 31.4 percent of girls working in the Pennsylvania silk weaving

---

[65] Ibid. Rauschenbusch had researched his topic in publications of the U.S. Bureau of Labor and Social Services Commission, cited on p. 187 and elsewhere in the book.

[66] Ibid., 191–92.

[67] Ibid., 194.

[68] Ibid., 195.

[69] Ibid., 212–13.

[70] Ibid., 223.

[71] Ibid., 227–28.

industry were paid under $2.00 per week.[72] Greed was the villain. Workers were at the mercy of employers; they had to accept low wages because they had to have some income to eat, but they had no guarantees of work and no security. Offering his ethical critique of capitalism, Rauschenbusch wrote, "Business as now conducted, has an interest in raising the value of things and keeping down the value of men. That makes property an enemy of life instead of its support."[73] From Rauschenbusch's perspective, "wherever life is held precious…there the law of Christ prevails. But in our economic system life is held cheap and wasted needlessly. The profit of the few has turned against the life of the many. God's reign will not come until the profit of all shall support the life of all."[74] Rauschenbusch is following the criteria of the greatest good for all. In his mind, the religious belief in the value of every person would be best supported by the growth of democracy, giving everyone a voice in society. Here, three ideas converge for Rauschenbusch: Christianity teaches the ultimate value of every soul, Socialism sees this for all people, and democracy is the path forward for participation by all.

Rauschenbusch also drew on Scripture to support his argument. In a pithy summary he wrote, "To set Things above Men is the really dangerous practical materialism. To set Mammon before God is the only idolatry on which Jesus warned us."[75] Rauschenbusch believed that materialism had become the highest American value. He described the divided hearts of American Christians: "When we try to keep both [Christ and Mammon] enthroned at the same time in different sectors of our life, we do what Christ says cannot be done…." He would never join the ministers who declared that capitalism was a Christian system of economics.

Criteria for Christianizing the Nation

Rauschenbusch raised the question of the direction that the church and the nation needed to take—to provide some constructive possibilities. He recognized that institutions change slowly; meanwhile, "we need a plan."[76] The starting point for Rauschenbusch was the criterion of justice: "The simplest and most fundamental quality needed in moral relations of men is justice."[77] In his view, justice was inherent in humanity: "We have a divine instinct for righteousness within us as a guide."[78] Rauschenbusch said that thus far we had justice only in theory in

---

[72] Ibid., 242–44.
[73] Ibid., 246.
[74] Ibid., 151.
[75] Ibid., 315.
[76] Ibid., 328, 331.
[77] Ibid., 332.
[78] Ibid., 326.

the United States, and society must begin by removing unjust privileges; he wrote that "logically this would be the first step; ethically it is the most important step; practically it is usually the last and hardest."[79] It was clear to him that change would have to come through legislation. the church should put its weight behind reforms so often called for by progressives.

Another criterion for Rauschenbusch in evaluating the economic system was the extent of freedom in society. Citing Jesus' declaration that he had come to set free the captive (Luke 4), he said that the spirit of Jesus made for freedom, and Christianity must necessarily be on the side of freedom.[80] The freedom Rauschenbusch sought was primarily economic. In the United States men had the vote, but this political democracy without economic democracy he described as "an unwashed promissory note, a pot without roast, a form without substance."[81] The possessing classes had managed to control the governing classes; hence the Progressives call for change in the political process.[82] He declared that the Christian religion had been "the strongest force in asserting the essential equality of all souls before God."[83] Rauschenbusch believed in forging a strong bond between Christianity and democracy. He affirmed that "democracy had become a spiritual hope and a religious force."[84] He believed that by working together Christianity and democracy would take the country in the direction of the reign of God.

A year before he published *Christianizing the Social Order* Rauschenbusch wrote, "One of the first ideals of American life has been democracy."[85] He directly combined religious and national values, writing, "Our democracy...is an essential part of our Christian and our American ideals.... In its teachings, too, the church should inculcate democracy as a distinctly Christian value."[86] At the end of his life Rauschenbusch wrote, "The American ideals of democracy have dominated my intellectual life. My literary and professional life for years has been characterized by the consistent effort to work and demonstrate interpretations of history, religion and social life."[87]

A third criterion for reforming the economic system was the ideal of fraternity. Rauschenbusch contrasted capitalism's competition with Paul's understanding of the church as an organism where the parts cannot work against one another and expect a healthy operation of the whole. Although it would be a "monumental

[79] Ibid., 337.
[80] Ibid., 352.
[81] Ibid., 353.
[82] Ibid., 355–362.
[83] Ibid., 363.
[84] Ibid.
[85] WR, "The Church and Social Questions," 105.
[86] Ibid., 107.
[87] WR, "A Valedictory Message: A Letter of Walter Rauschenbusch," 1409.

task," Rauschenbusch envisioned that a great cooperative system would eventually replace capitalism. Cooperation must prevail in the economic order if the kingdom of God were ever to come. The laws of the kingdom of God on earth include justice, collective property rights, democracy, human equality, and cooperation.[88] Rauschenbusch's criteria were not new. They appear to be inspired by the motto of the French Revolution: liberty, equality, and fraternity.[89] Rauschenbusch said that these ideas were constants in the moral universe, but they required implementation. In arguing for these criteria as Christian, Rauschenbusch merged political theory with liberal Protestant values for economic reform. This is not the only way to understand Christianization in the kingdom of God, but it was his, and it was a bold step of imagination and analysis. What is the church's responsibility to society, and how is it to be assessed?

The Way Forward

In the final part of his book Rauschenbusch suggests "methods of advance" in Christianizing the social order. Moving to the practical question of how to proceed, he proposes "to explain spiritual methods to bring about fundamental regeneration of the social order."[90] Rauschenbusch often acknowledged that the pace of reform was slow, but since the current mood was more progressive, people should take advantage of the present opportunity and act quickly.[91]

In this long book Rauschenbusch provides an extensive list of changes he hopes to see in American society: access by all to public schools, parks, playgrounds, markets, baths, libraries and hospitals, which lift the spirits and enhance the lives of everyone. But these amenities do not represent substantial economic reforms. Rauschenbusch repeatedly advocated an end to monopolies of services required in daily life—"railways, surface lines, elevated roads, subways, waterways, telegraph and telephone systems, gas and electric lights and power systems"—these were the irreducible minimum that needed to come under public ownership. He calls these "natural monopolies" and concludes that "competition in their case is economic nonsense."[92] He envisioned a nation Christianized by moving away from corporate capitalism to a collective economy, measured by the welfare of all citizens, and putting life's necessities within the reach of all.[93]

When he spoke to the Women's Home Mission group, Rauschenbusch was

---

[88] WR, *Christianizing the Social Order*, 372–73, 383.

[89] Rauschenbusch appealed to these same themes in calling his Baptist denomination to declaring "the task of the church is to Christianize the organized community life" (see WR, "American Christianity and National Life," 303–305).

[90] Ibid., 406.

[91] Ibid., 407, 410.

[92] Ibid., 435.

[93] Ibid., 451–53.

direct about the failures of the church. The chief charge against the church, he said, was "not positive wrong doing but inaction."[94] How, he asked, can Christian ministers "stand the scrutiny of God's justice if those who toil, have not, and those who toil not, have?"[95] Working people largely dropped out of the churches in the 1880s, he said.[96] So who comes to church? Teachers, clerks, and stenographers, but the church had lost the workers.[97] Again he pointed to the two great classes created by the modern economic system and asked where the churches had lined up. The answer generally had been with the propertied class; hence the loss of the workers.[98] As he declared to the women keen to support missions: "We have not won the world for Christ if this great class is alienated from the Christian religion.[99]

Christianizing the Social Order is a sustained and repetitious analysis and critique of the American economic system. Rauschenbusch gave the system such intense attention because he considered it to be the chief obstacle to bringing the kingdom near in American life. But the book is much more than an economic analysis. Declaring that his study is "a religious book from beginning to end," he concludes his exhaustive study with a direct appeal to the church.[100] His argument is that the church must come out of its spiritual isolation; it has ignored the existence of prostitution, child labor, and tenement crowding. The church itself needs salvation, which will come about only "by finding the purpose of its existence outside of itself, in the Kingdom of God, the perfect life of the race."[101] Rauschenbusch was convinced that the church, like the larger society, has also been corrupted by its quest for privileges and gain. He implores the church to change because "to concentrate on personal salvation as orthodoxy has done, or on soul culture, as liberalism has done, comes close to refined selfishness."[102] In his view both "orthodox" and "liberal" interpreters fail because they thought the Christian message was directed only to individuals for their personal benefit. The church must instead think in terms of the good of all. Only in this way will it find the path toward the kingdom of God.

Sydney Ahlstrom wrote that Rauschenbusch's interpretation of Jesus' message of love of God and humanity translates into ethical conduct, which is the

---

[94] WR, "Justice and Brotherhood," 183.
[95] Ibid., 181.
[96] Ibid., 183.
[97] Ibid., 184.
[98] Ibid., 180–84.
[99] Ibid., 176.
[100] WR, *Christianizing the Social Order*, 458.
[101] Ibid., 464.
[102] Ibid., 464–65.

supreme and sufficient religious act.[103] Rauschenbusch wrote,

> It is not this thing or that thing our nation needs, but a new mind and heart, a new conception of the way we ought to live together, a new conviction about the worth of human life and the use God wants us to make of our own lives. We want a renovation both inside and outside. We want a moral reservation of public opinion and a revival of religion.[104]

In this book he reiterated his view that the nature of religion is located in service. Claude Welch contends that Rauschenbusch's creativity centered on his emphasis on the idea of solidarity. He held that the kingdom of God is social, and so is evil. In Welch's view this was a new idea: Rauschenbusch "injected the new principle of a critical relation to social structures."[105] Rauschenbusch offered a new basis for understanding and implementing Christianity.

The book sold well, and Rauschenbusch was optimistic about prospects for the nation in 1912. Before exploring reception of the volume, a brief diversion is in order to notice two very small books Rauschenbusch published during this era.

The Bible and the Social Gospel

Protestant reform movements in the church's history almost invariably search the Bible to find scriptural support for justifying their fresh interpretation of Christianity. Rauschenbusch produced two very brief books, anchoring his social understanding of Christianity directly to Scripture. Both support the message he developed at length in *Christianizing the Social Order*. *Unto Me* is derived from Jesus' teaching in the gospel and explores the question, "What Is Christianity?"[106] The second book, *Dare We Be Christians?,* which also identifies the essence of Christianity, is derived from Paul's writing.[107] Rauschenbusch had no doubt that social Christianity was biblical, and in these brief studies he attempts to persuade readers of the biblical character of the social gospel.

Rauschenbusch published *Unto Me* in October 1912. The title of this little book refers to Jesus' famous teaching in Matthew 25 contrasting the professedly religious and the truly religious. Rauschenbusch pointed out that in determining those who truly follow God's will, Jesus identified those who fed the hungry and thirsty, welcomed the stranger, clothed the naked, and cared for the sick and imprisoned. These people found God by serving others in need. When "one of the least of these" was served, it was service to Christ.[108] Rauschenbusch paraphrases

---

[103] Ahlstrom, ed., *Theology in America*, 532.
[104] WR, *Christianizing the Social Order*, 459.
[105] Welch, *Protestant Theology in the Nineteenth Century*, 2:261, 265.
[106] WR, *Unto Me*, 9.
[107] WR, *Dare We Be Christians?*, 3.
[108] WR, *Unto Me*, 9–10.

as follows: "My life is so identified with my brethren that when ye fed and clothed them, ye fed and clothed me. God is living in these worn human bodies. When ye comforted them, ye comforted God."[109] The other group asks when they ever saw Christ in need and failed to minister to him. Again, Jesus so fully identified himself with all of humanity that when people in need are ignored, Christ is ignored. Rauschenbusch observed that thereby "they isolated themselves from their kind and missed contact with God who dwells in humanity."[110]

Unto Me called Christians to understand their faith in new terms: Christians demonstrate their love for God when they see Christ in other people and serve them. Here Rauschenbusch set forth the clearest biblical basis for the reform he sought: serving others is the key religious sensibility in this Gospel passage.

Rauschenbusch observed that these Christians bear the grief and misery of others, worry about causes of misery and exploitation, and suffer with others; social work is exhausting. Suffering for others is the kind of suffering Jesus experienced; it is the meaning of the cross. According to Rauschenbusch too many modern Christians seek to escape pain and avoid suffering instead of confronting evil and injustice. But those doing the work of relieving suffering and pain are following the path of the Christian life set by Christ.[111] In this essay Rauschenbusch affirms that true Christianity is not a mystical experience but rather an act of obedient response to the command to love one another. For him, profession of faith without action for others is false religion. This little book is a bold restatement of Rauschenbusch's central conviction. The power of the book rests on his appeal to the teachings of Jesus that forcefully contrast true and false religion. Jesus says those who merely profess commitment have not met the test of discipleship.

Two years after the appearance of *Christianizing the Social Order* and *Unto Me* Rauschenbusch published *Dare We Be Christians?*[112] This little book is an exposition of 1 Corinthians 13, Paul's famous passage on love. Rauschenbusch says that Paul borrowed from Jesus who "set love into the center of religion."[113] The

[109] Ibid., 9.

[110] Ibid., 10.

[111] Ibid., 28.

[112] The book had its inception in a sermon preached to students at Iowa State College. See WR to Professor F. W. Berkman, December 23, 1914, and C. W. Beaven to WR, January 2, 1915. Rauschenbusch revised the sermon and submitted the manuscript in July in order for it to appear in time for Christmas sales. His editors suggested the title *Dare We Be Christians?* See Parris T. Farwell to WR, September 2, 1914. The Letters cited in this note are from box 46, Rauschenbusch Family Papers.

[113] WR, *Dare We Be Christians?*, 44. Several correspondents admitted they had slighted Paul and looked only to Jesus for direction regarding social ethics. Rauschenbusch's exegesis rehabilitated Paul for them. See the collection of reviews of *Dare We Be Christians?*, box 46, Rauschenbusch Family Papers.

"dare" is whether Christians will actually put the practice of love into action.[114] The concerns Rauschenbusch expressed in *Christianizing the Social Order* are reinforced here. "Collective love," he says, "is the real cement of society."[115] Rauschenbusch repeatedly refers to the polarity between love and selfishness in this little volume. He challenges Christians with a dare because putting love into action "needs personal agents."[116] Several reviewers were reminded of Henry Drummond's popular little volume *The Greatest Thing in the World*.[117] But Rauschenbusch's "dare" moves the message from devotional piety to a call for devotion resulting in action. Christianity is "sounding brass and tinkling cymbals,"—hollow words—unless worked out in service to others. The words of 1 Corinthians 13 are familiar and cherished. But Rauschenbusch asks if they are actually put into practice. Both of these gems of exegesis offer convincing biblical support for interpreting Christianity in terms of action. In both these studies, Rauschenbusch seeks to revive the active dimension of the faith.

Reception of *Christianizing the Social Order*

Responses to *Christianizing the Social Order* came in an avalanche of letters to Rauschenbusch, along with many reviews of the book.[118] The letters are informal and unstructured. As sources of American religious opinion, they reveal how readers (primarily middle-class students, ministers, and academics) reacted to Rauschenbusch's proposals of service-oriented Christianity.

Most of the letters to Rauschenbusch were positive.[119] Archibald McClure, a McCormick Theological Seminary student, wrote, "I just want to send you a line to say how thoroughly I enjoyed reading *Christianizing the Social Order*." He noted that the book "brought so many keen and interesting ideas to my mind that I only hope in some way that I may be used to stimulate others to a truer appreciation of life thru [sic] having read it."[120] The note expressed both gratitude for stimulating ideas and strengthened motivation for this student's future ministry. David E. Schnable, an older student, also wrote to thank Rauschenbusch for his book. He reported that he had been a working man (a mechanic) and now was working his way through college and preparing for the ministry. He wrote, "I

[114] *Dare We Be Christians*, 30.

[115] Ibid., 24.

[116] Ibid., 47.

[117] See reviews of *Dare We Be Christians?*, box 46, Rauschenbusch Family Papers. See also Drummond, *The Greatest Thing in the World*, 11–77.

[118] See Rauschenbusch Family Papers, especially boxes 26, 27, 46, and 94. The letters reveal an extraordinary breadth of private opinion.

[119] There is no way to tell what letters may have been lost or thrown away. They do contain critiques, but few are dismissive.

[120] Archibald McClure to WR, July 21, 1913, box 27, Rauschenbusch Family Papers.

have experienced strike, etc. incident to industrial life and now feel that I have the point of view of the working man. I am without a house and have 'roughed' life in the city and country for several years...."[121] Rauschenbusch's writing helped the student name his identity:

> Heretofore I have never classified myself, but now after reading your book I feel that I am a Christian Socialist.... I believe thoroughly in your principles as set forth in your books.... To some, I know, there seems to be no special cause for broadening the influence of the Church beyond its present effort...but I am quite sure that in my generation the Church will be compelled to take notice of existing conditions or loose [sic] her power.[122]

Schnable recognized the loss of influence of the church in American society, and he cited specific evidence: "I have my friends who have left the church altogether, thinking that God wasn't needed...." He affirmed "the Good Old Gospel," but now saw that "it will require greater application."[123] Here was a student broadening his perspective on the mission of the church. He had adopted what Rauschenbusch was fond of calling "a larger view of Christianity."

Seminary professors also expressed their appreciation to Rauschenbusch. George G. Groat at Ohio Wesleyan University had heard Rauschenbusch deliver the Merrick lectures that became *Christianizing the Social Order*. He wrote to congratulate Rauschenbusch on the book, now greatly expanded from the original lectures. Groat was pleased to recall the lectures, to see Rauschenbusch's additions, and to recall Rauschenbusch's voice when lecturing the material. He also reported on Rauschenbusch's personal impact on students: "Your influence, started from the lectures that you gave here, is still alive among the students, I find, a fact that is very unusual when one considers the passing nature of a student body."[124] The students might not have read his works, but they had heard him and were favorably impressed.

Christian sociologists also praised the book. Hartford, Connecticut, resident Robert A. McJunkin wrote that he was "enthused with the rigorous, courageous, helpful message that the book carries. The chapter on Justice is a classic."[125] He hoped that this book would be one that would aid in "showing the way from this earth to the better one that is to come." He noted that many people believed that a life filled with adversity was essential to producing strong churches. "In other

---

[121] David E. Schnable to WR, November 13, 1913, box 27, Rauschenbusch Family Papers.

[122] Ibid.

[123] Ibid.

[124] George G. Groat to WR, December 10, 1912, box 26, Rauschenbusch Family Papers.

[125] Robert A. McJunkin to WR, December 18, 1912, box 26, Rauschenbusch Family Papers.

words, they deify *want* as *the* great incentive." He told Rauschenbusch that he did not deny the value of discipline, but also did not believe God willed lives to be filled with adversity and want. Poverty, he noted, meant lack of opportunity.[126] Clearly, Rauschenbusch's message resonated with McJunkin. J. W. Barnett of the Religious Brotherhood of the Barrie Congregational Church in Barrie, Vermont, wrote that he had convened a group of young working men—some of them socialists—for weekly discussion of *Christianizing and the Social Order*. He reported that they felt they were getting something worthwhile from the book and wanted to thank Rauschenbusch for writing it.[127]

Many pastors expressed gratitude to Rauschenbusch. S. J. Wallace, the pastor of the Zumbrota Methodist Episcopal Church in Zumbrota, Minnesota, wrote, "Dear Friend, after reading your book *Christianizing the Social Order* I feel I can address you as friend although I have never personally met you. I cannot forbear expressing to you that the book has been immensely profitable. It is incomparably the best of its kind I have ever read." He had also read *Christianity and the Social Crisis* but considered *Christianizing the Social Order* "far and away better...larger, truer and sweeter interpretation of the Kingdom" than any he had seen. He was deeply grateful that Rauschenbusch had published this book.[128]

Thomas E. Boord, an impoverished minister among working class people in Pittsburgh, Pennsylvania, wrote that his salary barely covered living expenses. He needed surgery "which is beyond my reach unless I avail myself of public charity, which is extremely humiliating."[129] He praised Rauschenbusch for the clarity of his writing and its truth: "From the standpoint of a fellow minister of the gospel I will say you have fully expressed many of my own convictions, have given shape to others that were undefined in my own mind, and have provided much food for thought."[130] He wrote that living in strong socialist communities and reading so much of their literature made him reluctant to align with a movement that placed a premium on ungodliness and "scoffs at Christianity and hisses the name of Christ."[131] His letter depicts the poverty that Rauschenbusch hoped to remedy and also conveys the problem for Christians of identifying with socialism as a tool for reform.

Strongly convinced by Rauschenbusch's argument, some ministers also sought guidance in implementing his proposal. Henry W. Stringer wrote a word of appreciation to Rauschenbusch for the book: "It fell into my hands in an hour

126 Ibid.

127 J. W. Barnett to WR, February 36, 1913, box 27, Rauschenbusch Family Papers.

128 S. J. Wallace to WR, November 10, 1913, box 28, Rauschenbusch Family Papers.

129 Thomas E. Boord to WR, December 26, 1913, box 26, Rauschenbusch Family Papers.

130 Ibid.

131 Ibid.

of deep discouragement and crisis, and it has given me a new vision, and prompted me, instead of giving up, to attempt a new service for the kingdom."[132] Stringer was pastor of the South Broad Street Baptist Church, Philadelphia. He described it as a "downtown" church with its attendant problems:

> The one-time purely American population has largely emigrated, and the neighborhood is largely preempted now by Americanized Italians, nominally Romanist, but largely out of touch with any church. Less than thirty percent of my membership live within eight blocks of the church and our work, carried on in the usual conservative methods, does not meet the needs. After doing all in my power, with available resources, I felt the time had come to move when your book came to me. It put new heart into me.[133]

Stringer clearly described the social dislocation that challenged many inner-city churches and sensed the futility of traditional methods of ministry. He reported that his church had now voted to devote Sunday evenings to "Social Service" meetings, with appropriate speakers and programs. He invited Rauschenbusch to his church and to a ministers' conference, paying him the compliment of being "the direct inspiration" for the social movement. He assured Rauschenbusch that his presence would benefit his church effort and "would greatly help the 'Christianizing the Social Order' for the ministers to hear you face to face." Stringer had made a beginning of creating a social conscience and ministry in his church, but in his postscript he welcomed "any suggestions that you may care to make out of your knowledge of practical experimental work on this line in other churches."[134] Rauschenbusch's theories inspired. However, implementation of social Christianity was a huge hurdle for the average minister, and his listeners did not find any practical guidance from Rauschenbusch for implementing social Christianity. These letters themselves expose the great flaw in Rauschenbusch's agenda.

Following publication of *Christianity and the Social Crisis* several of Rauschenbusch's readers had looked for a sequel. Theo Fisher, who wrote from Colorado Springs, Colorado, was a good example. Having read the earlier book he now wrote, "Your new book is a most satisfactory answer to this pressing need. I cannot begin to tell you how wonderful your book is to me. It's a veritable encyclopedia on the subject and I find myself going to it again and again for information on many points."[135] But Fisher needed yet more help, and he probed with specific questions: "To me one of the biggest questions is that of how the Church can best get its members working along the lines of the new interest to which the

[132] Henry W. Stringer to WR, February 5, 1913, box 27, Rauschenbusch Family Papers.
[133] Ibid.
[134] Ibid.
[135] Theo M. Fisher to WR, July 19, 1913, box 27, Rauschenbusch Family Papers.

social evangel calls them."

A second issue for Fisher was that he did not see any reference to the question so often raised by churchmen that since Socialism is a political matter and a political party, the Church should not preach it or align itself with it: "All this matter of the Church taking sides for Socialism rather than for the single tax etc. etc. I do not find made clear by you."[136] Fisher's letter points out the practical difficulty of implementing Rauschenbusch's proposals, and he raises the ongoing problem of how the church can move from worship to advocation of social reform without alienating many members. The association with socialism was a two-edged sword. It helped Rauschenbusch understand and analyze the problems of the nation and offer solutions, but the stigma attached to socialism made it difficult to appropriate it as an ally for Christian reform. Fisher concluded his letter with the observation, "However, if I read you aright your whole thesis is for the identification of sociology and religion.... [if so] our religion will function through the Church in a multitude of ways now outside its scope."[137] In his closing line this writer said that he would be glad to have further light on the matter. Clearly, he agreed that Rauschenbusch had correctly identified the problem, but he had found no clear way to actually begin a process of reform.

Ordinary readers of *Christianizing the Social Order* were motivated to do more. Many also described to Rauschenbusch their numerous personal struggles and church problems and offered their opinions and critiques based on their experiences. A large number of readers regarded *Christianizing the Social Order* a greater book than *Christianity and the Social Crisis.* Despite the fact that Rauschenbusch proposed to offer concrete suggestions for reform, he seems to have fallen short. Many still sought additional pragmatic assistance in finding actual methods for implementing his grand vision of creating a more Christian nation. Rauschenbusch's writing informed and inspired ministers and others to engage in social reform. The problem was that churches had no power to carry out reform. The changes Rauschenbusch envisioned would require legislation.

Well known religious leaders also commented on the book. Their letters to Rauschenbusch were generally more analytic and challenging. Rauschenbusch heard from Charles M. Sheldon of Topeka, Kansas, author of *In His Steps*, who espoused a different understanding of social Christianity. Sheldon's famous novel is now viewed as an early expression of social gospel teaching. In it Sheldon created ethical dilemmas for characters who then raise the recurrent refrain, "What would Jesus do?" Sheldon's book recognized the need for Christian action, but it was not nearly so sweeping in its call for structural social reform as Rauschenbusch's proposals. Sheldon wrote that he had just been re-reading *Christianizing*

[136] Ibid.

[137] Ibid.

the Social Order and noted Rauschenbusch's reference to *In His Steps.* Rauschenbusch had observed that the standard set by the question "What would Jesus do?" "convicts our social order but does not reconstruct it."[138] Sheldon responded that he understood Rauschenbusch's point, but he nevertheless defended his approach: "After all what will reconstruct the social order, except such a reconstructing of individual purposes and passions as will make men do the things they ought to do. What standard can we find in Christ's teachings which is not in the region of ideals? We [cannot] abandon it for something easier, which we say is 'practical.'" Sheldon assured Rauschenbusch that he was not writing in a spirit of criticism. He did, however, ask Rauschenbusch to "consider the ultimate standard for human conduct. How shall men govern themselves except by the example of the perfect Man?"[139] Here is an alternative argument that calls on the church to change society, but it will be accomplished through individuals striving to live an ideal life of following Christ.[140] In many other contexts it is clear that Rauschenbusch also believed that individual commitment was the essential starting point for Christianization. Even in this passage he emphasized that it was the source of conviction. But what he found missing in Sheldon is the necessity of systemic reconstruction of society based on the criterion of justice.

Most advocates of the social gospel agreed on the goal of justice. However, they differed on the actual method of implementing this goal. Rauschenbusch had analyzed the fundamental difference between the theories of capitalism and socialism. Responding to his fellow Baptist professor, Shailer Mathews at the University of Chicago, Rauschenbusch laid out the differences in their respective positions:

> Between your modified capitalism and my modified socialism there will, as you say, probably be little difference. But if you leave the instruments of production in the hands of the capitalist group and merely try to cut down their rents and profit and compel them to contribute more service to the common good, you have your job to do over and over. Every time the social value of property increases, you would have to coerce them to give it up. I'll resign rather than keep up that game to the end of time. I prefer to vest the property rights in the community and then work out the problem how to give the ablest fellows elbow-room and incentive enough to serve the rest.[141]

Rauschenbusch's position began with the community and required fundamental structural readjustment in the economy. His was a more thorough-going

---

138 WR, *Christianizing the Social Order,* 46.

139 Charles M. Sheldon to WR, December 26, 1913, box 27, Rauschenbusch Family Papers.

140 For a superb treatment of Sheldon's views see Miller, *Following in His Steps.*

141 WR to Shailer Mathews, February 25, 1913, box 27, Rauschenbusch Family Papers.

proposal than that of either Sheldon or Mathews.

Charles A. Strong, son of Rochester Seminary president A. H. Strong, represented a different view altogether. He wrote to Rauschenbusch, "Your book has made a profound impression upon me…it enlarged my acquaintances with the facts, made me understand better the workings of the capitalist system, and deepened my sense of its injustices. You have become a master of these subjects." Two years Rauschenbusch's junior, Charles Strong was born to wealth, and in his letter he defended capitalism. His grandfather had owned a Rochester newspaper. The tone of his letter is totally different from most of Rauschenbusch's correspondents. After his polite opening commendation of Rauschenbusch's book, Strong wrote, "Since I became a capitalist, I have tried to keep down my expense…. I felt that to own a motor-car was a sin of which I should probably never be guilty…. It was not easy to know how to use the money well. I have favored education. Now I am building a house in Italy (one must have a home)," he said.[142] Then he proceeded to "point out certain pro-capitalist considerations" and defend at length the advantages of the present social-economic system. His was a forthright defense of moneyed interests—with little concession to Rauschenbusch's reform goals. It is an isolated response among the numerous letters sent in support of Rauschenbusch's ideas, but it fairly represents capitalist sentiment. Strong reminded Rauschenbusch that "the income of all our colleges and libraries and museums, and of your own theological seminary, is derived from invested capital." He agreed that "the workers get less than their share, and that the capitalist gets very much more than his share." He recognized the injustice but thought it was inevitable because of "inequalities of gift and character among men."[143] Clearly the wealthy such as Strong were not drawn to Rauschenbusch's proposals. They were enjoying their privileges, justified their positions, and found little incentive to change.

These letters offer a glimpse into local parish life of the era, especially the aspirations and struggles of ministers. Some had financial difficulties; others, health problems; still others needed a confessor; and all seemed to struggle with the nature of their call and experience conflict with the expectations of their church members. Many were inspired because of the new energy conveyed by Rauschenbusch's vision. Others felt that they were in a conservative bind. They wanted to act on Rauschenbusch's proposals but thought they would meet resistance from their congregations. Still others appreciated the goals proposed but did not know how to implement them. The letters reveal much about the complex dynamics of reception of the social gospel message as well as the mentality of ministers and laymen in Protestant churches in 1912–1913.

---

142 C. A. Strong to WR, April 7, 1913, box 27, Rauschenbusch Family Papers.

143 Ibid.

These letters expose the greatest flaw in Rauschenbusch's thought. He assumed that people could be persuaded to follow a path toward the Kingdom of God. In more realistic moments he affirmed the selfishness of people who would not give up their privileges for the benefit of all citizens. He could inspire readers and make justice come alive in their consciousness, but the church had no leverage to change society on its own. This is why the goals of the social gospel—such as the forty-hour work week, minimum wages, factory protection, and child labor—all had to be reformed through legislation led by the Progressive Party. This outlook is what caused successors rightly to declare Rauschenbusch naively too optimistic and unrealistic. Although he acknowledged difficulties, Rauschenbusch nevertheless sustained hope for a transformed America. It was that vision that became his legacy.

Rauschenbusch did not succeed in re-shaping the American social structure, but he aroused the conscience of leaders in the church, and the church accepted its responsibility to address the causes of poverty. Society has changed in many ways during the past century, but the problems of poverty and the sources of injustice Rauschenbusch addressed still plague the nation and its churches every day. Readers then and now have reckoned Rauschenbusch to be the most articulate and forceful advocate of the early social gospel. Because he constantly assaulted injustices in society, because he did not spare the church, and because he saw things in a new and compelling way, readers then and later often called Rauschenbusch a prophet.[144] By this they meant that he spoke truth to power in his own society. In turn, he was opposed, and he suffered criticism that wounded his feelings, but he sustained his crusade for establishing justice in America, which he interpreted as a thoroughly Christian goal.

---

[144] See, for example, Hudson, "Rauschenbusch—Evangelical Prophet," 740.

CHAPTER 11

CHRISTIANITY AS BELIEF: *A THEOLOGY FOR THE SOCIAL GOSPEL*

Throughout his life and in his writings, Rauschenbusch was energized by religious purpose. He wrote a book of prayers affirming the centrality of spirituality to Christianity. He gave even more attention in his writings to ethical application of Christianity. As a boy he had aspired to help others, and he channeled this devotion to work for social justice. He also understood the long-standing place of theology in the Christian life. In writing "Why I Am a Baptist," Rauschenbusch declared that there is an intellectual element in all religions: he insisted that religion appeals to the whole man, including the mind.[1] He acknowledged the importance of theology and took full advantage of the opportunity to explore his understanding of the subject in a systematic fashion.

For years Rauschenbusch had said Christians should be revolutionary. He was not happy with the way he had been taught theology. To his good friend Will Munger he wrote,

> Yes, you are right, blessed is the man who trusts in the free Spirit, for he shall grow. Is not that trust in freedom and in the inward illumination of God's spirit the way in which the demand for faith comes to men whose work lies along intellectual lines? Is not Rochester Seminary trying to walk by sight in its theology? And has not the usual punishment for that attempt come upon it in clear-sighted short-sightedness? Men are not taught by Dr. Strong to trust themselves in a birch canoe on the ocean of God's being, and so he traces up a lot of men, who timidly creep around shores and never discover new continents. I have often thought how curiously faithlessness takes new forms and hides under the very guise of faith.

His old professor was too conservative for Rauschenbusch's taste, so he shaped his own approach to theology, beginning with challenges to traditional theology while he was a student. He left the "shores" of familiar theological restatement and landed to "discover" a new way of formulating theology.

Toward the end of his career, Rauschenbusch had occasion to articulate his

---

[1] WR, "Why I am a Baptist: My Fourth Reason," 156; also box 40, Rauschenbusch Family Papers.

theology. Rauschenbusch's *A Theology for the Social Gospel* had its genesis in a series of lectures. After a decade as a highly visible religious leader, fellow church historian Williston Walker wrote to Rauschenbusch inviting him to deliver the 1917 Nathaniel W. Taylor Lectures at Yale. Rauschenbusch replied his acceptance with gratitude for the honor and outlined his concept for the lectures:

> It seems clear that the immense moral and spiritual interests involved in the conception of applying the saving power of Christianity to the social order ought to affect systematic theology as well as pastoral theology, liturgies, etc. It seems to me to demand an expansion in the conception of redemption and a consequent revision and readjustment of the doctrines connected with redemption.[2]

Rauschenbusch had given lectures touching on theological issues for the Gates lectures at Grinnell College in Grinnell, Iowa, and the convocation lectures at Bangor Theological Seminary in Bangor, Maine. Since the lectures were unpublished, he asked if they could be used in an expanded version, and Walker replied that they could.[3] This was doubtless a great relief to Rauschenbusch. He was working on three major projects at once, including *The Social Principles of Jesus* and *Social Redemption.* (The latter book was scheduled for publication in fall 1914, but as Rauschenbusch wrote, "The mental distress which we all felt last Fall in consequence of the War made it impossible for me to finish it."[4] *Social Redemption* was never published.) Now he would add his theological justification of the social gospel. When Rauschenbusch accepted, Walker replied, "It is a great satisfaction to us of the Yale School of Religion, that you will give the lectures for us."[5] Following the lectures in April, during the summer he put them "in shape for print."[6] His typescript reveals something of how he worked. He often typed one paragraph per page, giving himself ample space for editorial changes. Then he edited his text by hand with pen.[7] Rauschenbusch was usually contending for a position in his writing, trying to persuade people to consider a new understanding of their practice of Christianity. But to the end of his career he sought to avoid attacking others by name. Concerning *A Theology for the Social Gospel,* he wrote to his publishers, "[as] in all my previous books. I gave [the book] a last revision from the point of view of Christian love, cutting out everything that might needlessly hurt."[8]

---

[2] WR to Williston Walker, December 31, 1915, box 40, Rauschenbusch Family Papers.

[3] Williston Walker to WR, January 8, 1916, box 40, Rauschenbusch Family Papers.

[4] WR to Williston Walker, December 31, 1915, box 40, Rauschenbusch Family Papers.

[5] Williston Walker to WR, January 18, 1916, box 40, Rauschenbusch Family Papers.

[6] WR to Leighton Williams, June 16, 1917, box 27, Rauschenbusch Family Papers.

[7] See WR, *The Social Principles of Jesus*, typescript, box 154, Rauschenbusch Family Papers.

[8] WR to George W. Coleman, November 8, 1917, box 32, Rauschenbusch Family Papers.

Rauschenbusch had serious misgivings about publishing his lectures on *A Theology for the Social Gospel.* Friends had warned against it. Rauschenbusch does not say why, but it is presumably because the New Theology he embraced was sharply criticized by conservatives. His apprehension on approaching publication of his ideas is palpable in his letter to Harold Marshall, Macmillan representative:

> My book, *A Theology for the Social Gospel*, is completed. Just as I was to give the word for its release, several of those nearest me greatly disturbed my mind by warning against its publication at the present time. They feared that there is so much antagonism abroad that this will be taken as an occasion to knife me in some way. They think that it is much safer for me to say nothing at present.... I concluded, however, to go ahead.[9]

Marshall replied, "My own feeling is that some of your friends are over-timid. I have no doubt that there will be more or less controversy over your book; indeed it would not be worth printing at all if it were not...."[10]

In the foreword to the book, Rauschenbusch addressed the fact that he was not trained in theology. However, he justified accepting the lectureship by noting that "theology has often received its most fruitful impulses when secular life and movements have set it new problems."[11] He expressed his conviction that he had devoted his life to the most pressing sort of problem: "events of life have laid social problems on my mind."[12] Moreover, he observed that there might be some advantage to approaching theology "from outside."[13] New issues and a new perspective might yield fruitful results. But he was keenly aware that his treatment of doctrines would not be traditional. Despite Rauschenbusch's expressed reservations, Claude Welch declared that Rauschenbusch was the most theologically able among the many exponents of the mainline American social gospel and was recognized as the leading prophet in the decade after 1909.[14]

Rauschenbusch took full advantage of the opportunity to explore Christian theology in a systematic fashion. He had several goals. First, he proposed to offer a social interpretation of the Christian message of sin and salvation. Second, he proposed to restate Christian doctrine in a way that included the social perspective "in some organic form," and he offered several concrete examples.[15] He would try to contribute to theology by approaching the task from the insights into the understanding of Christianity he had gained by interpreting life from a social

---

[9] WR to Harold Marshall, November 8, 1917, box 40, Rauschenbusch Family Papers.
[10] Marshall to WR, November 10, 1917, box 40, Rauschenbusch Family Papers.
[11] WR, foreword to *A Theology for the Social Gospel*, 1917 ed., n.p.
[12] Ibid.
[13] Ibid.
[14] Welch, *Protestant Thought in the Nineteenth Century*, 2:161.
[15] WR, *A Theology for the Social Gospel*, 1997 ed., 167.

perspective. But the categories of sin and salvation constituted the core of the book.

Adjusting Theology to Modern Society

Rauschenbusch opened the book with three chapters seeking to persuade listeners/readers to be willing to consider new perspectives and a new interpretation of Christian theology. He wrote that "in these introductory chapters my aim is to win the benevolent and serious attention of conservative readers for the discussions that are to follow."[16] He was well aware that he was approaching theology from a new perspective. Ritschl was the dominant influence in his theology.[17] He was contesting the old evangelism. He assumed that accepting the Social Gospel was a huge hurdle for his audience. He presumed that much of the audience interpreted Christianity in traditional Protestant theological categories.

In 1904 Rauschenbusch had published "The New Evangelism," a seminal essay calling the church to recognize that society had shifted from agrarian to industrial economies and that it must adjust its message accordingly.[18] In 1907 he elaborated what he had in mind by identifying the social crisis, and in 1912 by suggesting paths of reform. In this book he offers theological justification for his vision of applying Christian ideas to American society. In Donald Shriver's assessments, he was "crafting an ethic for the industrial age." His task in this book was to "underpin that ethic with theology."[19]

Rauschenbusch's succinct and arresting opening to his theology affirms, "We have a social gospel. We need a systematic theology large enough to match it and vital enough to back it. This is the main proposition of this book."[20] Rauschenbusch cites much evidence to support his claim that the social gospel had become a "permanent addition" to spiritual outlook, including testimonies of college students, workers, and ministers as well as implementation by foreign missionaries and by interdenominational groups such as "Men and Religion Forward Movement."[21] Rauschenbusch chooses his words carefully. Throughout his opening chapter he calls for "readjustment" in theological outlook, affirming that since the social gospel is "a new stage in the development of the Christian religion," it calls for a theology to match it.[22] His perspective that the church undergoes development means that he can argue that social Christianity should be added to

[16] Ibid., 23.
[17] Smucker, *The Origins of Walter Rauschenbusch's Social Ethics*, 77, 87, 94.
[18] WR, "The New Evangelism," 1054–59.
[19] Shriver, introduction to *A Theology for the Social Gospel* by Walter Rauschenbusch, xv.
[20] WR, *A Theology for the Social Gospel*, 1997 ed., 1.
[21] Ibid., 2–4.
[22] Ibid., 2.

individual Christianity.

Not calling for tossing out the old individually focused religion is an important strategy throughout much of his writing. He stresses the importance of traditional emphasis on individual salvation but then strenuously argues that individual Christianity by itself does not constitute all that is included in true Christianity; hence, his use of the language of "adjustment" and "enlargement."[23] Many scholars note how the theme of theological readjustment (relating theology to modern thought) represents one of Rauschenbusch's key contributions to theology.[24]

Rauschenbusch recognizes the psychological difficulty involved in the process of changing theological views and often addresses this problem. Lessons learned and sermons heard early in life do much to shape religious opinions of most people. Added to these realities, there is the widely held assumption that religion teaches the truth and that truth does not change. However, he reminds readers that the task of theology is to aid in the preaching of salvation, and theology should make the essential message of Christianity clear. The church reiterates only that we need to regenerate the individual, that salvation is for the life to come, and that it is not the task of the church to deal with economic problems. Rauschenbusch says that these are "half-truths."[25] So in addition to adjustment and enlargement, Rauschenbusch finds that old traditions are sometimes just wrong. He does not hesitate to criticize what he finds to be wrong or deficient in traditional Christianity.

Rauschenbusch noted that seeking to persuade people to change their beliefs "causes apprehension and distress because religious truth is truth souls live by and is too dear to be scrapped or made over." Moreover, "to grant the possibility of need for change means loss of assurance, and that hurts."[26] Hanford Burr wrote to Rauschenbusch, "I have just finished your new book. It reminds me at every stage of a process of reinterpretation which I had to go thru [*sic*] with a number of years ago. I think it will be immensely useful to the ministers who were brot [*sic*] up in conservatism and minister to conservative congregations, but still sense the new current about them."[27] During his own theological education, Rauschenbusch had experienced turmoil over this issue himself, and he clearly recognized the traumatic dynamic involved in reconstruction of beliefs. He wrote that he had "entire sympathy for the conservative instinct."[28]

Rauschenbusch developed several approaches to the problem of adjusting

---

[23] Ibid., 1–7.

[24] Hutchinson, *Modernist Impulse,* 2. Hutchinson preferred the term "adaptation."

[25] Ibid., 8.

[26] Ibid., 10.

[27] Hanford Burr to WR, February 13, 1918, box 40, Rauschenbusch Family Papers.

[28] WR, *A Theology for the Social Gospel*, 1997 ed., 10.

one's beliefs. He argued that change required for accommodating the social gospel is a matter of addition, not subtraction or substitution. If readers adopted a historical perspective, they would learn that the church's important early decisions were made by people who were not infallible. He wrote that "theoretically it [the church] is the great organization of unselfish service. Actually it has often been profoundly concerned for its own power and authority. But its authority rests in large part on the stability of its doctrine."[29] Although the church was slow to change, he went on to urge that "theology needs periodical rejuvenation."[30] Another argument Rauschenbusch used was his emphasis on the ethical dimension of theology. He criticized theology often for being too esoteric and speculative; it had become an "affair of experts," whereas "the working creed of the common man is usually very brief."[31] Rauschenbusch affirmed that the social gospel "deals with the ethical problems of the present life with which the common man is familiar.... Yet it appeals to God, his will, his kingdom; to Christ, his spirit, and his law."[32] He noted that people are becoming more aware of collective sins such as child labor, the manufacture of shrapnel and bombs, and low wages that keep men in poverty.[33] Rhetorically he asks if the old theology eases these burdens, implying that it does not.[34] Earlier Rauschenbusch had expressed his views about theology:

> Personally I should be well content with making the Savior's statement the basis of membership. The Church has taken religion away from the babes and given it to the rabbis by intellectualizing the gospel. This would reverse the process. It would shift the obligation from the domain of intellect to that of the will and the power of loving.
>
> As to an unassailable and final theology,—I think we shall never have it. But you are wholly right that our theology must not be in plain and shocking contradiction to the facts about the universe and about human life which are the common property of our age. Theology should give adequate intellectual support to the living religious convictions of modern men. It is defective if it teaches things which the best minds find hard to believe. It is also defective if it fails to teach things which arouse the deepest religious feelings and stir the best minds to religious action.[35]

Rauschenbusch asserted that the social gospel is neither alien nor novel.[36]

---

[29] Ibid, 12.
[30] Ibid.
[31] Ibid., 16.
[32] Ibid., 16–17.
[33] Ibid., 18.
[34] Ibid., 19.
[35] WR, *The Church, the People, and the Age,* 315.
[36] WR, *A Theology for the Social Gospel,* 1997 ed., 27.

He noted that although in the nineteenth century most theologians were very traditional, others began to perceive and introduce social dimensions of life for theological reflection. These including Schleiermacher, Rothe, Ritschl, and Troeltsch in Germany; Maurice and Kingsley in Great Britain; and William A. Brown, William H. P. Faunce, Rufus Jones, Shailer Mathews, Francis G. Peabody, and many others in North America.[37] His full list of people who had embraced new theological perspectives is much longer, and he concluded his introductory remarks asserting "a strong probability is established that the social gospel is not a passing interest, but that it is bound to become one of the permanent and commanding ingredients of theology."[38] Asked at the height of his career if his opinions had changed, Rauschenbusch replied ambiguously,

> I cannot say that they have. Indeed I have not had any great changes and revulsions in thought. My thought on the whole has followed along straight lines, sloughing off a good deal that was antiquated and absorbing new thought as far as I could, but not abandoning anything of any great importance. On the whole I feel that my later thought confirms what I was trying to reach out for in my earlier years. I had to unlearn a good deal which I had taken over from traditional moral and religious thought.[39]

After making overtures to his audience to consider theology in new ways, his next task was to clarify the essential problem for theology—the problem of sin and evil—and reformulate Christian theology.

The Kingdom of Evil: Rauschenbusch's Analysis of the Problem

Commentators pointed to Rauschenbusch's treatment of the doctrine of sin and evil as perhaps the most original contribution of this book.[40] Devoting about one-fourth of the book to sin and evil, he gave it a more thorough treatment than any other doctrine. He had written extensively about the kingdom of God throughout much of his career. Here he offers an extended analysis of its sin and evil—the essential problem for theology.

Rauschenbusch states that the theology of the social gospel has no interest in speculative doctrine. Instead, its concern is with social relations. For him the two essential Christian doctrines are sin and salvation. The interest of the social gospel is "with the eradication of sin and the fulfillment of the mission of redemption."[41] He was not alone in sensing a need to articulate anew a statement

---

[37] Ibid., 28–30.

[38] Ibid., 30.

[39] WR to H. G. Roller, March 12, 1915, box 14, Rauschenbusch Family Papers.

[40] See Shailer Mathews to Macmillan Co., January 5, 1918, and Henry Ferris to WR, January 2, 1918, box 40, Rauschenbusch Family Papers.

[41] WR, *A Theology for the Social Gospel*, 1997 ed., 31.

of theology. Both Helen Montgomery and Vida Scudder wrote to him expressing their gratitude for his candid revisions of theology. Traditional speculative theology had resonated with neither of them.[42]

Rauschenbusch calls attention to the universal consciousness of sin.[43] He cites several examples in common human experience: "We commit acts of sensuality, cruelty or dishonor, which nothing can wipe away...[we fall into] harmful habits...defilement of soul and the perversion of...intimate life."[44] In short, we "feel deep consciousness of sin."[45] Violations of conscience are compounded by wasted years and betrayals: no one escapes conscience. The Lord's Prayer itself assumes this condition; it contains the petition to "forgive us our trespasses and lead us not into temptation."[46] Furthermore, traditional definitions have overlooked social sins. Recalling some of his favored themes, Rauschenbusch asserts that traditional theology has addressed neither exploitation of the poor nor war, the supreme evil.[47] To illustrate, he tells one of his folksy stories: a Mennonite farmer delivered his milk, but the inspector labeled his cans of milk unfit. In a fit of rage the angry farmer swore on an oath. The Mennonite church excluded him for swearing but said nothing about his threatening the health of young children by selling tainted food.[48] Rauschenbusch uses this little parable to call attention to the social dimension of sin, too long overlooked by the church, but capable of far more damage to lives than an individual oath. Rauschenbusch likens the modern church to Jesus' judgment on those who strained out gnats and swallowed camels, "judiciously laying the emphasis on the minor sins and keeping silence on the profitable major wrongs."[49] He cites contemporary examples in the churches, recalling a New York City minister who preached that the chief marks of a Christian were attending church, reading the Bible, and contributing to the support of public worship. Another said that the four sins to avoid were drinking, dancing, card playing, and attending movies. Perhaps Rauschenbusch's Pietism restrains his attack on these familiar examples of sin, but he nevertheless is willing to marginalize them since the social sins he identifies appear to him so much more damaging.[50] Sadly the churches have been unaware of the depth of sin at social levels,

---

[42] Vida D. Scudder to WR, February 27, 1918, box 40, Rauschenbusch Family Papers; Helen Montgomery to WR, n.d., box 40, Rauschenbusch Family Papers.

[43] "The Consciousness of Sin" is the first of Rauschenbusch's six chapters on sin and evil (*A Theology for the Social Gospel*, 31–37).

[44] WR, *A Theology for the Social Gospel*, 1997 ed., 32.

[45] Ibid., 36.

[46] Ibid., 32.

[47] Ibid., 35.

[48] Ibid.

[49] Ibid.

[50] Ibid., 36.

and one of his goals is to awaken the church to the evils perpetuated by structural sin.

Rauschenbusch takes up the question of the fall of man, the traditional idea that depravity and death come to all because of the disobedience of Adam. He believes that by being so fully preoccupied with Adam the church has taken a wrong path. Jesus, he notes, did not concern himself with the origin of sin, but rather with its present reality as a force in people's lives. Furthermore, by directing all attention to one catastrophic event related to Adam, the interpretation "blocks the way for important advance in the consciousness of sin."[51] It has "diverted our minds from the power of social transmission."[52] For him, the sense that sin is universal does not in practice rest on reconstruction of one biblical narrative but rather on the pervasive presence of immoral behaviors leading to such problems as syphilis, war, and debt. Awareness of these current realities sharpens the "consciousness of sins" far more than all of the weight most people give to the narrative of Adam and Eve.[53] A. E. Murphy, a pastor in Peru, Indiana, wrote to thank Rauschenbusch for publishing the book despite opposition it would generate. He wrote, "Out here in Indiana 95% of the Baptists still put the Adam and Eve story at the center of their system.... I am wondering how you got your courage up to do it."[54] Doubtless it did take courage to point out the limitations of long-held theological views; Rauschenbusch was challenging ordinary grass roots theological positions in order to press a corporate understanding of sin drawn directly from modern experience.

In his discussion of the nature of sin, Rauschenbusch identifies multiple causes: humanity's powerful appetites, rampant instincts, ignorance, inertia, and sensual pleasures.[55] For Rauschenbusch the best definition of sin is selfishness. Selfishness can only be defined in relation to other people. It is therefore a social definition, and "is proof of the unquenchable social spirit of Christianity."[56] Before his Yale audience he concluded that "if theology absorbs this understanding of the nature of sin [as selfishness], it will become a strong intellectual support of the social gospel...."[57]

In describing the transmission of sin, Rauschenbusch defends the doctrine of original sin, saying that it has been one of the few attempts of "individualistic theology" to affirm the solidarity and unity of people.[58] Rauschenbusch rejects

---

[51] Ibid., 43.
[52] Ibid., 67.
[53] Ibid., 43.
[54] Rev. A. E. Murphy to WR, January 4, 1918, box 40, Rauschenbusch Family Papers.
[55] WR, *A Theology for the Social Gospel*, 1997 ed., 45.
[56] Ibid., 47.
[57] Ibid., 56.
[58] Ibid., 57.

complete depravity. He thinks Augustine was wrong to emphasize a biological transmission of sin, but he does find much evidence for social transmission of sin. "Sin is lodged in customs and institutions…[and] runs down the generations."[59] He develops the idea that society exercises its authority in defining and shaping opinions on morality. As examples, he discusses at some length society's changing views on alcohol consumption and war. According to his perception, in the case of alcoholism we can watch a gradual breaking down of a great evil. In the case of war, he says that we [in 1917 in the midst of World War I] are watching the reverse. Whereas public opinion previously condemned war, and "enthusiasm for peace was one of the clearest social convictions of the church…in the course of three years we have swung around [with the argument that military discipline] would improve the American character."[60] Even the church gave up its convictions concerning peace. Those who maintained peace convictions were now considered extremists. Rauschenbusch here is speaking autobiographically.

Rauschenbusch lists what he believes are still considered in the churches to be standardized sins—"drink, over-eating, sexualism, vanity and idleness," which he calls "transient acts and vices of individuals."[61] But gigantic evil comes from "the love of money and the love of power over men…[and] is the most difficult and most urgent field of practical redemption."[62] This dimension of "gigantic evil" is carried forward not by biological transmission but rather by the human choice and selfishness.

Rauschenbusch also addresses "the super-personal forces of evil."[63] He explores the tremendous ethical power of collective bodies, such as militarism and war, which can elevate or debase the lives of individuals. He declares that the social gospel recognizes the power of these super-personal forces, and modern theology must also recognize them if it is to come to grips with its essential task of redemption.[64]

In his final chapter on sin and evil, Rauschenbusch notes that the ideas he has identified all converge in one collective idea—the kingdom of evil. This was a brilliant linguistic move—a phrase that serves as counterpoint to the kingdom of God and calls attention to the social character of evil.[65] Rauschenbusch declares, "These two doctrines combined—the hereditary racial unity of sin, and the

---

[59] Ibid., 60–61.

[60] Ibid., 64–65.

[61] Ibid., 67, 90.

[62] Ibid., 67.

[63] Rauschenbusch shifts the language from sin to evil in his final two chapters on sin and evil.

[64] Ibid., 76.

[65] Ibid., 125. Rauschenbusch credits Ritschl with renewal of the concept of the kingdom of God; he notes that Ritschl did not have the advantage of social ideas (sociology) in order to

supernatural power of evil behind all sinful human action—created a solidaristic consciousness of sin and evil, which I think is necessary for the religious mind."[66] Finally Rauschenbusch, citing Schleiermacher, asserts that sin has been understood "as expressions of individual consciousness."[67] Instead, sin should be understood as "expressions of the common consciousness," defined here to designate all of humanity.[68] The key point is how seriously Rauschenbusch takes sin and evil. It is a powerful force.[69] Resisting sin calls for tremendous effort. It requires social redemption. Rauschenbusch analyzed sin from numerous perspectives. His approach is pragmatic, and his text is easily understood by the ordinary reader. In his survey of the conception of original sin in American theology from 1700 to 1950, H. Shelton Smith cited William Adams Brown who wrote in 1928 that in contemporary religion there was almost no reference to sin by ministers.[70] Smith concedes that the idea of sin was downplayed by many ministers but cites Rauschenbusch as the notable exception. He wrote, "There is an element of realism in his [Rauschenbusch's] conception of human nature that cannot be found in the thought of any other new theologian."[71] He documents Rauschenbusch's expressions of optimism, but finds that with the war raging in Europe in 1917, the *Theology* "became suffused with a realism concerning human nature which cannot be duplicated in the writings of any other American theologian of this period."[72] Smith recognized in Rauschenbusch a rare perception of evil. A decade later Sydney Ahlstrom, another significant interpreter of the history of American theology, also recognized that Rauschenbusch's "realistic spirit" regarding evil influenced the following generation of neo-orthodox theologians.[73] In the present generation, Gary Dorrien has repeatedly made similar assertions in many of his writings. Rauschenbusch ran against the tide of his day: he recognized the power of evil that resisted the kingdom of God.

The Kingdom of God in Rauschenbusch's Thought

Having developed multiple dimensions of the notion of the kingdom of evil

---

implement the notion of the kingdom of God (ibid., 138–39, fn. 1).

[66] Ibid., 90.

[67] Ibid., 92–93. Rauschenbusch credits Schleiermacher with the concept of the "kingdom of evil" but says he did not use the actual phrase. See WR, *The Social Teachings of Jesus*, typescript, ch. 9, p.17, box 154, Rauschenbusch Family Papers.

[68] WR, *A Theology for the Social Gospel*, 1997 ed., 93.

[69] Ibid., 11.

[70] Smith, *Changing Conceptions of Original Sin*, 198.

[71] Ibid., 200

[72] Ibid., 202.

[73] Ahlstrom, "Theology in America: A Historical Survey," 77.

in the first half of his book, Rauschenbusch turned in the second half to an extended discussion of the kingdom of God, the second of the twin themes of the book. Early in his career Rauschenbusch found the idea of the kingdom of God to be the doctrine that best captured the goal and tasks of the church, and he continued to write on this theme throughout his life. Here he summarizes key themes relating to the kingdom of God. Although the exact definition of the kingdom of God idea was elusive, Rauschenbusch ventured to state its characteristics, its direction, and examples of its establishment. The kingdom remained a goal to be fulfilled in the future—but always to be strived for in the present. This is the sense in which it functioned for Rauschenbusch. In these lectures Rauschenbusch wrote that the kingdom is "always but coming."[74]

Rauschenbusch offers the proposition that the kingdom of God is "the commonwealth of cooperative service.... [Thus] a productive life includes useful labor in service to others."[75] His notion of the kingdom of God understands selfishness as the root of sin and evil. In Rauschenbusch's estimation, even traditional understandings of salvation are self-centered and selfish. He says, "To be afraid of hell and purgatory and desirous of a life without pain or trouble in heaven was not in itself Christian. It was self-interest at a high level."[76] "Pure Christianity" is realized in seeing God in others and loving and serving God through them.[77] Selfishness is expressed at social as well as personal levels, and the social group dominates the individual; for example, the power of the city of the state over the individual.[78] The strategy of bringing the kingdom of God is short sighted if it fails to work for social change.

Rauschenbusch calls the kingdom of God the "marrow of the gospel."[79] In his view, theology must be revised to give the kingdom of God and the redemption of the social order central place. For many the church has replaced the kingdom of God. Jesus, he reminds the reader, spoke of the church only twice, but of the kingdom of God frequently. However, this emphasis was reversed in the course of church history. The church became central, and the kingdom of God was relegated to a distant future millennial era in the minds of many.[80] The reversal meant loss of Jesus' social ethics and genuine Christian fellowship: whereas the church "breeds" priests and theologies, the kingdom of God "inspires great ideas."[81] His language here is highly pejorative against the failings of the church.

[74] WR, *A Theology for the Social Gospel*, 1997 ed., 141.
[75] Ibid., 103.
[76] Ibid., 108.
[77] Ibid.
[78] Ibid., 110.
[79] Ibid., 131.
[80] Ibid., 132.
[81] Ibid., 133–34, 137.

Rauschenbusch had an important public platform, and he meant to use it. He says that the church looks to the past; the kingdom of God to the present and the future.[82] The kingdom of God is "the energy of God realizing itself in human life," and it is "always coming, always big with possibility, and always inviting immediate action."[83] But one can never say, "Lo, here"; there is no historical consummation of the kingdom.[84]

Rauschenbusch further develops his definition of the kingdom of God, suggesting that it may be understood as "humanity organized according to the will of God." This would be a society that promotes the highest development of personality; practices the qualities of love, unity, and liberty; and works to end exploitation, hunger, and war.[85] The kingdom embraces the whole of human life and seeks the transformation of the social order. In this book Rauschenbusch is proposing theological justification for his goal of redeeming society.

In Rauschenbusch's view, traditional theology has sought to take a point of view that is positioned above history. The social gospel, on the other hand, "sees the progress of the Kingdom of God in the flow of history." It is historically minded.[86] Christ initiated the kingdom of God; he "set in motion the historical forces of redemption which are to overthrow the Kingdom of Evil."[87] Whereas traditional theology has focused on the two natures of Christ, the social gospel is concerned with the ethical question of "how the divine life of Christ can get control of human society."[88] He shifts the theological focus from the metaphysical to the personal Jesus who releases revolutionary forces in history.[89] Rauschenbusch focuses on personality because he believes the "mysteries of the spiritual world take place in the will."[90] Citing Fichte, Rauschenbusch notes that full consciousness of the absolute unity of human and divine life did not exist before Jesus.[91] But Jesus experienced God in a new way—not as a judge, but as a father-forgiver who asks only for love, trust, and obedience. Rauschenbusch accepts the New Theology notion that Jesus experienced full consciousness of God—that God is love.[92] It is the historical force of Jesus' spirit that has transformed the world.[93]

---

[82] Ibid., 141.
[83] Ibid.
[84] Ibid., 227.
[85] Ibid., 142–43.
[86] Ibid., 146.
[87] Ibid., 147.
[88] Ibid., 148.
[89] Ibid., 148–52.
[90] Ibid., 150.
[91] Ibid., 153.
[92] Ibid., 154.
[93] Ibid., 160.

Rauschenbusch sees Jesus as a "force" in history, and he even uses scientific language of his day, likening this force to a "current" [of electricity].[94] The kingdom of God is "not a concept nor an ideal merely, but an historical force."[95] For Rauschenbusch Christianity is not merely above history; it operates precisely in the midst of history. He envisions a dynamic "where religion and intellect combine, [where] the foundation is laid for political democracy. Where people have...the spirit of democracy, they can curb economic exploitation...and predatory gain."[96] When fraternal feeling grows and develops into love for one's fellow man, then people are not far from the kingdom of God.[97] Rauschenbusch summarizes, "My main purpose in this book has been to show the social gospel as a vital part of the Christian conception of sin and salvation."[98] Rauschenbusch treats additional doctrines including God, biblical inspiration, atonement, and eschatology more briefly, and in discussing these traditional categories of theology, he raises the social implication of each. Rauschenbusch identifies the heart of theology as redemption. Claude Welch argues that Rauschenbusch's "most creative contribution in the *Theology* was his interpretation of human solidarity in sin and salvation." He coordinated the kingdom of God with "a real, superpersonal kingdom of evil."[99] He essentially recast systematic theology into two categories—the kingdom of evil and the kingdom of God—in order to explain the meaning of the Christian faith.

Reception of Rauschenbusch's *A Theology for the Social Gospel*

The reaction to Rauschenbusch's *Theology* was decidedly mixed. Some readers praised him. Others endorsed his general idea but offered corrections from their understanding of Christianity. A third category of reviews sharply criticized his interpretations of Christian theology.

Rauschenbusch's premise in his *Theology* was that the church needed to revise its theology. Society had changed, especially in an economic sense, but the church had failed to relate its teaching to current perspectives. Rauschenbusch proposed to use the language of traditional theology, but he gave old doctrines new meanings, ignored some doctrines, and emphasized those he believed were most useful for his argument. He was seeking to construct a theology relevant to current conditions in church and society. Regarding his premise, Shailer

[94] Ibid., 164; also, 188.
[95] Ibid., 165.
[96] Ibid.
[97] Ibid.
[98] Ibid., 167.
[99] Welch, *Protestant Thought in the Nineteenth Century*, 1:265.

Mathews, dean of Chicago Divinity School, agreed. He wrote, "The social movement is so much more really an expression of the creative forces of today, that it is inevitable that it should begin to rethink its religion from its own point of view."[100] Many people commented on the task that Rauschenbusch set himself—to let the social message find its place in the theological enterprise. Vida Scudder wrote, "I feel that you have brought out the inevitable social significance of the old doctrines…in a way to enrich orthodoxy and not disturb it."[101] This was Rauschenbusch's apparent intent, but his effort did disturb some readers. P. W. Crannell, president of Kansas City Theological Seminary, said he liked Rauschenbusch's approach of proposing an "adjustment" of theology but added that he personally would propose somewhat less adjustment.[102] Several people commented on Rauschenbusch's proposal to connect the old and the new in religion. Rev. Wallace Petty affirmed that the old theology did support individualism and the language needed revision in order to carry the new message: "we were looking for just such a rational statement of truth as you have given us."[103] Rauschenbusch would be alternately criticized for his boldness and complimented for his courage. His proposal to use traditional terminology and just add insights of the social movement proved problematic.

Henry B. Robins, professor of religious education and Rauschenbusch's colleague at Rochester, was not optimistic about the prospect of the success of Rauschenbusch's approach. The language remained but in Rauschenbusch's hands traditional theological terms had taken on quite different meanings. Robins challenged his good friend with humor, writing, "Certainly you have blazed a new trail for theology. I cannot be sure, however, that many professional theologians will rush to join you in making the trail a highway for theology."[104] On the other hand, W. G. Ballantine, professor at the Y.M.C.A. College in Springfield, Massachusetts, thought the traditional language of theology should be totally abandoned: "You have tried to put [new wine] into old bottles of an antiquated theological system. Those bottles never looked so old and dried and worthless. Any intelligent reader will lose some of the new wine. Is such an attempt worthwhile?"[105] He follows his generalization with critiques of Rauschenbusch's restatement of individual doctrines.

---

[100] Shailer Mathews to Macmillan Publishing Co., December 28, 1917, box 40, Rauschenbusch Family Papers.

[101] Vida Scudder to WR, February 27, 1918, box 40, Rauschenbusch Family Papers.

[102] P. W. Crannell to WR, January 7, 1918, box 40, Rauschenbusch Family Papers.

[103] Rev. Wallace Petty to WR, December 25, 1917, box 40, Rauschenbusch Family Papers.

[104] Henry B. Robins to WR, December 16, 1917, box 40, Rauschenbusch Family Papers.

[105] W. G. Ballantine to WR, January 21, 1918, box 40, Rauschenbusch Family Papers.

The image of the Old Testament prophet is of a loner who opposes injustices in society and speaks out on behalf of the oppressed. Many writers once again complimented Rauschenbusch by calling him a prophet. Henry Ferris wrote that he had thought Rauschenbusch was a radical, but now he thanked him for "stabbing me awake. I am a new friend."[106] Rauschenbusch described the ruling class as "parasites" who lived off the labor of others.[107] This language stung the conscience of Oberlin College Old Testament professor Kemper Fullerton so deeply that he described to Rauschenbusch the guilt he felt after inheriting property for which he had not worked.[108] Fullerton wrote that "the church's voice has almost sunk to a whisper," but that Rauschenbusch had "a knife with an edge on it that can lay bare with one cut the hidden cores of our conventional self-satisfied church life."[109] John Wright Buckham, professor of theology at Pacific School of Religion, wrote of the prophetic "fires" that characterized Rauschenbusch's books and of his "searching message to the church and to all who have the cause of social redemption at heart."[110] The descriptions by these two professors certainly suggest the style and tone of a prophet. It was precisely his prophetic spirit that also worried Rauschenbusch on occasion. Some of his friends knew about his anxiety over publishing a radically different approach to theology. Harry Ward, secretary of the Methodist Federation for Social Services wrote that he knew Rauschenbusch had been under pressure about whether or not to publish the book, and he was very glad that he decided to publish. He went on to reassure Rauschenbusch that if there were negative reactions, there also would be "no lack of both personal friends and adherents of the social gospel who will be only too glad to have the opportunity to join the issue."[111]

The most penetrating comments to Rauschenbusch came from thoughtful academics whose influence in many cases outlasted their own lifetimes. Not inclined to accept theology secondhand, they were also grappling with working out a meaningful theology. Vida Scudder, social activist and Episcopalian professor of literature at Wellesley, wrote tellingly of her youthful thinking:

> My own theology is not at all systematic, I fear; it doesn't begin with the consciousness of sin. When I was young I used to try to make it, and my attempt was a dead failure. Then I gave up, and began my theology with thinking about the nature of God, and got on better, and as I found myself following the order of the historic creeds as well as the Lord's Prayer, I decided I couldn't be so much

[106] Henry Ferris to WR, January 2, 1918, box 40, Rauschenbusch Family Papers.

[107] WR, *A Theology for the Social Gospel*, 1997 ed., 19.

[108] Kemper Fullerton to WR, January 20, 1918, box 40, Rauschenbusch Family Papers.

[109] Ibid.

[110] John Wright Buckham to WR, December 24, 1917, box 40, Rauschenbusch Family Papers.

[111] Harry F. Ward to WR, November 14, 1917, box 40, Rauschenbusch Family Papers.

> out of the way. But I suppose we of the laity are allowed to follow that order, while perhaps a scientific treatise might begin at the other end.[112]

Helen Montgomery found in Rauschenbusch's thinking echoes of her own experience. She wrote, "I think that the part which gripped me most was the discussion of supra-personal sins in the chapter on the atonement. As a child I used to try to feel guilty of killing Jesus but could never make it real. Whereas it is very plain to me that I have often been one of the crowd who stood consenting to some detestable wrong."[113] Clearly the old theology did not match the religious experience of these correspondents as it had not for Rauschenbusch.

The *Publishers' Weekly* review singled out Rauschenbusch's attempt to address present conditions in his *Theology*: "Most books that have been written on theology have one common failing—their total divorce from the contemporary currents of the world's life and thought and need.... Rauschenbusch has kept the content within the life of humanity...."[114] The writer suggested that the book was primarily for "younger ministers who have been trained in the thought of the new movement steadily gaining strength within the church.... But the book is for...all who are profoundly dissatisfied with present creeds and catechisms, for all who want a theology to which they can give their allegiance and yet preserve their self-respect."[115]

Hanford Burr, who taught at the Y.M.C.A. College in Springfield, Massachusetts, praised Rauschenbusch's approach to theology. Burr's lifework was with college students whose religious outlook he described:

> they were the cream of our churches and associations but who are so indifferent to the theology in which we were brot [*sic*] up as they are keen for a religion of self-sacrificing service. Ten years ago they knew the language of theology; now they are both ignorant and indifferent. But they flame to the appeals of a religion of dynamic conduct.... These men turn their backs on the old phrases which mean so much to us.[116]

Burr praised Rauschenbusch for recovering a usable theology for the young men who were drawn to the Y.M.C.A. He accurately captured the appeal that the book had for many Protestant youth who expressed religious sensibilities, but in a new idiom. The students needed a restatement of theology.

People invested in ministerial training were also drawn to Rauschenbusch's proposals. Lutheran minister O. H. Pannkoke commended Rauschenbusch on

---

112 Vida D. Scudder to WR, February 27, 1918, box 40, Rauschenbusch Family Papers.

113 Helen Montgomery to WR, n.d., box 40, Rauschenbusch Family Papers.

114 "A Prophet Becomes a Theologian," *Publishers' Weekly*, clipping, n.d., box 94B, Rauschenbusch Family Papers.

115 Ibid.

116 Hamford Burr to WR, February 13, 1918, box 40, Rauschenbusch Family Papers.

his energetic style of writing:

> The most commonplace material becomes alive and replete with a new interest at his hand. He writes with a peculiar earnestness. If eloquence means to speak out on a subject then his books are eloquent. He pours himself out. The thoughts rush out in phalanx and not in single file. They seem to be part of himself, a living thing. Those were characteristics of his earlier books. They are also of this.[117]

Pannkoke says that Rauschenbusch's conclusions are "extremely liberal. In many cases he retains the terms, but they have entirely changed meaning."[118] But Pannkoke also judged that "the social movement in the church...has certainly been the most striking phenomenon in theological thought in this generation." "Further," he declared, "it is a pity that more pastors will not read books like this and be jarred loose in mind...from the accretions of formal thought and formal faith."[119] Like Rauschenbusch, he emphasized how the world had changed. He appealed to the example of Luther who spoke fearlessly to the society and church of his day. He concluded that Lutheran pastors today also had the opportunity of "making the pulpit a power for this day."[120] This reviewer sought to inspire fellow Lutherans to embrace the program and theology presented by Rauschenbusch.

One of the ablest critiques of the *Theology* came from John Wright Buckham, professor of theology at Pacific School of Religion. Although he praised Rauschenbusch as a prophet, he did not like all of his theological revisions, beginning with Rauschenbusch's dismissal of "Greek theology and metaphysics in general." Buckham was profoundly convinced that this was part of "the full Gospel...including the Social Gospel."[121] Second, he thought Rauschenbusch had not done justice to mysticism "which is so essential an element in religion." Third, he thought Rauschenbusch should do much more "to incorporate the doctrine of God and the Incarnation...nor do I think you have given sufficient emphasis to the Living Christ as the vital Power in bringing in the new social order."[122] The buoyant Vida Scudder was also just as forthright with her criticisms as with her praise. She began matter of factly, "Of course," and continued,

> I differ from you, as usual. I hate your way of assuming that vital Christianity stopped about 200 A.D. and began again with the Reformation. To me the Medieval Church bore a far nobler social witness than Protestantism has ever borne.

[117] Pannkoke, "A review of *A Theology for the Social Gospel*," 247–48.
[118] Ibid., 248.
[119] Ibid.
[120] Ibid.
[121] John Wright Buckham to WR, December 24, 1917, box 40, Rauschenbusch Family Papers.
[122] Ibid.

> And I also deprecate your suggestion about the dangers of mysticism, and your constant implication that it is an unsocial force.[123]

She went on to argue ways in which the mystical experience produced love in others. Buckham and Scudder raised significant critiques, but they remained sympathetic academics simply offering their candid corrections to his thought.

Major outright rejections of Rauschenbusch's proposals for theology appeared in print rather than in letters. The anonymous reviewer for *The Presbyterian* seriously questioned moving the doctrine of the kingdom of God to the central place in constructing a theology and then "pruning or expanding all other doctrines to make them harmonize with one's conception of this doctrine." The writer said that Rauschenbusch had departed far from traditional doctrine: "Jesus is little more than the initiator of the Kingdom of God." Moreover, the reviewer wrote that in Rauschenbusch's view, developing the doctrine of the two natures of Christ had put people on a false trail. And the reviewer found the idea that we must democratize the conception of God both "absurd and irreverent." This Presbyterian reviewer ended by introducing and defending the thought of John Calvin and Abraham Kuyper as part of his review. He was dismissive in his conclusion: "There is much that is suggestive about the book, but as a contribution to theology it is hardly to be taken seriously."[124] R. Osgood Morse recognized Rauschenbusch's intense earnestness and honesty but had reservations about his theology. "Has Dr. Rauschenbusch been successful in dealing with these great doctrines constructively and in no way destructively? Candidly I cannot say that he has.... His adaptation of some of them...seems to have robbed some of them of certain vital force."[125]

The reviewer in the *Post Express* offered a direct and strong critique of Rauschenbusch's whole approach to Christianity: "The fallacy of Rauschenbusch lies in his assumption that sociology is a branch of theology.... When we read the first three pages we find that his real purpose is to use theology as a justification for his socialistic opinions."[126] This, of course, was a criticism he had endured for a long time. The next point was also too familiar to him:

---

[123] Vida Scudder to WR, February 27, 1918, box 40, Rauschenbusch Family Papers.

[124] Review of *A Theology for the Social Gospel*, in *The Presbyterian*, n.d., box 94B, Rauschenbusch Family Papers.

[125] R. Osgood Morse, review of *A Theology for the Social Gospel*, n.d., box 94B, Rauschenbusch Family Papers.

[126] Review of *A Theology for the Social Gospel*, in *Post Express*, December 28, 1917, box 46, Rauschenbusch Family Papers.

> The Christian religion aims at saving men's souls and not feeding their bodies. It does not seek to change the social order. Salvation is not a social but an individual and spiritual question. Dr. Rauschenbusch wants the minister of the Gospel to become a social reformer. The answer to his demand is that this is not the business of a clergyman.[127]

This became the accepted reading of Rauschenbusch in circles that opposed the social gospel. It remains a common and widely held, albeit a seriously distorted, view of Rauschenbusch. The reviewer's third point was that theology "must necessarily from its very nature deal with individuals and not with groups of communities.... Its appeal is to souls." The author further declared, "It is a narrow and vulgar idea that Christ was 'on the side of the poor;'...[instead] we find not 'Blessed are the poor,' but blessed are the poor in spirit.'" The author found Rauschenbusch's eschatology "exceedingly fantastic" with a resemblance to reincarnation. Moreover, "the very thought of Christ as a social agitator is repulsive." Finally, socialists cannot prophesy. The reviewer declared that Rauschenbusch was attempting to cover his socialism with the Christian religion. This review is filled with rebuttals at every point. It found nothing positive about Rauschenbusch or his book.[128]

What emerges more clearly than ever before in the letters to Rauschenbusch and the published reviews is the divided alignment of American Protestantism.[129] Rauschenbusch had taken on the arena of theology. Here his liberalism was not implicit. It was more evident than ever before that he challenged tradition. It is no surprise that the division between Protestant interpretations over Rauschenbusch's thought emerged most sharply in the reception and rejection of his *Theology*. C. L. Church was pleased with the book but feared that it would generate bitter words: "Unfortunately we have many people who have never grasped an inkling of the social gospel. And there are many...who love eschatology very much." His outlook was pragmatic. He continued, "We must also do what we can to prevent a split in the Baptist church. People who interpret religion and the Bible in the eighteenth century way are likely to break with more modern men and women. I should regard this as unfortunate."[130]

---

[127] Ibid.

[128] Ibid.

[129] In a notable study, Grant Wacker demonstrated that Protestants of differing opinion nevertheless cooperated far more readily from 1850–1900 than in the decade following 1900 (see "The Holy Spirit and the Spirit of the Age in American Protestantism, 1880–1910," 45–62). Wacker wrote, "it is precisely because there has been so much acrimony between liberals and evangelicals throughout most of the twentieth century that the commonalities of the 1880s and 1890s are so striking" (51). Rauschenbusch certainly faced some sharp criticism of his views.

[130] C. L. Church to WR, February 11, 1918, box 40, Rauschenbusch Family Papers.

Whereas Rauschenbusch did not call names in published works, he could not resist occasional jabs at followers of current premillennialism whose mental capacity, he said, was inversely proportionate to their enthusiasms for apocalyptic ideas.[131] He argued all his adult life that Christians should be revolutionary and support new causes, but this view was never going to appeal to all Christians. Rauschenbusch said he was writing to persuade conservatives, and he tried to soften the implications of updating theology. He spoke his mind without finding a way forward that convinced both liberals and conservatives. Instead, he became for many a polarizing figure—a prophet with a great vision of the kingdom of God for the present day or a socialist whose thought undermined true Christianity. Support came especially from Christians who indicated that the old theology did not resonate with them personally. They also thought the old theology was a serious problem for the modern church, which desperately needed to adapt the message for the modern world. But it was exactly this adapting that conservatives resisted and rejected. This would be a central point of contention in American Protestant debate throughout the following century.[132]

The Basis for Christian Ethics: *The Social Principles of Jesus*

The year before his *Theology* appeared, Rauschenbusch published *The Social Principles of Jesus* (1916). This book was designed as one of numerous textbooks prepared for "The College Voluntary Study Courses," a noncredit program of study for college students. The Association Press of the national Y.M.C.A. published The Everyday Life Books Series [Big Books in Small Compass] on behalf of several student groups. The books were pocket size.[133] The Committee on Voluntary Study enlisted several authors to provide stimulating guides for twelve weeks of study and reflection in Sunday school classes or campus student study groups as well as for general use in the church. The most prolific among the authors of the series was the young Harry Emerson Fosdick who published *Manhood of the Master* (1913) as well as his "Meaning" classics: *Meaning of Faith* (1917), *Meaning of Prayer* (1915), *Meaning of Service* (1920).

The format of *The Social Principles of Jesus* is different from Rauschenbusch's weightier volumes. Each of the twelve chapters contains a substantial Bible selection for the day, followed by Rauschenbusch's commentary. Rauschenbusch demonstrates familiarity with the biblical text, selecting appropriate readings to illustrate his themes. He had preached and written lessons on many of these texts, and he taught New Testament during his early years at Rochester as a professor in the German department. The next section of each chapter, titled "Study for

---

131 WR, *A Theology for the Social Gospel*, 1997 ed., 209.

132 See Hutchison, *The Modernist Impulse in American Protestantism.*

133 WR, *The Social Principles of* Jesus, 1927 ed. (dust jacket description).

the Week," is in effect a brief essay devoted to Rauschenbusch's analysis of the theme developed in the readings of the week. The final section of each chapter is a series of "Suggestions for Thought and Discussion" where Rauschenbusch offers an extended list of questions for student reflection. The questions are designed to provoke students to think through the professions they will follow, examine current ethical issues, recognize their responsibilities to create a more just society, and adopt an attitude of compassion for the poor. Through this extended list of questions, the reader finds many examples of the issues that concerned Rauschenbusch, and often his own opinion emerges from the way he formed the questions.[134]

In this volume Rauschenbusch devoted himself to study "the fundamental conviction of Jesus about the social and ethical relations and duties of men."[135] He concluded the book by emphasizing that Jesus' religion always sought an ethical and social outcome.[136] Examining Jesus' social principles was not a side project for Rauschenbusch. He believed it was the very heart of Jesus' message. He explored numerous aspects of American society, especially those that needed reform. He believed that practicing ethical Christianity would help create a nobler America.[137]

The book is readily accessible. For example, rather than leave "kingdom of God" with its somewhat vague biblical connotations, he explains to the youthful readers that a better translation would be "the reign of God."[138] In this book he seeks to motivate impressionable students to consider examples of injustices in society and form opinions about what they could do to shape a fairer American social and economic system. This was Rauschenbusch's first major book following *Christianizing the Social Order*. Perhaps because of its intended audience and pedagogical format and tone, it has not been as carefully examined as his other major writings.[139] Moreover, for this student audience, Rauschenbusch revisits major previously developed themes, including a critique of capitalism, affirmation of the dual nature of Christianity, and exploration of the nature of the kingdom of God.

The book is devoted principally to social ethics and Christian decision making. Along with *Christianizing the Social Order* it addresses the tasks of applying Christian principles in daily life. Rauschenbusch organized this book in four parts

---

[134] He wrote 240 questions, an average of twenty for each of the twelve chapters.

[135] WR, introduction to *The Social Principles of Jesus*, n.p. In the introduction, Rauschenbusch asserts that the book is neither a life of Christ, nor an exposition of his religious beliefs, nor a doctrinal statement about his life and work.

[136] WR, *Social Principles of Jesus*, 1927 ed., 193.

[137] Ibid., 196.

[138] Ibid., 49. He uses this terminology occasionally in this book (see pp. 70 and 80), but he normally retains the biblical language of "kingdom of God."

[139] Gustafson, "From Scripture to Social Policy and Social Action," 160.

with three chapters each. He starts with the teachings of Jesus about the value of life, social relationships and helping the weak. The second section deals with three dimensions of the kingdom of God as the highest good. The third division explores three major forces working against Jesus' ideal—political, economic and religious. The final section declares that to advance the kingdom will require struggle, suffering, and action.

Social ethicist James Gustafson discovered in *The Social Principles of Jesus* useful insights for contemporary ethical analysis and provided a perceptive analysis of the book. In his analysis the reformer must accomplish three goals—identify what is wrong, provide motivation for action, and set out the areas of the envisioned social reform.[140] These categories provide a useful framework for summarizing Rauschenbusch's social ethics. Gustafson was particularly struck by Rauschenbusch's statement that "the will of God is identical with the good of mankind."[141] This line was for Gustafson the "hinge" on which Rauschenbusch constructed his interpretation.

Rauschenbusch addresses all three of Gustafson's criteria for social moral enquiry. As in most of his writing, Rauschenbusch singles out ways in which entrenched political, economic, and religious forces resist social reform by holding onto the money, power, and privileges they enjoy. In addition, he considers Christian views of sin and evil, especially their social dimensions. Rauschenbusch discusses leadership, contrasting ambitious leaders who exercise power over others for personal gain with leaders who use their position to serve others.[142] He points out that Jesus warned about the danger of wealth far more than about licentiousness or drunkenness. In a stinging remark Rauschenbusch also notes that the modern church has revised Jesus' message: It has set aside the teaching of Jesus on wealth because the leaders of society seem to think there is something sacred about getting money.[143] Third, Rauschenbusch asserts that religion itself can inhibit social progress. He argues that Jesus' invectives against scribes and Pharisees were directed against perversions of religion that neglect justice, mercy, and good faith. This was a battle Jesus waged throughout his ministry. The criteria of good religion, says Rauschenbusch, is its ethical value.[144] There are other obstacles to the kingdom that are built into human nature. Rauschenbusch describes the human animal as naturally lazy and selfish, inclined to live for today.[145] Moreover, he informs readers that in its social expressions, evil became more

---

[140] Ibid., 161.

[141] Ibid., 162–63, 166, citing WR, *Social Principles of Jesus*, 1927 ed., 128.

[142] WR, *Social Principles of Jesus*, 1927 ed., 100.

[143] Ibid., 124, 126. Rauschenbusch is in part relying on Edward A. Ross, progressive American author of *Sin and Society* (1907) and *The Old World in the New* (1914).

[144] WR, *Social Principles of Jesus*, 1927 ed., 132–35.

[145] Ibid., 73, 152.

complicated and powerful than sins of individuals. He declares that this is true not only of gangs, but also of structures of economic and political oppression.[146]

Rauschenbusch takes many opportunities to motivate students to act. A reviewer notes that Rauschenbusch made a persistent appeal to young college students "to face the social demands of the faith of Christ" by living life for others.[147] He describes situations and poses related questions involving social decisions that affect the conditions of neighbors, notably to refrain from actions that would hurt others. He asks readers to form decisions about right courses of action. The book is filled with creative motivational scenarios, especially in the numerous questions Rauschenbusch formulated for student consideration.

Gustafson's third guideline is to state the reformer's aim or purpose of social reform. For Rauschenbusch the aim is to work toward establishing the kingdom of God or the reign of God (also described by Rauschenbusch as a better society, human solidarity, or the good of mankind). In ordinary language the ultimate goal is to create "a nobler America."[148] Gustafson's analysis notes that Rauschenbusch's Christian social ethic employs two criteria in making moral judgments on society—Scripture and "what is good for mankind."[149] Rauschenbusch assumes Protestant reliance on scriptural authority. In this book he cites eighty-four extended passages of Scripture, mostly from the Gospels. He is anchoring social Christianity squarely in the Bible. According to Gustafson, Rauschenbusch's other criteria for recognizing moral wrong is human reaction to "a violation of something which is part of man's natural life, such as prostitution, race, contempt, war, and excessive profits."[150] These are wrong and should be opposed because they violate "the good of mankind." Gustafson concludes that Rauschenbusch's social ethic is based on the correlation of the two authorities: the will of God and the good of mankind.

The next logical step, says Gustafson, is for the ethicist to make a critical examination of Rauschenbusch's assumptions and his twofold authority. Gustafson contends that to do so is not quite fair because this would "press questions of an academic sort on a man whose intentions were not critically to analyze the ethic they imbedded in his work, but were of a practical sort."[151] This generous concession is made with full awareness of many critiques of Rauschenbusch's social theory already made by generations of ethicists. Instead, Gustafson points out that Rauschenbusch was not asking the questions in the way modern ethicists

---

[146] Ibid., 160–62.

[147] Review of *The Social Principles of Jesus*, in *The Continent*, December 7, 1916, box 46, Rauschenbusch Family Papers.

[148] WR, *Social Principles of Jesus*, 1927 ed., 196.

[149] Gustafson, "From Scripture to Social Policy and Social Action," 163, 164.

[150] Ibid., 165.

[151] Ibid., 168.

would, nor did he try to construct an ethical method.[152] Nevertheless, because of his commitment to change in America, Rauschenbusch sought to establish a basis for social action. Gustafson reminds readers that Rauschenbusch was "a Christian reformer, not primarily an academic analyst of ethical thought."[153] Because contemporary ethicists have better resources for biblical interpretation and for understanding society, Gustafson contends they are obligated to do better work than Rauschenbusch did.[154] But he also argues that Rauschenbusch's limitations should not detract from his "historical significance nor from the greatness of the integrity of his thought, his action, and his person."[155] Gustafson's analysis helps identify the assumptions behind Rauschenbusch's social ethic. His assessment is a tribute to Rauschenbusch for attempting to provide a Christian rationale for working toward a more just society. Gustafson (1925–1988) was a major leader in Christian social ethics. His careful appropriation of Rauschenbusch is a superlative tribute to Rauschenbusch's principles on social ethics.

Rauschenbusch was keenly conscious of writing to seventeen- to twenty-one-year-old students in this book. He sought to convert them to his vision of a more just society. He defined the kingdom of God in terms of the American ideals of freedom and justice. Since students were in the midst of preparing for their future careers, Rauschenbusch pointedly asked them what their studies were for—"to fit ourselves for exploiting our fellows or to show them the way to the kingdom of God?"[156] He probed the conscience of readers with many questions having ethical implications. Rauschenbusch did not consciously distinguish among Gustafson's three analytical categories. Instead, he described problems of injustice to be addressed, suggested goals of a transformed society, and offered as much motivation as he could through relevant selection of Scripture, his own reflections, and his probing questions.

The process of writing *Social Principles* is well documented. Association Press representatives Richard H. Edwards and Frederick M. Harris proposed that Rauschenbusch write the book. Rauschenbusch reported that he made up his outline between morning and afternoon during Edwards's first visit.[157] Correspondence began in August 1915, and by September the press had sent comments of several reviewers. The contract followed, dated January 20, 1916. The committee was pleased with Rauschenbusch's work. Harris invited him to write a companion volume on Paul's social message and encouraged him regarding sales, reporting that Harry Emerson Fosdick's *The Meaning of Prayer* had enjoyed a wonderful

---

152 Ibid., 160.
153 Ibid.
154 Ibid., 169.
155 Ibid., 160.
156 WR, *Social Principles of Jesus*, 1927 ed., 77.
157 "Outline of Proposal for Book," typescript, box 46, Rauschenbusch Family Papers.

success: "During the six months it has been out it has sold over 40,000 copies."[158]

Writing the book energized Rauschenbusch. He wrote to Reverend G. Herbert Elkins of Pittsburgh indicating that he was writing a textbook for the student movements on "The Social Principles of Jesus" and that he saw "more freedom and power in his [Jesus'] teaching than ever."[159] At the same time, Rauschenbusch needed encouragement. He lamented as he looked at current affairs, "I have never seen so much greed, hate, insincerity, and hypocrisy in public life as at present.... [I] speak up, but my experiences thus far have shown me that it does absolutely no good, and merely results in cutting into my health and lessening my influence."[160]

There was much that needed to change. He was weary. The war weighed heavily on him. Perhaps the next generation would carry on, but his optimism was sharply tempered. In the book he wrote that the spirit of Jesus had never had more than half a chance in historic Christianity, but despite that it had accomplished much.[161] Rauschenbusch seemed discouraged, yet also hopeful. Perhaps he was simply being more realistic about the prospects for a social reformation of the nation. He now conceded that it might take fifty years before the social movement would be widely adopted by society.[162]

The welcome reception of this little volume was immediate. On September 20, 1916, an agent of Association Press wrote, "I am glad to report that we have already had the most hearty commendation of the volume from some of those [Y.M.C.A.] secretaries near at hand who have found time to examine the book."[163] Other reviewers were generally very favorable. Graham Taylor wrote, "It is one of those big little books which leads on and out to further study and progress."[164] A reviewer in *The Christian Century*, identifying Rauschenbusch as the leading author on the social application of Christianity, noted that "his books have been read by the tens of thousands" and that "this fine little volume...is no exception among his books."[165] The reviewer in *The Continent* was most enthusiastic, proclaiming that this book was "even more vital than his earlier books.... Rauschenbusch had put his whole heart" into this book. The author concluded

---

[158] Frederick Harris to WR, August 30, 1915, box 46, Rauschenbusch Family Papers.

[159] WR to G. Herbert Elkins, January 20, 1916, box 46, Rauschenbusch Family Papers.

[160] Ibid.

[161] WR, *Social Principles of Jesus*, 1927 ed., 72.

[162] Ibid., 73.

[163] D. S. Jillson to WR, September 20, 1916, box 46, Rauschenbusch Family Papers.

[164] Review of *The Social Principles of Jesus*, in *The Survey*, February 1917, box 46, Rauschenbusch Family Papers.

[165] Review of *The Social Principles of Jesus*, in *The Christian Century*, January 1917, box 46, Rauschenbusch Family Papers.

that "classes that use it can hardly be dull."[166] The book was in fact a great success. It had a ready market in Y.M.C.A./Y.W.C.A. study groups, and Rauschenbusch's influence reached many readers as a result. Four years after publication a letter came from H. S. Gott in Estonia to the Y.M.C.A. in New York City. He told a story in which he reported,

> Not long ago I was visiting our work at Petchovy situated in a famous monastery, and happened to be sitting in the room of the local secretary [of the Y.M.C.A.], a Russian, and also a priest, when one of the black monks breezed into the room with his long flowing robes, and said: "I say, Grievsky, where is that Social Teachings of Christ?"

Following his account of this story, Gott concluded, "The Secretary told me afterwards that he was not the only monk who was reading Rauschenbusch."[167]

The Social Principles of Jesus proved to be enormously popular.[168] This was a practical manual, characterized by a theological ethic sketched in nontechnical language. It reflects part of Rauschenbusch's theological assumptions, but it especially elaborated ethical guidelines useful in striving for a more Christian society. For Rauschenbusch, Jesus was the moral force behind the power of Christianity, and he also provided the principles for pursuing the kingdom of God.

History and Theology

Theology was formed in and by history. In Rauschenbusch's thought, theology must take history into account. Historians who adopted the new critical method of examining texts transformed "the perception" of Scripture and doctrine by demonstrating the historical nature of their composition. Christianity relies on authority, but since the late nineteenth century the nature of authority has been examined and revised in light of critical historical methods. Whereas history throughout much of church history had been written as providential, in the nineteenth century historians looked instead to human explanation in the shaping of history. It had, after all, been arguments, votes, and political pressures that shaped the most important doctrines of the church—the Trinity, and the Person of Christ. Moreover, following the Reformation, denominations summarized their beliefs in confessions of faith, and these did not agree. They too were

---

[166] Review of *The Social Principles of Jesus*, in *The Continent*, December 7, 1916, box 46, Rauschenbusch Family Papers.

[167] H. S. Gott to Y. M. C. A., New York City, 1920, box 46, Rauschenbusch Family Papers.

[168] The book sold 14,590 copies in 1916 and 13,275 in 1917, clearing Rauschenbusch $22,674 in a two-year period (royalty statements from Association Press, February 20, 1917 and February 1, 1918, box 106, Rauschenbusch Family Papers). In 1907 he was earning $3000 as a professor, the top salary paid to Rochester Theological Seminary faculty (See Minue, 141).

products of history, conditioned by time, place, and opposing interpretations. Liberalism accepted this historical reality rather than denying it: an important feature of Protestant liberalism was its openness to changing approaches to theology.

Rauschenbusch accepted the historical conditioning of theology early in his career, and his daily work as a church historian reinforced his conviction. When he introduced his book of theology, he declared that the church should be prepared to go through periods of "readjustment."[169] Over and over again Rauschenbusch reminded audiences that society had changed, and he implored the churches to adapt their thinking and action accordingly. His proposal of a social gospel seemed dramatic to many, but he could point to plenty of evidence of change in the industrial society of his day. In liberal approaches openness to new ideas was expected and welcome to communicate the gospel message to the present generation. The theology of liberalism itself gave way to neo-orthodoxy for many twentieth-century Christians, and neo-orthodoxy in turn gave way to liberation theology. "Readjustment" is normal—and valuable—for the church.

Theologian Albrecht Ritschl (1822–1889) focused attention on the historical Jesus and his message of the kingdom of God. His influence was profound for nineteenth-century theology. In his view, God works in the arena of history. It is precisely in the human arena that the kingdom of God contends with the kingdom of evil.[170] God would bring about the kingdom in history according to Jesus' message. Rauschenbusch drew deeply from the notion of the coming of the kingdom of God. Jesus' role is crucial in the work of God in history because he set in motion a force that has already changed the world for good. The task of the church is to help bring in the kingdom—in individual lives and in society.

A prominent way to recast the Christian message emerged as various expressions of personal relationships. The biblical summation of the gospel was love for God and love for fellow human beings. According to Jesus' words, these brief phrases summarized the gospel. In *What Is Christianity?* Harnack famously reduced the Christian message to simple formulas, notably, the Fatherhood of God and the brotherhood of mankind. Harnack's historical work led him to search for the core of early Christianity, which he did in his *History of Dogma*. In *What Is Christianity?* he wanted to convey the essence of the faith. It was an enormously successful book. Paul Tillich recalls Harnack telling him that in 1900 the main rail station in Leipzig was blocked by freight cars filled with Harnack's book,

---

[169] WR, *A Theology for the Social Gospel*, 1997 ed., 1, 10–22. Rauschenbusch was careful to develop this idea at the outset of his *Theology*, laying the groundwork for his restatement of theology. It is notable that he used the word in the letter to Williston Walker in which he explained his proposal for the Taylor lectures. See WR to Williston Walker, December 31, 1915, box 40, Rauschenbusch Family Papers.

[170] Evans, *Liberalism without Illusion*, 68.

which was translated into more languages than any book except the Bible and was being sent all over the world. Tillich concluded that this book had great significance to the educated people in 1900 who wanted to affirm "the Christian message in a form which was free from dogmatic captivity and at the same time very much rooted in the biblical message image of Jesus."[171] In a similar fashion, Rauschenbusch bypassed extended treatment of traditional doctrines and sought to communicate Jesus' teaching of the kingdom of God. He translated the Christian message into personal terms, never tiring of speaking of the infinite value of the human being. People were made in the image of God, and they and their society should be the object of love and redemption.

From a historical point of view, Rauschenbusch was fully aware of the debate over the relationship of the divine and the human that went on in the early church regarding the doctrine of the person of Christ. He rejected the ancient arguments as artificial, inconclusive, and without relevance for modern Christians. He wrestled with the doctrine of the work of Christ—how salvation should be understood. He rejected the traditional satisfaction theory of atonement, which focused on the necessity of the death of Christ, and instead adopted the outlook of the new theology, which stressed human love responding to God's love.[172] He believed that Jesus had full consciousness of God, and in this way initiated a new stage in history. Casting their narrative from a human point of view, nineteenth-century historians claimed that Jesus' influence had altered history, but they avoided the presumption of pronouncing what God had done in history. The common way to refer to the event was to declare that Jesus brought a new "force" into the world in his person.[173] Moreover, Jesus' central message of the kingdom of God is understood to be the reign of God in the lives of individuals and their relationships in homes, schools, churches, business, politics, and all social arrangements of people. The reward is the redemption of people—their physical and emotional welfare. The force that motivates people to live for others is the spirit of Jesus. Rauschenbusch was fully convinced that the power of Jesus' spirit persists today. Jesus was not a dead person from history but a living personality and force in the world.[174]

Rauschenbusch wrote a single-page theological statement that he called "An

---

[171] Tillich, *Perspectives on 19th and 20th Century Protestant Theology*, 222.

[172] Ironically, he dedicated *A Theology for the Social Gospel* to A. H. Strong, his theology professor, whose traditional theological views he rejected, but whom he personally respected.

[173] This terminology, widely used in Rauschenbusch's era, is still found useful by historians. For Rauschenbusch, see *Social Principles*, 194; "Our Attitude toward Millenarianism," 91; *A Theology for the Social Gospel*, 1997 ed., 127–28. For modern usage, see for example, Freeman, *A New History of Early Christianity*, 291.

[174] Hudson, ed., *Walter Rauschenbusch: Selected Writings*, 121.

Affirmation of Faith."[175] He laid out in four brief paragraphs the essentials of his theology. He began with his affirmation of the reality of the spiritual world, which included the elements of truth, holiness, prayer, duty, life eternal, and the reality of God. Second, he affirmed faith in the kingdom of God and its final triumph as well as his determination to live by its spirit in all of his day-by-day dealings. Third, he asserted his acceptance of all people and his solidarity with them, desiring the free flow of God's love through him to all other people. Finally, he affirmed his faith in life and its goodness, his desire to live a Christ-like life, and his confidence in redemption through the power of Christ.

Rauschenbusch reaffirmed in this one-page summary the traditional beliefs of the faith, including the reality of God, redemption through Christ to eternal life, and an ethical life based on the example of Christ. At the same time, he gave equal space to doctrines neglected but enormously important and meaningful in his understanding of Christianity, including his love of life and its goodness, his solidarity with all people, and above all, the full commitment of his belief and life to the kingdom of God. This statement, presumably written near the end of his life, neatly sums up Rauschenbusch's commitment not only to the essentials of Christian theology but also to the ethical practice of living out the Christian faith. These are the themes developed in his *A Theology for the Social Gospel* and *The Social Principles of Jesus*. Rauschenbusch devoted his life to making a better world. He inspired many readers, especially in the churches, to live and work for the kingdom of God. His influence would persist to the present moment. We turn next to highlight Rauschenbusch's legacy for the century following his death.

[175] WR, "An Affirmation of Faith," typescript, n.d., 1 page, NABHC archives.

CHAPTER 12

A CENTURY OF RECEPTIONS: RAUSCHENBUSCH'S CONTINUING LEGACY

This study has given particular emphasis to Rauschenbusch's major writings and their immediate reception. However, the evidence of Rauschenbusch's enduring significance lies in the fact that he is still being read today, a century after those first impressions. Rauschenbusch's ideas have resonated, and he has enjoyed remarkable staying power. His fuller legacy may be understood as the total impact of his continuing influence in American religion and culture during the past one hundred years. This, of course, is a vast topic represented by a constantly expanding body of academic literature. To account for his influence comprehensively would require a massive study, yet this is a logical place to extend the notion of reception from Rauschenbusch's first readers to his long-term influence. The purpose of this chapter is to sketch major contours of Rauschenbusch's abiding influence as spokesman for a Christian social gospel. He has stimulated extensive reflection on the idea of the Christian's role in creating a more just society and nation.[1]

During his lifetime and during the generation following, numerous readers declared that Rauschenbusch had done more than any other person to change the thought of American Protestantism in their generation.[2] Fifty years after Rauschenbusch's death, Harry Emerson Fosdick wrote, "Rauschenbusch did more after

---

[1] The legacy might be explored in several additional directions, including the formal acceptance of social Christian responsibility by one denomination after another, the ministries developed by Christian social activists, continuing opposition to the social gospel by many denominations, the acceptance of social responsibility by some evangelicals from Carl F. H. Henry in 1947 to the present, Rauschenbusch's role in missionary practice, and current students' lively desire to reach beyond individualistic worship and practice their Christianity by addressing human need in its many forms.

[2] See "The Social Gospel," an anonymous review of *A Theology for the Social Gospel*, published just before Rauschenbusch's death. Henry P. Van Dusen, president of Union Theological Seminary called Rauschenbusch, "the greatest single personal influence in the life and thought of the U.S. church in the last 50 years" (box 106, Rauschenbusch Family Papers). This statement was also printed in *Time* magazine (see "The Social Gospeler"). On April 5, 1937, giving the Rauschenbusch Lectures, Van Dusen said, "Probably the three most influential men in American Church History upon the thought of the church have been Jonathan Edwards,

his death than he ever did in his lifetime.... The essence of his message—the social and economic transformation involved in the coming of the kingdom of God on earth—is an integral part of the Christian gospel wherever intelligence and conscience are alive in the churches."[3]

W. H. P. Faunce wrote a note of sympathy and good wishes four months before Rauschenbusch's death. Aware of Rauschenbusch's illness, Faunce acknowledged the stress Rauschenbusch had experienced due to the war and then went on to express his personal gratitude. He wrote that nothing could "destroy my debt to you as long as I live. In that little church in New York you lived the social gospel in a way that made it real and vital to all the rest of us. Through your writings, as well as your teachings, you have since then reached an enormous circle and permeated American thinking. It is a great achievement, which ought to give you comfort and satisfaction morning, noon, and night."[4] Faunce had served as a fellow Baptist minister in New York before becoming president of Brown University. They remained good friends for life.

Rauschenbusch's long-term influence was assured when the Federal Council of Churches (1908) adopted his ideas of the social responsibility of the churches as part of their agenda. Under strong Methodist leadership, the newly formed organization attracted support of several Protestant denominations. Rauschenbusch's formulation of the social problem and its solution would undergo debate, criticism, and revision, but the fact that the churches formally accepted responsibility for supporting a just economic and social order meant that Rauschenbusch's main point had been accepted by mainline Protestantism. This was not merely an agenda item pursued for a few years; addressing social issues became a permanent fixture in American Protestantism. The Federal Council of Churches was renamed the National Council of Churches of Christ in 1950, and the central concern of the organization is often summarized as "peace and justice." Moreover, many individual denominations responded to the economic challenges posed by industrialization during this era and created departments devoted to addressing social issues. In his last book Rauschenbusch referred to personal and social salvation in the image of two concentric circles: he was always keen for the church to move beyond the individual and beyond the walls of the church to bring redemption to the wider culture.[5] In 1915 Rauschenbusch offered his own assessment of what he had achieved. He noted that when he began to look at social questions,

---

Horace Bushnell and Walter Rauschenbusch" (see box 106, Rauschenbusch Family Papers).

[3] Fosdick, introduction to *A Rauschenbusch Reader*, xxii.

[4] W. H. P. Faunce to WR, June 22, 1918, box 32, Rauschenbusch Family Papers.

[5] WR, *A Theology for the Social Gospel*, 1997 ed., 23.

> and to realize how deeply the teachings of Jesus differed from the teachings ordinarily accepted in the church, I dedicated myself to the task of re-establishing the teachings of Jesus Christ in the common thought of the church, and of establishing His precepts as the common principles of the social world. Whatsoever good there has been in my life has been along those lines.[6]

Rauschenbusch's influence has indeed endured.

An assessment of Rauschenbusch's academic achievements during his twenty years as professor is impressive. He made public addresses and published articles amid constant traveling. His works were translated into numerous other languages.[7] He was invited to present lectures at several universities, the most prestigious of which were his Nathaniel W. Taylor lectures at Yale. Rauschenbusch's sabbatical in 1891 and five invited lectureships became the bases for his three largest volumes: *Christianity and the Social Crisis*, *Christianizing the Social Order*, and *A Theology for the Social Gospel*.[8] Rauschenbusch published two additional influential volumes, *Prayers for the Social Awakening* and *The Social Principles of Jesus*. "Social" appears in the titles of Rauschenbusch's five major books. Depending on reviewer preference, each of these has been called Rauschenbusch's greatest work. These books have had lasting influence in defining American Protestant identity during the past century.

Print History of Rauschenbusch's Books, 1907–2017

Rauschenbusch's books were the most accessible and most enduring source of his ideas and influence. An outline of the print history of his five major books provides a snapshot of the fortunes of Rauschenbusch's century-long influence. The books considered here are *Christianity and the Social Crisis* (1907), *Prayers for the Social Awakening* (1909), *Christianizing the Social Order* (1912), *The Social Principles of Jesus* (1916), and *A Theology for the Social Gospel* (1918). One or more

---

[6] WR, "The Social Background, Spirit and Message of the Bible," address given at the Fifth National Convention of National Young Women's Christian Association, 1915; quoted in Sharpe, *Walter Rauschenbusch*, 425.

[7] Nixon listed translations into French, German, Norwegian, Swedish, Flemish, Russian, Japanese, and Chinese. See Justin Wroe Nixon, "Walter Rauschenbusch," typescript" (1947), 4, in American Baptist Historical Society, call no. 261, qN654R. Nixon's list of translations is in a typescript (1947).

[8] Rauschenbusch gave the Earl Lectures at the Pacific School of Religion, Berkeley, California (1910); the Merrick Lectures at Ohio Wesleyan University, Delaware, Ohio (1911); the Gates Lectures at Grinnell College, Grinnell, Iowa (1914); the Enoch Pond Lectures at Bangor Theological Seminary, Bangor, Maine (1915); and the Taylor Lectures at Yale Divinity School, New Haven, Connecticut (1917). See Rochester Theological Seminary, "Rev. Walter Rauschenbusch, D.D.," 36.

of his books was republished during each decade of the next century except for the 1930s and 1950s. Most of them were published in the United States or Europe (most frequently Switzerland and Germany), and some in China, Japan, Russia, and South America. All of these volumes were reprinted multiple times during the 1920s, suggesting that interest in the social gospel did not die with World War I as Rauschenbusch had feared—and as his critics have often declared. Especially noticeable are the many editions of the college study guide, *The Social Principles of Jesus*, published between 1916 and 1923. The book was distributed among soldiers as well as students, and it was published in Japan, Russia, and Switzerland as well as in the United States.

None of the books was republished during the 1930s, probably because of the economic hardships brought on by the Great Depression. The desperate economy likely affected both commercial printers and book buyers. In the 1940s *Christianizing the Social Order*, *A Theology for the Social Gospel*, and *The Social Principles of Jesus* were all republished. There was demand for the volumes during and immediately following World War II, with editions appearing in Geneva and Buenos Aires. Rauschenbusch's works were not reprinted during the post-war 1950s. The economy was booming. Americans focused on their jobs and their families during the decade, and churches flourished as never before. A Red Scare pushed society in a conservative direction. There did not seem to be a demand in the United States for revolutionary theology that challenged the status quo, but that was soon to change.

Rauschenbusch's works have been continuously reprinted since 1961. The next four decades were much better for book publishers. In the 1960s the United States experienced a huge cultural shift, which included challenges to the establishment—both secular and religious. The most important Rauschenbusch republication was *Christianity and the Social Crisis*, which appeared in the prestigious Harper Torchbook series in 1964, with a superb introduction by Columbia historian Robert D. Cross. Another edition appeared in 1971. Rauschenbusch's *Theology* volume was republished in 1960, 1961, 1968, 1971, and 1987, most frequently by the Methodist Abingdon Press. This volume had substantial staying power throughout this era. *The Social Principles of Jesus* and *Prayers for the Social Awakening* were immediately accessible to laity for devotional reading, and they proved to be the most widely disseminated of his books. Boston's Pilgrim Press had republished the *Prayers* book in the 1920s and published it again in 1984 as well as *Christianizing the Social Order* four years earlier (1980). Norwood, Folcroft, West, and Arden Library, all Pennsylvania presses, published *The Social Principles of Jesus* (Folcroft 1976, Norwood 1977, West 1978, and Arden 1985). Folcroft also published *Prayers* in 1977, and Norwood published it in 1978. In the 1990s the Presbyterian Westminster/John Knox Press republished both *Christianity and the Social Crisis* (1991) and *A Theology for the Social Gospel* (1997).

It was a press newly reorganized by merger and seeking to establish itself among academic publishers.

Resurgence of Rauschenbusch's works has flourished especially since 2000. Wipf and Stock has taken the lead, publishing all five major volumes between 2000 and 2011. Numerous other presses have joined in republishing Rauschenbusch. The total number of printings for the key volumes since 2000 is *Prayers* (2), *Christianity and the Social Crisis* (3), *Christianizing the Social Order* (4). *The Social Principles of Jesus* (4), and *A Theology for the Social Gospel* (6). The reasons for the increased frequency of publication since 2000 are ambiguous. On the one hand, advanced technologies make reprint editions easier and more cost effective. On the other hand, the Internet is also now seen as a rival and threat to print culture. Publishers presumably are responding to an ongoing demand or at least a perceived demand. In any case, no decade for a hundred years has matched the first decade of the twenty-first century in numbers of new editions of Rauschenbusch's work. To celebrate the Rauschenbusch centennial in 2018, Mercer University Press is publishing his key works in three volumes, complete with an introduction, photographs of Rauschenbusch and his family, and additional writings by other social gospel advocates of Rauschenbusch's era.[9] This reprint history in itself suggests that publishers and readers have found enduring value in Rauschenbusch's works. What is the heart of his thought that has sustained appeal for a century?

Rauschenbusch's Achievement

Gary Dorrien concluded that "the crucial figure in the historical narrative and religious vision [of the social gospel] is Walter Rauschenbusch because he conceptualized the social revolution, defined it, epitomized its spiritual character and legitimized it...."[10] Rauschenbusch's achievement came about in part through his considerable intellectual ability to assimilate, analyze, and systematize insights from several disciplines and subdisciplines. Perhaps the most noticeable development in his thinking was his ability to bring together his understanding of economics and Christianity, yet he declared that he "could not hope to be more than a popularizer in economics though I might reasonably hope to make a real contribution to the religious point of view."[11] Rauschenbusch modestly saw himself as an amateur in economics but better equipped in religion although various correspondents assured him that his economic analysis was sound. Rauschenbusch also expressed trepidation at publishing a volume on theology and presented a

[9] William H. Brackney, ed. *Walter Rauschenbusch: Published and Selected Works in Three Volumes* (Macon, GA: Mercer University Press, 2018).

[10] Dorrien, *Soul in Society*, 6.

[11] WR to Scott Nearing, April 21, 1913, box 14, Rauschenbusch Family Papers.

disclaimer in the preface of the book that this was not his chosen field of study.

Likewise, although he was profoundly immersed in the New Testament scholarship, he did not attempt to write a scholarly monograph on a particular aspect of biblical studies. In fact, he did not contribute a significant book or body of research even on church history, his chosen field of study. Instead, he used what he learned from history to understand and explain modern society, and he used his knowledge of church history to provide perspectives on the contemporary church in his writings. In the end Rauschenbusch focused all of his major writings on the social dimensions of Christianity. He was a synthesizer of his seminary curriculum. He drew from all its major fields of study: biblical, historical, theological, and practical. In addition, his reading in the disciplines of sociology, political science, education, and economics helped him analyze American society of his day, and his goal of Christianizing society led him to identify the economy as the central problem in American culture. He connected Jesus' message of the kingdom of God, spirituality, theology, and a vision of a transformed society to create the idea of the social gospel. Drawing on multiple resources, he effectively argued for the place of the social gospel in modern Christianity.

As Protestant spokesman Rauschenbusch's leadership passed with his early death, but his successful advocacy for the social gospel meant that he had reoriented the thinking of many Protestants of his day and in years following. Gladden, Ely and others had articulated the social gospel. But Rauschenbusch endures as the best-known spokesman for the movement. His contribution was to confront the church so effectively that the social gospel has remained a part of discussion and action in the church for a century. Rauschenbusch's vision of church and nation was bold and revolutionary. His language was strong; his biblical anchoring went beyond individual verses to show that justice permeated the whole tradition of the prophets, John the Baptist, and Jesus. Moreover, he had a unifying theme—the kingdom of God—and showed that it was at the heart of Jesus' message. Furthermore, he boldly denounced capitalism, which created suffering, and the church, which failed to take a stand for justice. Finally, the American social and political context was prepared for broad positive reception of his message. His ideas elicited strong responses—both negative and positive—and still do. Critics and detractors argued that Rauschenbusch moved too far from traditional Christianity. He seemed in the minds of many to substitute socialism and its goals for traditional Christian goals of personal salvation. His language and his categories stretched beyond traditional biblical and theological language. Even a sympathetic reviewer wondered, "What, for example, is the development of democracy going to do to our conception of God?"[12] But his views resonated with

[12] "The Social Gospel." This was an anonymous reviewer in *The Presbyterian*, and while the page number is missing, a copy of the review can be found in box 94B of the Rauschenbusch

many who judged his spirit and his agenda to be soundly Christian. Rauschenbusch gave Protestants a new vision of Christianity for their age and inspired them to new understandings of the role of the church.

Rauschenbusch refers to a favorable "psychological moment" which helped explain the unexpected success of his message. But his appeal was not due merely to an economic downturn or to some vague notion of the spirit of the times. Instead, he tapped a moral nerve that continued to move readers fifty years later and even one hundred years later. Rauschenbusch wrote to Scott Nearing, the radical economist, "My reading and thinking on social questions has been a labor of love under the pressure of moral and religious conviction which would not let me go."[13] The social gospel was no mere academic hobby for these two men. Both felt driven by a moral imperative to take up the task of seeking justice in the nation. Here Rauschenbusch articulated the reason his writing still commands response from members of the Christian community: the suffering of the poor elicits in every generation "moral and religious conviction" that will not let one's conscience go. He connected religious sensibility and human need. But he also acted on what his conscience told him. It took enormous courage to challenge tradition and propose that the usual understanding of Christianity was defective. Rauschenbusch's message is not likely going away as long as conscience calls people to pay attention to the suffering that always accompanies poverty and injustice. He was the foremost advocate for the social gospel.

Rauschenbusch's Followers to 1935

What were the early fortunes of Rauschenbusch's influence? During the two decades following his death his message for the church received significant attention. Charles C. Morrison observed that by the 1920s study of the social gospel was included in the curriculum of all major American Protestant seminaries of the North except the Lutheran. Many in the South also adopted the new study.[14] However, Gary Dorrien judged that whereas the clergy showed enthusiasm for the movement, the laity did not, and as a result the clergy did not promote the social gospel from the pulpit.[15] Dorrien argued, moreover, that immediately after World War I Americans lost enthusiasm for social crusades of any kind except the peace movement.[16]

From the outset of Rauschenbusch's writing, his message was designed for

Family Papers.

[13] WR to Scott Nearing, April 21, 1913, box 14, Rauschenbusch Family Papers.

[14] Morrison, *The Social Gospel and Christian* Culture, 15, cited in Dorrien, *The Making of American Liberal Theology*, 147.

[15] Dorrien, *The Making of American Liberal Theology*, 148.

[16] Ibid., 141.

the benefit of the lower classes but was addressed to the middle class. Rauschenbusch's own church did not respond to his proposals to aid workers, and his early publishing venture, *For the Right*, dedicated to the welfare of workers, failed in less than two years. Rauschenbusch recognized the problem in part, and he told the working class that they must embrace the movement themselves if it was ever to be successful.

The decade of the 1920s saw the largest number of translations of Rauschenbusch's major books. The influence of his writing was spreading not only to Europe, but also to Asia and Latin America. Also in the 1920s Rauschenbusch's work became the subject of academic investigation. In 1926 Anna M. Singer published *Walter Rauschenbusch and His Contribution to Social Christianity,* which was based on her dissertation. Because of his prominent role in the ecumenical movement, the opinions expressed by W. A. Visser t'Hooft carried significant weight. His perspectives on the social gospel appeared in *The Background of the Social Gospel in America.*

The letters to Rauschenbusch show that many ministers found new inspiration in Rauschenbusch's message. Ministers continued to be profoundly influenced by Rauschenbusch after his death. In 1934 Baptist minister Martin Leuschner wrote, "Walter Rauschenbusch and Our Day," an address he delivered at three separate ministers' conferences.[17] Rauschenbusch was clearly the guiding light for Leuschner's life as a minister. He chose his title because he was convinced that Rauschenbusch's influence was here to stay. He wrote, "None can think of his life as past, as belonging to history. He started something in the thought-life of the Christian church which is gaining momentum from year to year and makes him more alive today after his death than during the days of his pilgrimage on earth."[18] Moreover, "authors and leaders of the religious life of today have acknowledged their spiritual indebtedness to this interpreter of God's truth."[19] Leuschner indicated that during his seminary studies he had researched Rauschenbusch's influence on religious thinking and had found references to Rauschenbusch in some fifty books. He also listed an additional sixteen current titles to illustrate Rauschenbusch's influence on current writers of religious books, and he gives yet another list of books that were dedicated to Rauschenbusch.[20] Pauline Rauschenbusch had also shown Leuschner a letter indicating how Rauschenbusch had influenced Henry O. Wallace, secretary of agriculture, in his *Religion and Statesmanship*, and how former governor of Colorado, William Sweet, had been profoundly influenced by Rauschenbusch's idea of *Christianizing*

[17] Martin Leuschner, "Walter Rauschenbusch and Our Day."

[18] Ibid., 2.

[19] Ibid., 3.

[20] Ibid., 3–5.

the Social Order.[21] Leuschner affirmed that Rauschenbusch's major goal was "the possibility of [seeing] the Kingdom of God on earth...[and it involved] the task of bringing the power of God to bear upon all of life. This was the life-mission and life-fulfillment of Jesus as Rauschenbusch interpreted him."[22] Leuschner represented the perspective of an ordinary minister. What about the leading Protestant voice of the 1930s—Harry Emerson Fosdick, arguably the most influential minister of his era?

Fosdick, preacher and prolific author, wrote in his autobiography that he was "strongly influenced by him [Rauschenbusch].... a man of dynamic energy...remembered now as the author of influential books and as a famous professor at the theological seminary in Rochester."[23] Fosdick wrote that in order to understand Rauschenbusch's passion for the social gospel one had to go back to 1886 when he was pastor of a little church in New York City: "There in the overcrowded, health-destroying, crime-breeding slums was lighted his burning conviction that a merely individualistic gospel, taking no responsibility for the social conditions that condemn multitudes to physical and moral ruin, was both practically futile and profoundly unchristian."[24] Fosdick recalled that Rauschenbusch "made a momentous appeal to the social conscience of the Christian churches in the early nineteen hundreds."[25] He went on to say that his own early preaching "caught some of its flavor from his influence."[26] Fosdick (1878–1969) enjoyed a long life. He was already an influential writer by the time of Rauschenbusch's death in 1918. He became embroiled in the Fundamentalist controversy of the 1920s, but John D. Rockefeller admired Fosdick and promised to build a new church for him that was "international, interdenominational and interracial." Riverside Church was completed in 1931, and Fosdick remained as its senior minister until his retirement in 1946.[27]

Through his writings and the independence offered by the Riverside pulpit, Fosdick probably exerted more influence than any minister in the country. A measure of Rauschenbusch's impact is evident when comparing leading Protestant ministers before and after Rauschenbusch. Henry Ward Beecher, pastor of Plymouth Congregational Church, Brooklyn, New York, 1847-1887, was the leading Protestant ministerial voice during the Gilded Age. He was aware of economic problems but had little or no awareness of a social gospel to address them. Fosdick, on the other hand, clearly recognized that Rauschenbusch had

---

[21] Ibid., 8.

[22] Ibid., 12.

[23] Fosdick, *The Living of these Days*, 109.

[24] Ibid.

[25] Ibid., 110.

[26] Ibid.

[27] Balmer and Winner, *Protestantism in America*, 226.

introduced a new level of consciousness into the churches regarding poverty, and he profoundly influenced by Rauschenbusch. Fosdick wrote that Rauschenbusch's

> influence was wide and deep…and the effects of it still run powerfully on. His books were meat and drink to the generation he served…. Circumstances may alter his particular solutions in detail, but his basic presupposition and his message are yet valid. His conscious and unconscious disciples are uncountable, for he opened a new era in the thought and effort of American Christianity, and many who share it now have no idea how deeply indebted they are to Walter Rauschenbusch.[28]

Fosdick was deeply convinced of Rauschenbusch's ongoing influence during the 1940s. This was the case with ministers of many leading churches in the United States during Fosdick's era such as Ernest Fremont Tittle, George Buttrick, Ralph Sockman, and Henry Hill Crane.[29]

Followers of Rauschenbusch, especially his former students, created the Rauschenbusch Lectureship Foundation at Rochester in 1929. The idea was to sponsor annual lectures at the seminary devoted to social gospel themes. Conrad Moehlman wrote a ten-year anniversary essay on the "Life and Writings of Walter Rauschenbusch."[30] Scholars addressed Rauschenbusch's contribution each year throughout the 1930s. The Foundation lectureships provided the stimulus for many full-length books, several by leading Protestants. These included such works as Justin Wroe Nixon, *The Moral Crisis in Christianity* (1931); Charles Clayton Morrison, *The Social Gospel and Christian Culture* (1932); Shirley Jackson Case, *The Social Triumph of the Ancient Church* (1933); Reinhold Niebuhr, *An Interpretation of Christian Ethics* (1934); and Toyohiko Kagawa, *Brotherhood Economics* (1935). Nixon was Rauschenbusch's successor in church history at Rochester. He had written a superb sketch of Rauschenbusch's contribution to modern Christianity.[31] Morrison was editor of *The Christian Century*, the leading Protestant journal. Shirley Jackson Case was professor of New Testament at Chicago, a progressive Baptist, and a Rauschenbusch correspondent. Reinhold Niebuhr was a prolific author and professor at Union Theological Seminary who devoted much of his thought to ethical issues confronting the nation, and Kagawa was the most influential Asian voice being read by American Protestants. Nixon

---

[28] Fosdick, introduction to *Walter Rauschenbusch* by Dores Sharpe, xiii.

[29] Evans, *Liberalism without Illusions*, 74.

[30] Conrad H. Moehlman, "Life and Writings of Walter Rauschenbusch," 32-37. In 1930, Albert W. Beavan, president of Colgate-Rochester Divinity School, wrote to Pauline Rauschenbusch that Moehlman knew Rauschenbusch better than the other professors at the seminary and therefore would be the best equipped to write his biography (see Albert W. Beavan to Pauline Rauschenbusch, March 12, 1930, box 33, Rauschenbusch Family Papers).

[31] Nixon, "Walter Rauschenbusch—Ten Years Later," 1359–61.

embraced his mentor's vision but explained that Americans were so devoted to financial success that they were indifferent to the message of the social gospel.[32] Morrison thought that the social gospel had had limited success because it had not yet become a grassroots lay movement, yet its appeal remained strong among ministers. He declared that "one cannot name a northern seminary in which the social gospel is not taken for granted."[33]

In *The Social Triumph of the Ancient Church*, Case noted that "in perhaps half a century there has been an ever increasing conviction among Protestant leaders, sensitive to the injustices and evils in modern life that the present structure of society ought to be more thoroughly Christianized."[34] Case's Depression-era evaluation of the movement is measured. He wrote,

> It would be difficult to estimate in full the benefits that have resulted from the prophetic zeal with which this stirring social gospel has been preached by men of vision and consecration, like the late Professor Walter Rauschenbusch.... But, the tardiness with which the leaven of this new social vision has permeated life has, to say the least, had a very sobering influence upon our optimism.[35]

He concluded that "the challenging task of Christianizing society remains as yet largely unfulfilled."[36] Yet Case thought it reassuring to realize that the triumph of Christianity within the Roman Empire took centuries. Moreover, as the social environment changed, the early churches met further challenges. Case indicated that because the social gospel set out the "highest conceivable ideals," the result might appear meager, but he believed that like the early church, the social message would prevail in time.[37] The lectureship continued to inspire studies of Christianity and society into the next decade.[38]

It was increasingly clear to the Rochester faculty that their former colleague had made a unique contribution to American Protestant thought, and they determined to assemble a full Rauschenbusch bibliography. In 1934 *The Rochester Bulletin* published a helpful guide to sources about the career and thought of Rauschenbusch. The list of sources began with reference to the 1918 issue of the *Bulletin* that printed a bibliography of Rauschenbusch's publications. The 1934

---

32 Dorrien, *Soul in Society*, 78.

33 Morrison, 13, 15; cited by Dorrien, *Soul and Society*, 77–78.

34 Case, *The Social Triumph of the Ancient Church*, 226.

35 Ibid., 227.

36 Ibid.

37 Ibid., 228.

38 For example, see Holt, *The Nation under God*, and Johnson, *The Social Gospel Re-examined*. Continuing the series, following World War II, Baron published *Modern Nationalism and Religion*. Macmillan competed with Harper to publish the Rauschenbusch Lectures. See Macmillan's Ellen F. Shipper to Mrs. Walter Rauschenbusch, January 7, 1938, box 33, Rauschenbusch Family Papers.

Bulletin included additional comments on collections of his writings, biographical memoirs by his students (Justin Wroe Nixon, Henry Burke Robins and Conrad H. Moelhman), and references to accounts of Rauschenbusch's work in German, French, and English dictionaries.[39] The literature addressing Rauschenbusch's contributions was well under way. The bibliography was already impressive.[40]

In 1936, F. W. C. Meyer, professor in Rochester Seminary's German department, published an article celebrating the fiftieth anniversary of Rauschenbusch's ordination. Meyer reported that Edward C. Marsh, secretary of the Macmillan Company, had remarked shortly after Rauschenbusch's death that while he had observed the influence of many books, he believed "that no other publications of the new century have had so big an influence on the course of Christian thought and action" as those of Rauschenbusch.[41] Meyer also cited Professor Leonhard Ragaz of Zurich, translator of Rauschenbusch's *Theology*, who wrote, "Since the days of the New Testament there have been but very few to preach the gospel of the Kingdom of God as did he."[42] And Kagawa wrote that he was personally "set aflame with cooperative zeal by the reading of Rauschenbusch's books."[43] Meyer was deeply devoted to his German Baptist roots and its denomination, the North American German Baptists (now the North American Baptist Conference). He expressed gratitude and pride that Rauschenbusch was "the preacher, professor, and prophet who God gave us and signally honored as a spiritual stimulus to Christendom at large."[44] Preserving their ethnic and language distinctions and Pietistic tradition, this group of immigrant Baptists retained their separate identity. Although they dropped the word "German," they remained separate from the American Baptist Convention. Their churches flourished in the Midwest United States and Southern Central Canada. In 1949 they changed the name of their seminary to North American Baptist Seminary and moved it to Sioux Falls, South Dakota, to be closer to their constituency.

Today the seminary's deep appreciation for the contributions of August and Walter Rauschenbusch is evident in pictures on the walls, tributes on electronic bulletins, and in their archival holdings. Not everyone in this Baptist denomination approved of Rauschenbusch's social ideas, but most were happy to claim the famous man as one of their own. Meyer conveyed gratitude for the Rauschenbusch father and son, remarking that August had to serve as professor of "almost everything!" Walter served the German denomination by editing *Der Jugend-*

---

[39] "Concerning Walter Rauschenbusch," 286–87.

[40] In 1936, James Dombrowski offered a general study on Christian socialism; see Dombrowski, *The Early Days of Christian Socialism in America*.

[41] Meyer, "Rauschenbusch Aflame for God," 304.

[42] Ibid.

[43] Ibid.

[44] Ibid.

Herold, its youth paper, publishing a study course he had prepared, *Das Leben Jesu*, and helping edit two German hymnals. The Rauschenbusch father and son legacy is fondly remembered by an entire denomination as its leading light. But Meyer also conceded that the greatest contribution of Walter was his service to the wider church by "awakening its social conscience."[45] Many of the first-generation contributors to Rauschenbusch's legacy had known him as students or colleagues. They often imparted a sense of the effect Rauschenbusch had on them personally as well as assessing his interpretation of Christianity.

Rauschenbusch and the Age of Christian Realism: Niebuhr and Bennett and the Influence of the Social Ethos, 1935–1960

Gary Dorrien has written that U.S. social ethics in the twentieth century flow in three major streams: the social gospel, Christian realism, and liberation theologies.[46] According to Dorrien, the social gospel's influence continued into the 1930s. Reinhold Niebuhr's realism dominated the middle third of the century, and various forms of liberation theology flourished during the final three or four decades of the century. Rauschenbusch is identified as the founder of social ethics: there could hardly be a stronger affirmation of Rauschenbusch's significance in the history of American Christianity. Dorrien singled out Niebuhr as the preeminent American theologian of the twentieth century.[47] Niebuhr's relationship to the social gospel is complex. On the one hand he recognized Rauschenbusch as the "most brilliant and most generally satisfying exponent" of the social gospel.[48] At the same time he sharply criticized prominent features of the social gospel. The social gospel proposed nothing less than the transformation of society. However, it offered no workable mechanism to accomplish this goal. Rauschenbusch often wrote of a "cooperative commonwealth" to replace capitalistic competition, but he suggested that this could be achieved by Christian goodwill. The goal was to persuade the churches to contribute to the common good of society by living by the spirit of Jesus. This approach was idealistic and unworkable, and Niebuhr attacked it as a naïve proposal. He also thought theology should be applied to life, but the church needed a strong dose of realism in dealing with political and economic powers in the nation. Moreover, Niebuhr was constantly modifying his interpretations, depending on changing situations in soci-

---

[45] Ibid., 305.

[46] Dorrien, *Soul in Society*, vii.

[47] Ibid., 5.

[48] Handy, *The Social Gospel in America*, 253, cited from preface of Reinhold Niebuhr's *An Interpretation of Christian Ethics*.

ety. Niebuhr's relationship to theology of the previous generation was one of constant tension. Dorrien wrote, "For most of his extraordinary career, the greatest figure in modern American liberal theology never tired of expressing his disdain for Modern American liberalism....[49] [but] having begun his pastoral career as a social gospel liberal, he never completely broke from the tradition that first fired his imagination and idealism. Niebuhr never doubted that the church in America should be a force for social justice and democracy."[50] It would appear that while Niebuhr was critical of liberalism's idealism and failure to create a strategy for reform, he was nevertheless in agreement with its goal of seeking a more just society. Theologians often build on the recent theological past as well as criticizing it. Niebuhr was a social ethicist who addressed goals similar to those articulated by Rauschenbusch, but he was also a critic of notions of optimism, unrealizable progress, and lack of a workable method to bring about changes. Nevertheless, both Rauschenbusch and Niebuhr were powerfully drawn to devoting their lives to the quest for justice for American society.

Whereas Reinhold Niebuhr tended to be dismissive of the social gospel, H. Richard Niebuhr engaged in constructive analysis of the kingdom of God, the central theme of Rauschenbusch's theological reflection. Niebuhr wrote in his book, *The Kingdom of God in America*, that Rauschenbusch had set forth his "attempt to interpret the meaning and spirit of American Christianity as a movement which finds its center in the faith of the kingdom of God."[51] Having published *The Social Sources of Denominationalism* (1929), which demonstrated the influence of social factors such as race, class, and region, Niebuhr turned his attention to the study of the force driving American Christianity. The unifying idea that emerged for Niebuhr was the kingdom of God. In his reading, the notion of the kingdom of God had evolved from "the sovereignty of God" during the Puritan era, to the "reign of Christ" during the awakenings, to the "kingdom on earth" in the social gospel.[52] To identify as early as 1937 the recent shift to social Christianity as one of three major paradigms of the kingdom in interpreting American Christianity was a remarkable tribute to the rapid rise of the influence of the social gospel. In Niebuhr's view the kingdom is "neither an ideal nor an organization." Instead, "it is a movement"—a dynamic pattern.[53] Rauschenbusch shared a similar sense of kingdom. Niebuhr observed, "In Rauschenbusch especially the revolutionary element remained pronounced; the reign of Christ re-

[49] Dorrien, *Soul in Society*, 91.
[50] Ibid., 93.
[51] H. Richard Niebuhr, *The Kingdom of God in America*, vii.
[52] Ibid., x.
[53] Ibid., 164.

quired conversion and the coming kingdom was crisis, judgment as well as promise. Though his theory of the relation of God and man often seemed liberal he continued to speak the language of the prophets and St. Paul."[54] Richard Niebuhr understood the American quest for the kingdom in terms of the desire to Christianize the society.

Dorrien reminds readers of the prominent role of John C. Bennett's thinking as well as Niebuhr's in the era of Christian realism. In *Social Salvation* (1935), Bennett described a number of major changes in interpretation of the social gospel that had transpired since Rauschenbusch's death, but nevertheless affirmed that the thrust of social gospel theology of ethics was right because it recovered Jesus' compassion for the poor and his passion for justice.[55] Bennett also affirmed Christian realism and published a book by that title in 1941. He sought to make mainline Christianity relevant to the modern world but found that local churches reflected the dominant economic views of their members.[56] The legacy of Niebuhr and Bennett was to affirm a critical appropriation of the social gospel's quest for society that sought the good of all. In a retrospective essay, twenty years after Rauschenbusch, historian of Christian theology Arthur C. McGiffert assessed Rauschenbusch's thought, concluding that he gave too little attention to personal religion, and that by giving to the early church a social interpretation, he gave too little attention to reflection on the doctrines of the church, the atonement, and the incarnation.[57] He concluded that in 1938 theology was moving along three paths. First, there was the new conservative movement (neo-orthodoxy) that stressed the transcendence of God rather than God working in society. A second group retained the social gospel and sought to emphasize theism as well, while the third position of John Bennett, Walter Horton, and the Niebuhrs was "occupying a position between the two groups."[58]

In 1940 Charles Howard Hopkins published *The Rise of the Social Gospel in American Protestantism, 1865–1915*. Hopkins's work was followed in 1949 by Henry May's *Protestant Churches and Industrial America.* These studies were superb achievements of historical interpretation and served for decades as standard histories of the social gospel.[59] In addition to major theological assessments of Rauschenbusch, in 1942, Dores Robinson Sharpe published *Walter Rauschenbusch*, the first full-length biography of Rauschenbusch. Sharpe came from Canada to Rochester as a student in 1908, served as Rauschenbusch's secretary for a

[54] Ibid., 194.

[55] Bennett, *Social Salvation*, vii.

[56] Dorrien, *Soul and Society*, 171, citing Bennett, "Christian Ethics and Forms of Economic Power," 238.

[57] McGiffert, "Walter Rauschenbusch Twenty Years After," 96–109.

[58] Ibid., 104–105.

[59] May's book was reprinted by Octagon Press in 1963.

number of years, and knew him well. Sharpe's study had the advantage of including information from Pauline Rauschenbusch, who was still living and provided material for the book. Likewise, he had the benefit of input from readers who had known Rauschenbusch personally. He drew extensively from letters, diaries, sermons, lectures, press clippings, and magazines, as well as Rauschenbusch's published volumes.[60]

The idea of the social gospel was taking effect in a variety of ways. Measuring the full influence of Rauschenbusch is beyond the scope of this study, but one example—the autobiography of Canadian Baptist minister T. C. Douglas—is instructive. Douglas worked on his Ph.D. in Chicago in 1931. He never forgot the suffering he encountered doing case work in the city during the early years of the Depression. Reading Rauschenbusch and other social gospel writers convinced him that the church should be involved in society. He determined that he could serve the kingdom of God better in politics than in the pulpit, and when elected premier of Saskatchewan in 1944 he established hospital insurance for the entire population. Douglas's motivation for his action was born in recognition of the suffering brought about by poverty and of the social gospel message that the church should work for a better society.[61]

In 1950 Henry Steele Commager recognized the importance of Rauschenbusch's contribution in his magisterial history of American thought since 1880. He declared that with E. A. Ross's *Sin and Society*, *Christianity and the Social Crisis* was

> the best diagnosis of the moral confusion underlying the economic malaise that had yet appeared.... [Moreover], the argument of *Christianity and the Social Crisis* was primarily religious. The criticism of capitalism, the competitive system, the industrial revolution was familiar enough [but] Rauschenbusch's indictment of capitalism was not merely that it was antisocial but that it was anti-Christian, not that it stunted men and women in their physical growth and corrupted social and political life but that it stunted moral growth and corrupted the spirit of men.[62]

African-American scholar Benjamin Mays, president of Morehouse College for twenty-seven years, published an anthology of Rauschenbusch's works in 1950.[63] Rauschenbusch's message of social justice was clearly important to Mays.

---

[60] Sharpe, *Walter Rauschenbusch*, viii. At the same time, Sharpe was so close to Rauschenbusch that he tends toward hagiography rather than analytical assessment of his former professor.

[61] Douglas, *The Making of a Socialist*, 64–68. Douglas was part of a group of Canadian social gospel ministers turned politicians who formed what is today the New Democratic Party in Canada.

[62] Commager, *The American Mind*, 174.

[63] Mays, ed., *A Gospel of the Social Awakening*.

Despite the fact that Rauschenbusch did not address racial injustice as he did economic injustice, his fierce attack on injustice could be readily applied to race relations, evident in the thought of Martin Luther King, Jr., student of Mays.

In 1953, historian of American Christianity Winthrop Hudson wrote a thoughtful tribute to Rauschenbusch for *The Christian Century* in which he proposed to challenge superficial interpretations of Rauschenbusch by looking carefully at "the real structure and basic assumption of his thought."[64] Hudson wrote that in fact Rauschenbusch was not naively optimistic, as his critics often charged; instead, he rejected the notion of inevitable progress, which was popular during his day. Rauschenbusch also took seriously the doctrine of original sin, affirming that people are driven by self-interest, which Rauschenbusch believed had wrecked nation after nation. Thus personal regeneration was always the starting point for redemption. Rauschenbusch wrote, "Most social reformers claim that if only poverty and the fear of poverty could be abolished men would cease to be grasping, selfish, overbearing and sensual. We do not see it so."[65] He said that "no outward economic revolution will answer our needs."[66] For Rauschenbusch a new mind and a new heart were necessary. Hudson noted that Rauschenbusch understood that popular interpretations of the social gospel failed to account for the power of sin. The church's first task according to Rauschenbusch was to awaken faith in Christ, which transforms people into spiritual beings. The role of the church was indispensable since only here is this message heard. Hudson's article was designed to offer a corrective to popular misconceptions of Rauschenbusch by emphasizing key elements of his thought often ignored by critics, including Rauschenbusch's belief in the power of sin, his rejection of superficial optimism, and his emphasis on the necessity of personal regeneration. Hudson was an astute interpreter of Rauschenbusch, and his title "Evangelical Prophet" aptly captured the duality of Rauschenbusch's thought.

In 1954 Paul A. Carter added to the critical literature his historical analysis of the fortunes of the social gospel during the generation after Rauschenbusch's death.[67] Also in 1954 historians of Christian thought John Dillenberger and Claude Welch published *Protestant Christianity: Interpreted Through Its Development*.[68] This illuminating text included main themes of Protestant history, including full chapters on missions, the ecumenical movement, and "The Christian Criticism of Society." The authors treated the social gospel as a significant and

---

[64] Hudson, "Rauschenbusch—Evangelical Prophet," 740.

[65] Ibid., 741.

[66] Ibid.

[67] Carter, *The Decline and Revival of the Social Gospel.*

[68] This book proved useful, and the authors issued a second edition in 1988.

permanent dimension of American Protestantism. General textbooks on the history of American Christianity would follow the decision to include the social gospel when they began to appear a decade later. In 1955 historian H. Shelton Smith wrote that Rauschenbusch "was perhaps the foremost molder of American Christian thought in his generation.... He was undoubtedly the major architect of American Protestant social thought."[69] Rauschenbusch had firmly secured his place as initiator of the field of social ethics in the United States. Smith was well informed about the history of Christianity in the United States.[70] Rauschenbusch's reputation was holding up well in the estimation of leading scholars a half century after he contended for a social gospel in *Christianity and the Social Crisis*.

The fiftieth anniversary of Rauschenbusch's *Christianity and the Social Crisis* (1907) prompted several positive reflections on Rauschenbusch's work. In 1957 *Time* magazine reported that "a round table at the University of Chicago's Federated Theological Faculty honored author Walter Rauschenbusch with a discussion of his impact and influence on U.S. Protestantism."[71] The writer summarized Rauschenbusch's experience of the "jostling, exploiting, every-man-for-himself America" while ministering among the poor. Rauschenbusch found Pietistic Christianity inadequate to protect the oppressed and so interpreted the Bible "in a challenging new way" when he argued that the kingdom of God was "a corporate enterprise of salvation."[72] This informed reporter noted that "his Social Gospel became so powerful that it took U.S. Protestantism to opposite extremes, for church sometimes seemed to be turning into sanctified civic-betterment societies."[73] The writer noted that in 1957 the complaint was not so much about the workers' bodies as "that their souls are being stifled in too much benevolent prosperity."[74] This was the decade of the powerful critiques of American society by William H. Whyte's *The Organization Man* and David Riesman's *The Lonely Crowd.* Also in 1957 Robert Handy wrote a superb summary of Rauschenbusch's life and message. As a corrective to popular views that Rauschenbusch taught only social ideas, Handy stressed that the personal religious experience was the more significant beginning point:

> The key to understanding him is to see that his lifework was precisely the effort to keep both emphases with priority always on the first.... He warned against substituting social activities for religion; he insisted that not less religion but

[69] Smith, *Changing Conceptions of Original Sin*, 199.

[70] Smith, along with Robert Handy and Lefferts Loetscher would publish a collection of documents on American Christianity which for many years remained a standard collection of primary resources (Smith, Handy, and Loetscher, eds., *American Christianity*).

[71] "The Social Gospeler,"

[72] Ibid.

[73] Ibid.

[74] Ibid.

> more—of the right kind—was needed.... For Rauschenbusch the Kingdom of God was not an earthly utopia that man could create. He emphasized that it was divine in its origin, progress, and consummation. It was for him the revelation of the power, the righteousness, and the love of God.[75]

Handy concluded with a celebratory tone: "The light that Rauschenbusch lit half a century ago still burns in the activist cause-conscious heart of U.S. Protestantism."[76] Another fiftieth anniversary tribute came from the notable English Baptist leader, Ernest A. Payne. Payne described Rauschenbusch's shock at the degradation and exploitation brought on by poverty and his attempt to apply the Christian faith to society. He cited the earlier tributes by Van Dusen and Niebuhr and then added his own formulation of praise: "The sum of Rauschenbusch is one of which Baptists everywhere may well be proud. He represents one of the authentic and still needed streams within our varied tradition. What he said is true to the meaning of the New as well as the Old Testament and we shall forget it at our peril."[77] Payne identified the social message as one of several Baptist streams. Moreover, for his Baptist readers he emphasized its scriptural origins.

The fiftieth anniversary was also the occasion for publishing *A Rauschenbusch Reader*, a selection from Rauschenbusch's writings compiled by the author Benson Y. Landis. Henry Emerson Fosdick wrote an extended introduction to the volume. He began with the story of the publication of *Christianity and the Social Crisis* and the astonishing response to it. Rauschenbusch was surprised that most people were kind in their comments and only a few damned it.[78] Fosdick shared the surprise because the book attacked social ills and the church's failure to respond. He said that this book "struck home so poignantly on the intelligence and conscience of the churches that it ushered in a new era in Christian thought and action."[79] Fosdick summarized major steps in Rauschenbusch's life. He set the stage for understanding Rauschenbusch by describing Protestantism of the era:

> Only those who have lived in the late nineteenth century can easily conceive to what lengths the individualistic emphasis in the churches went.... The church's attention was centered not on seeing to it that the will of God was done on earth as it is in heaven but on seeing to it that individuals were prepared to escape from earth to the joys of heaven.... Into this tradition Walter Rauschenbusch had been born.[80]

Rauschenbusch's work near Hell's Kitchen brought him to what Fosdick

---

[75] Handy, "Walter Rauschenbusch, Evangelical Prophet," 6.
[76] Ibid.
[77] Payne, "The Prophet of the Social Gospel."
[78] Fosdick, introduction to *A Rauschenbusch Reader*, xiii.
[79] Ibid.
[80] Ibid., xv.

called his "second conversion."[81] Thereafter the "Reign of God in a redeemed society became the focus of Rauschenbusch's thought and the passion of his life."[82] Fosdick emphasized the balance Rauschenbusch held between individual and social redemption and also found in him a balance between optimism and realism.[83] Like other of the careful students of Rauschenbusch, Fosdick cautioned readers of Rauschenbusch that words change their meaning: "socialist" had a far more flexible meaning in Rauschenbusch's era; he said that in general it meant a theory of society that looked out for everyone. This could include income and inheritance, better housing, pure food and drug laws, limitations on hours of labor, establishment of minimum wages, labor unions, and safety regulations in factories.[84] Moreover, Rauschenbusch could speak of a Christian communism by which he meant collective sharing, "illustrated in the solidarity of a fine family."[85]

Rauschenbusch and Theologies of Liberation: 1960–1990

During the 1960s the dominance of Niebuhr and Bennett in the field of social ethics gave way to concerns addressed by liberation theologies, including liberation from poverty, racism, and sexism. Liberation theology found its most influential exponent in Gustavo Gutierrez, whose audience was the church in Latin America. Gutierrez's *A Theology of Liberation* (1973) emphasized God's special love for the poor, and he called for the church to take its stand with the poor.[86] Asked why it first appeared in Latin America, Gutierrez explained to Harvey Cox that the first question the poor asked was not middle class skepticism about the existence of God, but rather why the poor so constantly experienced deprivation and suffering.[87] Similarities between Gutierrez and Rauschenbusch are evident.[88] A variety of liberation theologies arose in the United States, however, to claim justice for specific groups of people: African Americans, women, Hispanics, and Native Americans. This decade welcomed reform. Rauschenbusch did not speak about injustices suffered by specific populations beyond poor workers, but marginalized groups had no problem appropriating his quest for justice as their own. Seminarians of this era were told repeatedly that the church must strive to be relevant to society.

Because of social upheavals over poverty, war, and civil rights, religion and

[81] Ibid.

[82] Ibid.

[83] Ibid., xix.

[84] Fosdick, introduction to *A Rauschenbusch Reader*, xx–xxi.

[85] Ibid., xx.

[86] Gutierrez, *A Theology of Liberations*.

[87] Cox, *The Future of Faith*, 194.

[88] For a comparison of Gutierrez and Rauschenbusch, see Sanks, "Liberation Theology and the Social Gospel: Variations on a Theme," 668–82.

ethical reflection in the 1960s was drawn to sustained attention on issues of social justice.[89] It is not surprising that some of the sharpest criticisms of Rauschenbusch appeared out of this context. Critics were quick to point out that Rauschenbusch failed to see and protest the forms of injustice suffered by African Americans and women of his era. This criticism has persisted to the present day. There is little doubt that Rauschenbusch's attitude toward women was patriarchal; he favored the role of women as homemakers and mothers, yet he was sympathetic with the suffering of working women and welcomed social changes on the horizon, especially the looming success of the suffragettes in securing the vote for women.

Rauschenbusch was keenly aware of the suffering of African Americans. He sharply condemned slavery of the past and lynching current in his day. After visiting Nashville and observing the plight of African Americans, he confessed that he had no solution to the problems they faced. These deficiencies in Rauschenbusch's thought must not be overlooked. However, Rauschenbusch's personal context was immigrant workers and their suffering. In 1967 Sydney Ahlstrom pointed out that during Rauschenbusch's era, "Agricultural dislocations, the racial caste system, ethnic prejudices, religious intolerance and civil rights were not prominent among their [social Christians'] concerns."[90] Rauschenbusch's interest was focused on finding ways to mitigate the plight of the workers rather than addressing the injustices of multiple groups in the United States. But his principle that the church should stand for justice and oppose injustice was easily applied to many forms of injustice, and he became an inspiration for later reformers dealing with other forms of injustice. Martin Luther King, Jr. is a prime example. King, the leader of the civil rights movement, explicitly acknowledged the influence of Rauschenbusch on his thinking about religion. In the notable *Christian Century* series, "How My Mind Changed," King traced his "Pilgrimage to Nonviolence." King's theological journey in seminary took him from his fundamentalist beginnings through liberalism, neo-orthodoxy, and existentialism. But after a decade of reading systematic theology and philosophy, he wrote, "I have become more interested in social ethics."[91] Social ethics was the point of intersection for King and Rauschenbusch. He recalled that during his seminary days he began "a serious intellectual quest for a method to eliminate social evil," and he "was immediately influenced by the social gospel."[92] He read Rauschenbusch's *Christianity and the Social Crisis* during the early 1950s. He said that this book "left an indelible imprint on my thinking."[93] Rauschenbusch had his flaws according to King, who

[89] Poverty remained a constant social problem in American society. It was addressed early in the 1960s by such studies as Harrington's *The Other America*.

[90] Ahlstrom, *Theology in America*, 75.

[91] King, "Pilgrimage to Nonviolence," 440.

[92] Ibid.

[93] Ibid.

found Rauschenbusch's belief in progress too strong. Moreover, King faulted Rauschenbusch for coming "perilously close to identifying the Kingdom of God with a particular social and economic system."[94] However, in King's judgment, in spite of these shortcomings Rauschenbusch gave to American Protestantism a sense of social responsibility that it should never lose:

> The gospel at its best deals with the whole man, not only his soul but his body, not only his spiritual well-being, but his material well-being. Any religion that professes to be concerned about the souls of men and is not concerned about the slums that damn them, the economic conditions that strangle them and the social conditions that cripple them is a spiritually moribund religion awaiting burial.[95]

In this passage King has clearly appropriated Rauschenbusch's central message.

The decade of the 1960s was a watershed in the discipline of the history of American Christianity. Scholars produced source collections, textbooks, atlases, and bibliographies.[96] The textbooks written by Winthrop Hudson (1965) and Edwin Gaustad (1966) have enjoyed long and well-deserved success.[97] Both are still in print a half century later in updated editions, and both treated the social gospel as a landmark in the development of religion in America. Numerous textbooks surveying the sweep of religion in America have been published since Hudson and Gaustad. They regularly include the social gospel in the story of American religious history. It is an established component of the American religious narrative from the academic historians' point of view.

During the 1960s Sydney Ahlstrom established a reputation for his work on the history of theology in the nation. In 1967 he edited *Theology in America*, which contained selections from thirteen American theologians along with Ahlstrom's extensive introduction and editorial notes.[98] In addition Ahlstrom wrote an extensive survey article on the history of American theology for the distinguished five-volume Princeton study published in 1961.[99] In both of these histories of theology, Ahlstrom gave a prominent place to Rauschenbusch's thinking. Ahlstrom observed that whereas H. Shelton Smith understood Rauschenbusch as the "foremost molder of American Christian thought of his generation," Winthrop Hudson "depicts him as a 'lonely prophet' whose thoughts 'ran counter to the

---

[94] Ibid.

[95] Ibid.

[96] In a 1964 article in the *American Historical Review*, Henry May announced that this discipline had come of age, and he cited an impressive list of works to support his claims (see May, "The Recovery of American Religious History," 79–92).

[97] Hudson, *Religion in America*; Gaustad, *The Religious History of America*.

[98] Ahlstrom, *Theology in America*, 531-586.

[99] Ahlstrom, "Theology in America: A Historical Survey," 232–321.

prevailing tendencies of the time.'"[100] Although the social gospel was not for everyone, Rauschenbusch offered an exciting viable new interpretation of Christianity. In Ahlstrom's judgment "the significance of Rauschenbusch, therefore, is very great."[101] In summarizing Rauschenbusch's thought, Ahlstrom noted that "he insisted that religion and ethics are inseparable, and that ethical conduct is the supreme and sufficient religious act."[102]

Ahlstrom noted that Rauschenbusch's "combination of liberal theology and ethical theory won extremely widespread acceptance...[and he] aroused social conscience...."[103] Moreover he found that Rauschenbusch's "realistic spirit" influenced the neo-orthodox theologians of the following generations both by exploring evil more deeply and by devoting thought to construction of a better society.[104] This is significant: rather than contrasting Rauschenbusch and neo-orthodoxy, Ahlstrom saw that they shared convictions about the power of sin. Ahlstrom also wrote the leading textbook on the religious history of America, where he again acknowledged the place of Rauschenbusch.[105]

In 1966 Robert T. Handy advanced the study of social gospel when he published *The Social Gospel in America, 1870-1920: Gladden, Ely, Rauschenbusch* in the distinguished series *A Library of Protestant Thought*. Handy assembled major writings from the three social gospel writers and provided critical introductions to each writer and to each selection. This volume provided a superb introduction to the main themes of social gospel thought. Handy followed his social gospel anthology in 1971 with *A Christian America's Protestant Hopes and Historical Realities*. Protestants in the late nineteenth and early twentieth centuries enjoyed cultural hegemony. Rauschenbusch shared with other Protestants a vision of a Protestant Christian America. As Handy noted, "The examination of the evangelical effort to mold a Christian civilization is important, not only for the understanding of religious history, but also for the interpretation of American social and cultural history."[106] Also in 1966 the Department on Church and Society of the World Council of Churches sponsored the publication of four books on social ethics in preparation for an international meeting. The books focused on a changing world, responsible government, economic growth, and man in community. What is especially noteworthy is the wide range of participants contributing to these studies. Prominent ethicist John C. Bennett wrote in his foreword,

---

[100] Ahlstrom, *Theology in America*, 531.
[101] Ibid.
[102] Ibid., 532.
[103] Ibid., 531.
[104] Ahlstrom, *Theology in America*, 77.
[105] Ahlstrom, *A Religious History of the American People*.
[106] Handy, *A Christian America*, x. Handy revisited this critical era from another angle in *Undermined Establishment: Church State Relations in America, 1880–1920*.

> In this volume, one writer is from the Eastern Orthodox Church. Three writers reflect the experience of Latin American Christians. One more is from Africa, and another is from Asia. One is from eastern Europe. Two others represent types of theological thought that have played little part in the ecumenical conversation: the neo-Evangelicals, who have often been suspicious of the emphasis on "social action" in the thought and work of the World Council of Churches, and a very fluid group of theologians who have been influenced in a central way by Rudolf Bultmann.... We are glad to welcome a Roman Catholic author.[107]

The 1960s also enjoyed a massive historiographical leap forward in Rauschenbusch studies with Max Stackhouse's publication of Rauschenbusch's *The Righteousness of the Kingdom* (1968). In 1891 Rauschenbusch wrote *Christianity Revolutionary*, but never published it. This edition of Rauschenbusch's earliest full statement of social Christianity, and Stackhouse's lengthy introduction offered access to a major stage in Rauschenbusch's intellectual development. Historians were especially interested in the origins and development of Rauschenbusch's social gospel thought—its timing and its sources. Stackhouse also carefully studied Rauschenbusch's sermons to look for the point at which he began to address social gospel topics from the pulpit. In the 1970s historian Klaus Juergen Jaehn continued the effort to trace the development of Rauschenbusch's social thought.[108] Rauschenbusch's challenges to the church were particularly compatible with widespread calls for social reform in America during the 1960s.

During Rauschenbusch's lifetime the Roman Catholic response to industrialization was articulated in Pope Leo XIII's famous 1891 encyclical *Rerum Novarum (Of New Things)* and in the United States by the writings of John A. Ryan. The Catholic Church remained sensitive to social ethics throughout the following century. Rauschenbusch would doubtless have been heartened by the 1986 publication of *Economic Justice for All: Pastoral Letter on Catholic Social Teaching and the U.S. Economy*, a major document issued by the Conference of Catholic Bishops. Also in 1986 William M. Ramsey published *Four Modern Prophets*, a study of Walter Rauschenbusch, Martin Luther King, Jr., Gustavo Gutierrez, and Rosemary Radford Ruether. This little book conveys the sensibility that modern prophets all speak for justice although the forms of injustice they encountered differed. This text effectively connected Rauschenbusch to modern varieties of liberation theology. During the 1980s Rauschenbusch also found another biographer, Paul Minus. In *Walter Rauschenbusch, American Reformer* (1988) Minus emphasized the development of Rauschenbusch's social ideas, the centrality of the kingdom in his thought, and his passion for justice. In the 1980s Rauschenbusch's writings were once again anthologized, but with an original perspective.

---

[107] Bennett, foreword to *Christian Social Ethic in a Changing World*, 17–18.
[108] See Jaehn, *Rauschenbusch: The Formative Years.*

Winthrop Hudson edited and published *Walter Rauschenbusch: Selected Writings* (1984) for the series *Sources in American Spirituality*. Hudson gave significant attention to spiritual resources found in Rauschenbusch's writings before 1900 and to his prayers. His selections and commentary demonstrated how important personal spirituality was to Rauschenbusch as the source of power for pursuing the goals of social Christianity.

Recovering Rauschenbusch for the Twenty-first Century: 1990–Present

In the 1990s scholars Ronald White, Ralph Luker, and Evelyn Higgenbotham addressed the social gospel and race, a dimension of the social gospel too long neglected.[109] Also Harlan Beckley published an analysis of three leading social ethicists, including Rauschenbusch.[110] He argued that Rauschenbusch was driven by a passion for justice, but that he believed justice would be impossible without Christianizing the social order.[111] In 1994 Donovan E. Smucker published *The Origins of Walter Rauschenbusch's Social Ethics* in which he helpfully identified the influences of four major strands in Rauschenbusch's development: Pietism, Anabaptist Sectarianism, social and religious liberalism and Christian socialist transformation.[112] Virtually a lifelong student of Rauschenbusch and social Christianity, Smucker cites personal correspondence with both Moehlman and Sharpe.

Since 2000 interest in Rauschenbusch has increased noticeably. A centennial edition of *Christianity and the Social Crisis* appeared in 2007, edited by Rauschenbusch's great-grandson, Paul Raushenbush. Phyllis Tribble, Tony Campolo, Joan Chittister, Stanley Hauerwas, Cornell West, James A. Forbes, Jr., and Jim Wallis contributed reflections on the book. The afterword is by the distinguished philosopher Richard Rorty, also a Rauschenbusch descendant. The respondents are leaders in Protestant American religious life today. The list is notable for its diversity in gender, ethnicity, and theology, suggesting Rauschenbusch's range of influence. Their varied comments provide yet another level of evidence underscoring enduring value of Rauschenbusch's thought a century after he wrote.

In recent years Rauschenbusch has received increasing attention from evangelicals. Following Carl F. H. Henry's call to fundamentalists to embrace social discussions of Christianity, the appeal has been repeated from time to time with

[109] See White, *Liberty and Justice for All*; Luker, *The Social Gospel in Black and White*; and Higgenbotham, *Righteous Discontent*.

[110] Beckley, *Passion for Justices*.

[111] Ibid., 35.

[112] This book was based on the author Donovan E. Smucker's University of Chicago dissertation of the same title (1957).

varying responses. Michael Clawson has recently recounted the story of evangelical social concerns since the 1960s. He adds to this literature the story of the emerging church movement's "turn toward social justice.[113] Tim Suttle provides documentation of this interest in his book *An Evangelical Social Gospel?: Finding God's Story in the Midst of Extremes.* This book found its inspiration in Suttle's reading of Rauschenbusch's *A Theology for the Social Gospel.*[114] A growing number of the current college student generation seems to be committed to social activism and ministry: they want to be involved in creating a better society.

In the present day it would be difficult to find more influential advocates for the importance and relevance of Rauschenbusch and the social gospel than Gary Dorrien of Union Theological Seminary and Christopher Evans of Boston University School of Theology. Dorrien established himself as the premier historian of liberalism in American Protestantism with his massive three volume work *The Making of American Liberal Theology* (1813 pages). Rauschenbusch received full treatment in volume two: *Idealism, Realism and Modernity, 1900–1950* (2003). Dorrien had already written a stirring defense of Rauschenbusch's originality and influence in *Reconstructing the Common Good and the Social Order* (1990). In *Soul in Society: The Making and Renewal of Social Christianity* (1995), Dorrien traced the course of social Christianity to 1995. Given the famous quote about Rauschenbusch by Reinhold Niebuhr that he was too optimistic and naïve about political reality, readers evidently dismissed Rauschenbusch without reading him. Dorrien, however, offers a revisionist view of popular perceptions, arguing that Niebuhr retained many of the same goals for society articulated earlier by Rauschenbusch. To be sure his "realism" dismissed Rauschenbusch's optimism, but Dorrien does much to rehabilitate the positive influence of Rauschenbusch during the century after his death. [115] In a closely related area of keen interest, Dorrien has recently demonstrated the vital presence of the social gospel in the African-American community.[116]

Historian Christopher Evans has also done superlative historical work to establish a reliable picture of Rauschenbusch's life and thought, addressing his failures as well as his successes. Based on thorough knowledge of the Rauschenbusch papers, he wrote the third and most comprehensive and balanced interpretative biography of Rauschenbusch, *The Kingdom Is Always but Coming* (2004). In 1999 Evans edited a volume titled *Perspectives on the Social Gospel.* This volume

---

[113] Clawson, "Emerging From What?," 212–84.

[114] Suttle, *An Evangelical Social Gospel?*, xv–xvi.

[115] Dorrien is by no means alone in his assessment. Niebuhr scholar Langdon Gilkey takes the same view. See Gilkey, *On Niebuhr: A Theological Study*, 231.

[116] Dorrien, *The New Abolition.*

included Ralph E. Luker's notable historiography, "Interpreting the Social Gospel: Reflections on Two Generations of Historiography."[117] Evans also edited *The Social Gospel Today* (2001), a collection of essays that recognize the ongoing influence of Rauschenbusch in the new century. Here the authors confront the engagement of the social gospel on not only the issues of race and women but also the issues of missions and world Christianity, evangelical social consciousness, homosexuality, theology, and pastoral care. The volume illustrates the wide-ranging application of principles of the social gospel and its quest for justice in society. In 2010 Evans published his monograph *Liberalism without Illusions: Renewing an American Tradition*, which makes the case for many constructive contributions of American Protestant liberals. In his latest book, *The Social Gospel in American Religion: A History* (2017), Evans recounts the major developments in the American social gospel movement.

Finally, Rauschenbusch's message is not confined to study by the academy. Appropriately, a century after the publication of *Christianity and the Social Crisis*, the National Council of Churches in the United States and the Church World Service published "A Social Creed for the 21st Century."[118] The language is changed to address specific modern concerns, but the spirit of the original "Social Creed" lives in the document. It remains a call to Christians and churches to strive for justice and to seek to honor the dignity and value of every person. The adoption of this new social creed coincides with the one hundredth anniversary of the publication of *Christianity and the Social Crisis.*

The brief survey in this chapter is severely limited, but it is indicative of Rauschenbusch's sustained and substantial influence. The evidence suggests that Rauschenbusch has left an important legacy to Christians throughout the century since his death. In every decade Christian leaders—ministers, historians, theologians—have acknowledged their debt to Rauschenbusch. They have critiqued his deficiencies, but many have also affirmed the value of his penetrating insights regarding church and society in the United States, and not a few acknowledge how Rauschenbusch's thought has changed them.

---

[117] Luker, "Interpreting the Social Gospel: Reflections on Two Generations of Historiography," 1–13.

[118] "A Social Creed for the 21st Century," approved by the General Assembly of the National Council of Churches Christ USA and Church World Service, November 7, 2007.

CONCLUSION

Walter Rauschenbusch was a creative religious thinker and campaigner. This book has explored his thought and vocation with particular attention to the positive reception he generated. Rauschenbusch did not discover the social gospel, but he became its most effective advocate. He hammered away on the theme over and over in scores of individual addresses and articles as well as in his books. He enjoyed a strong reception during his lifetime, and his message continued to resonate for many readers. When Rauschenbusch died, the editors of *The Standard* (Chicago) perceptively wrote, "We shall no longer hear his voice or look upon his face, but he will continue to speak to us through his books and to stimulate through the printed page a new generation of truth…."[1] Other readers later attacked his interpretation of the social gospel for its failures. However, at mid-twentieth century, theologian Roger Shinn eloquently called for a reassessment of Rauschenbusch's contribution to American religious life. He wrote, "There is little excuse for our generation, though it may have learned some things that the Social Gospel did not know, to sneer or condescend to Rauschenbusch. His prayers were so unquestionably generous and his enthusiasm so genuine that we would be foolish and ungrateful to forget his message."[2] Today there is a resurgence of interest in Rauschenbusch. What was Rauschenbusch's contribution to modern Christianity that still commands attention?

A New Understanding of Christianity

Rauschenbusch's move to New York City presented a great challenge to his Christianity. He responded by rethinking his religion. Rauschenbusch had a keen awareness of the society around him; so dominant was economic change in the United States following the Civil War that historians now regularly describe the era as the Age of Industry or the Gilded Age. The economic revolution brought on by the Industrial Revolution created serious social repercussions for workers in this new economy. Rauschenbusch's pastoral duties confronted him with the problem he would grapple with throughout his life. Encountering daily unrelenting suffering, Rauschenbusch rapidly developed empathy for the laborers and a great passion to alleviate their suffering. He was not content simply to preach on Sundays. If he was genuinely going to minister to this culture, he believed that he must understand American society and try to change it. In order to understand

[1] "Walter Rauschenbusch," 1408.

[2] Shinn, *Christianity and the Problem of History*, 125.

the new America, Rauschenbusch turned to current literature on economics and sociology. He developed a cluster of ideas as he articulated his new faith.

First, as Rauschenbusch read analyses of American society, he saw that American capitalism had created essentially two contending economic classes—the haves and the have-nots. Churches had addressed poverty through charity for centuries, and new organizations such as the Settlement Houses and the Salvation Army assisted the poor. The problem was that these responses failed to change conditions of life for workers. Widespread suffering continued. Poverty was structural; it was built into the capitalist system. He understood that people do not willingly surrender privilege: owners wanted to share as little wealth as possible with workers. Workers had only their labor to sell. As a Christian pastor, he could appeal to the wealthy to be generous and improve wages and working conditions, but only a tiny percentage of owners voluntarily changed their practice. Rauschenbusch came to the decision that the only way to reform American capitalism was to restructure the system. Legislation was essential to establishing structural changes that would end the injustices suffered by ordinary workers. He campaigned for a minimum wage, the 40-hour work week, insurance for workers, and to end child labor. In addition, he advocated public ownership of transportation and utilities in order to keep costs for essentials low.

Second, Rauschenbusch began to realize the centrality of economics for all of life: the economic dimension of life influences everyone in every society every day. Moreover, he was keenly aware of a contradiction between the American economic system and the teachings of Christian faith. The problem was that the new economy created by industrialization was based on competition. Rauschenbusch produced a devastating critique of the American economic order, declaring it to be unchristian. Few Christian thinkers had been so bold, penetrating, and clear in their analysis of the American economy. He believed that capitalism was based on selfishness and greed; on the other hand, he was preaching that Christianity was based on cooperation—an ethic of service and love—not competition. The nation needed to adopt a new socio-economic ethic. He envisioned moving from a capitalist model to an economy based on cooperation.

Third, the criterion for changing the nation should be the goal of justice. Rauschenbusch believed a good society would seek the well-being of all its citizens. Rauschenbusch was also enamored with American democracy, which aspired to political justice. He believed that liberty and justice for all implied not only granting the right to vote but also sharing the benefits of the nation's economy. Thus, achieving the American ideals of justice and democracy became the important criteria for Rauschenbusch's proposed reconstruction of society. Usually understood as secular categories, Rauschenbusch was nevertheless quick to appropriate these social values as Christian values, and he thought they were essential for a good society.

Fourth, the church should be involved in the redemption of the nation. The end goal of Rauschenbusch's reformulating Christianity for Protestants of his day was to engage the church in the construction of a better society. He loved the United States and all that it had offered him and many other new citizens. But because he found suffering permeating the economic order, he thought it was fully appropriate for churches to campaign for a nation dedicated to the welfare of all and to stand in solidarity with American workers by advocating for laws that would benefit and protect them. Instead of life based on competition, he envisioned American society moving to a cooperative commonwealth that looked out for the well-being of all citizens. The church should be an instrument for creating a more compassionate society, a better world for the future. This was Rauschenbusch's vision. But critics asked whether the church should focus on religious teaching rather than on social work.

Fifth, Rauschenbusch believed that the church was seriously hampered in addressing social ills because it had focused only on individual salvation. Searching for biblical justification for his views, he sought to show that biblical religion was inherently social—whether in the pronouncement of the Old Testament prophets, the message of Jesus, or the teachings of the earliest church. He declared that there were two great realities—the individual and the society. Both were in need of salvation. He held that Jesus' concept of the kingdom of God included both levels of redemption. This was the foundation of his teaching. The idea of social sin and the need for social salvation had been lost, but it was at the heart of Jesus' message and must be reclaimed.

Sixth, Rauschenbusch contended that the modern church must change. He often wrote that the revolutionary nature of the historical Jesus mandates that the church change. Although he shared much of the culture and religion of his day, Jesus sharply criticized aspects of current beliefs, and he also initiated a new religion. The coming of Jesus into the world provided a force that started something new. Rauschenbusch wanted the modern church to accept a new understanding of Christianity: it should accept that God's kingdom went beyond individual salvation and was meant to include the redemption of society. Keenly aware that churches tended to hold traditional views, he urgently made the case for change. In 1909 a newspaper reported on Rauschenbusch's speech "Revolutionary Religion," delivered at the People's Easter Sunday Evening in the National Theater in Rochester where Rauschenbusch declared, "I believe that Jesus was the greatest revolutionist that we ever had. The idea He set is so great, so vast, that all others seem small when compared to it."[3] Rauschenbusch believed that the contemporary church must be revolutionary if it was to be relevant to modern society. It must work for the salvation of the nation as well as the individual—the only way

[3] WR, "Revolutionary Religion", *Democrat Chronicle*, March 1, 1909.

it could hope to minister to masses of people in the changing industrial environment. Yet the church seemed to be stuck in the past, unwilling to change. Rauschenbusch insisted, "Real Christianity will always be seeing things that aren't right and hence will be continually making changes. If one is filled with that spirit which animated Christ, one will be unwilling to rest until everything is set right."[4] Rauschenbusch was a reformer with two goals in mind—salvation for individuals and for society.

Memories of Rauschenbusch the Man

People who knew Rauschenbusch personally could never separate the impact of the person from his message. Repeatedly people praised Rauschenbusch for his personal qualities. He was challenged by a serious handicap. He won the loyalty of students. He spoke his mind about injustices in America. He sought to live according to the spirit of Jesus. Many students, friends, and colleagues thought of him as the most Christlike person they knew. His personal spirituality was the basis for his entire Christian experience. His ideas were attacked often; his personal integrity, seldom. An unsigned and undated obituary reviewed Rauschenbusch's life achievements, and the author was also careful to include Rauschenbusch's personal qualities, noting that the way Rauschenbusch dealt with the loss of his hearing for the last thirty years of his life won the admiration of many. He retained his humor and carried on despite the difficulties deafness imposed. The obituary recalled:

> It was a deeply Christian impulse which led Walter Rauschenbusch, upon entering the ministry, to seek his field among the toilers and tenement house dwellers of New York City, when, having won recognition for ability of the first order, he might have claimed a more remunerative and less burdensome pastorate. It was the same spirit which led him, after a severe illness, to expose himself prematurely that he might serve the sick of his parish—an experience which ultimately cost him his hearing. How severely that handicap bore on his spirit only his most intimate friends knew: he had a genius for friendship, and deafness seemed a great barrier. However, both in social intercourse and in the lecture room he rose bravely and triumphantly above his great handicap. It helped to unite in him certain great native qualities of courage and compassion. His friend Dr. W. C. Gannett once wrote to him, "You have been my uncopied example—at once inspiration and despair! I think of you with a Bravo!" He had the gift of Humor and its keen appreciation with that gift he was himself able to help many another over a hard place.[5]

---

[4] Ibid.

[5] Anonymous obituary, n.d., box 38, Rauschenbusch Family Papers.

People also recognized Rauschenbusch's brilliant capacity to formulate concepts, to help people understand themselves, "to make articulate what they wished to say but could not."[6] This capacity coupled with great skill in public speaking and writing made him a superb communicator. Rauschenbusch's magnetism won the admiration of students and audiences.

> It was no wonder, then that friends from many lands made the pilgrimage to Rochester or that his students universally became not only his admirers but his fast friends and rejoiced in his friendship. He was the lure which drew many students to Rochester, and he never disappointed his students. Quite apart from his eminence as a social prophet, he had a well-deserved reputation as a teacher. There were no dry-as-dust hours in his classroom for the simple reason that he was singularly able to humorize his subject. His teaching was luminous.[7]

Rauschenbusch demonstrated unusual courage. He criticized the prevailing structure of society and those who exercised power. He matched the Old Testament prophets in condemnation of injustice. During his lifetime, countless people referred to Rauschenbusch as the prophet of his day. Insofar as his critical analysis still applies to American society, he remains a prophet for contemporary life. Few ministers or professors are ever given the designation of "prophet" during their lifetimes as was Rauschenbusch. Few dare to challenge society's norms as he did.

Rauschenbusch conveyed a powerful sense of his own personal religious commitment that drew people to him. A Universalist admirer wrote,

> Scholar and humanist as he was, the profoundest impression made upon his students was by a subtle religious quality in their revered teacher. He was, in the best sense of the term, a Christian mystic, and he so linked the mystic's faith with the scholar's knowledge and the humanist's altruism that the influence of his religious leadership was powerful and effective. He was a consistent and devoted disciple of Jesus, and no one could hope to understand him on his interpretation of the social order who left Jesus out of account.[8]

Edwin Dahlberg called Rauschenbusch "the most Christ-like man that I ever knew."[9] And Justin Wroe Nixon remembered him as "the greatest human being some of us have ever known."[10] These comments verge on the hagiographical but were meant sincerely. Stated with somewhat more restraint Paul Moore Strayer wrote that Rauschenbusch believed "profoundly in the penetrating and

---

[6] Ibid.

[7] Ibid.

[8] "The Passing of a Great Leader," 2.

[9] Dahlberg, "Edwin Dahlberg in Conversation," 211.

[10] Nixon, "Walter Rauschenbusch—Ten Years After," 1359.

inspiring power of religion."[11] For others, Rauschenbusch conveyed his spirituality through his writings. A reviewer of the French edition of *Prayers* wrote, "We have read this collection...and remain under a profound impression of the grandeur of soul of the author, of his high spirituality, of his intense power of sympathy."[12]

Admirers praised the Rauschenbusch they saw, but in his own heart Rauschenbusch carried pain and loss as well as optimism, humor, and a smile. Prophetic utterances generate resentment, and he was tortured by the thought that in difficult exchanges with others he probably had not forgiven or been forgiven. His feelings are evident in his final sermon at the end of his ministry in New York, when he confessed there had been conflict with some church members in the prayer he composed about hurting others, and in the poignant expression of his reflections three months before his death: "I leave my love to those of my friends whose souls have never grown dark against me. I forgive the others and I hate no man. For my many errors and weaknesses I hope to be forgiven by my fellows."[13] The war also ended his smiling disposition: he wrote, "Since 1914 the world is full of hate, and I cannot expect to be happy again in my lifetime."[14] He concluded, "I have carried a heavy handicap for thirty years and I have worked hard."[15] Rauschenbusch experienced life fully—its joys and its burdens. In his own mind he was no saint. But he was praised because of the way he coped with life's difficulties and spent his life working for a better society.

Reception is ultimately in the eye of the beholder. Rauschenbusch's assessment of life was quite different from friends who simply praised him. He was most candid when writing letters to his closest friends. The words he wrote to Leighton Williams were deeply informed by his personal experience and by the historian's struggle to understand other lives:

> As time goes on I feel sadly that even those nearest to us have only a fragmentary and sketchy comprehension of our life, and we should leave a brief tradition behind us that is somewhat historical, largely legendary or mythical, sometimes a haloed vision ready for our modern hagiology. Well, as long as God knows both what we have been and what we prayed to be![16]

---

[11] Strayer, "Walter Rauschenbusch," 627.

[12] Review of *Prayers*, in *Eclaireur*, January 1, 1914, box 92, Rauschenbusch Family Papers.

[13] WR, "Instructions in case of my death," March 31, 1918, typescript, box 39, Rauschenbusch Family Papers.

[14] Ibid.

[15] Ibid.

[16] WR to Leighton Williams, June 16, 1917, box 27, Rauschenbusch Family Papers

The Reception of Rauschenbusch

The early reception of Rauschenbusch's books recorded in letters addressed to him reveals spirited enthusiasm for his proposals. Minister after minister indicated that his ideas gave them renewed purpose for their vocations. They wanted to put his proposals into action for the welfare of their cities and the nation. The testimonies of the letters suggest a psychological lift for many of those in the profession who had been stifled by routines of worship and activities directed almost entirely to their own congregations. Rauschenbusch gave readers a new vision and a mandate to seek to transform American society beyond the walls of their churches.

Rauschenbusch's proposals faced difficulties; even those who enthusiastically embraced his views faced serious difficulties with them. Through apathy or belief that religion should be reserved for individual spiritual matters, especially legislation to protect workers and to provide for public (social) ownership of essentials, congregations often resisted Rauschenbusch's reform proposals. Rauschenbusch experienced this within his own congregation, and several ministers wrote to him that their congregations resisted his message. Ministers as a group might be excited about the prospects of the social gospel, but it would take congregational participation in order to implement new forms of ministry. The message was intellectually and morally satisfying to many ministers who accepted Rauschenbusch's reading of the Bible and the tasks for the church, but the message did not translate readily to a grassroots movement of change in many local churches.

Ministers therefore wrote to Rauschenbusch seeking advice on ways to implement his ideas in local congregations. Rauschenbusch wrote that he had received many requests since *Christianity and the Social Crisis* for practical advice in implementing Christianity, which was the reason he addressed the problem a second time in *Christianizing the Social Order.* In this long book he offered further extended analysis of the church's relationship to the economy, but again he did not provide sufficient practical suggestions for the means of changing society. He was an academic doing what he knew best, but it was a far reach to move from cogent analyses and articulated goals in books to structuring a workable method for implementing reforms in American society. Asked for advice, he rendered analysis.

The flaw in Rauschenbusch's proposal was that he relied on his hope for the spirit of Jesus to penetrate the lives of owners and workers. His proposal was too idealistic and unrealistic; hence the charges of naïve optimism that were later leveled against him. He believed in the power of religion to reform, and he recognized the necessity of individual transformation but also the necessity for individuals to personally commit to working for the benefit of all members of society rather than for themselves. But how this transformation would occur for a city or a nation was never made clear. Churches can change things internally, but they do not have leverage to change society. Although legislation could institute some changes, there was no way to coerce people to love one another enough to shift from a capitalist to a cooperative society. The church can only influence by persuasion and it cannot overcome self-interest. The whole proposal broke down at this point. Rauschenbusch realized that eloquent moving prayers were not enough: to achieve a good society a strong regulatory economy was essential. Otherwise people would revert to trying to gain advantages at the expense of others.

A great beginning was made in the reception of Rauschenbusch's proposals. When the Federal Council of Churches adopted Rauschenbusch's social ideas on economics as part of their agenda in 1908, this action insured the perpetuation of Rauschenbusch's ideas. To be sure, his ideas were flawed, but much of his analysis seemed solid. Especially important was the notion that society moves on rules, customs, practices that are systemic, and these must be addressed to effect lasting change. How that is to be done was not immediately apparent. Equally important, the churches committed themselves to work for justice, cooperation, and solidarity with workers. They accepted the task of social redemption as part of their responsibility. This decision marked a major shift in the history of Protestantism. Rauschenbusch planted an idea that seemed right to many Christians. He conveyed a vision and convinced many readers.

Rauschenbusch's creative combination of the Christian message and social analysis of human need generated powerful responses. Progressives of Rauschenbusch's generation accomplished what he could not by enforcing change through law. When so many in the nation suffered in the Depression, the welfare state was devised to protect the infirm and the elderly, symbolized by the creation of Social Security (1935). Denominations and churches have established ministries to the poor, and individuals have made personal commitments to working out their Christianity in service to others. The evidence suggests that Rauschenbusch left an important legacy to Christians in the century after his death in addition to his impact on his own generation. In every decade since Rauschenbusch's death, Christian leaders—ministers, historians, theologians—have acknowledged their debt to Rauschenbusch. Some have unsparingly critiqued his deficiencies, but many have also affirmed his constructive insights regarding church and society. The suffering of fellow human beings set the agenda for his life. Rauschenbusch's relevance for today is apparent when one begins to read his analysis of American society. Social analysts and historians increasingly understand the primacy of the economy in life. It affects everything from political agendas and elections to social policy and the well-being of every nation.

Rauschenbusch addressed with clarity failures of nation and church to address injustices embedded in the economic structure. Failures still abound. He often seems to be writing about our time as well as his own era when he describes economic inequities in terms of the one percent and the rest of the population, the suffering of the poor, and the need to remediate the situation with a living wage, the heavy toll taken by rent, politics controlled by powerful business corporations, the tendency of rich and poor alike to be driven by greed, the cultural captivity of the churches in their quest for success and their inability to critique the injustices in society. His analyses remain relevant to current American society as does his question to the churches about their level of response to injustices of all kinds in this nation.

BIBLIOGRAPHY

Books by Rauschenbusch

(original editions and subsequent editions used in this book)

Christianity and the Social Crisis. Edited by Robert D. Cross. New York: Harper and Row (Harper Torchbook), 1947.

Christianity and the Social Crisis in the 21st Century. Edited by Paul Raushenbush. New York: Harper Collins, 2007.

Christianity and the Social Crisis. New York: The Macmillan Co., 1907.

Christianizing the Social Order. New York: The Macmillan Co., 1912.

Christianizing the Social Order. New York: The Macmillan Co., 1926.

Dare We Be Christians? Boston: The Pilgrim Press, 1914.

Das Leben Jesu: Ein Systematisher Studiengang für Jugendvereine und Bibelklassen. Cleveland: P. Ritter, 1895.

Die Politische Verfassung Unseres Landes (*Civil Government of the United States*). 1902.

For God and the People. Boston: The Pilgrim Press, 1910.

Prayers for the Social Awakening. Boston: The Pilgrim Press, 1925. This is an expanded version of *For God and the People*, including several later prayers.

Righteousness of the Kingdom, The. Edited and introduced by Max Stackhouse. Nashville: Abingdon Press, 1968.

The Social Principles of Jesus, The. London: The International Committee of Young Men's Christian Association, 1916.

The Social Principles of Jesus, The. New York: Association Press, 1927.

Theology for the Social Gospel, A. New York: The Macmillan Company, 1917.

Theology for the Social Gospel, A. Introduction by Donald W. Shriver, Jr. Louisville, KY: Westminster John Knox Press, 1997.

Unto Me. Boston: The Pilgrim Press, 1912.

Articles by Rauschenbusch in Newspapers, Journals, Pamphlets, and Books

"$8,500." *For the Right* 1/6 (March 1890): 5–6.

"About the Anniversaries." *The Examiner*, June 23, 1892.

"'American Christianity and National Life.' An Address to the Northern Baptist Convention, May 22, 1915." *The Standard* 22/42 (June 19, 1915): 1303–305.

"The American Church," *The Congregationalist* (October 23, 1913): 562.

"Be Fair to Germany." *Rochester Evening Times*, November 13, 1914.

"The Brotherhood of the Kingdom," Brotherhood Leaflet No. 2, *Brotherhood of the Kingdom* (bound volume in ABHS archives).

"Centralization of Baptist Polity." *Thirteenth Annual Session of the Baptist Congress held in The Central Baptist Church in Providence, R.I. November 12th, 13th, and 14th, 1895*. New York: Baptist Congress Publishing Co., 1896. 57–60.

"Church and Social Questions, The." In *Conservation of National Ideals*, 99–122. New

York: Fleming Revell, 1911.
"Church and the Social Crisis, The." *The Baptist World Alliance Second Congress. Philadelphia, June 19–25, 1911, Record of Proceedings*. Philadelphia: Harper and Brothers Company, 1911.
"Church, the People, and the Age, The." In *The Church, the People, and the Age*, edited by Robert Scott and George William Gilmore, 315. New York: Funk and Wagnalls, 1914.
"Conceptions of Missions I." *The Watchman* 73/47 (November 24, 1892): 1.
"Conceptions of Missions II." *The Watchman* 73/48 (December 1, 1892) 1.
"A Conquering Idea." *The Examiner*, July 31, 1892.
"Crow's Nest, The." *For the Right* 1/4 (January 1890): 4.
"Culture of the Spiritual Life, The." *Rochester Baptist Monthly* 12/3 (November 1897): 17.
"Does the New Testament Provide a Definite and Permanent Church Polity?" *Twenty-Second Annual Session of the Baptist Congress*. New York: Baptist Congress Publishing Co., 1905. 108–15.
"Drop a Nickel in the Slot." *For the Right* 1/4 (January 1890): 3–4.
"Eight Hours." *For the Right* 1/9 (June 1890): 3.
"Emotionalism in Religion: Discussion." *Eleventh Annual Session of the Baptist Congress for the Discussion of Current Questions, held in The First Baptist Church, Augusta, GA., Dec. 5th, 6th and 7th, 1893*. New York: Baptist Congress Publishing Co., 1894. 33–34.
"First Christian Church, The." *The Inquirer*, July 17, 1892.
"First Christian Martyr, The." *The Inquirer*, August 28, 1892.
"Freedom of Spiritual Religion, The." Philadelphia: American Baptist Publication Society, 1910.
"From *Tongue of Fire*," *For the Right* (1/11)(August 1890), 6.
"Genesis of *Christianity and the Social Crisis*, The." *Rochester Theological Seminary Bulletin: The Record* (November 1918).
"Getting at the Crow's Nest." *For the Right* 1/5 (February 1890): 2.
"Good Men and Good Governance." *For the Right* 1/11 (August 1890): 2.
"Gracious Call, The." *The Inquirer*, February 7, 1892.
"Heretics in the Truth." *The Inquirer*, April 14, 1892.
"In Germany: Some Chapters in Social Reform." *For the Right* 1/7 (Spring 1891): 2–3.
"Influence of Historical Studies on Theology, The." *American Journal of Theology* 11/1 (January 1907): 111–27.
"Justice and Brotherhood." In *The Path of Labor: Christianity and the World's Workers*, by M. Katharine Bennett, Grace Scribner, John E. Calfee et al., 165–87. New York: Council of Women for Home Missions, 1918.
"Keep Them Separate." *For the Right* 1/4 (January 1891): 3.
"Letter to Dr. Lemuel Call Barnes, Field Secretary, American Baptist Home Mission Society, May 10, 1918." *Rochester Theological Seminary Bulletin*, November 1918.
"The Materials of Religious Education: Being the Principal Papers Presented At, and The Proceedings of the Fourth General Convention of the Religious Education

Association." Rochester, New York, February 5–7, 1907, (Chicago: Executive Office of the Association, 1907) 25–30.
"Modern Judaizers." *The Sabbath Outlook*, April [day?] 1892.
"Movement against Alcoholism in America, The." *Proceeding and Papers of the Fifth World Congress of Free Christianity and Religious Progress, Berlin, August 7, 1910*. Goerlitz, Germany: Hoffmann & Reiber, 1910.
"Natural and Artificial Monopolies." *Eighth Annual Session of the Baptist Congress*. New York: Baptist Congress Publishing Company, 1890.
"New Evangelism, The." *The Independent* 56 (January–June 1904): 1054–59.
"Our Attitude toward Millenarianism." *The Examiner*, September 24 and October 1, 1896.
"Prayer for Friendship, A." *The Watchman*, 7:10 (March 16, 1919): 297.
"Prefatory Note," *Tenth Annual Session of the Baptist Congress*. New York: Baptist Congress Publishing Company, 1892.
"Regenerate Church Membership," *Rochester Baptist Monthly*, 17/7, March 1903.
"Relation of Church and State: Discussion," *Eighth Annual Session of the Baptist Congress for the Discussion of Current Questions, held in The Jarvis Street Baptist Church, Toronto, Ont. Nov. 12th, 13th and 14th, 1889*. New York: Baptist Congress Publishing Co., 1890.
"Religion, the Life of God in the Soul of Man." *New York Times*, October 22, 1900.
"Religion: The Life of God in the Soul of Man." *Baptist Magazine* (May 1909): 1–8.
"Report of Talk to Sunday School", *Rochester Democrat and Chronicle*, January 25, 1913.
"Review of *The Life of Döllinger*." *American Journal of Theology* 7/4 (October 1903): 733–43.
"Revolutionary Religion," *Democrat Chronicle*, March 1, 1909.
"Speaking in Tongues—What Was It?" *Watchman* (September 30, 1897): 1251–52.
"State Conference of Religion to Be Held Next Week." *New York Times*, November 22, 1900.
"Story of Three Miners, A." *For the Right* 1/2 (1889): 2–3
"Thoughts on Prayer." *Rochester Baptist Monthly* 15/5 (January 1901): 33–34.
"Tradition as a Formative Force in Baptist Doctrine and Church Life." *Twelfth Annual Session of the Baptist Congress for the Discussion of Current Questions, held in The Woodward Avenue Baptist Church, Detroit, Mich., Nov. 13th, 14th and 15th, 1895*. New York: Baptist Congress Publishing Co., 1895. 36–38.
"The American Church," *The Congregationalist* (October 23, 1913): 562.
"Valedictory Message: A Letter of Walter Rauschenbusch to Cornelius Woelfkin," May 1, 1918, published in *The Standard* 65/49 (August 3, 1918): 1409.
"The Value and Use of History," *The Record* (November 1914): 31–42.
"Walter Rauschenbusch—His Personal Testimony." *The Watchman Examiner*, August 1, 1918.
"Way of Righteousness, The." *The Inquirer*, April 3, 1892.
"Weeping Prophet, The." *The Inquirer*, February 18, 1892.
"What Is a Christian Nation?" *The Standard* 54/21 (January 23, 1907): 757–58.
"Why I Am a Baptist—II." *Canadian Baptist* (Toronto, Canada), January 2, 1913.
"Why I Am a Baptist." *The Rochester Baptist Monthly*, "Why I Am a Baptist: Prelude,"

20/2 (November 1905): 2–3; "Why I Am a Baptist: My First Reason," 20/4 (December 1905): 85–88; "Why I Am a Baptist: My Second Reason," 20/5 (January 1906): 106–108; "Why I Am a Baptist: My Third Reason," 20/6 (February 1906): 134–36; "Why I Am a Baptist: My Fourth Reason," 20/7 (March 1906): 156–59.

"The Workers," *The Baptist Union*, February 26, 1898.

"Zurich Anabaptists and Thomas Münzer, The." *The American Journal of Theology* 9/1 (January 1905): 91–106.

American Church: Great Christian Groups Which Belong Together, The. Lewiston, ME: The Journal Printshop, 1914.

Unpublished Materials

Much of Rauschenbusch's materials remain unpublished. This includes a heavy volume of correspondence to and from Rauschenbusch, extended notes on his lectures, drafts of books or portions of books, notes on speeches, and an exhaustive collection of his sermons. Over 180 boxes of these papers are housed in the American Baptist Historical Society archival collection at Mercer University in Atlanta, Georgia (cited as ABHS archives or cited as Rauschenbusch Family Papers). A second center holding primary materials is the North American Baptist Heritage Commission archives housed in the Sioux Falls Seminary, Sioux Falls, South Dakota (cited as NABHC archives).

Secondary Sources

Acton, Lord. "Döllinger." *The English Historical Review* 5/20 (October 1890): 700–44.

Ahlstrom, Sydney E. *A Religious History of the American People*. 2nd ed. New Haven: Yale University Press, 2004.

———. "Theology in America: A Historical Survey." In *The Shaping of American Religion*, edited by James W. Smith and A. Leland Jamison, 232–321. Princeton: Princeton University Press, 1961.

———, editor. *Theology in America: The Major Protestant Voices from Puritanism to Neo-Orthodoxy*. Indianapolis: The Bobbs Merrill Company, 1967.

Arthur, William. *The Tongue of Fire; or, The True Power of Christianity*. New York: Abingdon-Cokesbury Press, n.d. Original publication, 1856.

"As Lectures Fill Many Engagements Professor Rauschenbusch Not Able to Meet All Demands," *Rochester Democrat and Chronicle*, April 16, 1911.

Baker, Ray Stannard. "Why Socialism Grows." *New York Times*, December 15, 1908.

———. *The Spiritual Unrest*. New York: Frederick A. Stokes Company, 1910.

Balmer, Randall, and Lauren Winner. *Protestantism in America*. New York: Columbia University Press, 2002.

Baptist Congress of 1901. *Proceedings of the Baptist Congress 1901*. New York: Baptist Congress Publishing Company, 1901.

Baptist World Alliance. *Congress Program Guide*. Falls Church, VA: Baptist World Alliance, 2010.

Barbour, Clarence Augustus. *Making Religion Efficient*. New York: YMCA Press, 1912.

Barnes, Lemuel Call. "Walter Rauschenbusch—His Personal Testimony." *Watchman Examiner*, August 1, 1918.

Barnes, Sherman B. "Walter Rauschenbusch as Historian." *Foundations* 12 (July–September 1969): 254–62.
Barnette, Henlee. "Walter Rauschenbusch: Baptist Thinker and Leader." *Baptist Leader*, January 1958, XIX:10, 6-7.
Baron, Salo Wittmayer. *Modern Nationalism and Religion*. New York: Harper and Brothers, 1947.
Baumer, Franklin L. *Modern European Thought: Continuity and Change in Ideas, 1650–1950*. New York: Macmillan, 1977.
Beckley, Harlan. *Passion for Justice: Retrieving the Legacies of Walter Rauschenbusch, John A. Ryan and Reinhold Niebuhr*. Louisville: Westminster John Knox Press, 1992.
Bennett, John C. "Christian Ethics and Forms of Economic Power." In *Christian Values and Economic Life*, edited by John C. Bennett, Howard R. Bowen, William Adams Brown, Jr., and G. Bromley Oxnam, 235-257. New York: Harper and Brothers, 1954.
———. *Christian Realism*. New York: Charles Scribner's Sons, 1941.
———. Foreword to *Christian Social Ethic in a Changing World: An Ecumenical Theological Inquiry*, edited by John C. Bennett, 17-19. New York: Association Press, 1966.
———. *Social Salvation: A Religious Approach to the Problems of Social Change*. New York: Charles Scribner's Sons, 1935.
"Best Books of 1907." *New York Times*, August 9, 1908.
Beversluis, Joel. *Sourcebook of the World's Religions: An Interfaith Guide to Religion and Spirituality*. Novate, CA: New World Library, 2000.
Bliss, W. D. P. "Seeks to Make Religion a Legislative Force." *New York Times*, February 8, 1914.
Boudens, Robrecht. Introduction to *Alfred Plummer: Conversations with Dr. Döllinger, 1870–1890*, edited by Robrecht Boudens, [pages?]. Leuven: Leuven University Press, 1985.
Bouyer, Louis. *A History of Christian Spirituality*. 3 vols. London: Burns and Oates, 1968.
Bowden, Henry Warner. *Church History in the Age of Science: Historiographical Patterns in the United States, 1870–1898*. Chapel Hill: University of North Carolina Press, 1971, xvi-xix.
Bowden, John, editor. *Encyclopedia of Christianity*. Oxford: Oxford University Press, 2005.
Bowler, Peter J. *Monkey Trials and Gorilla Sermons*. Cambridge: Harvard University Press, 2007.
Brachlow, Stephen. "Walter Rauschenbusch." In *Baptist Theologians*, edited by Timothy George and David S. Dockery, 368–71. Nashville: Broadman Press, 1990.
Breisach, Ernst. *Historiography: Ancient, Medieval and Modern*. Chicago: University of Chicago Press, 1983.
Brooke, Stopford A., editor. *Life and Letters of the Rev. F. W. Robertson*. 2 vols. London: Kegan, Paul Trench, Treubner and Co., 1865.
Bushnell, Horace. *Christian Nurture*. New York: Scribner, Armstrong and Co., 1876.
Carman, Augustus S. "A Great Theological Quintet." *The Examiner* 18 (May 2, 1912): 533–34.

Carrette, Jeremy, and Richard King. *Selling Spirituality: The Silent Takeover of Religion*. London: Routledge, 2004.
Carter, Paul A. *The Decline and Revival of the Social Gospel: Social and Political Liberalism in American Protestant Churches, 1920–1940*. Ithaca, NY: Cornell University Press, 1954.
Case, Shirley Jackson. *The Social Triumph of the Ancient Church*. New York: Harper and Brothers, 1933.
Catalogue of the Rochester Theological Seminary, Founded November 4, 1850, by the New-York Baptist Union for Ministerial Education, 1854–5. Rochester: Press of A. Strong & Co., Democrat Office, 1854.
Chadwick, Owen. *The Secularization of the European Mind in the Nineteenth Century*. The Gifford Lectures in the University of Edinburgh for 1973–1974. Cambridge: Cambridge University Press, 1975.
Chambers, John Whiteclay, II. *The Tyranny of Change: America in the Progressive Era, 1890–1920*. 2nd ed. New Brunswick, NJ: Rutgers University Press, 2000.
"Cheap Baths for the Poor: Walter Rauschenbusch Urges the Building of a Model House by the City." *New York Times*, April 16, 1894.
Cherry, Conrad. *Hurrying toward Zion: University Divinity Schools and American Protestantism*. Bloomington: Indiana University Press, 1995.
"Christianity and the Social Crisis." *The Watchman* 89/25 (June 20, 1907): 7.
"Christianity and the Social Crisis." *The Watchman* 90/6 (February 6, 1908): 7.
Clawson, Michael. "Emerging From What?: The Historical Roots of the Emerging Church Movement." PhD diss., Baylor University, 2017.
Commager, Henry Steele. *The American Mind: An Interpretation of American Thought and Character Since the 1880s*. New Haven: Yale University Press, 1950.
"Concerning Walter Rauschenbusch." *Rochester Bulletin*, March 1934.
Cox, Harvey. *The Future of Faith*. New York: Harper One, 2009.
Cracknell, Kenneth, and Susan J. White. *An Introduction to World Methodism*. Cambridge: Cambridge University Press, 2005.
Cross, F. L., and E. A. Livingstone, editors. *Oxford Dictionary of Christian Church*. 3rd rev. ed. London: Oxford University Press, 2005.
Cross, Robert D. *The Church and the City, 1865–1910*. Indianapolis: The Bobbs-Merrill Company, 1967.
———. Introduction to *Christianity and the Social Crisis* by Walter Rauschenbusch, viii-xx. New York: Harper, 1964.
Cross, Whitney R. *The Burned-over District: The Social and Intellectual History of Enthusiastic Religion in Western New York, 1800–1850*. New York: Harper, 1950.
Dahlberg, Edwin. "Edwin Dahlberg in Conversation: Memories of Walter Rauschenbusch." Transcribed by John E. Skoglund. *Foundations* 35/3 (July–September 1975): 209–18.
———. *Walter Rauschenbusch: Prophet of Social Christianity*. Rochester: Colgate Rochester Divinity School, n.d. 12-page leaflet, housed in North American Baptist Heritage Society, Sioux Falls Seminary, Sioux Falls, S.D.
Daniel, C. A. "Reminiscences of my friend Walter Rauschenbusch." North American Baptist Heritage Commission archives, #820.

Darwin, Charles. *The Origin of Species*. New York: Penguin, 1968.
DeWitt, Benjamin P. *The Progressive Movement: A Non-Partisan, Comprehensive Discussion of Current Tendencies in American Politics*. New York: The Macmillan Company, 1915.
Dictionary of American Biography. New York: Charles Scribner's Sons, 1946.
Dillenberger, John, and Claude Welch. *Protestant Christianity: Interpreted through Its Development*. 2nd ed. New York: Macmillan Publishing Company, 1988.
Dombrowski, James. *The Early Days of Christian Socialism in America*. New York: Columbia University Press, 1936.
Dorrien, Gary. *The Making of American Liberal Theology*. 3 vols. Louisville: Westminster John Knox Press, 2001–2006.
———. *Reconstructing the Common Good: Theology and the Social Order*. New York: Orbis Books, 1990.
———. *Soul in Society: The Making and Renewal of Social Christianity*. Minneapolis: Fortress Press, 1995.
———. *The New Abolition: W. E. B. DuBois and the Black Social Gospel*. New Haven: Yale University Press, 2015.
———. "Thy Kingdom Come: Walter Rauschenbusch, Vida Scudder and the Social(ist) Gospel." *The Making of American Liberal Theology*. Vol. II: *Idealism, Realism and Modernity 1900–1950*, 73–150. Louisville: Westminster John Knox Press, 2003.
Douglas, T. C. *The Making of a Socialist: The Recollections of T. C. Douglas*, edited by Lewis H. Thomas. Edmonton: University of Alberta Press, 1982.
Draper, J. William. *History of the Conflict Between Science and Religion*. New York: D. Appleton, 1874.
"Dr. Rauschenbusch Passes Away." *The Watchman-Examiner*, August 1, 1918.
Drummond, Henry. *The Greatest Thing in the World*. New York: James Pott, 1880.
Dupré, L. and D. Saliers, editors. *Christian Spirituality: Post Reformation and Modern*. New York: Crossroad Publishing, 1989.
Eisenstein, Elizabeth L. *The Printing Press as an Agent of Change*. 2 vols. New York: Cambridge University Press, 1979.
Ely, Richard. *Social Aspects of Christianity and Other Essays*. New York: Thomas Y. Crowell & Company, 1889.
Evans, Christopher H. *The Kingdom Is Always but Coming: A Life of Walter Rauschenbusch*. Grand Rapids: Eerdmans, 2004.
———. *Liberalism without Illusions: Renewing an American Christian Tradition*. Waco, TX: Baylor University Press, 2010.
———. "Walter Rauschenbusch and the Second Coming: The Social Gospel as Baptist History." In *Through a Glass Darkly: Uses and Misuses of Baptist History*, edited by Keith Harper, 145–71. Tuscaloosa: University of Alabama Press, 2012.
———. *The Social Gospel in American Religion: A History*. New York: New York University Press, 2017.
———, editor. *The Social Gospel Today*. Louisville: John Knox Press, 2001.
Evearitt, David J. "Interpreting Salvation, Personal vs. Social: A Late Nineteenth-Cen-

tury Case Study on Walter Rauschenbusch and A. B. Simpson." *Evangelical Theological Society Papers*. Portland: Theological Research Exchange Network, 1991.

"Faunce, William Herbert Perry." *Dictionary of American Biography*. New York: Scribners, 1946. V-VI: 299–301

Foner, Eric. *Give Me Liberty: An American History*. Vol. 2. New York: W.W. Norton, 2006.

Fosdick, Harry Emerson. Introduction to *A Rauschenbusch Reader*, edited by Benson Y. Landis, [pages?]. New York: Harper and Brothers, 1957.

———. Introduction to *Walter Rauschenbusch* by Dores Robinson Sharpe, vii-xiii. New York: Macmillan, 1942.

———. *The Living of These Days*. New York: Harper and Row, 1956.

Foster, O. A. Durwood. "Albrecht Ritschl." In *A Handbook of Christian Theologians*, edited by Dean G. Peerman and Martin E. Marty, 49-67. Nashville: Abingdon, 1965.

Fox, Richard W. "The Culture of Liberal Protestant Progressives 1875–1925." *Journal of Interdisciplinary History* 23/3 (Winter 1993): 639–60.

Freeman, Charles. *A New History of Early Christianity*. New Haven: Yale University Press, 2009.

Gabelmann, J. S. "The German Department of Rochester Theological Seminary." *The Home Mission Monthly* 20/9 (September 1898): 308–12.

Gaustad, Edwin. "Our Country: One Century Later." In *Liberal Protestantism: Realities and Possibilities*, edited by Robert S. Michaelsen and Wade Clark Roof, 85–101. New York: Pilgrim Press, 1986.

———, and Leigh E. Schmidt. *The Religious History of America*, rev. ed. New York: Harper San Francisco, 2002.

George, Henry. *Progress and Poverty*, Fiftieth anniversary ed. New York: Robert Schalkenbach Foundation, 1936. First published 1879 by D. Appleton & Co.

Gilkey, *On Niebuhr: A Theological Study*, (Chicago: Chicago University Press, 2001), 231.

Gillespie, Charles Coulston. *Genesis and Geology: The Impact of Scientific Discoveries Upon Religious Beliefs in the Decades Before Darwin*. New York: Harper Torchbook, 1959. First published 1951 as volume 58 of the *Harvard Historical Studies*.

Gould, Lewis L. *America in the Progressive Era, 1890–1914*. Harlow, England: Pearson Education, 2001.

Gladden, Washington. *Applied Christianity: Moral Aspects of Social Questions*. Boston: Houghton Mifflin, 1886.

Gustafson, James M. "From Scripture to Social Policy and Social Action." *Andover Newton Bulletin* 9 (January 1969): 160–69.

Gutierrez, Gustavo. *A Theology of Liberation*. Maryknoll: Orbis Books, 1973.

Halbrooks, Thomas. Preface to *The Social Gospel Today*, edited by Christopher H. Evans, xii–xiv. Louisville: Westminster John Knox Press, 2001.

Haldeman, I. M. *Professor Rauschenbusch's Christianity and the Social Crisis*. New York: Charles C. Cook, 1911.

Handlin, Oscar. *The Uprooted*. 2nd ed. Philadelphia: University of Pennsylvania Press, 2002.

Handy, Robert T. *A Christian America: Protestant Hopes and Historical Realities*. New York: Oxford University Press, 1971.
———. Foreword. *The Righteousness of the Kingdom,* edited by Max Stackhouse, 5-6.
———. *The Social Gospel in America, 1870–1920: Gladden, Ely, Rauschenbusch* in *A Library of Protestant Thought*, edited by John Dillenberger, et al. New York: Oxford University Press, 1966.
———. *Undermined Establishment: Church State Relations in America, 1880–1920.* Princeton: Princeton University Press, 1991.
———. "Walter Rauschenbusch: Evangelical Prophet," *Crossroad,* vol. 7, no. 3, (June 30, 1957) 4-6, 83.
Harnack, Adolph. *History of Dogma*. 7 vols. Translated from the 3rd German edition by Neil Buchanan. New York: Dover, 1961. First published 1895–1900 by Roberts Brothers, Little, Brown and Company.
———. *What Is Christianity?* Translated by Thomas Bailey Saunders. 2nd ed. New York: G. P. Putnam's Sons, 1903.
Harrington, Michael. *The Other America*. New York: Macmillan, 1962.
Hastings, Adrian. "History." In *The Oxford Companion to Christian Thought*, edited by Adrian Hastings, Alistair Mason, and Hugh Peter, 299-301. Oxford: Oxford University Press, 2000.
Hayes, Catherine D. "The History of the University of Rochester Libraries—120 Years." *University of Rochester Library Bulletin* 25/3 (Spring 1970): 59–122.
Hedley, John. *Science and Religion: Some Historical Perspectives*. Cambridge: Cambridge University Press, 1991.
Heelas, Paul, editor. *Spirituality in the Modern World: Within Religious Tradition and Beyond*. Oxford: Routledge, 2011.
Heelas, Paul, and Linda Woodhead. *The Spirituality Revolution: Why Religion Is Giving Way to Spirituality*. Oxford: Blackwell, 2005.
Henry, Carl F. H. *The Uneasy Conscience of Modern Fundamentalism*. Grand Rapids, MI: William B. Eerdmans Publishing, 1947.
Higgenbotham, Evelyn Brooks. *Righteous Discontent: The Women's Movement in the Black Baptist Churches, 1880–1920*. Cambridge: Harvard University Press, 1993.
Higham, John. "Ethnicity and American Protestants." In *New Directions in American Religious History*, edited by Harry S. Stout and D. G. Hart, 239-259. Oxford: Oxford University Press, 1997.
Hinson, Glenn. *A Miracle of Grace: An Autobiography*. Macon, GA: Mercer University Press, 2012.
Holder, Arthur. "Christian Forms of Spirituality." In *The Cambridge Dictionary of Christianity*, edited by Patte Daniel, 1183-1184. Cambridge: Cambridge University Press, 2010.
Holt, Arthur. *The Nation under God*. Chicago: Willett Clark and Co., 1939.
Hopkins, Charles Howard. *History of the Y. M. C. A. in North America*. New York: Association Press, 1951.
———. *The Rise of the Social Gospel in American Protestantism, 1865–1915*. New Haven: Yale University Press, 1940.
Hudson, Winthrop S. *American Protestantism*. Chicago: University of Chicago Press,

1961.
———. "From *Tongue of Fire*" in *For the Right* (August 1980), 6.
———. "Rauschenbusch—Evangelical Prophet." *The Christian Century*, June 14, 1953.
———. *Religion in America*. New York: Charles Scribner's Sons, 1965.
———, editor. *Walter Rauschenbusch: Selected Writings*. New York: Paulist Press, 1984.
Hutchison, William R. *Errand to the World: American Protestant Thought and Foreign Missions*. Chicago: University of Chicago Press, 1987.
———. *The Modernist Impulse in American Protestantism*. Durham, NC: Duke University Press, 1992.
Jaehn, Klaus Juergen. *Rauschenbusch: The Formative Years*. Valley Forge: Judson Press, 1976.
James, William. *The Varieties of Religious Experience*. London: Longmans, Green and Co., 1902.
Johnson, Ernest F. *The Social Gospel Re-examined*. New York: Harper, 1940.
Johnson, Paul E. *A Shopkeeper's Millennium: Society and Revivals in Rochester, New York, 1815–1837*. New York: Hill and Wang, 1978.
Jonas, Glenn. *A Critical Evaluation of Albert Henry Newman, 1852–1933, Church Historian*. San Francisco: Mellen Research University Press, 1992.
Jones, Carter Helm. "Comments." *Twenty-Second Annual Session of the Baptist Congress*. New York: Baptist Congress Publishing Co., 1905.
Keller, Ludwig. *Geschichte der Wiedertäufer und ihres Reiches zu Münster (History of the Anabaptists and their Kingdom at Münster)*. Münster: Verlag der Coppernrath'schen Buch-& Kunsthandlung, 1880.
———. *Ein Apostel der Wiedertäufer: Hans Denck (An Apostle of the Anabaptists: Hans Denck)*. Leipzig: S. Hirzel, 1882.
———. *Die Reformation und die älteren Reformparteien (The Reformation and an Alternative Reformation Party)*. Leipzig: S. Hirzel, 1885.
———. *Die Waldenser und die deutschen Bibelübersetzungen* (*The Waldensians and the German Translation of the Bible*) Leipzig: S. Hirzel,1886.
King, Ursula. *The Search for Spirituality: Our Global Quest for a Spiritual Life*. Norwich: Canterbury Press, 2009.
King, Martin Luther Jr. "Pilgrimage to Nonviolence." *Christian Century*, April 13, 1960.
Kraut, Alan M. *The Huddled Masses: The Immigrant in American Society, 1880–1921*. Arlington Heights, IL: Harlan Davidson, Inc., 1982.
Latourette, Kenneth Scott. *A History of Christianity*. New York: Harper and Brothers, 1953.
———. *A History of the Expansion of Christianity*. 7 vols. New York: Harper and Brothers, 1938–1945.
Lawrence, Brother. *The Practice of the Presence of God*. Published by Joseph de Beaufort in 1692 under the title of *Spiritual Maxims*.
Leo XIII, *Rerum Novarum*, May 15, 1891, *Christian Social Teachings*, ed. George W. Forell (Garden City, NY: Doubleday & Company, 1966) 339–44.
Leuschner, Martin. "Walter Rauschenbusch and Our Day." Handwritten address presented in 1934 and 1935, item #1043 in the North American Baptist Heritage Commission archives. Sioux Falls Seminary, Sioux Falls, SD.

Lippy, Charles H. *Introducing American Religion*. New York: Routledge, 2009.
Luker, Ralph E. "Interpreting the Social Gospel: Reflections on Two Generations of Historiography." In *Perspectives on the Social Gospel*, edited by Christopher Evans, 1-13. Lewiston, NY: Edwin Mellen Press, 1999.
———. *The Social Gospel in Black and White: American Racial Reform, 1885–1912*. Chapel Hill: University of North Carolina Press, 1991.
Main, Arthur Elwin. "The Seventh-day Baptist General Conference, 1802–1902." In *Seventh Day Baptists in Europe and America*, 2 vols. Plainfield, NJ: American Sabbath Tract Society, 1910.
Marney, Carlyle. "The Significance of Carlyle Marney for Today." *Foundations* 2/1 (January 1989): 13–26.
Marsden, George. *Fundamentalism and American Culture: The Shaping of Twentieth-Century Evangelicalism 1870–1925*. New York: Oxford University Press, 1980.
Martin, Hugh, editor. *Christian Social Reformers of the Nineteenth Century*. New York: George H. Doran, 1927.
Marty, Martin. *The Irony of It All, 1893–1919*. Vol. 1 of *Modern American Religion*. 3 vols. Chicago: University of Chicago Press, 1986.
———. *Pilgrims in Their Own Land: 500 Years of Religion in America*. Boston: Little, Brown and Company, 1984.
May, Henry F. *Protestant Churches and Industrial America*. New York: Harper and Row, 1949.
———. "The Recovery of American Religious History." *American Historical Review* 70 (October 1964): 79–92.
Mays, Benjamin, editor. *A Gospel of the Social Awakening: Selections from the Writings of Walter Rauschenbusch*. New York: Association Press, 1950.
Mazzini, Giuseppe. *The Duties of Man and Other Essays*. New York: Cosimo Classics, 2005.
McClymond, Michael. "Revivals." In *Religion in America*, edited by Philip Goff, 306-320. Oxford: Wiley-Blackwell, 2010.
McGerr, Michael. *A Fierce Discontent: The Rise and Fall of the Progressive Movement in America, 1870–1920*. New York: Free Press, 2003.
McGiffert, Arthur C. "Walter Rauschenbusch Twenty Years After." *Christendom* 3/1 (Winter 1938): 96–109.
McGinn, B., J. Meyendorff, and J. Leclercq, editors. *Christian Spirituality: Origins to the Twelfth Century*. New York: Crossroad Publishing, 1985.
McKelvey, Blake. "Walter Rauschenbusch's Rochester," *Rochester History* 14/4 (October 1952): 1–28.
Mead, Sidney. *The Lively Experiment*. New York: Harper and Row, 1963.
Meinhold, Peter. *Geschichte der kirchlichen Historiographie*. 2 vols. Freiburg: Verlag Karl Alber, 1967.
Meyer, F. W. C. "Rauschenbusch Aflame for God." *The Baptist Herald*, October 1, 1936.
Miller, David H. *God at Work: the Faith at Work Movement*. Oxford: Oxford University Press, 2007.
Miller, Timothy. *Following in His Steps: A Biography of Charles M. Sheldon*. Knoxville:

University of Tennessee Press, 1987.
Minus, Paul M. *Walter Rauschenbusch: American Reformer*. New York: Macmillan Publishing Company, 1988.
Moehlman, Conrad H. "Life and Writings of Walter Rauschenbusch." *The Colgate-Rochester Divinity School Bulletin* 1 (1928–1929) 32-37.
Moore, LeRoy Jr. "Academic Freedom: A Chapter in the History of the Colgate Rochester Divinity School." *Foundations* 10 (January–March 1967): 64-79.
Morris, Jeremy, editor. *To Build Christ's Kingdom: F. D. Maurice and His Writings*. Norwich: Canterbury Press, 2007.
Morrison, C. C. *The Social Gospel and Christian Culture*. New York: Harper and Brothers, 1933.
Ness, Peter Van, editor. *Spirituality and the Secular Quest*. New York: Crossroad Publishing, 1996.
"New York as It Ought to Be, An Address Before Baptist Ministers by the Rev. W. Rauschenbusch." *New York Times*, November 19, 1985.
Newman, A. H. *A Manual of Church History*. 2 vols. Philadelphia: American Baptist Publication Society, 1899, 1902.
Niebuhr, H. Richard. *Christ and Culture*. New York: Harper, 1951.
———. *The Kingdom of God in America*. Chicago: Willett, Clark & Company, 1957.
———. *The Social Sources of Denominationalism*. New York: Henry Holt and Co., 1929.
Niebuhr, Reinhold. *An Interpretation of Christian Ethics*. New York: Meridian, 1956. Original publication: *Rauschenbusch Memorial Lectures*, 1934.
Nineteenth Annual Catalogue of the Officers and Students of the Rochester Theological Seminary. Rochester, NY: Tracy and Rew, 1870.
Nixon, Justin Wroe. "Walter Rauschenbusch—Ten Years Later." *The Christian Century*, November 8, 1928.
Numbers, Ronald L. *Darwinism Comes to America*. Cambridge: Harvard University Press, 1998.
O'Connor, Joseph. "The Spirit of Discontent: Professor Rauschenbusch on the Problems of Christianity in the Social Crisis." *New York Times*, June 1, 1907.
Osgood, Howard. *A Short Synopsis of Introduction to The Pentateuch: for the use of classes in Rochester Theological Seminary*, printed, not published. Rochester, NY: Frank D. Phinney, printer, 1880.
Otto, Rudolf. *Das Heilige: Über das Irrationale in der Idee des Göttlichen und sein Verhältnis zum Rationalen* (Breslau, Germany, 1917; First English translation in 1923 as *The Idea of the Holy*). Translated by J. W. Harvey. Oxford: Oxford University Press, 1923.
Palmer, G. E. H., Philip Sherrard, and Kallistos Ware, editors. *The Philokalia*. London: Faber and Faber, 1983.
Pannkoke, O. H. A review of *A Theology for the Social Gospel*, in *American Lutheran Survey*, June 12, 1918.
Pattison, Thomas Harwood. *The Making of a Sermon: For the Classroom and Study*. Philadelphia: American Baptist Publication Society, 1898.
Payne, Ernest A. "The Prophet of the Social Gospel." *The Baptist Times*, December 19, 1957.

Payne, Richard J., and John Furina, editors. *The Classics of Western Spirituality*. New York: Paulist Press, 1981.
Persons, Stow. *American Minds: A History of Ideas*. Huntington, NY: Robert E. Kreiger Publishing Company, 1975.
Pierard, Richard V., editor. *Baptists Together in Christ 1905–2005: A Hundred-Year History of the Baptist World Alliance*. Birmingham: Samford University Press, 2005.
Pitts, Bill. "The Personal and the Social Christianity in Rauschenbusch's Thought." *American Baptist Quarterly* 26/2 (Summer 2007): 138–60.
———. "Rauschenbusch and the Reformation," *Baptist History and Heritage* 52/3 (Fall 2017): 32–46.
———. "Shaping a German Immigrant Church." *American Baptist Quarterly* 33/2 (Summer 2014): 194–214.
"Plan of Organization." In *Proceedings of the Baptist Congress 1901*. New York: Baptist Congress Publishing Company, 1901.
Pourrat, Philippe. *La Spiritualité Chrétienne*. 4 vols. Paris: Gabalda, 1918.
Raitt, J., editor. *Christian Spirituality: High Middle Ages and Reformation*. New York: Crossroad Publishing, 1987.
Ramaker, Albert J. *The German Baptists of North America*. Cleveland: German Baptist Publication Society, 1924.
Ramsay, William M. *Four Modern Prophets*. Atlanta: John Knox Press, 1986.
Rauschenbusch, August. *Leben und Wirken von August Rauschenbusch*. Completed and edited by Walter Rauschenbusch. Cassel: J. G. Oncken, 1901.
———. *August Rauschenbusch, Life and Ministry*. Completed by Walter Rauschenbusch and translated by Donald H. Madvig. Sioux Falls, SD: North American Baptist Heritage Commission, 2008.
———. *Saturday or Sunday: Which Should We Observe?* Translated by F. N. Jewett. New York: American Tract Society, c. 1908.
Rauschenbusch-Clough, Emma. *A Study of Mary Wollstonecraft and the Rights of Woman*. London: Longmans, Green & Company, 1898.
Renan, Ernst. *Life of Jesus*. London, 1864. First published 1863 in France.
Richey, Russell E., Kenneth E. Rowe, and Jean Miller Schmidt, editors. *The Methodist Experience in America: A History*. Vol. 1. Nashville: Abingdon Press, 2010.
Riis, Jacob. *How the Other Half Lives*. New York: Dover Publications, 1971. First published 1890 by Charles Scribner.
Roberts, Jon. H. *Darwinism and the Divine in America: Protestant Intellectuals and Organic Evolution, 1859–1900*. Madison: University of Wisconsin Press, 1988.
Robins, H. B. *Rochester Seminary Bulletin*. Rochester: Colgate Rochester Divinity School, 1918.
Robins, Henry Burke. "The Contribution of Walter Rauschenbusch to World Peace," *The Bulletin* (Rochester: Colgate Rochester Divinity School, May 1940, 34.
———. *Rochester Seminary Bulletin*, 1918, 34, cited in Sharpe, *Walter Rauschenbusch*, 433, n. 13.
"Rochester Takes a Step Forward." *The Baptist* 1/21 (June 19, 1920): 728.
Rochester Theological Seminary. "Rev. Walter Rauschenbusch, D.D." In *Rochester Theological Seminary General Catalogue, 1850–1920*. Rochester, NY: E. R. Andrews

Printing Co., 1920.
———. *Catalogue of the Rochester Theological Seminary, Founded November 4, 1850, by the New-York Baptist Union for Ministerial Education, 1854–5*. Rochester, NY: Press of A. Strong & Co., Democrat Office, 1854.
———. *Nineteenth Annual Catalogue of the Officers and Students of the Rochester Theological Seminary*. Rochester, NY: Tracy and Rew, 1870.
———. *Rochester Theological Seminary General Catalogue 1850–1920*. New York: E.R. Andrews Printing Co., 1920.
———. *Seventeenth Annual Catalogue of the Officers and Students of the Rochester Theological Seminary, 1867–68*. Rochester, NY: Baton and Andrews, 1867.
Roof, Wade Clark. *Spiritual Marketplace: Baby Boomers and the Remaking of America Religion*. Princeton: Princeton University Press, 1999.
Ross, Edward A. *Sin and Society: An Analysis of Latter Day Iniquity*. Boston: Houghton Mifflin and Company, 1907.
———. *The Old World in the New: The Significance of Past and Present Immigration to the American People*. New York: The Century Company, 1914.
Ryan, John A. *A Living Wage*. New York: Macmillan, 1906.
Sanford, Don A. *A Choosing People: The History of Seventh Day Baptists*. 2nd ed. Macon, GA: Mercer University Press, 2012.
Sanks, T. Howland. "Liberation Theology and the Social Gospel: Variations on a Theme." *Theological Studies* 52/2 (October, 2001): 668–82.
Schaff, Philip, editor. *Ante-Nicene Fathers*. 10 vols. New York: Christian Literature Publishing Co., 1885–1900.
———. *History of the Christian Church*. 3rd ed. 8 vols. New York: Charles Scribner's Sons, 1910.
———, editor. *Nicene and Post-Nicene Fathers*. 14 vols. New York: Christian Literature Publishing Co., 1885–1900.
Schneider, Carl E. "Americanization of Karl August Rauschenbusch, 1816–1899." *Church History* 24/1 (March 1955): 3–14.
Schubert, Hans von. *Outlines of Church History*. Translated by Maurice A. Canney. New York: G.P. Putnam's Sons, 1907.
Scott, David. "Prayer." In *Encyclopedia of Christianity*, edited by John Bowden, 963. Oxford: Oxford University Press, 2005.
———. "Spirituality." In *Encyclopedia of Christianity*, edited by John Bowden, 1137. Oxford: Oxford University Press, 2005.
Scougal, Henry. *The Life of God in the Soul of Man*. London: Charles Smith, 1677.
Sears, Charles H. *The Redemption of the City*. Philadelphia: Griffith and Rowland Press, 1911.
Seeberg, Reinhold. *The History of Doctrines*. Translated by Charles E. Hay. Grand Rapids, MI: Baker Book House, 1961.
Shantz, Douglas H. *An Introduction to German Pietism: Protestant Renewal at the Dawn of Modern Europe*. Baltimore, MD: Johns Hopkins University Press, 2013.
Sharpe, Dores Robinson. *Walter Rauschenbusch*. New York: Macmillan, 1942.
Sheldon, Charles. *In His Steps*. Chicago: Chicago Advance, 1896.
Sheldrake, Philip. *A Brief History of Spirituality*. Oxford: Blackwell Publishing, 2007.

———. *Spirituality and History: Questions of Interpretation and Method.* 2nd ed. London: SPCK, 1995.
Shinn, Roger. *Christianity and the Problem of History.* New York: Charles Scribner's Sons, 1953.
Shriver, Donald W. Introduction to *A Theology for the Social Gospel* by Walter Rauschenbusch, xi-xxiv. Library of Theological Ethics. Louisville: Westminster John Knox Press, 1997.
Singer, Anna M. *Walter Rauschenbusch and His Contribution to Social Christianity.* Boston: Richard G. Badger, 1926.
Smith, George Adam. *The Book of the Twelve Prophets.* 2 vols. London: Hodder and Stoughton, 1896, 1898.
Smith, H. Shelton. *Changing Conceptions of Original Sin: A Study in American Theology Since 1750.* New York: Charles Scribner's Sons, 1955.
———, Robert T. Handy, and Lefferts A. Loetscher, editors. *American Christianity: An Historical Representation with Representative Documents.* 2 vols. New York: Charles Scribners and Sons, 1960–1963.
Smucker, Donovan E. *The Origins of Walter Rauschenbusch's Social Ethics.* Montreal: McGill-Queen's University Press, 1994.
"Social Gospel, The." *The Nation,* July 20, 1918.
"Social Gospeler, The." *Time* 70/21 (November 18, 1957): 1066.
Spalding, John Lancaster. "The Country and City." In *The Religious Mission of the Irish People and Catholic Colonization,* 64–100. New York: Catholic Colonization Society, 1880.
Stackhouse, Max. "Editor's Introduction: The Continuing Importance of Walter Rauschenbusch." In *The Righteousness of the Kingdom,* edited by Max Stackhouse, 13–59. Nashville: Abingdon Press, 1968.
———. "The Formation of a Prophet: Reflections on the Early Sermons of Walter Rauschenbusch." *Andover Newton Quarterly* 9/3 (January 1969): 4–12.
Stead, William T. *If Christ Came to Chicago.* Chicago: Laird and Lee, 1894.
Stein, Stephen J. "Millennialism." In *Religion in America,* edited by Phillip Goff, 215–27. Oxford: Wiley-Blackwell, 2010.
Stelzle, Charles. *Christianity's Storm Centre: A Study of the Modern City.* New York: Fleming Revell, 1907.
Stevens, William Arnold. "Biblical Criticism." In *Introduction to the New Testament: Lectures and Notes.* Rochester, NY: Rochester Theological Seminary, 1905.
———. "Inspiration of the Apostles." *Baptist Quarterly Review* 8/1 (January 1886): 48–92.
———, and Ernest DeWitt Burton. *A Harmony of the Gospels for Historical Study: An Analytical Synopsis of the Four Gospels in the Version of 1881.* Boston: Bible Study Publishing Co., 1893.
Stout, Harry S., and Robert M. Taylor. "Studies of Religion in American Society: The State of the Art." In *New Directions in American Religious History,* edited by Harry S. Stout and Daryl G. Hart, 15–47. Oxford: Oxford University Press, 1997.
Strain, Charles R. "Toward a Generic Analysis of a Classic of The Social Gospel: An Essay-Review of Walter Rauschenbusch's *Christianity and the Social Crisis.*" *Journal*

of the American Academy of Religion 46/4 (December 1978): 525–43.
Strayer, Paul Moore. "Walter Rauschenbusch." *The Universalist Leader*, August 8, 1918.
"Strong, A. H." *Dictionary of American Biography*. New York: Charles Scribner's Sons, 1946. 17:142–43.
Strong, Augustus H. *Reminiscences of Early Rochester*. Rochester, NY: Rochester Historical Society, 1916.
———. *A Tour of the Missions: Observations and Conclusions*. Philadelphia: Griffith and Rowland Press, 1918.
Strong, Josiah. *The Challenge of the City*. New York: Missionary Education Movement, 1907.
———. *Our Country: Its Possible Future and Its Present Crisis*. New York: Baker & Taylor, 1885.
Suttle, Tim. *An Evangelical Social Gospel?: Finding God's Story in the Midst of Extremes*. Eugene, OR: Cascade Books, 2011.
Szasz, Ferenc Morton. *The Divided Mind of American Protestantism, 1880–1930*. Tuscaloosa: University of Alabama Press, 1982.
Tarnas, Richard. *The Passion of the Western Mind*. New York: Ballentine Books, 1991.
Taylor, Frederick W. *The Principles of Scientific Management*. New York: Harper Brothers, 1911.
Taylor, Jeremy. *The Rule and Exercises of Holy Living*, 1650.
———. *The Rule and Exercises of Holy Dying*, 1651.
"The Social Problem." *The Examiner* 85/29 (July 18, 1907): 902.
"The Passing of a Great Leader," *The Universalist Leader*, August 3, 1918.
The Westminster Dictionary of Spirituality. Philadelphia: The Westminster Press, 1983.
Tillich, Paul. *Perspectives on 19th and 20th Century Protestant Theology*. Edited by Carl E. Braaten. New York: Harper and Row, 1967.
Tseng, Timothy, and Janet Furness. "The Reawakening of the Evangelical Social Conscience." In *The Social Gospel Today*, edited by Christopher Evans, 114-125. Louisville: Westminster John Knox Press, 2001.
United States Catholic Conference. *Economic Justice for All: Pastoral Letter on Catholic Social Teaching and the U.S. Economy*. Washington, DC: United States Catholic Conference, 1986.
Veblen, Thorsten. *The Theory of the Leisure Class: An Economic Study of Institutions*. New York: Macmillan, 1899.
Vedder, Henry. *Balthasar Hubmaier, the Leader of the Anabaptists*. New York: G. P. Putnam's Sons, 1905.
Vidler, Alec R. *F. D. Maurice and Company*. London: SCM Press, 1966.
Visser 't Hooft, Willem Adolph. *The Background of the Social Gospel in America*. Haarlem: H. D. Tjeenk Willink & Zoon, 1928.
Wacker, Grant. *Augustus H. Strong and the Dilemma of Historical Consciousness*. Macon, GA: Mercer University Press, 1985.
———. "The Holy Spirit and the Spirit of the Age in American Protestantism, 1880–1910." *Journal of American History* 72/1 (June 1985): 45–62.
Wakefield, Gordon S. "Spirituality," In *The Westminster Dictionary of Spirituality*, 361–62. Philadelphia: Westminster Press, 1983.

"Walter Rauschenbusch." *The Standard* 65/48 (August 3, 1918): 1407–408.
Ward, Benedicta, translator. *Sayings of the Desert Fathers: The Alphabetical Collection*, rev. ed. Kalamazoo: Cistercian Publications, 1984.
Welch, Claude. *Protestant Thought in the Nineteenth Century*. 2 vols. New Haven: Yale University Press, 1972, 1985.
Wentz, Richard E. *American Religious Traditions: The Shaping of Religion in the United States*. Minneapolis: Fortress Press, 2003.
White, Andrew Dickson. *History of the Warfare Between Science and Theology in Christendom*. 2 vols. New York: D. Appleton and Co.,1896.
White, Ronald C. Jr. *Liberty and Justice for All: Radical Reform and the Social Gospel, 1875–1925*. San Francisco: Harper and Row, 1990.
"Why Socialism Grows." *New York Times*, December 15, 1908.
Williams, George Huntston. *The Radical Reformation*, 3rd ed., revised and expanded. Kirksville, MO: Truman State University Press, 2000; first published by Westminster Press, 1962.
Williams, Leighton, "The Brotherhood of the Kingdom and Its Work, Brotherhood Leaflet No. 10., *Brotherhood of the Kingdom* (bound volume in ABHS archives).
Woelfkin, Cornelius. *The Rochester Theological Seminary Bulletin: The Record*, LXIX (November 1918) 22.
Wuthnow, Robert. *After Heaven: Spirituality in America Since the 1950s*. Berkeley: University of California Press, 1999.
———. "The Great Divide: Toward Religious Realignment." In *The Restructuring of American Religion*, 133–72. Princeton: Princeton University Press, 1988.
Zinn, Howard. *A People's History of the United States*. New York: Harper Collins Publishers, 2001.

INDEX